P9-ARQ-298

--◦◦֍ MISSOURI ֎◦◦--

A HISTORY OF
THE CROSSROADS STATE

MISSOURI

A History
of the
Crossroads State

BY
EDWIN C. McREYNOLDS

University of Oklahoma Press
Norman

F
466
M2

By Edwin C. McReynolds

Oklahoma: A History of the Sooner State (Norman, 1954)
The Seminoles (Norman, 1957)
Oklahoma: The Story of Its Past and Present
(with Alice Marriott and Estelle Faulconer) (Norman, 1961)
Missouri: A History of the Crossroads State (Norman, 1962)

45551

LIBRARY OF CONGRESS CATALOG CARD NUMBER: 62–18052

Copyright 1962 by the University of Oklahoma Press, Publishing Division of
the University. Composed and printed at Norman, Oklahoma, U.S.A., by the
University of Oklahoma Press. First edition.

FOR EARL, RUTH, AND DOROTHY

--⋙ PREFACE ⋘--

THE HISTORY OF MISSOURI is significant chiefly in its relation to the main current of American development. It is not necessary or desirable to make a rigid separation between events outside the state's boundaries and developments within. The genius of Joseph Pulitzer may depend in great part upon his inheritance from ancestors who never saw Missouri, and the career of Senator Tom Benton may be closely related to his brother's activities in Nashville, Tennessee, or to a boyhood error of the statesman himself at Chapel Hill, North Carolina. The compromise measure proposed by Jesse B. Thomas of Illinois in the United States Senate on February 3, 1820, was clearly a matter of deep concern to Missouri and to the United States as a whole.

In this condensed narrative of Missouri the author has attempted to select materials that have proved valid contributions to the state's history, in the long view. If it is agreed that acquaintance with the past has value for an understanding of current society, then it must follow that no portion of the historical record may be ignored. Even the explorations that brought Missouri to the attention of Europeans must be touched upon. However, studies of the more remote past based upon acquaintance with geological concepts of the earth's crust and biological knowledge of modern man's development as an organism must be left to specialists in the fields of geology and anthropology.

Acknowledgments are due many persons who have given material aid in the writing of this book. The University of Oklahoma in 1959 and Cottey College in 1961, by reduction of the author's teaching load, made possible the completion of the project in 1962. Arthur McAnally, librarian, A. M. Gibson, archivist, and Miss Opal Carr, reference librarian, in the University of Oklahoma, gave a great variety of assistance, particularly with respect to making materials available and convenient. The library staff of the University of Missouri, Miss Sarah Guitar, of the State Historical Society of Missouri, Richard S. Brownlee, secretary of the State Historical Society, Percy Powell, of the Library of Congress, and Harold Hufford, of the National Archives, provided knowledgeable guidance in the author's search for source materials.

Miss Nellie Homes, librarian of Cottey College, was helpful in various ways in connection with articles in historical magazines and problems of composition. Robert B. Downs, of the University of Illinois, provided space in the library and made its resources available for a summer of research. Miss Dorothy Hill, of the public library in Nevada, Missouri; Paxton P. Price, of the Missouri State Library; Charles van Ravenswaay, of the Missouri Historical Society; and the staffs of the Mercantile Library in St. Louis, the Truman Library at Independence, and the public library in Joplin, all gave particular attention and valuable aid to the author in his search for books and documents. Claude Earp, of Nevada, Missouri, was consulted on a variety of questions concerning recent Missouri politics, the work of the Missouri Highway Commission, and notable persons with whom he has had long acquaintance. Miss Corinthia Gilbert, of Cottey College, gave useful suggestions in regard to the location of materials, historical sites, and persons with unique information. Hans Schmitt, of the University of Oklahoma, and Donald Lamore, of Cottey College, aided the author in French translation. Jim Atteberry, of Osceola, offered useful suggestions concerning the Osage Valley and the Osage Tribe.

Portions of the manuscript were read on request by the author's colleagues. Professors Donald Berthrong, Max L. Moorhead, and Charles C. Bush, of the University of Oklahoma, were among the readers who provided expert criticism and suggestions for revision. Professor Peter Ristuben, of Pacific Lutheran University, Tacoma, Washington, gave critical attention to the chapter on the Missouri fur trade. Dean John Caylor of Cottey College read critically a chapter on which his opinion was specifically requested; and President Blanche Dow of Cottey College took the time from her crowded schedule to read six chapters of the manuscript and to offer valuable suggestions for improvement. Mrs. Josephine Soukup did indispensable work in the preparation of the manuscript.

Lack of space prevents the separate recognition of help from many friends who have called attention to various materials, particularly newspaper articles on Missouri history, which have proved to be vitally useful pointers.

Edwin C. McReynolds

Norman, Oklahoma
September 29, 1962

CONTENTS

--◦⊰ ILLUSTRATIONS ⊱◦--

[xiii]

AFTER PAGE 370

Harry S. Truman
The Truman Library
Main Hall of Cottey College
Kansas City industrial area
Mississippi Lime Company plant
Kansas City grain elevator
Pea Ridge iron-mining project
Senator Thomas Hart Benton
Artist Thomas Hart Benton
Segment of Benton murals in the Capitol
The Capitol of Missouri

Maps

-‑⊸{ MISSOURI }⊷∘-

A HISTORY OF
THE CROSSROADS STATE

1

EXPLORATION BY EUROPEANS

THE SPANISH EXPLORERS

JUAN ORTIZ, naked like the Indians who brought him to Captain Baltasar de Gallegos and carrying in his hands a bow and arrows, had all but forgotten his native Spanish language. He was in danger of being slain by Hernando de Soto's mounted soldiers, who misunderstood the purpose of his visit. The horsemen dashed forward, and the painted Indian warriors fled before the strange beasts carrying strange fighters in armor; but Ortiz found the words for his deliverance: "For the love of God and of Holy Mary, slay not me; I am a Christian like yourselves and was born in Seville."

On May 25, 1539, the followers of Hernando de Soto, en route to Missouri, though completely unaware of their destination, had landed 620 men and more than 200 horses on the coast of Florida. They had come ashore at a place occupied by the party of Pánfilo de Narváez eleven years earlier, during one of the brief intervals between high optimism and cruel disaster in his tragic journey along the Gulf Coast.[1] Indian prisoners informed De Soto that Juan Ortiz, a Christian survivor of the Narváez expedition, was still living among them, in the possession of a chief. Although a meeting with Ortiz was arranged in advance, suspicion was so

[1] Richard L. Campbell, *Historical Sketches of Colonial Florida* (Cleveland, 1892), 10, 11; "Relations of Ranjel," *Narratives of the Career of Hernando de Soto* (E. G. Bourne, ed.; 2 vols., N. Y., 1904), 56, 57.

[3]

intense that the armed Indian visitors were regarded as spies, and the Spaniards did not at first recognize the survivor of Narváez's band as one of themselves.[2]

When Ortiz had established himself as a friend, the Spanish invaders were delighted to find an interpreter and guide. De Soto and his men were at the beginning of an adventure of great proportions—a journey through trackless forests from the coast of Florida to the hills of the Ozarks, beyond the great Mississippi. The native peoples, naturally hospitable and friendly to strangers, were to prove an almost impassable barrier to De Soto and his men. All the tribes from Florida to Missouri were determined, resourceful, hard fighters, and they quickly got the impression that the Spanish adventurers intended no permanent good to them.

The evidence is somewhat mixed in regard to the attitude of De Soto himself to the Indians. The Gentleman of Elvas, one of his followers, presents a moderate view; but Gonzalo Fernández de Oviedo y Valdés, a leading historian of the period, says that "this governor [De Soto] was much given to the sport of slaying Indians"; and after an account of De Soto's depositing in Seville one hundred thousand pesos in gold, he adds: "He decided to return to the Indies . . . and continue the employment, blood-stained in the past, which he had followed in the countries I mention."[3]

From the region on the Gulf Coast of Florida, which De Soto called the "fertile Province of Apalachi," the invaders set out toward the northeast. Their adventures on the journey to the Broad River in North Carolina, across the Blue Ridge Mountains, and back to the Gulf Coast are fascinating episodes in the exploration of North America; but we must push on to the area that was destined to be Missouri.

The fundamental conflict of interest between the Spaniards and the natives must have become clear to the head men of the Indian tribes living on the Gulf Coast. At Mabila, when Governor de Soto with a small guard entered the town under the impression that the Indians were docile and resigned to his giving orders through their captive chief, he suddenly found himself in the midst of a revolt

2 "Relation of Luys de Biedma," ibid., 3, 4.
3 Ibid., 59; Oviedo, Historia General y Natural de las Indias, 544ff.

and obliged to fight for his life. Twenty-two of his men were killed and 148 wounded, receiving "688 arrow wounds."

The Indians, according to the Spanish reports, had from 2,500 to 3,000 killed at Mabila. De Soto remained for four weeks after the battle to reorganize his army and allow the wounded to recover, and then marched north with Indian guides into the Chickasaw country. On December 17, 1540, he arrived at Chicaça, an Indian town that stood near the site of present-day Redland, in Pontotoc County, Mississippi.

The Spanish accounts are filled with stories of brutal injustices by the invaders and of suspicion and accusations of treachery against the Indians. In May, 1541, De Soto reached the Mississippi, and on June 18 moved his army to the west bank. He used boats constructed at the place of crossing—probably in present-day Tunica County, Mississippi, about thirty miles below Memphis. The Gentleman of Elvas described the stream at the point of crossing as "swift, and very deep." He added that the waters of the great river carried "trees and much timber" from above, and that there were "many fish of several sorts."

West of the Mississippi, the army of De Soto continued its search for riches and adventure. The Spaniards captured many men and women and seized clothing, blankets, and skins. The route described by the invaders is subject to a wide variety of interpretations; but frequent references to the river in the Spanish accounts seem to indicate that the ridge parallel to the Mississippi was followed from the point of crossing, southwest of Memphis, to the natural roadway that extends northward along the St. Francis River into Missouri. The land was fertile with abundant crops of corn and vegetables, wild fruits, pecans, and walnuts. The population was relatively dense in the area, where the sandy alluvial soil was easy to cultivate.[4]

At Pacaha, De Soto's army gained control after a skirmish, and the Indian leaders of the area became rivals for Spanish favor. The

[4] "Relation of de Biedma," *Narrative of De Soto*, 4–6; "Relation of Ranjel," *ibid.*, 61–70, 82–86, 89, 93, 127; "Narrative of the Gentleman of Elvas" (tr. by T. H. Lewis), *ibid.*, 172, 195–206; John Bartlett Brebner, *The Explorers of North America* (N. Y., 1933), 80.

head man of Casqui gave his daughter to De Soto and the chief of Pacaha gave his two sisters—Macanoche and Mochila—as tokens of love to be his wives. The Gentleman of Elvas described Macanoche as "symmetrical, tall, and full." Her expression was pleasant, her manners and features those of a lady. The same authority declared that "the other was robust."

There is no certainty about the limits of the territory claimed by the chief of Pacaha, but the area probably included portions of present-day Mississippi County, Arkansas, and extended north of New Madrid in Missouri.

De Soto rested his army for about six weeks near the principal town of Pacaha, and the rival Indian leaders daily sent supplies of food, splendid gifts, and messages indicating their friendship. Then the white invaders resumed their march, south and westward toward the St. Francis River. At Quiguate, one of the largest of the Indian towns discovered by De Soto, the cacique sent presents of food and clothing, including woven garments as well as skins of deer, bear, panther, and wildcat. The natives described the country to the south, down the St. Francis, as fertile and populous. Toward the northwest was Coligoa, in a mountainous region. The Spanish officers decided to march to the northwest, which offered greater possibilities, in their judgment, for the discovery of precious metals. Spanish records differ in the estimates of the distance from Quiguate to Coligoa—from 80 to 120 miles; but they agree that the area was rugged and mountainous. The region was probably near the headwaters of the St. Francis or the Black River.

Disappointed in their search for ore, the Spaniards continued their journey, turning southwest. They probably reached the Grand (or Neosho) River at an Indian town called Tanico, where the people were many and the cornfields productive. Farther south, De Soto "tarried a month," because the horses were well provided with maize. "The blade of it, I think, is the best fodder that grows," declared the Gentleman of Elvas. The army spent the winter at Antiamque, on a river that has generally been identified as the Arkansas.

The story of DeSoto's return to the Mississippi and of his death on May 21, 1542, is told in detail by his associates. The adventures of his followers, who continued their journey under Luis Moscoso de Alvarado, are essential parts of the history of North American exploration, but cannot be summarized here. De Soto had told the Indians that he and his Christian followers were immortal, so his successor tried to keep the fact of his death a secret from them. In September, 1543, when the band arrived by boat at the mouth of the Pánuco, in Mexico, there were 311 survivors from De Soto's original army of 620 men.[5]

THE FRENCH EXPLORERS

Access to the Mississippi Valley from the basin of the St. Lawrence and Great Lakes is easy in a number of places. In 1608 the French were established at Quebec on the lower St. Lawrence. By 1613, New France was so organized as to include the territory between Lakes Huron and Michigan and, by 1634, the territory from Lake Michigan to the Mississippi.

The search for a passage to the Pacific was a powerful incentive in French exploration. Before and even after French travelers reached the Mississippi, many of the missionaries and traders thought in terms of access to Asia by a water route. Some of them looked forward to exploration of the great river, familiar in the traditions of the Indians, as a certain means of reaching the western ocean. Count Frontenac in 1672 still expected to prove that the Mississippi flowed into the Pacific Ocean through the Gulf of California.

Father Jacques Marquette, who had come to Canada in 1666, had served in the missions at Sault Ste Marie, at St. Esprit far west on Lake Superior, and at St. Ignace on the Straits of Mackinac. In spite of warnings from the Christian Indians among whom he worked, he had for several years planned to attempt to convert the natives farther west. Louis Joliet, who was to join him on the western journey, at twenty-eight was an experienced explorer and woodsman. He had attended the Jesuit seminary at Quebec and

[5] *Ibid.*, 84; Thomas Nuttall's *Journal* (Cleveland, 1905), 254–56; Frederick A. Ogg, *The Opening of the Mississippi* (N.Y. and London, 1904), 36; "Narrative of the Gentleman of Elvas," *Narratives of De Soto*, 212n., 213, 215–22, 264, 267.

studied for the priesthood, but after a year spent in Europe, he came back to a life of adventure in Canada. In 1669 he searched for copper on Lake Superior and two years later helped in planting a trading post at Sault Ste Marie. He was the official representative of the French government on the expedition from St. Ignace to the Mississippi.

In December, 1672, Joliet arrived at St. Ignace and with Marquette proceeded toward the Mississippi the following May. The two Frenchmen, accompanied by five men whom they had employed as oarsmen, left St. Ignace on May 17, 1673. Two light birchbark canoes carried the men and their meager supply of arms and ammunition, Indian corn and dried venison.

The route of the party was through Green Bay to the Fox River, which the canoes ascended without difficulty up to the rapids. The friendly Mascotin Indians, under Christian influence since the time of Jean Nicolet's first journey west of Lake Michigan and already acquainted with Father Marquette, furnished two guides for the party to the Fox-Wisconsin portage. On June 17, 1673, the party reached the Mississippi.

For a week they moved south with the current, traveling by day and resting in midstream by night. At the village of an Illinois Indian band they went ashore for one night and welcomed the change in diet provided by the Indians. Then, ignoring the warnings of these natives, they resumed the journey down the Mississippi, in the waters of which they were able to catch in their nets an ample supply of fish.

The great muddy river from the west, emptying into the Mississippi a few miles below the mouth of the Illinois, made a deep impression upon Marquette. In his account of the journey he expressed the hope of reaching "the Red or California sea" by ascending the Pekitanoui (Missouri) at some later date. The Ohio, entering the Mississippi from their left, and the Arkansas, still farther south, from their right, convinced the leaders that their party was traveling toward the waters of the Gulf of Mexico, where Spanish influence among the native population was strong. Two months had elapsed since the party began its leisurely journey at St. Ignace. Their return, by way of the Mississippi, the Illinois, and the

Des Plaines rivers, required a few days longer. The total distance from Green Bay to the Arkansas and return was over 2,500 miles.

Joliet continued at once to Quebec, while Marquette rested for a few weeks at Green Bay to recover from dysentery, a disease which had attacked him while the party was on the Mississippi.

The explorations of Robert Cavelier, Sieur de la Salle, a contemporary of Joliet and Marquette, had direct bearing upon the opening of Missouri to settlement. La Salle had come to Canada in 1666 when he was twenty-three years of age. He established a fur-trading post on the St. Lawrence a few miles above Montreal, but after two years sold his interests there to raise funds for a journey to China, which he expected to reach by descending the Ohio River. He met Louis Joliet and exchanged views with him concerning the travel routes of the great interior of North America. He explored portions of Lakes Ontario, Erie, Huron, and Michigan, and at least a part of the Ohio River. After the descent of the Mississippi by Joliet and Marquette to the mouth of the Arkansas in 1673, La Salle gave up the idea of reaching the Pacific by following an easy water route from the vicinity of the Great Lakes or the upper Ohio. He knew that Spain was established on the Gulf of Mexico since Joliet and Marquette had encountered Indians on the lower Mississippi who were armed with weapons and supplied with powder made in Europe. The information obtained by Joliet from the Indians on the Missouri did not encourage La Salle to seek the great western ocean by following that stream. Instead of a new route to the Pacific, La Salle proposed to explore the obvious route to Spanish waters. An inland French empire, in which the Great Lakes and the Mississippi would be bound together by the military power of France, became his great objective.

The magnificent scope of La Salle's schemes appealed strongly to his contemporaries. On a visit to France in 1677, he obtained authority from the great minister of Louis XIV, Jean Baptiste Colbert, to explore in the western territories, to erect forts for the protection of his trade interests, and to exercise a monopoly on buffalo hides in the Mississippi Valley for five years. The energy, courage, and spirit of the man have gained the unqualified admiration of nearly all students of his career, though many Frenchmen of his

[9]

day, including some of his close associates, were cool in their estimates and even bitter in their denunciation of him.

La Salle began his most famous expedition—from Illinois to the mouth of the Mississippi—early in the year 1682. His party, besides himself and his lieutenant, Henri de Tonty, consisted of twenty-one Frenchmen, eighteen Indian warriors, ten women who were brought along by the braves to cook for them, and three of their children. The Indians were Algonquian-Mohegans from the region east of the Hudson and Abnakis from Maine—both tribes traditionally hostile to the Iroquois.

Traveling in canoes, La Salle and his followers reached the mouth of the Illinois on February 6, but were delayed for a week by floating ice on the Mississippi. On the thirteenth they set out again and, after traveling six leagues, came to the mouth of the Missouri (Ozage), "coming from the west." Six leagues below the junction with the Missouri, they passed a village of the Tamaroas. These Indians, a branch of the Illinois, were absent on a hunting expedition, and La Salle's men left signs of their peaceful visit with an indication of their route.

By Father Membré's estimate, the distance traveled from the Illinois to the Tamaroa village was twelve leagues, and from the village to the mouth of the Ohio (Quabache), forty leagues. The distance from the Illinois to the Ohio, on a straight line, is about 160 miles; along the river, it is nearly twice as far. "We went slowly, because we were obliged to hunt and fish almost daily," the missionary recalled.

Below the Ohio one of the hunters, Peter Prudhomme, was lost and, after wandering in the woods for nine days, was rescued. La Salle met Chickasaw Indians as he searched for the lost man and visited a town of the Arkansas tribe near the mouth of the river that is named for them. Father Membré was much impressed with the hospitality of these natives, whom he described as "lively, civil, generous people."

On April 6, 1682, La Salle and his men reached a point where the river divides into three main channels. Henri de Tonty was assigned the task of exploring the middle channel; Jean Bourdon

D'Autray the one on the east; and the leader himself that on the west. Three days later, the bands reunited, and La Salle took possession, in the name of King Louis XIV, of the "River Colbert" (Mississippi) and its tributaries. Father Membré estimated the distance from the mouth of the Seignelay (Illinois) to the Gulf of Mexico as "at least 350 leagues," and the total length of the river, 800 leagues.

La Salle's followers were out of provisions at the time the great new province was claimed for France and named Louisiana in honor of the reigning king. Some dried meat was found near the Gulf shore, "which we took," Father Membré recorded, "to appease our hunger. But soon after perceiving it to be human flesh, we left the rest to our Indians. It was very good and delicate."

The events of Sieur de la Salle's career after his return from the voyage to the mouth of the Mississippi are not closely connected with the history of Missouri. His memoir, delivered to Colbert's son, Seignelay, who had become minister of marine for Louis XIV, shows a clear intention of building a great French province in the middle of North America. The long-continued attempt of France to carry out that plan—for more than a century after La Salle's death—was a major factor in the European contest for colonial supremacy in the New World. Spain was the principal obstacle to the scheme for continental control, in La Salle's view, and he believed Spanish power could be overthrown with the aid of the North American Indians.

Louis XIV agreed to the principles of La Salle's scheme and gave him support for putting it into execution. Four ships were prepared for a sea voyage to the lower Mississippi, with 480 persons on board. Father Zenobius Membré and Henri Joutel were among them. The ships reached the Gulf of Mexico in December, 1684, "after a prosperous voyage," and cruised along the northern coast, seeking the channels of the Mississippi Delta. The party missed the mouth of the great river and traveled all the way to Matagorda Bay on the coast of Texas. Failure to locate the entrance to the Mississippi was the first of a series of misfortunes which followed La Salle on his last expedition. Eventually, through the treachery of some members of his party, he lost his life as he attempted to travel overland from Matagorda Bay to the Mississippi.

In their travels along the Mississippi, the members of La Salle's party undoubtedly made some brief excursions into the area that is now Missouri. Henri de Tonty's account of his excursion specifically refers to the west bank in the latitude of Missouri and shows some acquaintance with the Indians of that area. Next to La Salle himself, perhaps Tonty did more than any other person to introduce Missouri to Europeans.

Tonty's journeys along the Mississippi gave him some acquaintance with the Indians who lived west of the river. His location for the Missounta, Otenta, and Osage was "in the prairies, 150 leagues from the mouth of the Missouri." He said that there were few beaver below the mouth of the Ohio, but large numbers of "buffaloes, bears, large wolves, stags, and hinds . . . and some lead mines which yield two-thirds of ore to one of refuse." In 1700, he was with Iberville at the mouth of the Mississippi, and in 1702 performed his last public service—a visit to the Chickasaw Indians as agent of Louis XIV's government.[6]

[6] Reuben Gold Thwaites, *France in America*, 49–56; *Jesuit Relations* (R. G. Thwaites, ed.; 73 vols., Cleveland, 1896–1901), VIII, 295–96; XXIII, 275; LIX, 94, 95, 98–107; Francis Parkman, *La Salle and the Discovery of the Great West*, I, xxiv, 20, 32, 33, 49–72, 168–84, 223–37, 239–59, 273–74; J. G. Shea, *Discovery and Exploration of the Mississippi Valley* (Albany, 1903), 40–43, 111–49, 169–82, 216–17; *Old South Leaflets*, Vol. II, No. 46; *Historical Collections of Louisiana* (Benjamin French, ed.), I, 64, 79–80, 82, 195; II, 297; Brebner, *Explorers of North America*, 253n., 255, 302; Ogg, *Opening of the Mississippi*, 77; Louis Houck, *A History of Missouri*, I, 154–55; Muriel H. Wright, *The Indian Tribes of Oklahoma* (Norman, 1951), 218–19; Walter Williams and Floyd Calvin Shoemaker, *Missouri, Mother of the West*, I, 42–47.

2

NATIONAL RIVALRIES AND
EARLY SETTLEMENT

PIERRE LEMOYNE, Sieur d'Iberville, and his brother, Jean Baptiste Lemoyne, Sieur de Bienville, operating on the lower Mississippi and adjacent Gulf Coast between 1698 and 1722, established France as the principal rival of Spain in the area. A permanent settlement on Biloxi Bay, another at the site of Mobile, the founding of New Orleans, a fort at Natchitoches, and the explorations of Bernard de la Harpe to the region of lead ore north of the Arkansas River were among the tangible results of the French efforts. The Spanish officers at Pensacola were not unaware of French settlement in the vicinity of Biloxi Bay, and the governor showed his disapproval by a formal protest, followed by a series of attacks upon French ships in the Gulf of Mexico.[1]

In Europe, the fortunes of France and Spain were drawn together in the War of the Spanish Succession (1702–13), but four years after the death of Louis XIV in 1715, the prince regent for Louis XV, the Duke of Orleans, united with Great Britain and her allies in a war against Spain. Bienville led an expedition against Pensacola, principal stronghold of Spain on the northern shore of

---

[1] Williams and Shoemaker, *Missouri*, I, 53; Hiram M. Chittenden, *The American Fur Trade of the Far West*, I, 87; Campbell, *Historical Sketches of Colonial Florida*, 10, 11; Le Page du Pratz, *History of Louisiana* (New Orleans, 1947), 14; French, *Historical Collections of Louisiana*, I, 52–78 (Tonty's "Memoir"), III, 84; Pierre Margry, *Découvertes et établissements des Français*, VI, 243–306, 357–82; Houck, *History of Missouri*, I, 273.

the Gulf of Mexico, and captured it. In a counterattack, the Spanish governor recovered the fort, only to lose it a second time to Bienville before the end of the war. The treaty of peace in 1720 gave control of Pensacola to Spain, but recognized French title to the settlements in the lower Mississippi, which were, in effect, a wedge driven between the Spanish possessions in Florida and those in Mexico.

Charles Claude du Tisné, serving under Bienville, traveled up the Missouri in 1718 beyond the mouth of the Gasconade and to the lower Osage basin. He reported that the Osage Indians lived in villages about eighty leagues southwest of the Osage's confluence with the Missouri. He gathered much useful information about the forests of the lower Missouri and its tributary streams. He found navigation of the great river out of the Northwest to be filled with difficulties and was finally turned back from his visit to the Panoussas Indians by the opposition of the Missouri tribe.

Du Tisné returned to Kaskaskia and made a new start to the west, crossing the Mississippi near the site of Ste Genevieve and proceeding across the Meramec and Gasconade valleys. He visited the Osages, Pawnees, Padoucahs, and Panoussas, traveling beyond the present western limits of Missouri. His report mentioned the discovery of lead and other ores in the vicinity of the Osage villages and rock salt near the Panoussas.[2]

In 1720, Don Antonio Valverde Cosio, Spanish governor at Santa Fe, made an effort to investigate and perhaps to challenge French expansion in the Missouri Valley. It is doubtful that he attempted to carry out an elaborate program of settlement at this time, as one French contemporary suggested in his account of the project. Governor Cosio gave command of the military expedition to Don Pedro de Villasur, who set out from New Mexico toward the northeast in June, 1720. Accounts of the number of men in his expedition vary, but Bienville's report in 1721 to the Council of the

---

[2] Thwaites, *France in America*, 78, 79; Le Page du Pratz, *History of Louisiana*, 100–105, 317; Herbert E. Bolton and Thomas M. Marshall, *The Colonization of North America* (N.Y., 1936), 295; French, *Historical Collections of Louisiana*, I, 148–50, 153–54; Houck, *History of Missouri*, I, 256–57 (Houck quotes Bossu, *Travels in Louisiana*, I, 202).

Regency (which must be viewed with caution) stated that two hundred Spanish horsemen with their Indian allies were destroyed by the Otoes and Missouris as Villasur attempted to invade the French settlements of the Illinois region.

The "Spanish Caravan," whatever its size, probably furnished the impulse for the establishment of Fort Orleans. Sieur de Bourgmont undertook the task of establishing friendly relations with the Indians of the upper Missouri. He reported at New Orleans to Governor Bienville, who was instructed to furnish him with necessary supplies and men, and in Illinois presented himself to M. Boisbriant. With a small party of soldiers Bourgmont pushed along the Missouri beyond the Gasconade and the Osage and past the Chariton on the north bank. Above the mouth of Grand River he selected a place to build a fort, opposite the principal Indian town of the area, which was on the south bank in present Saline County. No permanent settlement resulted—in fact, the site has completely vanished as the result of Missouri River floods. During his career as an explorer, however, Bourgmont used Fort Orleans as a starting point for important western expeditions.

In 1724 he traveled to the country of the Kansas (Canzés) and the Padoucah Indians. There he became ill and had to be carried on a litter. He became worse and was forced to return to Fort Orleans. After a month, however, he was sufficiently recovered to try again, and in September, 1724, he traveled by boat to the Kansas village, situated about halfway between the Grand and the Kansas rivers. A council of the Otoes (Othos), Iowas (Ayoois), and Kansas (Canzés) tribes was urged by the French leader as a means of making peace between those bands and the Osage, Panimaha, and Illinois Indians. The principal Kansas chief offered his daughter to Bourgmont in marriage, but the French leader explained that he was married and that he was forbidden by his country's laws to have two wives. The chief then proposed that his daughter become the wife of Bourgmont's son, who thus would become the great chief of the Kansas Indians. To this the Frenchman answered that his son was too young for marriage, but that when he was older, he might, if he wished, marry the Indian girl. With this promise the Indians were satisfied.

[15]

From the Kansas village Bourgmont marched west to the vicinity of present-day Kansas City; then southwest about one hundred miles to the Padoucahs. The principal men of his command certified that he had satisfied the terms of his assignment by establishing friendly relations with the Indians of the Missouri Valley. M. de St. Ange signed the document as acting major; La Renaudière, as superintendent of the mines; and Dubois, as sergeant of the military unit.[3]

THE EARLY MINING SETTLEMENTS IN MISSOURI

It was during the administration of Governor Bienville that the first settlements were made in the mineral region that extends westward from the Mississippi River to the headwaters of the St. Francis. Lead deposits had been reported in the area much earlier, and Iberville had shown great interest in Missouri mining. Shallow mines to supply lead for trade with the Indians were recorded in the accounts of Bernard de la Harpe, Father Jacques Gravier, and Le Page du Pratz.

La Mothe Cadillac, first governor of the Louisiana Province after the establishment of Antoine Crozat's trade monopoly in 1712, was especially interested in silver mining. He traveled to the Missouri lead mines and visited, among others, the diggings that came to be called Mine La Motte. Philippe Renault, the son of a well-known ironmaster in France, came to America in 1719 to engage in mining on a large scale. He brought with him to the Illinois country some two hundred miners from France and five hundred Negro slaves purchased in Santo Domingo. Renault's miners explored for minerals in the vicinity of Kaskaskia and crossed to the west side of the Mississippi. Traces of silver were discovered, but

[3] Margry, *Découvertes* . . . , VI, 386, 409, 448–49; Bolton and Marshall, *Colonization of North America*, 279, 284, 291, 296; LeRoy R. Hafen and Carl Coke Rister, *Western America* (N.Y., 1941), 58; Houck, *History of Missouri*, I, 250–55, 258–60, 264–67; Adolphe F. Bandelier, *The Gilded Man* (Jean l'Archeveque); Gilbert J. Garraghan, "Fort Orleans on the Missoury," *Mo. Hist. Rev.*, Vol. XXXV (1941), 373–84; Joseph Wallace, "Fort de Chartres—Its Origin, Growth, and Decline," *Transactions of the Illinois State Historical Society*, Vol. VIII (1903), 105–13.

lead was the metal that was produced in marketable amounts. For more than twenty years Renault refined ore in crude furnaces and carried the lead to Fort Chartres in "horse-collar" molds, placed around the necks of pack horses. After Ste Genevieve was founded on the right bank of the Mississippi, probably in 1735, a road was made from that settlement to the nearest lead mines, eventually extending to Mine à Breton. Two-wheeled French carts, *charettes*, were used instead of pack horses for transporting pigs of lead to the river along this road, the oldest path for wheeled vehicles in Missouri.

From Fort Chartres, at the beginning of the mining operations by the French, and later from Ste Genevieve, surplus lead was conveyed to New Orleans by flatboats, and from that river port to Europe.

Many of the reports published in France were exaggerated and unduly optimistic. Particularly, reports on gold and silver were subject to exaggeration. After exploring the valley of the Meramec, Sieur de Lochon declared that the region contained large quantities of excellent silver ore; Don Antonio, experienced in Mexican mining, obtained freedom from galley slavery and a job in the mineral districts of Missouri by boasting of his skill as a miner; and a Canadian named Matthew Sagan, by creating the impression that he had discovered gold in the upper Missouri, caused an expedition to be prepared for him to command. All of the predictions of vast wealth from precious metals proved false. Lead mining, in the aggregate, was not disappointing, and the mineralogists were not indulging in fantastic dreams when they pointed out the enormous variety of useful minerals to be found in Missouri.

Permanent settlements had been planted in Illinois: Cahokia on the Mississippi in 1699; Kaskaskia, five miles above the mouth of the Kaskaskia River, in the following year; and, before the end of 1733, Fort Chartres, St. Philippe, and Prairie du Rocher. French Canadians from the Illinois settlements probably mined in Missouri for several years before forming any permanent settlement on the west bank. After Ste Genevieve, at an established crossing on the Mississippi, became a community with year-around resi-

dents about 1735 and other clusters of cabins grew up in the vicinity of active mining centers, Illinois men were for many years the
principal immigrants.

Ste Genevieve, in addition to being located at a convenient river
crossing, had the advantage of being close to workable salt springs.
Salt was second to lead among the products shipped to New Orleans. A serious impediment to the growth of the town, however,
was its precarious position on a river bank that was steadily reduced by the waters of the Mississippi during flood times. For
nearly fifty years, Ste Genevieve held its own; then, as the caving
banks began to threaten cabins with destruction, the town moved
three miles upstream to higher ground. The period of removal to
the new site covered about ten years, 1781 to 1791, the flood season
of 1785 giving positive impetus to the change.[4]

MISSOURI UNDER SPANISH RULE

Between June and October, 1759, British forces in North America
wrenched control of Niagara, Louisbourg, and Quebec from the
French. During the following year Montreal fell to the English,
and, with the surrender of Miami, Detroit, Mackinac, and St.
Joseph, France had lost all of her American territory except Louisiana. In other sections of the global war, British armies and fleets
were almost uniformly victorious. Senegal in Africa was occupied;
a French fleet was beaten in Far Eastern waters; Hawke, Bos-
cawen, and Rodney crushed French naval power in European
waters. An attempt by the French general, Chevalier du Lévis, to
recapture Quebec was turned back by the superior artillery fire of
the British in a second battle on the Plains of Abraham, April 18,
1760.[5]

It is probable that William Pitt, with a free hand to continue the

---

[4] French, *Historical Collections of Louisiana*, I, 52–78; *Jesuit Relations*, LXV,
105; Le Page du Pratz, *History of Louisiana*, 158, 163, 195–96; Bolton and Marshall,
Colonization of North America, 277–78, 282; Williams and Shoemaker, *Missouri*, I,
60, 61; Houck, *History of Missouri*, I, 280–84; Capt. Philip Pittman, *The Present
State of the European Settlements on the Mississippi* (Cleveland, 1906), 84–92;
Wallace, *loc. cit.*, 105–13.

[5] Bolton and Marshall, *Colonization of North America*, 379–81.

war against France, would have made an effort to complete the conquest of North America by adding Louisiana to British possessions; but the new king of England, George III, was inclined to end the conflict. However, the family compact between Louis XV of France and Charles III of Spain was revived, and, with Spain in the war, England was under the necessity of further naval campaigns. Admiral Rodney captured Martinique in February, 1762, and on August 13 the English occupied Havana. Less than two months later the city of Manila in the Philippines was taken by the British eastern squadron.

Peace was signed at Paris on February 10, 1763, by the principals in the contest for control of North America. France was practically expelled as an active colonial power in America. England held Canada, Cape Breton Island, and all the territory east of the Mississippi except the Isle of Orleans. Florida came under British control, and Havana was returned to Spain. The former French territory west of the Mississippi and the Isle of Orleans on the lower left bank were turned over to Spain. Probably both French and British statesmen regarded the Spanish title to Louisiana as temporary. Certainly few men of any country realized the potential value of the vast domain west of the Mississippi or predicted the occupation of Louisiana by a new American republic within a period of less than fifty years.

During the years of international maneuvering over the title and occupation of Louisiana, 1762–69, steps were taken in New Orleans to keep the fur trade of the Missouri moving down to that port on the lower Mississippi. In 1762 the firm of Maxent, Laclede and Company received from Governor Kerléric a grant to trade on the Missouri River, a privilege which the Superior Council of Louisiana refused to confirm as a monopoly; but in November of the following year Pierre Laclede Liguest arrived at Fort Chartres, accompanied by a band of frontier settlers—mechanics, boatmen, hunters, and trappers. His boats contained merchandise from France to open trade with the Indians of the Missouri. Antoine Maxent was one of the wealthy merchants of New Orleans, and his backing of the Louisiana Fur Company was a guarantee of financial support during the experimental stage of the enterprise.

Maxent was a brother-in-law of Governor Luis de Unzaga and the father-in-law of Governor Bernardo de Gálvez. Like his partner Laclede, Maxent was a man of energy and acumen.

Fort Chartres in 1763 was a new structure, built on the site of the old settlement established by Pierre, Duc de Boisbriant in 1719–20. Chevalier de Macarty constructed new fortifications in 1751 on plans submitted by Lieutenant Jean B. Saussier, a French engineer who settled and lived to a ripe old age in Cahokia. Neyon de Villiers, who led the force from Fort Duquesne that captured George Washington's little party of Virginians at Fort Necessity in 1754, succeeded Chevalier de Macarty at Chartres. Villiers was commandant when Laclede Liguest wintered at Fort Chartres with his settlers for the new trading post.

In February, 1764, Laclede was ready to start building his trading post at a carefully selected location on the west bank of the Mississippi, below the mouth of the Missouri. Associated with him in the planning and actual building of the post was young Auguste Chouteau, whom the trader placed in charge of erecting the first storehouse and cabins. In April, 1764, Laclede named the new settlement St. Louis, in honor of King Louis IX. Along the river, Laclede laid out *La Rue Royale*, later to be called Main Street, and planned other roadways parallel to it: *La Rue de l'Église* and *La Rue des Granges*, in more recent times Second and Third streets. He built his own house near the center of the village, on a square that was bordered by *La Rue Royale*. On the spot where Laclede first cleared the timber for his trading post, Barnum's Hotel and the Merchants' Exchange were later erected.

The first wave of settlers to St. Louis came from the French towns in Illinois, whose people preferred the rule of Spain to that of the British. In 1765 the French commandant, St. Ange de Bellerive, removed his garrison from Fort Chartres to St. Louis. Under the Louisiana Fur Company grant, Laclede had no authority to plat the settlement or to give title to lots in St. Louis. He made specific assignments to settlers, however, and St. Ange, for five years after his arrival in 1765, followed the trader's example by granting real estate titles in the name of the French government. St. Ange's garrison included, besides the commandant, "two lieutenants, a fort major, one sergeant, one corporal, and twenty men."

In 1770, Governor O'Reilly sent Don Pedro Piernas to take formal possession of Upper Louisiana from the French. A census report by Piernas in December, 1773, showed the following population figures for the two major settlements of Missouri:

	Whites		Slaves	
St. Louis	Males, 285	Females, 159	Males, 105	Females, 88
Ste Genevieve	" , 251	" , 149	" , 149	" , 127
Total	" , 536	" , 308	" , 254	" , 215

The successor of Piernas as lieutenant governor in Missouri was Francisco Cruzat, who was followed in a short time by Fernando de Leyba. Spanish aid for George Rogers Clark in his Revolutionary campaign north of the Ohio was supplied by shipments of arms, ammunition, provisions, and money from New Orleans, while De Leyba was in charge at St. Louis. Spain joined in the alliance against England in 1779, probably with the purpose of adding territory east of the Mississippi to her possessions in the great valley. Governor Bernardo de Gálvez captured British posts on the lower Mississippi, besides Mobile and Pensacola on the Gulf of Mexico. Gálvez was active in supplying De Leyba with goods and financial aid for the campaign of the British colonies against England in the Northwest Territory.

In February, 1780, Captain Emanuel Hesse mobilized a force of 950 Indians and traders—both French and English—on the Fox and Wisconsin rivers for an attack on St. Louis. This movement, started on the order of Lieutenant Governor Sinclair, was a part of the British plan to recover the Northwest Territory and, at the same time, strike a blow against Spain. The Sac, Fox, Menominee, Puant, and Ottawa Indians were led by Matchikuis, who was called "General" and presented with a brilliant British uniform.

At Prairie du Chien the force captured a boat from Cahokia, and at the lead mines a party of seventeen miners was taken, with a store of supplies and fifty tons of ore. The craft captured at Prairie du Chien was laden with goods which were of great use to the invading British force, and it was charged by Americans in the Illinois country that Charles Gratiot of Cahokia was engaged in the business of supplying the hostile Indians with munitions and guns. George Rogers Clark had found it expedient to investigate similar charges against French traders of the Illinois country during his campaign from the Wabash to the Mississippi. The merchant Jean Gabriel Cerré of Kaskaskia was charged by his neighbors with hostility to the American cause. After hearing the merchant and comparing his account of his activities with that of his accusers, Clark permitted him to take the oath of allegiance to the American Union. "In short, he became a most valuable man to us," Clark wrote in his journal. Cerré's daughter Thérèse married Auguste Chouteau.[6]

In Louisiana, Spain depended upon French traders to maintain harmonious relations with the Indians instead of upon the missions, as in the earlier colonies. Licensed traders, under careful instructions from the government, cultivated friendship with the tribes, and officials in Spanish posts distributed presents to the chiefs and other influential Indians. On questions of loyalty to countries of Europe involved in war or bound by an alliance, the individual Indian could not be depended upon to follow the general course of his tribe. Nor was every man of French descent in America ready to support the combination against England when the diplomats in Paris agreed upon such a policy. The French traders who accompanied Captain Hesse in the attack on St. Louis were joined with a powerful enemy against an ally of France.

In 1780 the population of St. Louis was about eight hundred, mainly French settlers from Illinois. During the sixteen years since

[6] *Ibid.*, 398; Houck, *The Spanish Régime in Missouri*, I, Introduction, xv, xvi; II, 1–4; William R. Shepherd, "The Cession of Louisiana to Spain," *Political Science Quarterly*, Vol. XIX (1904), 439–58; Arthur S. Aiton, "The Diplomacy of the Louisiana Cession," *American Historical Review*, Vol. XXXVI (1931), 701–20; Chittenden, *The American Fur Trade*, 97–101; *Collections of the Illinois State Historical Society*, Vol. X, 435 (material on the Kerléric grant to Maxent, Laclede & Co. The same volume contains material on "The Critical Period, 1763–65," edited by Alvord and Carter); *Dictionary of American Biography*, IV, 92–95 (articles on Auguste Pierre Chouteau, Jean Pierre Chouteau, René Auguste Chouteau, by William H. Ghent); and on Pierre Chouteau, by Stella M. Drumm); *ibid.*, X, 520–21 (article on Pierre Laclede by William H. Ghent); Williams and Shoemaker, *Missouri*, I, 63–65.

Pierre Laclede had laid out and named the settlement, more than one hundred stone dwellings had been constructed and the people had firmly established fur trading as the principal occupation of the area. De Leyba had offered to send aid from St. Louis to George Rogers Clark immediately after the capture of Kaskaskia by the Americans in July, 1778, in the event of an Indian attack from Detroit; and in the spring of 1780, a letter from Governor Patrick Henry of Virginia to St. Louis probably contained Colonel Clark's warning that Emanuel Hesse and his allies were on their way to attack the river settlements.

Captain de Leyba called in the soldiers and militia from Spanish posts in the vicinity, St. Charles and Carondelet, and prepared his defenses for St. Louis. Earthworks were thrown up to protect the 29 regulars and the militiamen, who numbered 281. On a platform commanding the main road into town from the north, five cannons were stationed, and from this position De Leyba supervised the defense maneuvers. Lieutenant Silvia de Cartabona, who had marched reinforcements from Ste Genevieve, was in charge of 20 men assigned the task of protecting De Leyba's house, where a party of women and children had taken refuge.

The invaders reached St. Louis on May 26, 1780. The traders and their Indian allies were astonished, perhaps, by the well-planned defense and by the determination of the men under De Leyba's command. After a brief period of feeling out the town's defenses, Hesse withdrew from St. Louis and turned his attention to pillaging the nearby farms. Accounts of the casualties vary, for the invasion was aimed at both St. Louis and Cahokia and some action took place on the Illinois side of the Mississippi. Perhaps, too, some exaggerations crept into the reports of British officers and the stories told many years after the event by aged survivors among the defenders.

An account that was probably based upon De Leyba's official report states that fifteen whites and seven slaves were killed, six whites and one slave wounded, and fifty-seven whites and thirteen slaves taken captive. Lieutenant Governor Sinclair said that Dominique Ducharme and Joseph Calvé, interpreters who accompanied the expedition, were guilty of treachery, that there was no element of surprise in the attack, and that the French-Canadian traders of Hesse's party were timid and half-hearted.

The presence of George Rogers Clark in the vicinity, although he did not actually cross to the west side of the river, might have been a factor in the hasty withdrawal of Hesse's men. Clark came up to Cahokia and sent Colonel Montgomery to pursue the retreating British force with a party composed of regular American troops, French recruits from the Mississippi bottoms, and Spanish militia from St. Louis. This counterattack had the effect of relieving the Missouri and Illinois settlements from the threat of British-commanded Canadian Indians. Colonel Montgomery attacked the Indian villages on Rock River, burning some of the houses.

De Leyba died on June 28, 1780, and his executive functions were taken over by Lieutenant de Cartabona until the return of Francisco Cruzat, who was sent to the command at St. Louis for the second time. In January, 1781, Cruzat organized an expedition to take the offensive against the British east of the Mississippi; and in a winter attack this party captured Fort St. Joseph on the southeastern shore of Lake Michigan. This victory entered into the discussions of the territorial settlements at Paris in 1783 and perhaps had an indirect bearing upon the award of the land east of the Mississippi to the United States.[7]

Travel on the Mississippi during the last year of the American Revolution was perilous. In August, 1782, Governor Bernardo de Gálvez reported the capture of Madame Cruzat, wife of the commandant at St. Louis, as she traveled by barge up the river from New Orleans. The party that surprised and seized the boat was composed of former British citizens of Natchez, who had been

[7] Pittman, *Present State of the European Settlements*, 94; Houck, *The Spanish Régime in Missouri*, I, 61, 66–75, 167–68; II, 37–38; Houck, *History of Missouri*, II, 37–46; Bolton and Marshall, *Colonization of North America*, 400–401; C. E. A. Gayarré, *History of Louisiana*, III, 104–34; James A. James, "The Significance of the Attack on St. Louis, 1780," *Proceedings of the Mississippi Valley Historical Association, 1908–09*, II, 197–217; Walter B. Douglas, "Jean Gabriel Cerré—a Sketch," *Transactions of the Illinois State Historical Society*, VIII, 275–84; Frederic L. Billon, *Annals of St. Louis in Its Territorial Days* (St. Louis, 1888), 165; Sara John English, "George Rogers Clark," *Journal of the Ill. State Hist. Soc.*, Vol. XX (1928), 540; Williams and Shoemaker, *Missouri*, I, 67.

driven out by the Spanish conquest of the lower valley, and an allied group of Chies Indians.

Don Estevan Miró reported the loss of a barge belonging to Pourèe *dit* Beausoleil, bound for the Illinois from Natchez. Juan Toorner (John Turner), "rebel Captain of Natchez," with a party of ten Englishmen and three Negroes, took the barge by means of a surprise attack. But Picote de Belestre and the barge's crew, some four hours after the capture, suddenly reversed the situation by freeing themselves from their bonds and throwing their captors into the river. Six of the Englishmen and two Negroes were killed with oars, while the others swam ashore. The barge returned to Natchez and afterwards set out for Illinois with a convoy.

The United States of America replaced England as the neighbor of Spanish Louisiana by the terms of the Treaty of Paris, in 1783. The major settlements of Lower Louisiana were New Orleans, which grew to 5,338 by 1788; Natchitoches, 1,021 in the same year; and Arkansas, 119. In Missouri, St. Louis had 925 inhabitants in 1799; Ste Genevieve, 949; St. Charles, 875; New Madrid, 782; and Cape Girardeau, 521. The census ordered by the commandant, De Lassus, disclosed a total population of 6,028 in the year 1799, a growth of about 5,000 during the three decades of Spanish rule. Missouri products included 265,047 bushels of wheat, an equal crop of Indian corn, 28,627 pounds of tobacco, 1,340 quintals of lead, about 1,000 barrels of salt, and furs valued at $75,000.

Indian disorders were relatively few under Spanish rule, as they were under French administration. By comparison, the English colonies were harassed by attacks on outlying settlements, raids and massacres, and Indian wars. The fundamental reasons for the better relations of French and Spanish settlers with the native population were to be found in the important trade that grew up along the Missouri and elsewhere in Louisiana, a commerce in which the Indians shared in the advantages. In all the English colonies the basic motive for settlement was land for agriculture, but in Missouri the motives were quite diverse. The Spanish authorities recognized at once the importance of the fur trade and the other commercial ventures that were related to it—construction and management of river craft, maintenance of storage depots, and exchange of articles which were in demand by the Indians, trappers, and merchants. Leaving Indian relations in the hands of French traders was a practical solution of a difficult problem by the Spanish government.

The growth of religious liberty on this frontier was based in part upon the same conditions that operated in favor of freedom in early Massachusetts, Virginia, and Maryland. Enforcement of religious conformity was not practicable in a land where population was sparse, transportation difficult, and even communication between officials and citizens no simple matter. The strong and persistent demand for laborers, farmers, miners, trappers, boatmen, and other producers discouraged attempts that might have been made to enforce religious uniformity.

The movement of French population from Illinois into Missouri continued for a full decade after the Treaty of Paris. American settlers came to St. Louis in increasing numbers after 1795, and many families from Tennessee, North Carolina, or Kentucky moved across the Mississippi into the Cape Girardeau or the New Madrid district. In 1796, Ste Genevieve was visited by Moses Austin, who had mined lead in Virginia during the American Revolution. Austin settled with his family near Mine à Breton and devoted his attention to the production of minerals.

Pierre Louis Lorimier, born of French parents in Canada and best known as an Indian trader, agent, and interpreter for the British during the American Revolution, came to Missouri in 1787. He built his house near the site of present St. Mary's and engaged in trade with the Indians of the vicinity. The Spanish government employed him as an Indian agent, with headquarters on Apple Creek—an arrangement which led to his persuading many Shawnees and Delawares to remove to Missouri. Spanish officials regarded these new Indian settlers as support for their defense against the Osages.

For his services to the Spanish provincial government, Lorimier received six thousand arpens of land from Governor Carondelet in 1796 and thirty thousand arpens later, from Marquis de Casa Calvo. He was given a license to trade with the Indians on the

Arkansas, St. Francis, and White rivers. He married a woman of mixed blood, Shawnee and French, and, after her death, took a second wife, also Shawnee and French. One of Lorimier's sons by his first wife attended the United States Military Academy at West Point and received the customary commission in the United States Army upon graduation.

Lorimier brought many settlers besides the Delaware and Shawnee Indians into Missouri. Like John Law, he had a distinct preference for German immigrants and the settlement of Swiss-Germans who came to the White River in the Cape Girardeau district were congenial neighbors for the Indian agent. Joseph Neyswanger, John Freimann, Daniel Krentz, Valentine Lorr, and John Probst were immigrants from North Carolina, all of Swiss-German descent. Major John Bollinger brought with him from Lincoln County, North Carolina, the first German Protestant preacher who settled in southeastern Missouri. Bollinger's Mill on White River with the cabins of people who established themselves north and south of it—many of them relatives of the Major—was for a time the western limit of settlement in the Cape Girardeau district.

Other settlers from the states east of the Mississippi included the numerous members of the Randall family from Hamilton County, Virginia, Joseph Waller from Tennessee, Hypolite Mariot, a French hunter brought to Missouri by Louis Lorimier, and David Bowie. William Lorimier, son of Louis, held land near the forks of Cape la Cruz Creek. Moses Hurley, Pierre Dumay, Joseph Chevalier, and George Henderson settled on land north of Cape Girardeau—the last on a grant of land obtained by Louis Lorimier.

Another man who attempted to found a colony during the Spanish period was George Morgan of Philadelphia. As a land speculator he had interests in the region north of the Ohio River and in a colonial grant of 2,862 square miles in western Virginia. During the Revolution, Morgan served as United States Indian agent and in the army attained the rank of colonel. After the war, he lived on a farm near Princeton, New Jersey, where he carried on experiments in scientific agriculture. His investigation of the Hessian fly, a menace to wheat-growers, attracted wide attention.

Encouraged by Diego Gardoqui, Colonel Morgan laid out his

town on a well-chosen strip of land about twelve miles below the mouth of the Ohio on the Missouri shore, naming the settlement New Madrid. He planned wide streets, a convenient marketplace, a central warehouse, and a field for the subsistence of newcomers. The first settlers erected cabins, fenced garden spots on their half-acres of ground, and helped to build the storehouse and prepare the common field.

After a brief period of ostensible support, Governor Miró began to use his influence against the growth of the Morgan colony. General James Wilkinson, who was attempting to take advantage of the uncertain and confused loyalties of United States citizens in the West, conspired with Miró to separate these western people from the states of the Atlantic Coast. Colonel Morgan's colony on the Mississippi would be an obstacle to the smooth development of this plan; and Miró, urged on by Wilkinson, abruptly ended Morgan's connection with the colony. He then offered him one thousand acres of land in the Natchez district, and an additional tract for each of his sons, provided he would continue in the Spanish colonial service. Miró also assured Morgan that settlers who came to New Madrid would be favorably received and given the protection of a fort.[8]

Colonel Morgan did not accept this offer of new employment, but retired to his farm in New Jersey. He later removed to "Morganza" in Pennsylvania, where he spent his final years as a gentleman farmer. The New Madrid district continued to grow, and at the end of Spanish rule in Louisiana contained about fifteen hundred settlers, of whom two-thirds were immigrants from the United States.[9]

During the time of George Washington's administration as President, when the French Republic was represented in America by Charles Genêt, schemes for French recovery of Louisiana were many. George Rogers Clark worked with Genêt to organize a mili-

[8] Houck, *The Spanish Régime in Missouri*, I, 36, 46, 76, 211–34; Houck, *History of Missouri*, II, 187–92; 108–34; Gayarré, *History of Louisiana*, III, 215, 406; *Dictionary of American Biography*, XI, 413 (article on Pierre Louis Lorimer by Stella M. Drumm).

[9] *Ibid.*, XIII, 169–70 (article on George Morgan by Max Savelle).

tary force of western settlers for the invasion of the Spanish province. This armed band, augmented by a party of Creek warriors, was to descend the Ohio and Mississippi rivers under the command of Auguste de la Chaise, a native of Louisiana. At New Orleans, Baron de Carondelet strengthened his fortifications and organized his militia forces to meet the threat. His report indicated that he could put six thousand men in the field and that he was prepared to concentrate them rapidly to meet any aggression.

The attitude of President Washington probably had a decisive effect in preventing the invasion. He had not supported Genêt's ambitious schemes at any time, and he cautioned citizens of the United States against becoming involved in an unlawful attack upon the neighboring province. The governor of Georgia also warned the people of his state against Genêt's efforts to enlist the Creeks in the movement and against Clark's designs upon Spanish Florida.

The recall of "Citizen" Genêt, followed by the diplomatic triumph of Thomas Pinckney in obtaining from Spain the right of deposit on the lower Mississippi in the Treaty of San Lorenzo el Real, solved a pressing problem for western American settlers and relaxed the tension between Spain and the United States along the Louisiana border. The House of Representatives voted impeachment charges against Senator William Blount of Tennessee in 1797, and the Senate, in a separate action, expelled Blount for engaging in a conspiracy to seize the Floridas and Louisiana Territory. The impeachment case was settled in February, 1799, when the Senate decided that it was without jurisdiction. Blount's "conspiracy" was quite popular among the people of Tennessee.

The period of calm on the western frontier was short. Napoleon Bonaparte, First Consul of the French Republic, turned his restless attention to the valley of the Mississippi. He ordered his ministers to collect information on the Spanish province and on the people and products of the Ohio River, which the French still regarded as a part of Louisiana. M. de Pontalba, who had become acquainted with the topography, native population, and commercial possibilities of Louisiana by many years of residence, prepared a *memoir* for Napoleon, in which he suggested the potential wealth of the Mississippi Valley and called attention to Spain's failure to take revenue from her province.[10]

Two weeks after the message of Pontalba was presented to Napoleon, the Treaty of San Ildefonso was signed by the French and Spanish authorities. This agreement provided that France, in return for the cession of Louisiana and of Parma and its dependencies, should elevate the Duke of Parma to the title of king in Etruria. Because of the war between France and England the terms of this treaty were not made public, but gradually the secret became known to European and American diplomats.

The steps by which Napoleon Bonaparte became discouraged in his scheme for re-establishing the French colonial empire in America cannot be traced here. In the history of Haiti, the career of Toussaint L'Ouverture has an important place; and the failure of Napoleon's armies on the island, traceable in part to the great Negro leader's skill as a warrior, had a direct bearing upon the Emperor's decision to give up Louisiana. At the very time when the Jefferson administration was becoming deeply concerned about the changed diplomatic status of New Orleans and was considering means for acquisition of the lower left bank, Napoleon was moving toward a decision to rid himself of the vast area west of the Mississippi.

On March 2, 1803, Secretary of State James Madison sent credentials to Robert R. Livingston and James Monroe in Paris, authorizing them to negotiate for the acquisition of "New Orleans and of West and East Florida, or as much thereof as the actual proprietor can be prevailed on to part with." After some exchange of offers and maneuvering for advantage in the prospective deal, with Livingston and Monroe pretending an indifference which they did not feel and Bishop Talleyrand, representing Napoleon, shuffling the diplomatic cards with his customary indirection, the French Secretary of the Treasury, Barbé-Marbois, was drawn into the conversations. A proposition from Talleyrand to sell the whole of Louisiana was met by Livingston's suggestion that the United

[10] Gayarré, *History of Louisiana*, III, 337–39, 341–42, 410–45; Williams and Shoemaker, *Missouri*, I, 66–75.

States might be willing to pay twenty million francs for it. The Frenchmen apparently regarded that amount as too low for consideration and requested the Americans to give the matter of a serious offer some thought.

The negotiations were carried on at a time when the western American settlers were wildly excited over the announcement that right of deposit at New Orleans was to be withdrawn. Livingston wrote the French minister of exterior relations that the people of the American West faced ruin in the closing of the river to their goods. "All the produce of five States is left to rot upon their hands," he declared. Senator Ross of Pennsylvania had for some time been urging drastic action on the part of the United States. He said that the people of the West had an "undoubted right from nature to the free navigation of the Mississippi." He thought that the process of negotiation was too slow for the relief of the American settlers. "Plant yourselves on the river, fortify its banks, invite those who have an interest at stake to defend it; do justice to yourselves when your adversaries deny it; and leave the event to Him who controls the fate of nations," he urged.

The diplomats at Paris came to an agreement on terms of the cession and signed the treaty on April 30, 1803. Louisiana was ceded to the United States for eighty million francs, of which twenty million were assigned to the payment of United States citizens for obligations from France. The third article provided for incorporation of Louisiana's people "in the Union of the United States" and their admission "as soon as possible, according to the principles of the Federal Constitution, to the enjoyment of all the rights, advantages and immunities of citizens of the United States; and in the meantime they shall be maintained and protected in the free enjoyment of their liberty, property, and the religion which they profess."

The French Colonial Prefect, Pierre Clement Laussat, took formal possession of Louisiana Territory at New Orleans in December, 1803, some months after the treaty of purchase by the United States. He authorized Captain Amos Stoddard of the United States Army to act for France in receiving the upper territory from Spain at St. Louis on March 9, 1804; and the same officer took possession for the United States in a flag-raising ceremony witnessed by Captain Meriwether Lewis, Antoine Soulard, and Charles Gratiot.

The majority of the people in St. Louis and Ste Genevieve in 1804 were French; but Captain Stoddard estimated that English-speaking settlers in the Cape Girardeau district, New Madrid, and scattered through other parts of Missouri, made up at least half of the ten thousand total population.[11]

[11] Houck, *History of Missouri*, II, 346–48; III, 355–75; IV, 160–61; Gayarré, *History of Louisiana*, III, 477, 479, 481–508, 523, 524, 540–49, 580, 582–88, 608–16, 620; IV, 7, 9, 12, 15.

3

MISSOURI TERRITORY, 1803-1821

THE NEW AMERICAN PROVINCE

PRESIDENT JEFFERSON, under authority of the law providing temporary government for Louisiana Territory, named Amos Stoddard commandant of the upper district. From March 10 until September 30, 1804, Captain Stoddard remained in St. Louis as acting governor. In the meantime, Congress made two separate territories of Louisiana: Orleans, with its own government, in the region south of the 33d parallel, the approximate southern boundary of present-day Arkansas; and the District of Louisiana, all the region north of the dividing line. Temporarily, the District of Louisiana was to be under Indiana Territory.

On October 1, 1804, the day set for the beginning of administration by Indiana officers, Governor William Henry Harrison arrived in St. Louis accompanied by the territorial judges, Thomas T. Davis, Henry Vanderburgh, and John Griffin. Five administrative districts had been provided for the settled portion of the upper territory, which contained at this time about ten thousand inhabitants. St. Charles had 1,400 white citizens and 150 slaves; St. Louis, 2,280 whites and 500 slaves; Ste Genevieve, 2,350 whites and 520 slaves; Cape Girardeau, 1,470 whites and 180 slaves; and New Madrid, extending south into present Arkansas, 1,350 whites and 150 slaves.

Under explicit instructions from President Jefferson, Captain Stoddard had made no changes in the local government as acting

45551

executive of the upper territory. He took little part in the affairs of
the province except in the organization of militia units at St. Louis,
Ste Genevieve, Cape Girardeau, and New Madrid. He estimated
that 60 per cent of the population were Americans of English descent. The St. Charles and St. Louis districts contained a large
element of French population, while in New Madrid and Cape
Girardeau the American settlers were in definite majority.

The people of the District of Louisiana were not pleased at
the prospect of being attached to Indiana Territory. Their protest
against government by nonresidents and neglect of property rights
which they enjoyed under Spanish rule was framed by elected
representatives from the five administrative districts. A petition,
prepared by eighteen agents from the five districts and signed
by fifteen of them on September 29, 1804, was presented to Congress by Auguste Chouteau and Eligius Fromentin. Although the
officers were French and eight of the fifteen who signed the Re-
monstrance were of French descent, there were powerful representatives of the American settlers, some of whom had been distinguished citizens of eastern seaboard states during the American
Revolution. George Frederick Bollinger was one of the prominent
men from North Carolina; Stephen Byrd, a settler from Watauga,
came originally, also, from North Carolina; Colonel Christopher
Hays, one of Morgan's men from Pennsylvania, had commanded a
regiment in the war against the British and had held many civil
offices.

Eligius Fromentin, who was born in France, was the best-edu-
cated man among the delegates, and probably the author of the
memorial. He began his career as a Jesuit priest in France but
withdrew from the clerical order and removed to Maryland, where
he was married. He settled in New Madrid soon after the acquisition of Louisiana by the United States.

On March 3, 1805, Congress passed an act setting up a separate
government for the Territory of Louisiana, with boundaries to include the people of the five districts. The governor, appointed by
the President for a three-year term, and the three appointed judges
of the territory were entrusted with the legislative power. A territorial secretary in charge of records and with authority to act for

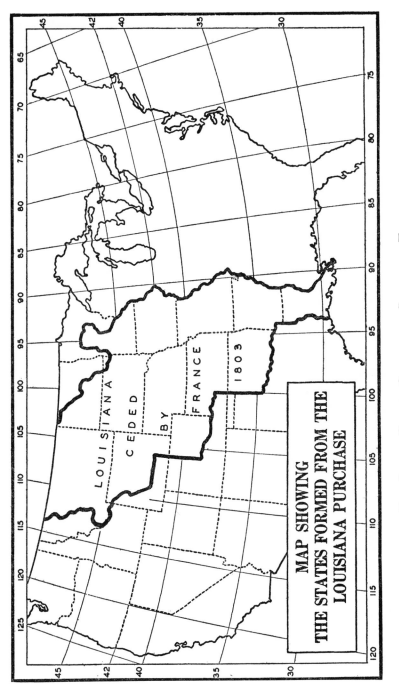

MAP SHOWING
THE STATES FORMED FROM THE
LOUISIANA PURCHASE

LOUISIANA CEDED BY FRANCE 1803

The States Carved Out of the Louisiana Territory

the governor in his absence was also appointed by the President. Four-year terms were provided for the judges and the secretary. Inferior courts might be established by the governor and judges, acting in their legislative capacity. The governor was to serve as commander of the territorial militia and as commissioner of Indian affairs. Jury trials were provided for all criminal cases and for civil suits involving property worth more than one hundred dollars.

President Jefferson appointed General James Wilkinson governor and Joseph Browne, a brother-in-law of Aaron Burr, secretary of the new territory. John B. C. Lucas, John Coburn, and Rufus Easton were selected for the three judicial posts. In a letter dated February 12, 1806, Albert Gallatin warned the President about James Wilkinson: "Of the General [Wilkinson] I have no very exalted opinion; he is extravagant and needy and would not, I think, feel much delicacy in speculating on public money or public lands. In both those respects he must be closely watched; and he has now united himself with every man in Louisiana who had received or claims large grants under the Spanish Government (Gratiot, the Chouteaus, Soulard &c)." Gallatin added that he did not think Wilkinson capable of betraying the United States to a foreign country.

In regard to Auguste Chouteau, Gallatin had written the President on August 20, 1804: "I had two conversations with Chouteau; he seems to be well disposed but what he wants is power and money. He proposed that he should have a negative on all Indian trading licenses, and the direction and all the profits of the trade carried on by the government with all the Indians of Louisiana, replacing only the capital. I told him this was inadmissable. . . . As he may be either useful or dangerous I gave no flat denial to his last request. . . . As to the government of upper Louisiana, he is decidedly in favor of a military one, and appears much afraid of civil law and lawyers."[1]

[1] Amos Stoddard, *Sketches of Louisiana* (Philadelphia, 1812), 226; Jonas Viles, "Population and extent of Settlement in Missouri before 1804," *Mo. Hist. Rev.*, Vol. V (1911), 189–213; *The Life and Papers of Frederick Bates* (T. M. Marshall, ed.; St. Louis, 1926), I, 20, 237–47; Lucien Carr, *Missouri, a Bone of Contention*, 82–87; Louis Houck, *History of Missouri*, II, 376–401. Fromentin removed to Louisiana and became U. S. senator in 1812.

In spite of steady support from the Jefferson administration, General Wilkinson failed to give reasonable satisfaction as governor of the new Louisiana Territory. He held the office from July, 1805, to August, 1806, and during his year in St. Louis became the bitter enemy of many leading citizens there. Rufus Easton, first postmaster, Judge Lucas of the territorial court, Edward Hempstead, clerk of the Legislative Council, Colonel Samuel Hammond, formerly commandant of the District of St. Louis, and Colonel Hammond's nephew, whom Wilkinson charged with the "wanton murder" of an Indian—all were in solid opposition to the governor.

In August, 1806, about the time Aaron Burr was beginning his much debated expedition to the lower Mississippi, General Wilkinson was sent to the Sabine border to meet a rumored Spanish threat in that quarter. The relationship of Burr and Wilkinson, whether treasonable conspiracy or innocent land speculation on a Spanish grant or a plan to engage in Mexican revolution, served to increase the suspicions of St. Louis citizens against the General. Perhaps it would be more accurate to say that his enemies acquired evidence of the elusive character of Wilkinson's loyalty and the ambiguous tone of his government service, while his friends took a firmer hold upon the view that Wilkinson was too fine a man to do the things he obviously was doing.

When he was sure that the Burr expedition from Blenerhassett's Island was not so formidable as to threaten United States control of the western territories, Wilkinson planned to betray his confederate by causing his arrest and court-martial in New Orleans. The General was brought to Richmond, Virginia, to give testimony in Burr's trial for treason; and the attorneys for the government found his evidence so evasive that they gave up their plan to file new charges.

There is evidence that General Wilkinson, in command on the Sabine border, provided himself with insurance by warning Jefferson that a plan was under way to separate Louisiana from the United States and to invade Mexico. He sent a messenger to the Spanish viceroy asking financial support for his part in stopping the threatened invasion of Mexico. During these maneuvers, he kept Burr's confidence in his faithful adherence to their original plans, and he held Jefferson's support long after the President had broken relations with Burr and prosecuted him for treason.

The opponents of Wilkinson in St. Louis accused him of interference with the Board of Commissioners on land titles, of giving his support to wealthy French landowners in preference to American settlers, and of preferring military rule to government by legislature and courts. He was called a despot, a Burrite, a Federalist, and a Royalist. Aaron Burr's visit to Dr. Joseph Browne, his brother-in-law, had added greatly to the rumors of attempted revolution in the West and to the pleas for Wilkinson's removal. The President removed him and appointed a new governor on March 3, 1807.

Alexander McNair came from Pittsburgh to St. Louis in time to see Captain Stoddard acknowledge transfer of the province from France. McNair had commanded a militia company at Pittsburgh in President George Washington's expedition against the Whisky Insurrection, and afterwards had held a commission as first lieutenant in the United States Army. In 1805, Governor William Henry Harrison appointed him an associate justice in the recently established court of common pleas at St. Louis, with Charles Gratiot, J. B. C. Lucas, John Coburn, Rufus Easton, Richard Caulk, James Richardson, and John Allen. During that year he was married to Marguerite Susanne de Reilhe, daughter of a well-to-do French merchant in St. Louis.[2] In 1807 he became governor.

THE LEWIS AND CLARK EXPEDITION

With acceptance by Congress of the bargain made in 1803 by Livingston with the agents of Napoleon, the people of the American Republic quickly adjusted themselves to their new position. President Jefferson, recovering promptly from his doubts concerning the legality of the Louisiana Purchase, published such information

[2] Houck, *History of Missouri*, 404–408; Carr, *Missouri, a Bone of Contention* (Boston and N.Y., 1888), 87–92; *Dictionary of American Biography*, III, 314–21 (article on Aaron Burr by Isaac J. Cox); *ibid.*, XII, 147–48 (article on Alexander McNair by H. Edward Nettles); *ibid.*, XX, 222–26 (article on James Wilkinson by Isaac J. Cox); Walter B. Stevens, "Alexander McNair," *Missouri Historical Review*, Vol. XVII (1922), 3–21; *The Writings of Thomas Jefferson* (Paul L. Ford, ed.; 12 vols., N.Y., 1904–1905), X, 110–11.

as he could obtain on the geography and resources of the new territory and took steps to explore the great river valleys. For exploration of the Missouri, he commissioned his friend and fellow scientist, Meriwether Lewis, to organize and equip a small band of soldiers and frontiersmen.

Instructions were explicit with respect to exploration of the Missouri and its principal tributaries. Careful observation of the native peoples was urged upon the adventurers, with especial consideration for the names and numbers of the tribes, the extent of their territorial claims, relations with other peoples, language, occupations, war, food, clothing, housing, prevalent diseases, laws, customs, and potential commerce. The President also suggested the usefulness of learning the state of "morality, religion, and information" among the various Indian tribes, as a means of "extending and strengthening the authority of reason and justice among them."

Specific directions were given for obtaining information on the Pacific Coast relative to the fur trade and other commercial ventures. Open letters of credit were placed in the explorer's possession as a possible means of obtaining passage on the return by an ocean voyage, in the event that travel overland proved "imminently dangerous."

In December, 1803, Captain Lewis traveled from Washington to St. Louis, chiefly by means of river boats. He was joined at Louisville by Captain William Clark, younger brother of the American Revolutionary commander in the Northwest Territory. Recruits for the expedition went into camp on the Illinois shore opposite the mouth of the Missouri, while the American government awaited official approval from Spanish officials still in control at St. Louis. On May 14, 1804, the explorers were ready to break camp and begin the long and hazardous journey up the Missouri.

Fourteen volunteers had been obtained from the regular army, and in addition, nine young men from Kentucky who were enlisted also as private soldiers. Nine watermen, a corporal, and six soldiers were assigned to the task of helping with defense in case of attack, and to assist in carrying the supplies up to Mandan, the place selected for the first winter quarters. Two French watermen, an interpreter and hunter, and Captain Clark's Negro servant, York, completed the original party—a total of forty-five men, including the sixteen with temporary assignment. Two pack horses were provided for the hunters, who were expected to keep the men supplied with fresh meat.

A keelboat fifty-five feet long, equipped with a large square sail and twenty-two oars, was the principal means of transportation used by the party. A ten-foot deck in the bow and another in the stern, a middle section in which lockers might be raised quickly for a breastwork, and ample storage space were among the conveniences provided by this craft. Two open boats, "one of six and the other of seven oars," also made the journey.[3]

The journey from Wood Creek (opposite the mouth of the Missouri) to the "Kanzas River," which enters the Missouri near the site of Kansas City, required forty-seven days—from May 14 to June 29, 1804. A month later Lewis and Clark were planning a council with the various Indian tribes in the vicinity of Council Bluffs, which was recorded in the Journal at 41 degrees, 17 minutes North Latitude. Thus, two and one-half months were spent in present-day Missouri and on the borders of Missouri on the upstream portion of the expedition.

The value of the exploration to Missouri, however, is not to be measured by milage or direct contact of the adventurers with the area that was eventually incorporated in the state. The hinterland of the river town St. Louis was to be extended to the outermost limits of the Northwest by the settlement of that vast region, and new terminal points were to be established on the Missouri for commerce with the great Southwest along the Osage and Kansas rivers, the Santa Fe Trail, and elsewhere. The explorations of 1804–1806 were significant and dramatic, not only in the adventures of the men who took part in them but in the appeal their discoveries made to the imaginations of ambitious men responsible for future development.

[3] Meriwether Lewis, *History of the Expedition under the Command of Captains Lewis and Clark* (5th ed., 1924, James K. Hosmer, ed.), I, Introduction, xvii–xxxv, xli–xlvi, xlvii–liii, 2, 3; *Journals of Lewis and Ordway* (Milo Quaife, ed.; Madison, 1916), 79; *Original Journals of the Lewis and Clark Expedition* (R. G. Thwaites, ed.; 8 vols., N.Y., 1904), VII, 357–58.

At two o'clock on May 16, the party arrived at St. Charles, on the north bank of the Missouri—a town of one long street, one hundred wooden houses, and a chapel. Its population of 450 were largely descendants of French Canadians, a people who, in their manners, "unite all the careless gayety and the amiable hospitality of the best times in France." In Sergeant Ordway's words, "an old French Settlement and Roman Catholick—some Americans settled in the country around."

At a camp of Kickapoo Indians an exchange of commodities was made: the Indians gave four deer for two quarts of whisky. Osage Woman River, Devil's Race Ground—where the large boat nearly capsized—a three hundred foot cliff with names and paintings on the walls, a French village called St. Johns (more commonly, La Charette), the "last settlement of whites on this river"—these were some of the places noted in the journals during the first ten days.

From time to time, the out-bound travelers met traders' canoes or rafts laden with peltries from the Osage, Pawnee, Kansas, or other western Indians. Near the mouth of the Gasconade, one hundred miles and thirteen days from the Mississippi, George Shannon killed a deer, Joseph Whitehouse was lost, hunting, and Reuben Fields killed a deer. Later, the cause of Whitehouse's delay in returning to the party was explained: he had discovered an interesting cavern—"the most remarkable cave I ever Saw in my travels," in the words of his own journal. The width of the Gasconade at its mouth was reported as 157 yards and the depth, 19 feet.

At 133 miles the Osage River was reached. Two major bands of Osage Indians lived on this stream the explorers stated: the Great Osages, with 500 warriors, and the Little Osages, with 250. The Arkansas Osages, who had removed to the Vermillion River under Chief Bigfoot, had at this time about 600 warriors. Plentiful game was reported—bears and deer—in this part of the journey, and there were occasional meetings with traders on their way to St. Louis with peltries. After passing the Big and Little Chariton rivers, the explorers met several French trappers who camped for the night with them. Captain Lewis persuaded Pierre Dorion, who had lived among the Sioux more than twenty years and was able to speak several Indian languages, to join the expedition.

Above the Grand, one of the Indian hunters reported that he was stalking deer near a small lake when he heard a snake "making a gutteral noise like a turkey." When he fired his gun, the noise became louder. A Frenchman confirmed the story of the vocal snake.[4]

In the rich, wooded land north of the river above the mouth of Grand, the party obtained ash timber for new oars. Here also the hunters "provided two deer and two bear." After passing a point where the current was so rapid that the men were "obleged to waid & Toe the boat over sand bars," the party camped. "Their is Beautiful high Good praries on the South Side pleasantest place I have ever Seen," wrote Sergeant Ordway. And a few days later: "Several men went out hunting killed . . . 4 Deer and one bear, they inform us that their is handsome praries & very good land on the South Side of the River." On June 19, Ordway's record included: "We passed a beautiful large prarie on the North Side, high Rich Bottom on South Side."

The camp on June 29 was near the mouth of the Kansas River in the vicinity of present Kansas City. Two villages of Kansas Indians lived on this stream, the first at a distance of twenty leagues, the second, forty leagues up from its confluence with the Missouri.

On July 8 the expedition passed Ordway's Creek, and beyond it, Little Nodawa Island, Great Nodawa—five miles long and embracing seven or eight thousand acres of good land—and near its western end the mouth of Nodawa River, seventy yards wide and navigable.

Discipline was maintained among the enlisted men by corporal punishment. John Newman's court-martial at noon on October 13, near the present line between North Dakota and South Dakota, considered the charge that he had "uttered repeated expressions of a highly criminal and mutinous nature, to the obvious subversion of discipline and loyalty on the part of the members of the expedition." The jury of nine soldiers convicted him and pronounced sentence—seventy-five lashes on the bare back—and he should be

---

[4] *Journals of Lewis and Ordway*, 48, 49, 80, 81 n. 5, 85, 86 n. 4, 102–103 n. 2, 398–402; J. K. Hosmer, *The Expedition of Lewis and Clark* (Chicago, 1902), I, 4; Lewis, *History*, I, 8–14.

"henceforth discarded from the permanent party engaged for North Western discovery." The severity with which the corporal punishment was executed may be judged from the report that the Arikara chief who witnessed the whipping "was affected to the point of weeping."

Early in November, 1804, the followers of Lewis and Clark were building their cabins at the place selected for the first winter quarters, seven or eight miles below the mouth of Knife River on the east bank of the Missouri. From that time until April 7, 1805, the party remained at Fort Mandan, cultivating the acquaintance of the Indian tribes in the vicinity, repairing and replacing equipment, and employing a few new persons for the continuation of the expedition. On the sixteenth of November, Sergeant Ordway recorded a heavy frost—"Such a frost I never Saw in the States." On that day the men erected the frame for a "provision & Smoak house 24 feet by 14 f." Captain Clark reported, "All hands work at their huts untill 1 o'clock at night." On Saturday, November 17, "The party all moved into the huts."

Corn and other provisions were obtained from the Mandan Indians. On Monday, November 19, the hunters of the exploring party brought in a boat load of wild game: "5 buffalow, 11 Elk & 30 Deer also several kinds of small game." The French interpreter, Toussaint Charbonneau, arrived with four horses "loaded with peltry meat &c."

A Shoshoni woman named Sacajawea, wife of Charbonneau, was unquestionably one of the most interesting and most important persons on the expedition. From Fort Mandan up to the headwaters of the Missouri, across the divide and along the Snake to the Columbia, thence westward to the Pacific, Sacajawea and her infant son were to accompany the explorers. Long before the return of Lewis and Clark to the Mandans, the woman of the Snake tribe (of Shoshonean linguistic stock and related to the Utes, Paiutes, and Comanches) was to prove her value as an interpreter and as a scout, thoroughly acquainted with the upper Missouri and familiar with the habits of the Indian tribes in the area.

Sunday, April 7, 1805, was clear and pleasant at Fort Mandan. A multitude of errands, ceremonies, and conferences were in order as Lewis and Clark set out for the upper Missouri. At the same time the barge began the return trip to St. Louis in charge of Corporal Richard Warfington, with six private soldiers, the pilot Joseph Gravellin, and two French rivermen.

Of the equipment for the party up the Missouri, Captain Lewis wrote: "Our vessels consisted of six small canoes and two large perogues. . . . Altho' not quite so rispectable as those of Columbus or Capt. Cook, were still viewed by us . . . with quite as much anxiety for their safety and preservation." The men under Captains Lewis and Clark included three sergeants (Patrick Gass, Nathaniel Pryor, and John Ordway), twenty-three private soldiers, two interpreters (George Drouillard [or Drewyer] and Toussaint Charbonneau), Sacajawea and her infant son, Charbonneau, Jr., and York, the Negro servant of Captain Clark. Sergeant Gass, thirty-three years of age and thus one of the older men of the party, had been elected by the men to take the place of Sergeant Charles Floyd, who had died after a short sickness on August 20, 1804. A Mandan Indian also accompanied Lewis and Clark as an emissary of peace to the Shoshonis.[5]

The journey up the Missouri, from Fort Mandan to Three-Thousand-Mile Island on the Jefferson River, required four months. On August 12, 1805, Captain Lewis's advance party succeeded in reaching the highest source of the Missouri and crossing the top of a ridge which descended on the west to a tributary of the Columbia River. On the following day he made satisfactory contact with a band of Shoshoni Indians under the leadership of Cameahwait; but after several days of meetings with them, had not succeeded in allaying their suspicion of all white men. The Shoshonis, like Lewis's men, were almost entirely without food, and the Captain's generosity in dividing with them three deer killed by George Drouillard seemed to gain some of their confidence.

It was not, however, until the second party under Captain Clark

[5] *Journals of Lewis and Ordway*, 105 n. 5, 153, 164, 180, 191, 212, 221, 229–31, 233, 239, 254, 255, 266, 272, 277, 315, 320, 371, 390; *The Journals of Lewis and Clark* (Bernard De Voto, ed.), 17, 18, 20; *Original Journals* (Thwaites, ed.), VII, 355–57.

came up with Sacajawea and Charbonneau on August 17 that complete understanding was established between the explorers and the Indians. The Shoshoni woman immediately recognized her fellow-tribesmen, even at a distance mounted on horses; and when she sat down in a tent to interpret for Cameahwait, she recognized in the person of the chief her own brother.

Sacajawea had been captured by the Gros Ventre Indians about four years previously when her own tribe was in camp on the Jefferson Fork of the Missouri. Two or three of the Shoshonis were killed in the attack, and Sacajawea, then about twelve years old, was taken prisoner along with several other children and women. She became the property of Charbonneau by purchase or gambling, and was one of his several wives. When the Indian woman recognized Cameahwait as her brother, she was so overcome that it was impossible for her to continue in the conference as an interpreter.

When Captain Lewis attempted to purchase horses from Cameahwait, he was assured that the explorers might have the use of pack horses and that the chief would aid the party's crossing of the mountains in every way possible. On the journey across the divide and down the rivers of the Northwest to the Pacific, help from the Shoshonis was an important factor. Sacajawea herself proved her great worth. The contrast between the estimates by Lewis and Clark of the French interpreter, Charbonneau, and his Indian wife is pronounced. "Your woman who accompanied you that long dangerous and fatigueing rout to the Pacific Ocean and back deserved a greater reward ... than we were able to give her at the Mandans," Clark wrote to Charbonneau. "As to your little Son (my boy Pomp) you well know my fondness for him and my anxiety to take and raise him as my own child."

The explorers spent the winter of 1805–1806 near the Columbia River at a place which they called Fort Clatsop. Captain Lewis selected the site, a few miles south of the Columbia and seven miles back from the coast on a small stream which the explorers named Netul Creek, now called Lewis and Clark River. The fort consisted of a log stockade fifty feet square and seven cabins, "a row of three ... facing another one of four," with a parade ground between. The cabins were not completed until January 1, 1806, and on March 23, the explorers departed on their homeward journey.

On July 2, Captain Lewis called for six volunteers to go with him on a northern route, up the Marias River, and on the following morning the two parties proceeded on their separate ways. The leader's purpose in thus dividing his men was to explore a larger area than the entire band, traveling as a unit, could cover. Lewis intended to go by the most direct route to the Great Falls on the Missouri, where a part of his men would prepare carriages for the portage around the falls, while the others would explore the Marias River, which Lewis regarded as the limit of Louisiana Territory.

As Lewis and his little band were about to begin the return from the upper Marias, on July 26, 1806, they encountered a party of eight Piegan Indians. George Drouillard was scouting on the opposite side of the stream, and for the moment held the full attention of the Indians. After establishing amicable contact with them, Captain Lewis proposed that the two parties encamp together for the night. To this the Piegans agreed. Captain Lewis noted that the Indians had in their possession only two rifles. He had a long talk with them, in which he indicated that his party had come into the upper Missouri region and on to the Pacific to ask the Indians to be at peace with each other and with the United States. He also invited the Blackfeet and their people to visit the trading houses and exchange goods with white traders.

Captain Lewis, not entirely satisfied of the good intentions of the eight native plainsmen, posted Reuben Fields as guard over the horses. The Indians arose early in the morning (July 27), and as they crowded around the fire, one of them suddenly seized the two rifles belonging to Joseph and Reuben Fields and started off with them. Joseph Fields, who had taken his brother's place as guard, immediately called Reuben. At the same time two other Blackfeet seized the rifles of Drouillard and Captain Lewis.

After fifty or sixty yards Reuben Fields overtook the Indian who had stolen the two rifles and, in struggling with him for possession of the guns, stabbed him through the heart with his knife. The Indian ran off a few steps and fell dead. Drouillard also grappled with the Indian who had taken his rifle and recovered it. Captain Lewis with his pistol pursued the other Blackfoot and compelled him to drop the rifle he had stolen. Lewis also prevented his companions from firing upon the Indians until he discovered that they were trying to drive off all the horses. Then Lewis and his men fought for their property and, in the confusion that followed, recovered all of their horses but one and took four of the Piegans' horses.

With his pistol Captain Lewis shot the Indian who was still armed, at the distance of thirty paces; and, firing as he sprawled on the ground, the Indian fanned Lewis's hair with a rifle ball. Of the baggage left behind by the retreating Indians, Lewis took only some buffalo meat, one gun, two bows and quivers, and four shields. The four Indian horses were found to be very good animals, and the explorers traveled with all speed possible, expecting an attack by a larger force.

The separate bands of Lewis and Clark eventually united just above the mouth of the Little Missouri on August 12. In a hunting accident on the previous day Captain Lewis had been wounded painfully by Peter Cruzat. Although he was quite ill from the wound—he fainted once while Clark was dressing it—he was able to walk in about two weeks. The party reached Fort Mandan on August 14.

Sacajawea, Charbonneau, and their little son remained at the Mandan village. John Colter, youngest man on the expedition, received permission to go back with Joseph Dickson on a trapping expedition, and one of the Mandan head men, Big White (Sheheke), was persuaded to go down to St. Louis with the explorers as the first stage of his journey to Washington to meet President Jefferson. On September 23, 1806, the Lewis and Clark party arrived at St. Louis, where they "fired three Rounds" and the populace "gathered on the Shore and Hizzared three cheers."[6]

[6] Lewis, *History*, I, 139–41, 378–408; II, 119, 214–18, 364, 365, 385–86, 429, 443, 499; *Original Journals* (Thwaites), II, 37, 39, 283, 361, 366; I, xxxiii; II, 10, 130, 132, 155–58, 172, 175, 181, 225; III, 60; V, 348, 358, 365, 373–80; VII, 334–37; *Journals of Lewis and Clark* (De Voto, ed.), 203, 294–336, 415–42; *Journals of Lewis and Ordway*, 382 n. 1; F. W. Hodge, *Handbook of American Indians North of Mexico* (2 vols., Washington, 1905), I, 870; John C. Ewers, *The Blackfeet*, 45–51.

EXPEDITIONS OF ZEBULON M. PIKE AND STEPHEN H. LONG

Other great explorations in Louisiana Territory, none perhaps of such direct importance to Missouri as that of Lewis and Clark, were undertaken during the period before Missouri statehood. Outstanding in these ventures into the unknown were two journeys of Zebulon Montgomery Pike—one to the upper Mississippi, the other to the headwaters of the Arkansas—and the Stephen H. Long expedition up the Missouri and overland to the Rocky Mountains, intended also for Red River exploration but resulting in a journey along the Canadian. Lieutenant Pike was sent by General Wilkinson to explore the source of the Mississippi River while Lewis and Clark were on their journey up the Missouri. This party explored a branch which Pike thought to be the source of the Mississippi, a supposition that was later found to be in error, and the expedition returned to St. Louis on April 30, 1806.

Two months later preparations were almost complete for another, more extensive exploration under Lieutenant Pike. A second commissioned officer, Lieutenant James B. Wilkinson, son of the Governor, was sent along with Pike on this exploration of the Southwest. The party started up the Missouri on July 15, 1806. As a gesture of friendship, Pike and Wilkinson returned to their tribe a delegation of Osage Indians who had recently visited President Jefferson in Washington. The explorers also took with them some Indian women and children captured by Potawatomis and ransomed by government officials. The return of captives proved on this occasion, as on many others, to be the most effective means of winning the confidence of wild Plains Indians.

From the Great Bend of the Arkansas, Lieutenant Wilkinson explored that stream to the Mississippi while Pike continued westward, where he found the distinctive mountain which eventually appeared on maps as Pikes Peak. The party in the Rocky Mountains crossed the Sangre de Cristo range and spent the latter part of the winter on the Río Grande. Here they were arrested by a Spanish military force and taken to Santa Fe. Afterwards they were sent on to Chihuahua and then returned to the United States, being well treated throughout this involuntary extension of their journey.

The Stephen H. Long expedition to the Rocky Mountains began at Pittsburgh on May 1, 1819, and during that month descended the Ohio in the steamer *Western Engineer* to the Mississippi. The two-volume report of the exploration by Dr. Edwin James—who was the botanist, geologist, and surgeon of the party—gives a colorful view of the settlements and the countryside of the Missouri and Illinois banks of the Mississippi. This is the only published narrative of the expedition by a participant, and in writing it Dr. James had access to the notes of Major Long, Captain J. R. Bell—who joined the party at Council Bluffs in May, 1820—and Thomas Say, the naturalist.

The party left St. Louis on June 21, 1819, entered the Missouri, and proceeded up that stream past St. Charles. Thomas Say and three companions, in their capacity as scientific observers, traveled by land up to Loutre Island, carrying their tent, blankets, and provisions on a pack horse, while Major Long and the rest of the explorers continued the journey in the *Western Engineer*. Dr. William Baldwin, the botanist who had become so ill at Pittsburgh that he considered turning back and who had been treated by Dr. Daniel Drake at Cincinnati, would have preferred to accompany Say and his party, but was still unable to walk the necessary distance.

The party went into winter quarters at "Engineer Cantonment" near Council Bluffs. With new instructions from the War Department, Long pushed west in the spring of 1820 to the source of the South Platte. After three weeks of exploration in the upper waters of that stream and along the Arkansas, one group of nine, under Major Long, crossed the upper Cimarron, and after six days began the descent of the Canadian River, which they supposed to be the Red. Captain Bell and the rest of the men traveled down the Arkansas. Dr. James accompanied the band which explored the Canadian, while Thomas Say rode with Captain Bell.

The failure of the Long-Bell party to find the Red River was of little consequence in the broad results of Southwestern exploration. Dr. James's account of the Canadian is of primary interest in the study of the region that was set apart as the home of the Indians, and has an important, though less direct, bearing upon the western trade of the Missouri River. Thomas Say's record of the journey along the Arkansas, with his notes on the Indians of the area, was lost by the desertion of three men on August 30, 1820. The deserters took all the manuscripts prepared by the scientist and his assistants. Furthermore, since they also stole the best of the horses, Captain Bell was unable to catch them.

Major Long reached Fort Smith on September 13, four days after the arrival of Captain Bell. They traveled together down to the Cherokee towns in Pope County, Arkansas, and from that point across country to Cape Girardeau, Missouri. Dr. James and Lieutenant Swift made a little additional tour, from the Cherokee towns to Hot Springs, Arkansas, already well known to the Indians. From Cape Girardeau Major Long and Captain Bell proceeded to Washington.[7]

[7] *The Expeditions of Zebulon Montgomery Pike* (Elliott Coues, ed.), II, 583; *Zebulon Pike's Arkansaw Journal* (Stephen H. Hart and Archer B. Hulbert, eds.; Colo. Springs and Denver, 1932), lxiii–xcvi; *The Journal of Captain R. Bell* (Harlan M. Fuller and LeRoy Hafen, eds.), 13–25; James's *Account of Stephen H. Long's Expedition* (vols. XIV–XVII of Thwaites' *Early Western Travels*), XIV, 10, 11, 18, 84–87, 132–57, 229–50; XVII, 11–41.

4

MATERIAL GROWTH, GOVERNMENT, AND SOCIETY, 1804-1820

THE PATTERN OF SETTLEMENT

AFTER ITS ACQUISITION by the United States, Louisiana Territory increased rapidly in population. The settlements of Upper Louisiana contained 20,845 inhabitants in 1810 and 5,000 more according to the special census of 1814. The next six years saw an impressive growth from 26,000 to 70,000. Missouri was definitely ready for statehood in 1820.

In St. Louis most of the 180 houses in 1804 were built of hewn timber set on plates laid upon a stone foundation or planted in the ground. One-story dwellings were the general rule, sometimes with porches on all four sides, covered by an extension of the roof sloping from the comb of the main structure. Spaces between the upright timbers were filled with stone and mortar. Wooden pins rather than iron nails were used for fastening timbers together. The larger houses had a fireplace at each end, or perhaps a single large chimney in the center with fireplaces on both sides of it, one for each of the two rooms. Two-story houses became more common as the people who were engaged in commerce at St. Louis grew more affluent. The first brick house was erected by Manuel Lisa at the corner of Main and Chestnut streets during the ninth year of American occupation. Before the end of the War of 1812, the town's population had grown to 2,600, and at the time of statehood in 1821, to 5,600.

La Charette, near the site of Marthasville, was fifty miles up the

Missouri from St. Charles and the westernmost settlement of whites visited by Lewis and Clark in 1805. The people were pushing farther west every year, along the Missouri and elsewhere. Only two families lived on the Gasconade in 1808, but three years later the militia muster roll for that area contained 250 names.

In 1814, the county seat of Cape Girardeau district was moved to the new town of Jackson, ten miles west of the river port. Four years later the population of Jackson was about 300, with more than sixty dwelling houses, five stores, two shoemaker shops, one tannery, and two schools—one for boys, the other for girls. Observers disagreed about the character of the people. John Mason Peck said they were "more moral, intelligent, and truly religious than the people of any village . . . in the territory." Timothy Flint, on the contrary, regarded these same people "ignorant, bigoted, and devoid of interest," to a greater degree than any other people in Missouri. "Their country is a fine range for all species of sectaries, furnishing the sort of people in abundance who . . . think by devotion to some favored preacher or sect, to atone for the want of morals and decency, and everything that appertains to the spirit of Christianity."

The dwellings, courthouse, and jail were built of logs. In 1820, Major Long was impressed with the fine, thriving appearance of the town and also by the superior manners of the people.

A straggling settlement on Loutre Island near the mouth of the Gasconade, attacked by a band of eight Potawatomi Indians under Chief Nessotinaineg in 1810, was able to raise a pursuit party of but six men. This party, led by Stephen Cole, was all but annihilated. Nine years afterwards, when Major Long's explorers visited the area, the island was well settled, and a town was planned at the mouth of the Gasconade to bear the name of the river. In three years the number of families in the neighborhood of Côte sans Dessein had increased from 30 to 800. The town of Franklin, settled only two years earlier, contained 120 log houses, thirteen stores, a press that issued a weekly newspaper, two grain mills, two blacksmith shops, four taverns, a courthouse, a log jail, two billiard halls, and a post office. Two brick buildings had been erected and several two-story frame houses.

Boonville, on the south bank across the Missouri from Franklin, had only eight houses; but Major Long in 1819 predicted that its position, secure against river flood waters, would result in more substantial growth for the smaller town—a prophecy that was quite accurate. On Thrall's Prairie, some miles back from the river in the vicinity of present-day Columbia, settlements were made after the War of 1812. In addition to Augustus Thrall, William Baxter, Reuben Gentry, John Berry, and William Berry and their families were among the earliest immigrants to the Columbia neighborhood.

The Boonslick settlement, established at the site of a salt-making enterprise begun by the sons of Daniel Boone in 1807, had seventy-five families four years later. William and Charles Canole had established a blacksmith shop in the community, and Lindsay Carson, father of the famous scout "Kit" Carson, had settled with his family near Fort Kinkead. At Lindsay Carson's house, in 1810, his daughter Elizabeth was married to Robert Cooper. "Kit" Carson, one year of age when the family moved to the Boonslick country, grew up there to the age of seventeen before he ran away from service as a saddler's apprentice in Franklin to the more adventuresome life of a scout in the Rockies. His father had been killed by a limb falling from a tree when "Kit" was nine.

Dr. John Sappington came to Missouri in 1817, lived for a time near Glasgow, and in 1819 moved farther west to Arrow Rock in present Saline County. He fought malaria with quinine, developing Sappington's Anti-Fever Pills, which became well known along the low river valleys that produced many mosquitoes. The first settlers came to Chariton in 1818, and in one year the town grew to about 500 population. The pressure of immigrants in the territory was steadily westward, and by 1819 the areas of present Carroll and Clay counties had permanent settlers. In 1816 a trading post at the mouth of Grand River purchased peltries from the Sac and Fox Indians, who still hunted for deer, elk, bear, and beaver along the stream. Henry Becknell ran a ferry across the Missouri below the mouth of Grand River. The Becknell ferryboat consisted of two large canoes lashed together and covered by a frame on which livestock could be transported across the river.

It was inevitable that settlers should penetrate the country remote from the larger streams. For example, John Pettijohn moved up the White River from Arkansas to settle with twenty-two other families in the vicinity of present-day Springfield. Jeremiah Pierson constructed the first mill on the Pomme de Terre, and Augustine Friend built his house on White River in 1819. James Fisher and William Holt, who lived in a region that is now a part of Taney County, acted as guides for Henry Rowe Schoolcraft through the Ozarks in 1819. Zimri Carter settled near the site of present Van Buren, in Carter County. In this area there are many natural wonders, including the Big Spring, which has a maximum daily flow of 84,000,000 gallons of fresh water, one of the largest springs in the United States.[1]

MISSOURI AND THE WAR OF 1812

Missouri was a part of that western area of the United States which was most hostile toward British policies and activities during the decade preceding the outbreak of war in 1812. The natural clash of interest between the fur traders of Canada and the people of St. Louis and New Orleans who sought to develop the Missouri River trade continued after the Louisiana Purchase in 1803. In place of the French trappers and traders backed by Spanish authority during the period 1763 to 1803, British fur merchants and their agents found themselves confronted by the same persons operating under the new American Republic, with the addition of adventurous "Big Knives," American trappers who penetrated remote river valleys and mountain areas of the great Northwest.

Regis Loisel, who investigated British activity on the upper Missouri in 1803, met Lewis and Clark on his way back to St. Louis. Probably Loisel learned from Jefferson's explorers that Louisiana Territory had been transferred formally to the United States.

[1] Houck, *History of Missouri*, II, 280–82; III, 140, 146–48, 157–60, 166–69; Carr, *Missouri, a Bone of Contention*, 86; *Dictionary of American Biography*, II, 441–43 (article on Daniel Boone), and III, 530–32 (article on Christopher Carson), both articles by William J. Ghent; XI, 291 (article on Manuel Lisa, by Irving B. Richman); Henry Rowe Schoolcraft, *Scenes and Adventures in the Ozark Mountains* (Philadelphia, 1853), 48.

The principal grievances expressed by Missourians against the British were concerned with the influence of agents who supplied Indian bands with weapons and incited them to hostility against traders and settlers from the United States. The clash between Captain Lewis's men and the Piegans on the Marias in 1806 and the raid on Loutre Island in 1810, previously related, were incidents of an extensive and bitter warfare on the Missouri frontier. Henry M. Brackenridge reported many attacks and robberies by the Indians in 1811 and the killing of a member of his own party in a clash with the Potawatomis.

The Sacs and Foxes who lived west of the Mississippi under the leadership of Quashquama met with William Clark in St. Louis and assured him of their friendship toward the United States. In 1812 a delegation of Osages, Delawares, Shawnees, Sacs, and Foxes accompanied Clark from St. Louis to Washington and again declared their friendship; but the Rock River Indians of the Sac and Fox tribe were definitely pro-British during the war. Raids in the vicinity of Salt River, at Fort Mason near the site of Hannibal, and at various points north of the Missouri River prompted Governor Benjamin Howard to call out the territorial militia. At St. Charles, Captain Timothy Kibby and the Governor organized a company of rangers composed of frontiersmen who lived in the settlements along the Missouri—one of whom was Nathan Boone. This company patrolled the area from Fort Mason on the Mississippi westward to Loutre Island. Edward La Gouthrie, a trader at Prairie du Chien, was sent by Superintendent Robert Dickson to obtain the support of Black Hawk and his Rock River Sacs and Foxes for the British. Gouthrie brought presents in the form of money and ammunition to these Indians and the Winnebagoes, who joined Black Hawk in an attack on Fort Madison. When this attempt failed, the eastern Sacs and Foxes joined the British force at Green Bay.

Governor Howard's vigorous use of Missouri militia held the Indians west of the Mississippi in check for a time. British agents were never able to obtain the united support of any major tribe, perhaps because the Indians were not fundamentally in favor of having their land taken by either Englishmen or Americans. Like the Creeks and Seminoles of the South, the Plains Indians of the

Northwest were inclined to regard the British as the lesser of two evils, since the prospect of their settlement on Indian hunting grounds was not an imminent threat. When Governor Howard resigned his office in Missouri to become a brigadier general in the United States Army, President Madison appointed William Clark to take his place as governor. Perhaps no better choice could have been made, particularly in view of the fact that Indian affairs were of first importance in the territory during the war. Clark had the confidence of many Indian leaders and was highly regarded by the people of Missouri. Quashquama's Sacs and Foxes offered to enter the war against the British, but were advised to take a neutral stand.

In spite of the vigilance of Governor Clark's militia, Sacs and Foxes from the Rock River area attacked isolated settlements along the west bank of the Mississippi. Raids at Gilbert's Lick, above the mouth of the Missouri, and at Portage des Sioux led John McNair to attempt retaliation. His party of twelve was ambushed and wiped out, on the Illinois shore.

The people of Missouri constructed a line of stockade forts along the portion of the Mississippi frontier most exposed to Indian attacks. St. Charles was alarmed by attacks on settlers near the town, and the people of St. Louis were sufficiently concerned, in one meeting, to pass a resolution for erecting fortifications. In regions of sparse population, the settlers commonly built log houses with a projecting upper story and convenient loopholes for their firearms.

During the year 1813 Indian hostilities continued, and the Missouri troops were active. Major Henry Dodge, later advanced to the rank of general, Alexander McNair, afterwards governor of Missouri, Major Nathan Boone, Lieutenant Colonel Daniel M. Boone, and many other noted men of the territory saw active service. Captains Allen Ramsey and Peter Craig, both of Cape Girardeau, were killed—Ramsey in a skirmish in 1813 near St. Charles, and Craig at the battle of the Sink-Hole.

In September, 1814, General Henry Dodge with 350 horsemen marched to western Missouri, where the small, widely scattered settlements were hard to defend against fast-moving Indian raiders. Dodge's rangers were composed of five companies, under Captains W. Thompson of St. Louis, Isaac Van Bibber of Loutre Island, Ralph Daugherty of Cape Girardeau, Robert Poston from the Flat River country, and Benjamin Cooper of the Boonslick settlement. Two majors, Daniel Morgan Boone and Nathaniel Cook, served under Dodge, and during the campaign Captain Cooper was elevated to the rank of major. A man who was later to be elected one of the United States Senators from Missouri, David Barton, was a private in the St. Louis Company. The Apple Creek Indians, Shawnees and Delawares, supported Dodge with a small force that included the famous old Shawnee war leader, Papiqua, and a younger Shawnee chief, Kishkalewa.

General Dodge and his men pursued and overtook a party of hostile Miamis on the south side of the Missouri at a place that is now called Miami's Bend, in Saline County. The Indians—31 warriors and 122 women and children—prepared to fight behind hastily constructed earthworks; but when they saw that the attacking force, which completely surrounded them, had vastly superior numbers, they were ready to negotiate for surrender. Kishkalewa opened the talk for General Dodge, who promised, all of his officers agreeing, that the Miamis should be received as prisoners, with safe conduct back to the settlements. However, when the Boonslick men found in possession of the Indians a rifle which had belonged to a settler from their community who had been recently ambushed, they threatened to repudiate the promise. General Dodge confronted Captain Cooper with drawn sword, demanding that the Boonslick company be ordered to carry out the terms of the surrender. Major Boone took his place by the side of the General. Captain Cooper reluctantly obeyed, and the Boonslick men fell in line.[2]

After the Treaty of Ghent was agreed upon by the representatives of Great Britain and the United States, ratified, and proclaimed in the United States, warfare on the Missouri frontier subsided but slowly. Colonel Edward Nicholls in Florida and the

[2] *Tabeau's Narrative of Loisel's Expedition to the Upper Missouri* (Annie Heloise Abel, ed.; Norman, 1939), 20–28; *Original Journals of the Lewis and Clark Expedition* (Thwaites), I, 29; VI, 270; Houck, *History of Missouri*, III, 98–139; William T. Hagan, *The Sac and Fox Indians*, 48–53.

lower Mississippi, laboring to keep Creek and Seminole resentment active and at the same time to arouse the British ministry to renewal of the war, was only one of the officers in North America who were not satisfied with the results. In June, 1815, the Sacs, Foxes, Iowas, and Winnebagoes, with more than twelve hundred warriors on the Rock and Des Moines rivers, were still on the warpath and still receiving from Robert Dickson and other British agents encouragement to hostility along with materials for waging war.

At Portage des Sioux, early in 1815, the Indian leaders who had been at war with the United States were invited to meet with government officials to consider new treaties and the confirmation of older agreements. Governor William Clark, Ninian Edwards of Illinois, and Auguste Chouteau were selected by President Madison to act for the United States. The Sacs living on the Missouri River confirmed the treaty of February 21, 1805, between the United States and the united tribes of the Sacs and Foxes. The Indian leaders also agreed to "remain distinct and separate from the Sacs of Fox River, giving them no aid or assistance whatever, until peace shall be concluded between the United States and the said Sacs of Fox River."

The Indians of the Rock River area refused to attend the conference that resulted in this agreement; but on December 30, 1816, their chiefs met with the United States commissioners and confirmed the Treaty of St. Louis, made by Governor William Henry Harrison on November 3, 1804 (ratified February 21, 1805). The United States agreed to place this hostile portion of the tribe on the same footing that they had enjoyed before the war, provided the Indians would surrender to the commanding officer at Cantonment Davis on the Mississippi River all property seized in raids on white settlers since the Fox River Sacs had been notified that peace had been concluded at Ghent on December 24, 1814. The Sac and Fox leaders agreed to a permanent peace with the United States.

In order to protect themselves from the hostile Indians, settlers in Missouri frequently constructed what they called forts—usually just large log houses with projecting upper stories fitted with loopholes for firearms, but sometimes more conventional blockhouses placed at the corners of large rectangular areas enclosed in log stockades. In all of the settlers' forts, however, an attempt was made to insure a water supply in the event of a siege. For example, water was the factor that determined the location of Fort Wood, near Big Spring at the site of present Troy, and of the second Fort Cole, on a bluff above Missouri River, in present East Boonville, where water could be drawn up by means of a rope and windlass in the event of a strong Indian attack. Cooper's Fort, near present-day Glasgow on the Missouri River, supplied food for residents of the stockade by planting a common field of 250 acres. During the worst of the Indian attacks, twenty families and some unattached young men occupied this fort, and took part in the cultivation of the field.

The relation of Indians in Illinois and Missouri to the fur trade in St. Louis under the jurisdiction of the United States and in Canada under the British created many problems of loyalty for the native population. White traders were not entirely free from the perplexing aspects of the situation, and in at least one instance, an officer of high rank in the United States Army deliberately permitted his name to be linked with both major parties in the war.

Thomas Forsyth was a secret agent for the United States who frequently obtained the release of American prisoners captured by the Indians. A former British trader, he concealed his new allegiance to the United States and received rough treatment from an American military force that captured him at Peoria and left him with other prisoners, British and Indian, at a place on the Mississippi below Alton. After being rescued, he complained to the American authorities that his treatment as a prisoner of war was inhuman. *Niles' Weekly Register* for August 20, 1814, reported that Major Forsyth had conducted to Greenville "160 Pottawatamies, 750 Shawanese, 100 Delawares, 193 Wiandots, 150 Miamies, 50 Kickapoos, 30 Weas, and 20 Senecas," all of whom had accepted "the American tomahawk, and [were] willing to fight against the enemies of the United States." It was also reported in the same newspaper that Robert Dickson, the fur trader who had become British Indian superintendent in the Northwest and whose wife was the sister of Chief Red Thunder of the Dacotah tribe, had offered to pay the Winnebagoes two thousand pounds sterling in merchandise for Forsyth's head. Dickson was also accused of trying to hire a Sac warrior to assassinate Governor William Clark.[3]

THE GOVERNMENT OF MISSOURI TERRITORY, 1812–1821

An act of Congress in 1812 made Missouri a territory of the highest class. This Organic Act provided for an elected House of Representatives, one member to each five hundred white male residents; a Legislative Council of nine members; and a governor appointed by the President. The two houses with the governor constituted the General Assembly, which had the power to enact civil and criminal laws, establish inferior courts, and provide details for the duties of local officers. The members of the council were appointed by the President of the United States with the consent of the Senate for a term of five years, the nine members to be selected from a list of eighteen nominated by the territorial House of Representatives. Only male residents of Missouri, twenty-five years of age and owners of at least two hundred acres of land in the territory, were eligible to sit in the Council; but the House was open to all white men who were freeholders, taxpayers, and residents of Missouri for one year prior to the election.

Five counties—St. Charles, St. Louis, Ste Genevieve, Cape Girardeau, and New Madrid—took part in the election of the first territorial House of Representatives and the first delegate to Congress. Edward Hempstead, a young attorney who was admitted to the bar in Connecticut, who had come out to Vincennes in 1805 and walked to Missouri from that Indiana town, was elected delegate. During his brief practice of law at St. Louis, he had served as clerk of the Legislative Council, deputy attorney-general for St. Charles and St. Louis districts, and attorney-general for the Territory of Louisiana.

[3] *A Compilation of All the Treaties Between the United States and the Indian Tribes Now in Force* (Washington, 1873), 734, 735–37; Williams and Shoemaker, *Missouri*, I, 73–74; *The Indian Tribes of the Upper Mississippi Valley and Region of the Great Lakes* (Emma Helen Blair, ed.; 2 vols., Cleveland, 1912), II, 181 n. 61; *Dictionary of American Biography*, VI, 536 (article on Thomas Forsyth, by Louise Phelps Kellogg); *Niles' Weekly Register*, Vol. VI (August 20, 1814), 426–27.

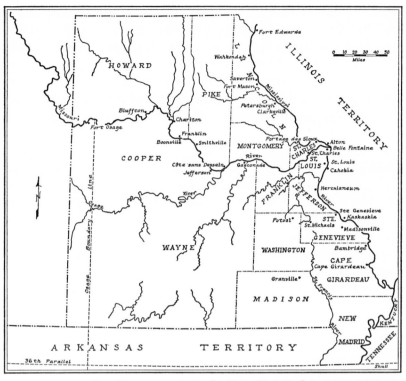

Based on a map from the State Historical Society of Missouri

MISSOURI TERRITORY
(after a portion of Arkansas County was included in the new
Territory of Arkansas in 1819)

Party politics had little to do with elections in Missouri during territorial days. Most of the people who came west of the Mississippi to settle the land were young and inclined toward liberal principles; but the commercial activities of St. Louis and other towns on the great river highways and the limited view of democractic government that was characteristic of the old French traders and their countrymen gave the new territory a complicated pattern of politics. Force of character and competitive spirit were large factors of success in Missouri politics, as in other western territories.

The first territorial House of Representatives, with thirteen members met at the Robidoux house in St. Louis on December 7, 1812. After Judge John B. C. Lucas administered the oath of office to each member, the House elected William C. Carr of St. Louis as speaker. Eighteen residents of Missouri were nominated for the Legislative Council, and President Madison sent his list of the nine who were to serve. Best known among the members of the House, perhaps, were Speaker William C. Carr and member George Bollinger, an old resident of the Cape Girardeau area. In the Council, James Flaugherty of St. Charles, Auguste Chouteau and Samuel Hammond of St. Louis, and John Scott of Ste Genevieve were well known throughout the territory.

Secretary Frederick Bates acted as governor in the absence of Benjamin Howard, who had resigned his office in Missouri when he accepted an appointment as brigadier general in the United States Army; but when the General Assembly met in July, 1813, Governor William Clark was ready to assume the duties of the office. Washington County was created, west of Ste Genevieve, with a population of about 1,000. The total number of inhabitants in the territory was over 26,000, including about 2,000 slaves and free Negroes. The name of Stephen F. Austin, representing Washington County, appeared among the members of the House in 1815 and the later sessions of the territorial legislature; and Arkansas County, containing most of the present state of Arkansas, was detached from New Madrid and given one representative in the House.

Eighteen new counties were created in Missouri during the

years 1818 and 1820, ten of which were organized by the first
General Assembly of the new state in 1821. The establishment of
the line between Missouri and Arkansas was an essential part of
the maneuvering in Missouri's struggle for statehood. Eventually
the line was defined as follows:

> Beginning in the middle of the Mississippi River, on the parallel of
> thirty-six degrees of north latitude; thence west along that parallel of
> latitude, to the St. François River; thence up, and following the course
> of that river, in the middle of the main channel thereof, to the parallel
> of latitude of thirty-six degrees and thirty minutes; thence west along
> the same, to a point where the said parallel is intersected by a meridi-
> an line passing through the middle of the mouth of the Kansas River,
> where the same empties into the Missouri River . . . .

Suffrage in Missouri was held by white male citizens twenty-one
years of age, who had lived in the territory for one year and paid a
county or a territorial tax. By a law of 1816, Congress abolished
appointment of Council members. The qualified voters in each
county were entitled to elect one member for a term of two years
(instead of five years). The changes provided by this act were in
harmony with the democratic tendencies of the West and of the
country as a whole after the War of 1812.

The most striking change that marked the transfer of Louisiana
Territory to American control was the shift of authority from the
lieutenant governor and his district commanders to elected officials
and territorial administrators responsible to the government at
Washington. Political discussion among the American settlers was
a factor in public affairs from the beginning of occupation by the
United States; and the influence of Missouri people upon territorial
government is obvious in the reaction of Congress to popular demands. The old French population took little interest in politics;
in fact, after a few years they and their descendants had practically dropped out of the contests for public office.

SOCIETY AND THE BEGINNINGS OF AMERICAN CULTURE

The transfer of government to American authorities from Spanish
officials who had been effective in making arrests and prompt in

applying punishment was not achieved without loss of order. The departure of the Spaniards who, backed by the military arm, had exercised despotic power was accompanied by a strong and increasing wave of settlers. Many of the people who came to Missouri were venturesome frontiersmen, unaccustomed to restraint in the pioneer settlements of North Carolina, Tennessee, Kentucky, Indiana, or Illinois, from which they came. A few were fugitives and some were certain to create disorder in any region that 'they inhabited. The net result in territorial Missouri was an excess of violence—duels, riots, brawls, and assaults in great variety. Protection for the Indian against lawless whites was seriously reduced; theft of livestock and various forms of abuse were so common as to give ample motive for Indian hostility toward the United States during the War of 1812.[4]

Education and refinement were not unknown in the territory, however, as the testimony of many residents and travelers proves. Edward Hempstead, Connecticut born and possessed of more than ordinary education and legal training, characterized the society of St. Louis in 1805 as "good." George Sibley wrote that the society of St. Louis in 1816 was "pretty good and daily improving." Christian Schultz spoke highly of the modesty, agreeable manners, beauty and good taste of the ladies of St. Louis. Other visitors mentioned the fact that private libraries were not unknown in early Missouri, and movements for establishing public libraries were begun in St. Louis and Franklin before the year of statehood.

People who traveled in the back-country, however, were sometimes shocked by the displays of brutality that came to their attention. Henry R. Schoolcraft, relating his experiences in 1818 on the upper waters of the White River in the Ozarks, wrote: "In their childish disputes, boys frequently stab each other with knives, two instances of which have occurred since our residence here. No correction was administered in either case, the act being rather looked upon as a promising trait of character."

Schoolcraft considered the lack of schools, general ignorance of books, neglect of religion, and absence of moral restraint as ele-

[4] Houck, *History of Missouri*, II, 412; III, 1, 2, 6–16, 55–57, 182, 183, 268; *United States Statutes at Large*, III, 545.

ments of a "truly deplorable" state of society "for the rising generation." Apparently without entire recognition of the significance of his statement, Schoolcraft called attention to the self-reliance of young Missourians: "They begin to assert their independence as soon as they can walk, and by the time they reach the age of fourteen, have completely learned the use of the rifle, the arts of trapping beaver and otter, killing the bear, deer, and buffalo, and dressing skins and making mockasons and leather clothes."

Gambling was a popular form of amusement among all classes. Taverns and other public places maintained facilities for playing a great variety of games. Merchants, Indian agents, lawyers and physicians, boatmen—including the new class who braved the dangers of steam navigation—trappers visiting in St. Louis between their ventures in the wilds of the upper Missouri, and many other citizens tried their hands at cards or dice. Even the Negro slaves were known to find the opportunity for risking their meager possessions in games of chance. The professional gambler made his appearance at an early date, in St. Louis, New Madrid, and on the river boats. The third General Assembly of the territory, along with acts chartering the Bank of Missouri, providing a bounty for killing panthers, wildcats, and wolves, and granting a charter to the Potosi Academy, also established several lotteries. The sale of lottery tickets was a common form of raising public money.

The duels in Missouri Territory involved many persons of prominence, including army officers, attorneys and physicians, and territorial officials. In 1807, William Ogle, a Cape Girardeau merchant, challenged Joseph McFerron, clerk of the district court, because of a real or fancied injury. They fought on Cypress Island, and McFerron's bullet struck Ogle in the head, killing him instantly. Although McFerron resigned his position in the district court, public opinion was so strongly in his favor that he was called upon in a short time to resume his post.

Young lawyers, contesting for advancement in the rough society of the territory, were especially prone to settle their disputes by dueling. An island in the Mississippi adjacent to St. Louis was so much in demand by the duelists that it came to be called "Bloody Island." Dr. Bernard Farrar fought there with a young attorney named James A. Graham in 1810. Graham died later from the wound he received. In 1816, Henry S. Geyer wounded George Kennerly in a duel on Bloody Island, but the injured man lived and became a close friend of Geyer. Charles, the son of Judge John B. C. Lucas, survived a first duel on Bloody Island with Thomas Hart Benton, but in a second meeting fell with a bullet in his heart. Joshua Barton, recently appointed federal district attorney for the state of Missouri by President James Monroe, was killed by Thomas Rector in a duel.[5]

ECONOMIC PROGRESS: LEAD-MINING, AGRICULTURE,
AND THE FUR TRADE

Before Missouri statehood, the people of Ste Genevieve regarded the mining of lead on public lands as one of their rights, based upon Spanish law and provisions of the Louisiana Purchase treaty. William C. Carr, employed by the United States government to investigate land claims, reported to Albert Gallatin's Treasury Department in December, 1805, that $50,000 worth of ore had been taken from the mines on public property during the previous summer. As an indication of the potential wealth in the mineral lands, Carr stated that a single laborer at Mine à Breton, "part of which is claimed by Moses Austin, Esquire," had obtained for one day's work the sum of one hundred dollars. Secretary Gallatin recommended that official permission should be required of all persons who desired to dig for lead on public land.

The first shot-tower in Missouri and in all the West was established by John N. Macklot at Herculaneum in 1809. Ten years later two other towers occupied points on the bluffs above the Mississippi at this port, and Christian Wilt with his partner, John Honey, had erected a shot-tower at Illinois Station. In 1818 the average cost of transportation from the lead mines at Potosi or Mine à Breton to Herculaneum, distances under forty miles, was seventy-five cents per hundredweight, whereas, the cost of trans-

[5] Henry Rowe Schoolcraft, *Journal of a Tour into Missouri and Arkansas, 1818–1819* (London, 1820), 48–50; William Nisbet Chambers, *Old Bullion, Senator from the New West*, 50–53, 72–76; Houck, *History of Missouri*, I, 57, 72, 73, 74–79, 82.

porting an equal weight one thousand miles by steamboat, from the river port to New Orleans, was seventy cents.

Lieutenant Colonel George Bomford, reporting for the Army Ordnance Department to Secretary John C. Calhoun in 1822, gave a summary of lead production in Missouri Territory. Most of the mines were in Washington County and adjacent areas, he stated, about thirty-five miles south of the Missouri River. From thirty-three to forty-five mines were active in the group that included Mine la Motte, Mine à Breton, Shibboleth mines, Mine à Martin, Mine Renault, and Bryan's mines. The productive Shibboleth mines, Bomford said, were claimed by "a Mr. Smith . . . and also a Mr. Lebaume"; and the rich, extensive Mines à Dubuque, "in the territory detached from the State of Missouri," had claims against their titles by the heirs of Dubuque and by Auguste Chouteau.

"Great injury is supposed to have resulted to the United States," the officer wrote, "from those and other claims not having been satisfactorily adjusted by the former commissioners." Lieutenant Colonel Bomford repeated the charge of an informant that the government had not properly supported lessees of the mining lands against claims based upon old Spanish grants and against intruders. He advocated small leases, on the ground that "no beneficial effects have resulted" from the "large leases or monopolies of large tracts." The Shibboleth mines, he declared, "might have been made to produce to the United States about $10,000 per annum."

The Bomford Report quotes Henry R. Schoolcraft to the effect that Missouri lead mines produced three million pounds in 1818, "a much greater amount" in 1821. Land Commissioner George Graham, also basing his estimates upon the findings of Schoolcraft, stated that fifty-five million pounds of lead from Missouri had been smelted between the acquisition of Louisiana in 1803 and December, 1819. This product, he thought, had an average value of $149,728 a year.

The French settlers had developed a system of farming in which the common field was the dominant factor, both in Missouri and on the lower Mississippi. Perhaps the maintenance of a common levee was sufficient reason for the survey of land in long strips along the Mississippi, where overflow was a constant threat. In

Missouri the system was explained by the necessity of prompt group action against Indian attack and the economy of fencing in large tracts. Probably the long, narrow strips, one arpent (192 feet, 6 inches) wide and forty arpents deep, were modeled without conscious imitation upon the medieval system, in which peasant holdings were similarly patterned. French agricultural colonists on the St. Lawrence and in Illinois, as in Missouri and on the lower Mississippi, employed the common field, with fences under the supervision of an official and the people living in villages. In Missouri under Spanish rule a board of umpires reported to the syndic in regard to the condition of fences and ruled on disputes. The common field at Ste Genevieve, in the fertile Mississippi bottom, contained about 3,500 acres extending several miles along the river.

Many observers, before and after the purchase of Louisiana by the United States, criticized the French farmers for their failure in thorough cultivation and for their use of crude wooden implements. The explorers on the Lewis and Clark expedition described the French inhabitants of the St. Charles area as poor farmers.

In the territorial period, most of Missouri's land was still wild and uncultivated, but the planting and cultivation of crops grew steadily in importance as the population increased. The clearing of timber from the land for the purpose of farming was intimately connected with the development of wood products in great variety. Rail fences, log houses, and wood for fuel were among the early and obvious uses of timber by the settlers. Major Long noted that a farmer on Loutre Island cut two hundred sturdy fence rails, eleven feet long, from a single walnut tree and thirty thousand shingles from one cottonwood.

American farmers from Kentucky, Virginia, and other regions of older settlement brought new standards of cultivation to Missouri. The Stephen H. Long expedition, traveling along the two great rivers in the summer of 1819, recorded ample evidence of progress in agriculture during the interval of fifteen years since Captain Lewis made his journey up the Missouri. Long took notice of a fine wheat field near the river on the land of a settler from Virginia. The Talbot farm on Loutre Island, a few miles below the mouth of the Gasconade, was a well-cultivated tract, and its owner was able to furnish the travelers with a supply of vegetables and poultry. Above Loutre Island, the evidences of careful soil cultivation were not so numerous; but large clearings in the Boonslick country showed clearly the intention of the settlers to farm there. Hannah Cole, with her nine children, crossed to the right bank of the Missouri, settling in the region that is now Cooper County. Indian hostilities during the War of 1812 forced Hannah and her children, together with Stephen Cole and his family of six, to take refuge in Forts Kinkead and Hempstead north of the river. These white settlers had regarded the Sacs of Moniteau Creek as good neighbors, "kind and obliging." Samuel Cole later recalled that he had often hunted with Quashquama, Keokuk, and the half-blood Blundo, and that he was well acquainted with young Black Hawk.

Because the Boonslick country had a plentiful supply of elk, deer, bear, and a variety of small game, pioneer settlers were attracted to the area. Of greater importance for the future, it came to be known as a region of deep, fertile soil, where corn flourished and pasturage for livestock was abundant without planting or cultivation. An ample water supply and the presence of salt in the region were added incentives to settlement. In November, 1819, it was reported that three thousand persons passed through St. Charles in the month of October, "bound principally for Boon's Lick."[6]

A change in Missouri's economic life which came with American settlers was the sharp rise in the price of uncleared land. Under Spanish rule speculation was discouraged, and the demand for unimproved land was so slight that it was practically disregarded on the market; but by 1820 such land was the object of much interest to American investors. The increase of local markets for farm products, as well as growth of mining and salt making, and a huge increase in the fur trade brought a positive upward trend in the prices of all grades of land.

The great era of the fur trade in Missouri began in territorial days. After the purchase of Louisiana and the explorations of

[6] *Ibid.*, 45, 46, 152, 154, 190; II, 232–35; *American State Papers, Public Lands,* III, 563–64; *The Lewis and Clark Expedition* (Hosmer, ed.), I, 4, 5; Williams and Shoemaker, *Missouri,* I, 190–202.

Loisel and Tabeau, Lewis and Clark, and Zebulon Pike, competition began in earnest for the hides and furs of the upper Missouri and the Southwest. Manuel Lisa, the most talented and one of the most intrepid of the fur traders, was an outstanding figure in the enterprise until his death in 1820. Ensign Nathaniel Pryor, René Jesseaume, George Drouillard, and John Colter utilized their knowledge of the great Northwest in serving the new trading companies; and the Chouteau family of St. Louis, already well established in a variety of business enterprises, continued their activities in furs and hides.

Pierre Chouteau accompanied Ensign Pryor on his journey up the Missouri in 1807 for the return of Chief Sheheke to his tribe, the Mandans. Apparently, Frederick Bates took enough interest in the chief's safe conduct to try to exact from Manuel Lisa a promise that he would accompany Chouteau's party; but the promise, if given, was evaded, and the return of Sheheke was prevented by the Sioux and Arikaras. Ensign Pryor and Pierre Chouteau held Manuel Lisa responsible for the attack on their party by hostile Indians, charging him with bad faith; but it is doubtful that he actually encouraged the attack or displayed more selfishness in providing for his own safety than was shown by his principal competitors in the fur trade.

By 1809, the Missouri Fur Company, with a capital of forty thousand dollars, was expanding its operations from St. Louis under the leadership of Manuel Lisa, William Clark, and Sylvester Labadie. During the War of 1812 the fur trade reached a low point, but it revived after the Treaty of Ghent. By 1819, fifteen hundred buffalo hides were being delivered in St. Louis annually. Robidoux and Papin were competing with the Missouri Fur Company for Pawnee, Oto, Omaha, Sioux, and Iowa trade by that time; Bernard Pratte and A. F. Baronet Vásquez, with a post near Omaha Village, traded with the same tribes; and the Chouteaus traded with the Osage and Kansa tribes.

Manuel Lisa planned to open overland trade with Santa Fe before his first important trading venture up the Missouri in 1807, but the scheme was abandoned, probably because of Spanish opposition. Other traders in Missouri were interested in the possibilities of Santa Fe trade, however, particularly after Zebulon Pike returned from his expedition to the Southwest and reported the wide disparity between the low prices of provisions and livestock, on the one hand, and the high prices of manufactured goods, on the other.

"New Mexico . . . sends out about 30,000 sheep annually, tobacco, dressed deer and cabrie skins, some furs, buffalo robes, salt, and wrought copper vessels of superior quality. It receives in return, from Biscay and Mexico, dry goods, confectionery, arms, iron, steel, ammunition, and some choice European wines and liquors; from Sonora and Sinaloa, gold, silver, and cheese. . . . Flour sells per hundred, at $2; salt, per mule load, $5; . . . horses, each, $11; sheep, each, $1; beeves, each, $5; mules each, $30; superfine cloths, per yard, $25; fine cloths, per yard, $20; linen, per yard, $4; and all other dry goods in proportion."

The American traders, pushing out toward Spanish lands, and occasionally passing beyond the limits of Louisiana Territory, were not always successful in returning with the goods they obtained in the Southwest. The Spanish boundary was not defined until John Quincy Adams and Luis Onís agreed upon terms of the Florida Purchase treaty in 1819. In the main, the Santa Fe trade was forced to wait until Mexico had established its independence.[7]

[7] Houck, *History of Missouri*, II, 208; III, 155, 178–81; Thomas Nuttall, *Travels into the Arkansas Territory* (Vol. XIII of Thwaites' *Early Western Travels*), 77–79; Chittenden, *The American Fur Trade*, I, 119–24, 137–58; *The Life and Papers of Frederick Bates*, I, 199, 247; *The Expeditions of Zebulon M. Pike* (Coues, ed), II, Part III, "Observations on New Spain," 718–806.

5

THE NEW STATE OF MISSOURI

MOVEMENT FOR STATEHOOD; REACTIONS IN CONGRESS

THE MISSOURI TERRITORIAL DELEGATE, John Scott, presented a petition to Congress on March 16, 1818, praying for statehood. During the three years following, the problem of Missouri's admission to the Union proved to be the most absorbing political question in Washington and the country at large. Writers on the history of the period have given the subject detailed attention. Differences of opinion exist, however, not only about the emphasis that is due the various aspects of compromise, but upon the difficult puzzle of individual motives and political cross-currents. The constitutional disputes were numerous and the sectional bitterness that characterized the debates was clearly related to the hostility that grew into war four decades later.[1]

John Scott's petition and the earlier statehood proposals were turned over to a select committee of which the delegate from Missouri was chairman. A month later, Scott reported a bill for the admission of Missouri as a state, but it was referred to the Committee of the Whole and not acted upon before adjournment of the first session.

[1] Frederick Jackson Turner, *The Rise of the New West, 1819–29* (N.Y., 1906), 149–71; Houck, *Missouri*, III, 243–44; William Plumer, Jr., *The Missouri Compromises and Presidential Politics* (St. Louis, 1926), 3n.; James Albert Woodburn, "The Historical Significance of the Missouri Compromise," *American Historical Association, Annual Report*, 1893, XX, 249–97; Frank H. Hodder, "Side Lights on the Missouri Compromises," *American Historical Association, Annual Report*, 1909, IX, 151–61.

The rapid settlement of Missouri and other parts of the West had brought about a struggle for control between the North and South. Fundamentally it was a contest of money crops produced by slave labor and small-farm production, free labor, rising industry, and consequent growth of commerce. The steadily increasing advantage in northern population was the product of immigration and the combination of industry and commerce that supplemented small-farm production. The three-fifths rule—by which slaves were given this fractional weight in apportioning members in the House of Representatives—together with the relatively fast growth of population in the free states, had shifted control of the House to the North. Theories concerning the constitutional power of Congress to exclude slaves from the territories were not merely academic exercises. The demand for slave labor in the Southwest and the resulting trend upward in the market value of Negroes injected bitterness into the debates over expansion of slave labor. Southern politicians, alarmed by their minority status in the House of Representatives, were determined to hold their equality of members in the Senate.

Sectional rivalry was to become a dangerous, unhealthy political phenomenon during the three years of conflict over the admission of Missouri. It was the misfortune of the South that the owners of slaves, a small minority of the population, succeeded in maintaining the false concept that their property interests were synonymous with the welfare of the entire section.

Between the establishment of the Constitution with its slavery compromises and the beginning of agitation in Missouri for the admission of that territory as a slave state, Congress had maintained a balance between the two sections. Vermont, the eighth free state, had been followed by the admission of Kentucky and Tennessee, to restore equality in the Senate; Ohio, Indiana, and Illinois, north of the Ohio River, had been balanced by the admission of three slave states, Louisiana, Mississippi, and Alabama.

In the three new states north of the Ohio River, proslavery sentiment of the southern population was offset by the antislavery provision of the Northwest Ordinance, which discouraged the growth of slave property but did not free Negro slaves already in the area. In the contest over the labor system in Ohio, Indiana, and Illinois, at statehood, the vested interests of slaveowners were not enough to maintain their property rights against the settlers from both sections who opposed slavery on principle. Edward Coles, a Virginian who had freed his own slaves with a dramatic flourish when he came to Illinois in 1819, quickly assumed leadership of the antislavery men in the new commonwealth. During one of the periodic contests to legalize slave property, he was elected governor, in 1822. He helped to defeat a determined drive of the proslavery men in 1824 to call a convention for amending the constitution. Their principal object was to legalize slave labor, so that Illinois might compete with Missouri for the immigrant slaveowners who were pouring into the undeveloped western lands.

In Missouri the owners of land along the Missouri and Mississippi rivers who had brought their slaves with them to the territory were active in politics. The legal status of slavery was bolstered by article three of the purchase treaty, which guaranteed "that the inhabitants of the Territory shall be . . . admitted . . . to the enjoyment of all the rights, advantages, and immunities of citizens of the United States . . . and protected in the free enjoyment of their liberty, property, and the religion which they profess." Without doubt, the right of the former French citizens to their slave property was included in the broad provisions of this article, and thus slavery as an established, legal institution in Missouri gave great advantage to slaveowners in the struggle to protect their property interests.

In February, 1819, Congress was ready to consider the question of passing enabling acts for Alabama and Missouri. On the Missouri statehood bill, James Tallmadge of New York proposed an amendment in the following words: "Provided, that the further introduction of slavery or involuntary servitude be prohibited, except for the punishment for crimes whereof the party shall have been duly convicted; and that all children born within the said state after the admission thereof into the Union shall be free, at the age of twenty-five years."

Debate on the Tallmadge Amendment in the House was brief but sharp. Speaker Henry Clay took the floor against the proposed conditions, arguing that restrictions upon Missouri, denying powers exercised by other states, were unconstitutional. Previously Clay had taken a stand in favor of gradual emancipation in Kentucky, but he now expressed the sophistry that diffusion would lessen the bad effects of the slave system.

In the Senate, Rufus King, already known as a leader of antislavery sentiment, led the fight in favor of restrictions. "The Constitution declares that Congress shall have power to . . . make all needful rules and regulations respecting the territory . . . of the United States," King said. "The power . . . to determine what regulations are needful: and if a regulation prohibiting slavery . . . be, as it has been, deemed needful, Congress possess the power to make the same, and moreover to pass all laws necessary to carry this power into execution." Senator King had not even clothed the theory of national supremacy in a new garb of conservatism, and such an argument was not acceptable in Missouri. Resolutions of mass meetings and editorials in Missouri newspapers made it clear that people of the territory were not favorably impressed by sentiments against popular sovereignty and the growth of western power.[2]

The opposition to slavery on economic grounds in Maryland, Virginia, and North Carolina, where declining profits in tobacco had long since removed the strongest incentive for owning slave property, was not duplicated in Missouri. Frontier land was in the process of being cleared, and slaveholders confidently predicted that great fortunes would be made in cotton, hemp, tobacco, timber, and simply in property improvements. Planters in the border states and generally in the upper South were interested in providing Negroes for the new West as a means of relieving their own problem of surplus slaves.

On February 16, 1819, the House of Representatives voted on the two proposals of the Tallmadge Amendment separately: on prohibiting the further introduction of slavery into Missouri, the vote was 87, yes; 76, no; on freedom for children born after admission of the state at the age of twenty-five years, 82, yes; 78, no. Eleven days later the amendment was defeated in the Senate by a

[2] *Niles' Register*, Vol. XVII (Dec. 4, 1819), 215.

vote of 22 to 16. The House contained 105 members from free states to 81 members who represented slave states; but in the Senate, the sections were balanced, with 22 members from free states and an equal number from slave states.[3]

The newspapers of Missouri were generally opposed to the restrictions and sharp in their criticism of political motives among the antislavery men. Some editors charged that the Eastern members of Congress regarded "with a jealous eye the march of power westward, and are well aware the preponderance will soon be against them." Other writers denounced restriction upon Missouri as an attempt to control the sovereign state. A Montgomery County meeting on April 28, 1819, passed a strongly worded resolution against the "usurpation of sacred rights," inherent in the attempted restrictions.

Resolutions passed by many of the eastern state legislatures urged Congress to adopt the restrictions of the Tallmadge Amendment. "It cannot be pretended," the resolution from Pennsylvania declared, "that the rights of any states are . . . affected, by refusing to extend human bondage over the . . . West." This resolution expressed the view that opening the West to slaves would "increase their number . . . open a new and steady market . . . and render all schemes for obliterating this blot upon the American character, useless and unavailing." The southern legislatures generally sent resolutions against the Tallmadge restrictions—although the slave state of Delaware urged Congress to take a stand against extension of slavery to the new territories.[4]

THE MISSOURI COMPROMISE: FIRST PHASE

In December, 1819, Congress approved the constitution of Alabama and admitted the territory to statehood. The House of Representatives passed a bill for the admission of Maine, Massachusetts having agreed to the change in status for her former province.

---

[3] Woodburn, *loc. cit.*, 255; *Annals of Congress*, 15 Cong., 2 sess., I, 1170, 1214.
[4] Hodder, *loc. cit.*, 153–54; Turner, *Rise of the New West*, 156–57; *Annals of Congress*, 16 Cong., 1 sess., 300–11.

James Barbour of Virginia, president pro tempore of the Senate, delivered three long addresses on the Missouri question. Senator Benjamin Ruggles of Ohio spoke for several hours against joining Maine with Missouri in considering statehood for both. William Pinkney of Maryland, ill but determined, addressed the Senate for three hours in reply to Rufus King. Pinkney's major speeches on the Missouri question consumed a total of more than eight hours.

The Maryland senator maintained his reputation as a master of subtle phrases, an orator almost unrivaled in diction, foremost in rhetoric if not in his powers of reasoning. "I confess to you . . . that some of the principles announced by the . . . gentleman from New York [King] . . . did, when they were first presented, startle me not a little. . . .

"My reliance is that these principles will obtain no general currency; for if they should, it requires no gloomy imagination to sadden the perspective of the future. My reliance is upon the unsophisticated good sense and noble spirit of the American people. . . . The people of this country, if I do not wholly mistake their character, are wise as well as virtuous. They know the value of that Federal association which is to them the single pledge and guarantee of power and peace."

William Plumer, Jr., representative from New Hampshire, wrote to his father that Pinkney was a great disappointment to him, as an orator. "He succeeded perfectly in convincing those who were, before, of his opinion."

Senator William Smith of South Carolina, after admitting that he had little hope the Senate would believe any further light could be shed upon the Missouri question, made three long speeches against restrictions. In spite of an act by the Massachusetts legislature on June 19, 1819, clearing the way for statehood in Maine, Senator Smith was still contending eight months later that the people of Massachusetts were "far from wishing Maine a separate state."

Senator Jesse B. Thomas of Illinois seized upon the opportunity provided by Maine's application for statehood to frame a compromise measure. He proposed as an amendment to the Missouri statehood bill that Maine should be admitted as a free state, Missouri as a slave state, and that slavery should be prohibited north of 36 degrees, 30 minutes in the rest of the Louisiana Purchase. This amendment passed the Senate on February 17, 1820, by a vote of 34 to 10; and on March 2, 1820, the terms of compromise proposed by Senator Thomas were finally accepted in the House, by a vote of 90 to 87.[5]

THE MISSOURI CONVENTION

Passage of the Enabling Act, approved by President Monroe on March 6, did not end the bitter struggle over Negro slavery in Missouri. Before the final admission of the state, a second compromise had to be fought through the House of Representatives over the clause in the Missouri constitution concerning free Negroes. The Enabling Act provided that all free white male citizens of the United States "who shall have arrived at the age of twenty-one years, and have resided in the Territory three months previous to the day of election," were eligible to be elected "and authorized to vote" in the election of delegates. Apportionment of the forty-one delegates was as follows: Franklin, Jefferson, Lincoln, Madison, Pike, and Wayne counties, one each; Montgomery and New Madrid, two each; Cooper, St. Charles, and Washington, three each; Ste Genevieve, four; Cape Girardeau and Howard, five each; and St. Louis, eight. The new state was entitled to send one member to the United States House of Representatives.

The eighth section of the Enabling Act provided that "in all that territory ceded by France to the United States, under the name of Louisiana, which lies north of thirty-six degrees and thirty minutes north latitude, not included within the limits of the State contemplated by this act, slavery and involuntary servitude, otherwise than in the punishment of crimes, whereof the parties shall have been duly convicted, shall be, and is hereby, forever prohibited."

The area defined in the Enabling Act included the land of the present state, with the exception of the Platte Purchase of 1837,

---

[5] Woodburn, *loc. cit.*, 261–63; *Annals of Congress*, 16 Cong., 1 sess., 101–108, 259–75, 278–87, 313–35, 374–417, 846–50; Glover Moore, *The Missouri Controversy*, 86–90, 101–103.

six counties lying between the Missouri River and the meridian originally established as the western border.[6]

Perhaps the most important issue in the election of delegates, although it created a contest in but few of the counties, was the question of restrictions on slavery to be included in the constitution. The candidates who were opposed to restrictions won in every instance, with an opposition vote of about 400 in St. Louis County and a total of 425 restriction votes in four other counties. The non-restrictionists in St. Louis began their celebration upon receiving news of the passage of the Enabling Act by displaying transparencies with the names of northern congressmen who had voted against restrictions—six senators and fourteen representatives—and by speeches in which patriotism was identified with extension of slavery, unrestricted, into Missouri. Members from southern states had stood "united as a Spartan band, forty days in the pass of Thermopylae, defending the people of Missouri, the Treaty of Cession, and the Constitution of the Republic."[7]

John B. C. Lucas became the leader of St. Louis voters who opposed extension of slavery in Missouri. David Barton, at the head of the anti-restriction men, had powerful support in St. Louis and elsewhere in the state. Alexander McNair, able, well informed, and popular, was a native of free Pennsylvania, but was strongly opposed to restrictions upon slavery by Congress or by the Missouri Convention. General Bernard Pratte, the son of a Ste Genevieve merchant and a fur trader himself, with extensive business interests, owned slaves and had grown up under a system in which slave labor had a large part in the plans for land development. Edward Bates, elected to the convention, and his elder brother, Frederick, secretary and often acting governor of Missouri Territory, were Virginians and active advocates of slavery extension. Pierre Chouteau, Jr., a St. Louis member of the convention, be-

6 *United States Statutes at Large*, III (Richard Peters, ed., 1846), 16 Cong., 1 sess., chap. 22 (March 6, 1820), 545–48; Ben: Perley Poore, *Federal and State Constitutions*, II, 1102–1104; Floyd C. Shoemaker, *Missouri's Struggle for Statehood*, chap. V; "Fathers of the State" section, *Missouri Historical Review* (Oct., 1915), 1–52; Hodder, "Side Lights on the Missouri Compromises," *American Historical Association, Annual Report* (1909), 151–61.

7 Quoted in Hodder, *loc. cit.*, 155.

longed to a family of traders who had little sympathy for the anti-slavery movement, particularly in the undeveloped lands of the West. Thomas F. Riddick, another St. Louis delegate, was a Virginian and an outspoken opponent of restrictions on slavery. John C. Sullivan was a Kentuckian who had served as collector of revenue and surveyor in Missouri Territory. He also represented St. Louis in the convention. Duff Green, who had come from Kentucky to Missouri after serving as a soldier in the War of 1812, had been the first postmaster at Chariton and had established the first stage line with a contract for carrying United States mail west of the Mississippi River. He represented Howard County.

Of the forty-one members, only six were born in free states or territories that adopted constitutions prohibiting slavery, plus two natives of the British Isles, where slavery was not permitted by law. Henry Dodge, born in Indiana more than thirty years before statehood and five years before the Northwest Ordinance put a check upon slavery there, had little acquaintance with the doctrine of abolition in actual practice. His family had moved to Ste Genevieve before Napoleon obtained title to Louisiana in 1800, and Dodge never became an advocate of slavery restriction.

Joseph McFerron, a native of Ireland, had been in Missouri about twenty years, and his repeated election to office in Cape Girardeau County is evidence of his adjustment to the system of slave labor in the region. John Rice Jones, who was born in Wales, had come to America during the Revolution, fought with George Rogers Clark in the Northwest Territory, and lived for a time in Vincennes. He came to Missouri with the first large wave of settlers after the Louisiana Purchase and was thoroughly adjusted to the system of slave labor in the Mississippi bottom. Not one of the foreign-born or the free-state men was an advocate of restriction upon slavery in Missouri; probably any such stand would have prevented his election to the convention. Judge Lucas' "independent ticket" in St. Louis, where antislavery sentiment among the voters was strongest, received only half as many votes as the "lawyer junto," which united on Barton, Bates, Chouteau, McNair, Pratte, Rector, Riddick, and Sullivan. In a different environment, it is possible that Benjamin Emmons, a native of New York who came to Upper Louisiana from Vermont, would have taken a stand against slavery extension; but as a member from St. Charles he was strongly resentful, along with many other citizens in Missouri, of what was regarded in the West as an attempt by Congress to control the new state. Emmons had lived in Missouri for many years, at first on Dardenne Creek, then in the town of St. Charles, where he was proprietor of a hotel.

Perhaps it is significant that twenty-five members were born in border slave states—the tobacco area where expansion of slavery to the West would afford some relief from oversupply of slave labor. It is equally worthy of note that thirty-three of the total, more than 80 per cent, were born and reared in regions where slavery was fully accepted as a permanent part of the economic structure of society.[8]

The convention met on June 12, 1820, in the dining room of the Mansion House Hotel in St. Louis. Organization was accomplished quickly, with the election of David Barton as president and William G. Pettus as secretary. Edward Bates, one of the youngest members of the convention, moved the appointment of a drafting committee; but the convention organized, instead, four groups which were to submit their work to a central committee to be combined into a single document. This product was to be referred to a revision committee, of which Edward Bates was named chairman. Frank H. Hodder, considering the relative claims of prominent Missourians to authorship of the first state constitution, wrote in 1909: "Mr. Bates occupies, with reference to the first constitution of Missouri, the position which Gouverneur Morris occupies with reference to the Constitution of the United States."

However, the work of the Missouri Convention in 1820 was based solidly upon Kentucky's second constitution, which was framed by a convention and put into effect on January 1, 1800, without being submitted to the people. Even the article relative to control of slavery in Missouri had provisions similar to Article VII of the Kentucky constitution, with an added grant of power to the General Assembly: "It shall be their duty to prevent free negroes

8 Woodburn, *loc. cit.*, 252, 253, 265; Hodder, *loc. cit.*, 154-55; Houck, *Missouri*, III, 249-65.

from coming to and settling in the State on any pretext whatever." This clause was to be the subject of an additional Missouri Compromise in 1821.[9]

As president of the convention, David Barton did not dominate the members or plan the work of making the constitution. Other delegates besides Edward Bates left deeper marks upon the basic law than the convention's chairman. Alexander McNair, who was recognized as a competent student of government, had the facility of clear speaking and writing which enabled him to make a sizable contribution. Bringing earlier state constitutions into the meetings, he called the attention of committee members to their provisions. Duff Green, a Kentuckian who had spent few of his years in Missouri, perhaps had a larger part in the actual work of the convention than the presiding officer with his relatively routine activities.

The attitude of Missouri's citizens is suggested in the words of the preamble: "We the people of Missouri . . . do mutually agree to form and establish a free and independent republic, by the name of the 'State of Missouri,' and for the government thereof do ordain and establish this constitution." Professor Hodder regarded the election of a proslavery convention as not so much due to "any very strong sentiment in favor of slavery as to a fierce resentment bred by the congressional attempt at dictation."

That the hostility toward restriction was pronounced is true; but that the Missouri Convention, without Congressional annoyance, would have set up a free-state constitution is to be doubted. Southern men elected to the convention represented the interests of politically active slaveholders; a restriction aimed against their immediate property interests seemed to them a monstrous threat to human liberty. It was the political habits and background of voters and candidates in Missouri, combined with the economic interests of men who had their capital invested in land and slaves, that caused the election of a proslavery convention. The liberties and constitutional rights of western communities provided fuel for the debates in Congress and the discussions in Missouri concerning restrictions in advance of statehood upon a "sovereign" state.

[9] Hodder, loc. cit., 156; Poore, Constitutions, I, 657–68.

Library of Congress

JEAN BAPTISTE LEMOYNE, SIEUR DE BIENVILLE
three times governor of French Louisiana.

Missouri Historical Society
SUPPOSED PORTRAIT OF PIERRE LACLEDE
who built a trading post on the west bank of the Mississippi
below the mouth of the Missouri in 1704 and
called it St. Louis after King Louis XV of France.

Missouri Historical Society
AUGUSTE CHOUTEAU
who was associated with Laclede
in building the post and who was the principal founder
of the prominent Missouri family.

WILLIAM CLARK
explorer, Indian commissioner, and Missouri territorial governor.
From a painting by Gilbert Stuart.
From William Clark Kennerly, *Persimmon Hill.*

DANIEL BOONE
who followed his son to Missouri and lived there from 1799 until
his death in 1820. From a painting by Chester Harding.
From William Clark Kennerly, *Persimmon Hill.*

Massie photograph, Missouri Commerce and Industrial Development Division
RECONSTRUCTED FORT OSAGE
which was built originally in 1808 on the
right (south) bank of the Missouri, about twelve miles
from present Independence, to protect the
Osage Indians and their domain.

Detroit Institute of Arts

"THE TRAPPERS' RETURN"
from a painting by George Caleb Bingham.

Missouri Historical Society

MANUEL LISA
pre-eminent fur trapper and trader.

Missouri Historical Society

MANUEL LISA'S WAREHOUSE AT ST. LOUIS

Smithsonian Institution

SAC AND FOX INDIANS
on the St. Louis shore in April, 1833. From an engraving
of a drawing by Carl Bodmer in *Maximilian's Travels* (1843).

The Missouri constitution provided for biennial sessions of the General Assembly. It limited the House of Representatives to one hundred members, elected for two years and apportioned among the counties on the basis of population, but with each county entitled to at least one representative. The Senate was composed of members elected for four years from single member districts, not to exceed thirty-three and not fewer than fourteen in number. Clergymen of all faiths were excluded from membership in the General Assembly. Representatives were required to be twenty-four years of age with a residence of two years in Missouri and to live in the counties which they represented. The minimum age for a senator was thirty years, and the residence requirement four years in Missouri, one year in his district. Suffrage was extended to all free white male citizens of the United States who had been residents of Missouri for one year.

The governor, to be elected by the voters for four years and not eligible for immediate re-election had the authority to appoint, with the consent of the Senate, the auditor and secretary of state. His power to "take care that the laws be distributed and faithfully executed" and his power to command the militia provided in effect for his appointment of the attorney-general and adjutant-general. These executive officers were to serve four-year terms. To be eligible for the chief executive post, one had to be a natural-born citizen of the United States or a citizen of the United States at the time of the adoption of the federal constitution "or an inhabitant of that part of Louisiana now included in the State of Missouri at the time of the cession thereof from France to the United States." Minimum residence of four years in Missouri immediately preceding the election was required. The governor did not possess the power to veto a bill if a majority of all the members elected to each house still voted for the bill after considering his objections to it.

The treasurer was chosen by the General Assembly for a term of two years. The office of the chief executive was not modeled upon that of state governors in the Revolutionary period. In many instances these early governors had been chosen by the legislatures for short terms and had extremely limited authority over appointments. The lieutenant-governor of Missouri, also elected by the voters for a term of four years, was *ex officio* president of the Senate.

It is true that Thomas Hart Benton influenced the work of the convention without being one of its members, a fact that he often called to the attention of his audiences during his long political career. Among the other public men who exercised an indirect influence upon the convention, Nathaniel Beverly Tucker deserves consideration. He served as judge of the district court, before and after statehood. He was an ardent supporter of state rights, and his economic views found backing among southern planters and the rural population in the West. Perhaps his theories belonged to a declining social order, but the weight of his influence in 1820 cannot be denied. His thinking was shaped, in part, by the views of his half-brother, John Randolph; he had no confidence in democracy and felt a strong antipathy toward northern industrialism.

Tucker was a Virginian, and in 1832 he was to return to his native state as professor of law at William and Mary College. He reached his greatest influence later, as a member of President John Tyler's unofficial advisory group. He advised public men in Missouri that the state government, already organized and being administered under the new constitution, had the right to continue as a "Sovereign State."

The people of Missouri were not in the majority ardent supporters of slave labor. Their stand in favor of slavery, so far as the common man upheld the institution, was in the nature of tolerance for the property interests of political leaders. When men like Judge Beverly Tucker, however, presented the restriction movement as an effort by Federalists in the national capital to perpetuate control of communities in the West, recruits were made for the extension of slavery. Like John Randolph of Roanoke, Beverly Tucker was inclined toward brilliant flights of rhetoric, eccentric behavior, and irresponsible extremes of political position. In Missouri he presents the strange spectacle of an aristocrat with little sympathy for the common man, leading a raw commonwealth of plain citizens who were soon to demonstrate a powerful leaning toward Jacksonian democracy.

Thomas Hart Benton, old enough to be a member of the United

States Senate but by no means mature in his judgment of Tucker's complicated pattern of thought, was deeply impressed by the Virginian's bold defense of state sovereignty. An editorial in Benton's St. Louis *Enquirer* for March 31, 1819, stated: "There seems to be no ground whatever for apprehending the passage of the Bill clogged with the odious restrictions which New England policy engrafted upon it." Would Missouri submit to the indignity of restriction? "No! Never!"[10]

The convention completed its work on July 19, 1820, thirty-eight days after it was first called to order. Not only was the constitution put into effect without waiting for the approval of Congress, but also without the democratic process of popular vote. The *Schedule*, added by the convention to the thirteen articles of the constitution proper, provided that "all writs, actions, prosecutions, judgments, claims, and contracts . . . shall continue as if no change had taken place." Territorial laws were to remain in force "until altered or repealed by the general assembly." Election of state and local officers and a congressman was ordered for the fourth Monday in August, 1820; the president pro tempore of the Senate was directed to examine the returns in the presence of both houses of the General Assembly and to declare the results.

Putting a new state constitution into operation without approval by a popular vote was not an uncommon procedure. In fact, the Revolutionary state governments were generally launched in that fashion, after constitutions were written by the colonial legislatures. With the growth of western population and the admission of western states, the popular referendum became more widely accepted as normal procedure. Maine, which was admitted as a part of the Missouri Compromise, ratified its constitution by a vote of the people in 1820—affrmative, 9,040, negative, 796. Of six

[10] Poore, *Constitutions*, II, 1104–17; Hodder, *loc. cit.*, 156–57; Houck, *Missouri*, III, 10–11, 248, 250, 253, 268; Beverly Tucker, letter to John C. Calhoun, "Correspondence of John C. Calhoun" (edited by Chauncey S. Boucher and Robert P. Brooks), *Annual Report of the American Historical Association* (1929), 258–62; *Dictionary of American Biography*, XIX, 36, 37 (article on Nathaniel Beverly Tucker by Carl Bridenbaugh). The *Enquirer's* editorial is quoted in Moore, *The Missouri Controversy*, 260.

states that called conventions to write new constitutions during the decade of the Compromise of 1820, Missouri was the only one that did not submit its constitution to popular vote.

In the election of August 28, 1820, Alexander McNair was chosen governor, receiving 6,575 votes to 2,556 for William Clark, who ran second. William Ashley was elected lieutenant-governor over Nathaniel Cook by a small plurality; and John Scott, who had served as territorial delegate since 1816, was elected representative to Congress, unopposed. The General Assembly met on September 19, less than a month after the election, at the Missouri Hotel in St. Louis. The lower house elected James Caldwell speaker, and Governor McNair made his selections for executive posts: Joshua Barton, secretary of state, William Christy, auditor, and Edward Bates, attorney-general. As justices of the Supreme Court he appointed Mathias McGirk, John D. Cook, and John Rice Jones. Pierre Didier became the first state treasurer.

In the election of United States senators by the General Assembly, David Barton was the favorite candidate from the start. He had emerged from the work of the convention without arousing powerful opposition in any quarter, and he was assured of a majority before the voting began. In a joint session of the House and Senate, each of the fifty-two members was entitled to cast two votes for Missouri's two senators. Thomas Hart Benton was able to obtain the promise of twenty-six votes—one short of a majority— and to promote the support of one more member.

A meeting was called at Auguste Chouteau's house, where Benton was given a chance to express his views on the validity of the land claims under old Spanish grants. Judge Lucas, who had powerful support in the legislature, was known to regard many of the Spanish grants as invalid. Marie Philippe Leduc was a member of the General Assembly and, like the Chouteau group, claimant of a large area of land under Spanish grants. Benton had met Charles Gratiot, an old French settler who was married to Auguste Chouteau's sister, when the young Tennessee lawyer first arrived in St. Louis, five years before the statehood convention. Gratiot had invited Benton to occupy a room in his house, and legal employment was quickly found for the new settler. Benton had been engaged in a number of cases in which the claimants based their suits upon Spanish grants.

Judge Lucas, as land commissioner, had been responsible for the rejection of many claims based on Spanish grants in which fraud could be established as a factor in the original concession. Judge Lucas himself had become a land speculator and was interested in opening the way for new investors by voiding the old grants. Charles Gratiot and the Chouteaus, Jean P. Cabanné, Silvestre Labadie, and Marie Philippe Leduc all had good reason to suppose that Benton, as United States senator, would be more friendly toward their land claims than Judge Lucas. The meeting at Auguste Chouteau's house obtained for Thomas Hart Benton the promise of his twenty-seventh vote. Even with Leduc among his supporters, however, an element of uncertainty was created by the severe illness of Senator Daniel Ralls, another Benton man. On the day of the final vote on the candidates, Ralls was carried from his sickbed to the Assembly Room, where he voted for Benton and Barton. The results were as follows: Barton, thirty-four; Benton, twenty-seven; Lucas, sixteen; Henry Elliott, eleven; Nathaniel Cook, eight; and John Rice Jones, eight. Barton and Benton, each having a majority, were declared elected to the United States Senate.[11]

THE MISSOURI COMPROMISE: FINAL PHASE

When the second session of the Sixteenth Congress assembled, John Scott claimed his seat as the elected representative from the state of Missouri. He was not accepted as a member, and when the Speaker called for the "Delegate from the Territory of Missouri," Scott did not respond. He was admitted to a seat on the floor of the House, and in the Senate, Barton and Benton were accorded the same recognition. They could listen to the debates on the Mis-

[11] Poore, *Constitutions*, I, 700, 711, 788, 983, 995; 32, 48, 76; II, 1104, 1341, 1465, 1548, 1667, 1677; Houck, *Missouri*, III, 247–52, 265–67; Chambers, *Old Bullion, Senator from the New West*, 61–65, 97–100; Billion, *Annals of St. Louis*, II, 162. The New York convention of 1821, of which Rufus King was a member, submitted their product to popular vote, in which it was ratified 74,732 to 41,402. Poore, *Constitutions*, II, 1341.

souri question, but they could not participate as members of Congress. Hear the debates they did, and a flood of correspondence went back to their friends in Missouri, along with regular progress reports to the home newspapers. Senator Benton predicted, in a letter to the *Missouri Intelligencer*: "In the Senate we apprehend no difficulty. In the House of Representatives the struggle of last winter will be renewed, and it is apprehended that the restrictionists will prevail."

On December 12, 1820, the Senate considered a resolution declaring the consent of Congress to admission of Missouri into the Union and accepted it by a vote of twenty-six to eighteen. As it was passed, the resolution carried an amendment introduced by John Eaton of Tennessee: "Provided, That nothing herein contained shall be so construed as to give the assent of Congress to any provision in the Constitution of Missouri, if any such there be, which contravenes that clause in the Constitution of the United States which declares that 'the citizens of each State shall be entitled to all privileges and immunities of citizens in the several States.' "[12]

The House of Representatives, after a sharp debate on the clause concerning exclusion of free Negroes, voted against the Senate's proposal for the admission of Missouri. The division of the House was almost exactly sectional, with only one of ninety-three votes against admission coming from a slave state and five of seventy-nine in favor of admission from free states.

Henry Clay attacked the problem of compromise in a committee selected by the House for that purpose, and on February 10, 1821, reported for his committee an amendment to the Senate resolution. Under Clay's proposal, Missouri would be admitted if its legislature agreed, before the fourth Monday of November, 1821, that "the said State shall never pass any law preventing any . . . persons from coming to and settling in the said State who are now or hereafter may become citizens of any States of this Union."

The resolution with Clay's amendment received eighty affirmative votes in the House to eighty-three in opposition. Finally,

[12] *Annals of Congress*, 16 Cong., 2 sess., 43–50, 99, 116, 118–19; Plumer, *Missouri Compromises*, 12, 13, 44, 98; Hodder, *loc. cit.*, 157; Moore, *Missouri Controversy*, 144, 146.

Clay's persistence resulted in the selection of a conference committee of thirty—twenty-three representatives and seven senators; and when he submitted its compromise resolution to the House on February 26, he had the satisfaction of obtaining an affirmative vote of eighty-seven to eighty-one. John Randolph, duty-bound to oppose any measure that named a condition for Missouri's entrance into the Union, was the only southern representative who voted against Clay's final effort to frame a bill acceptable to both sections. The condition, as the conference committee phrased it, required that the free-Negro clause of the Missouri constitution should "never be construed to authorize the passage of any law . . . by which any citizen of either of the States in this Union shall be excluded from any of the privileges and immunities to which such citizen is entitled under the Constitution of the United States." It was provided further that the legislature of Missouri should, "by a solemn public act . . . declare the assent of the said State to the said fundamental condition."

The United States Senate accepted this final phase of the compromise on February 28, 1821, with eleven senators from free states joining seventeen from the South to make the vote decisive, twenty-eight to fourteen.

The authority to refuse admission, after Congress had voted to accept the Thomas compromise, was disputed in the debates of 1820–21, and has been a question of endless confusion down to the present day. A recent book on the Missouri controversy calls attention to the fact that two-thirds of the northern members of the House were willing to adopt a new measure of restriction in February, 1821: acceptance by Missouri of gradual abolition as a condition to admission as a state. This is evidence, the author says, that two-thirds of the free-state representatives were ready to repudiate the Missouri Compromise within a year of its passage; that they did not look upon it as "sacrosanct," but simply as undesirable legislation, which they would gladly repeal, when they were able to muster enough votes.

Such a statement of the case blandly ignores the fact that the compromise agreement, from the point of view of Congress, was not complete with the passage of the Thomas amendment. In February, 1821, the issue had shifted to the clause in the Missouri constitution which made it the duty of the legislature to exclude free Negroes from entering Missouri on "any pretext whatsoever." The members who voted for the new restriction did not regard Missouri as a state until the convention was able to meet all the requirements of the Constitution of the United States. Missouri statehood was challenged particularly for the alleged violation of the clause of Article IV of the federal Constitution which declares, "The citizens of each State shall be entitled to all privileges and immunities of citizens in the several States." Certainly the basic law of Missouri was open to the charge of containing a direct contradiction of a clause in the federal constitution.[13]

On December 9, 1820, Senator Harrison Gray Otis, debating the questionable provision of the Missouri constitution, stated that Missouri had been authorized by an act of Congress to "form a constitution, subject to certain limitations and conditions." Congress had the duty of determining whether or not the conditions had been met. "We have the right to ascertain whether she has established a republican or a monarchial government," he said; "whether she arrogates the power of making peace and war, regulating commerce, collecting imposts, or other powers inhibited in express terms of the Constitution, to the several States." Would Missouri have met all the constitutional requirements for statehood, if she had made her governor a lifetime officer or if she had made her senate an hereditary body? Or, was it the duty of Congress to ascertain whether or not discrepancies existed between the law of the state and the federal Constitution?

Otis quoted the fourth of the thirteen Articles of Confederation in support of his view on interstate rights: "Free inhabitants of each of these States . . . shall be entitled to all privileges and immunities of free citizens in the several States, and shall have free ingress and regress," etc. To deny that free Negroes might be citizens of any one of the states would be to deny the right of the state "to confer that capacity upon them." But all persons born in Massa-

[13] *Abridgment of the Debates of Congress*, 1789–1856 (Thomas Hart Benton, ed.), VI, 682–87; Moore, *Missouri Controversy*, 168–69.

chusetts of free parents were citizens, and all persons residing in the state were either citizens or aliens.

The legislature of Missouri declared the state's acceptance of the final phase of compromise, "by a solemn public act," in the summer of 1821. At the same time, the insistence of the lawmakers upon including a statement of Missouri's equal right with other states to discriminate against free Negroes, coupled with the well-known fact that many states, north and south, had laws that did in fact violate Article IV of the federal Constitution, gave an atmosphere of defiance to the acceptance. President Monroe received a copy of the Missouri legislature's act and proclaimed the admission of Missouri as the twenty-fourth state.[14]

[14] *Annals of Congress,* 16 Cong., 2 sess., 89–98; *Abridgment of the Debates of Congress,* VI, 682–87; Moore, *Missouri Controversy,* 168–69.

6

COMMERCE OF THE CROSSROADS

THE SANTA FE TRADE

BETWEEN MISSOURI'S ADMISSION to statehood and the Treaty of Guadalupe-Hidalgo twenty-seven years later, three major developments in the American West gave emphasis to the lower Missouri Valley as a crossroads area. Many economic changes that took place outside of Missouri affected directly the character of commerce along the two great rivers of the state. Most obvious of the outside influences were the opening of the Santa Fe Trail, rapid development of the fur and peltry trade throughout the great West, and the migration of the Mormons to Missouri and to Utah. The Mexican War, expansion of the United States in the Southwest, and settlement of the Oregon question were vital elements of Missouri's history.

In the same year that Missouri achieved statehood, Mexico won her independence from Spain. Because of the considerable population that grew up in Spanish New Mexico and Chihuahua and the surplus goods in those provinces, attempts had already been made to establish trade connections between Santa Fe and St. Louis. French trappers had penetrated the upper Arkansas and traded with the Indians of the Rocky Mountains before the surrender of western Louisiana to Spain. Between 1763 and 1800, while Spain held title to Louisiana as well as New Mexico, Pedro Vial had been sent from Santa Fe to St. Louis by Governor Fernando de la Concha to open up trade relations. Pedro Vial said that he could have marched from New Mexico to St. Louis in twenty-five days—a statement that might have resulted from his need to inspire Baron Carondelet with his own optimism.[1] No important commerce grew up as a result of Vial's efforts, however.

After the United States purchased Louisiana, traders found hostile Indians and natural obstacles of the trail increased by the suspicion of officers at Santa Fe. Spain's control of Mexico was slipping, and offers from Missouri to open trade with the upper Río Grande appeared to the Spanish governors as an added threat.

After the successful revolution and establishment of the Mexican Republic in 1821, trade between the Missouri River and Santa Fe rapidly took root. Two expeditions by William Becknell of Franklin were of such basic importance as to obtain for him, by common consent, the title "Father of the Santa Fe Trade." Becknell organized his little band of men at Franklin, the principal town of Howard County, on the Missouri River. "Our company crossed the Missouri River near Arrow Rock ferry on the first day of September, 1821, and encamped six miles from the ferry," Captain Becknell wrote in his account of the expedition.

The party moved across Little Osage Plain in present Saline County, covering thirty miles on the second day. During the ten weeks that followed, Becknell and his men endured hardships, overcame difficulties of the pioneer trail, and witnessed many events that were astonishing, some delightful, and, on occasion, terrifying. On November 16 the party arrived in Santa Fe, where Captain Becknell was received by the governor—a courteous, friendly, and well-informed host.

William Becknell and his men disposed of their goods at a fair price. Some of the party remained at San Miguel. Becknell and one companion began the return trip on December 13, 1821, reaching the Arkansas on the seventeenth day and arriving at Franklin in forty-eight days. In spite of the small amount of trade goods carried by the party, there is evidence that the project was regarded as a brilliant financial success. It was reported that Becknell and his associate "dumped heaps of dollars on the sidewalks of Franklin" before the startled eyes of their fellow-townsmen, and

[1] Houck, *History of Missouri*, I, 132; II, 58, 90; III, 155.

that one citizen who had invested $60 in the enterprise received $900 in return. In addition to the evidence of trade possibilities, Becknell brought back a message of welcome from the Spanish governor at Santa Fe.[2]

On his second expedition William Becknell crossed the Missouri at Arrow Rock on May 22, 1822, and collected his followers as he moved west. In addition to the pack horses, three wagons laden with goods for the Santa Fe trade gave particular significance to this expedition.

At the first encampment beyond the Arkansas River, which the Becknell wagons had crossed with some difficulty, a minor disaster befell the traders. Twenty horses, frightened by buffalo during the night, scattered across the prairie and had to be hunted the following day. All but two were recovered; but in hunting for the strayed horses, two of Becknell's men were seized by a party of Osages, stripped of their possessions, horses, guns, and clothing—and "barbarously whipped." A message from Auguste Pierre Chouteau informed Becknell that he had recovered the horses and guns taken by the Osages and would deliver them to their owners. The traders found the Indian camp deserted and another message written on bark instructing them to follow Chouteau and the Osages up the Autawge River. "This we declined, thinking that his precipitate retreat indicated some stratagem or treachery," Becknell recorded. He added that in crossing Osage territory, traders should maintain strict guard against forays by these Indians.

Instead of following the route of his first expedition through Raton Pass, this time Becknell led his wagons across the Cimarron Desert southwest from the Arkansas. The weather was excessively hot, and the party had no water after leaving the Arkansas except the meager supply that was carried in jugs. It was exhausted on the second day, and real suffering followed. The mules, hauling

[2] Josiah Gregg, *Commerce of the Prairies*, 9–11; Ray Allen Billington, *The Far Western Frontier, 1830–1860*, 23–25; Rupert N. Richardson and Carl C. Rister, *The Greater Southwest*, 129; Hafen and Rister, *Western America*, 246–56; *Dictionary of American Biography*, XII, 111–12 (article on Robert McKnight, by Stella M. Drumm); F. F. Stephens, "Missouri and the Santa Fe Trade," *Mo. Hist. Rev.*, Vol. X, No. 4 (July, 1916), 234–38; Houck, *Missouri*, III, 155–56; Chittenden, *The American Fur Trade*, II, 489–514.

heavy loads along a route not previously marked for wheeled vehicles or staggering under heavy packs, panted for water and were
unable to hold even a moderately fast pace. Some of the men became so desperately in need of liquid that they resorted to cutting
off mules' ears and trying to ease their thirst by drinking the hot
blood. Afterwards they reported that the experiment gave no relief
to their parched throats.

As the party was about to turn back toward the Arkansas, which
they could not have reached in their exhausted condition, one of
the men caught sight of a large buffalo which had just come up
from the Cimarron River, with its sides distended by the water it
had drunk. The animal was slain and the traders hastened to
quench their thirst with the liquid from its stomach. In his account
of the journey, one man stated that no beverage he ever tasted,
before or afterwards, was so satisfying as this drink from the interior of the slaughtered buffalo. A few of the stronger members
went on to the Cimarron to obtain a new supply of water. All the
men recovered, and within a few days the caravan arrived at San
Miguel.

Great difficulty was encountered near Rock River in moving the
wagons "up some high and rocky cliffs by hand"; but Mr. Heath's
party, which had joined them on the Arkansas, proved to be not
only congenial companions but also skilled helpers in the labors of
the trail. The two bands separated at San Miguel "for the purpose
of trading more advantageously."[3]

On the return trip, Becknell reached Fort Osage in forty-eight
days. He advised other Missourians who might embark upon the
Santa Fe trade, to "take goods of excellent quality and unfaded
colors. . . . A very great advance is obtained on goods, and the trade
is very profitable; money and mules are plentiful, and they do not
hesitate to pay the price demanded for an article if it suits their
purpose, or their fancy."

After a trapping expedition from Santa Cruz to the Green River,
Becknell accepted the task of carrying the mail to George Sibley's

[3] "The Journals of Captain Thomas Becknell, from Boone's Lick to Santa Fe,
and from Santa Cruz to Green River," *Mo. Hist. Rev.*, IV, No. 2 (Jan., 1910), 65–
84; Billington, *The Far Western Frontier*, 23–25; Chittenden, *The American Fur
Trade*, II, 502–504.

surveying party which was marking the trail from Fort Osage to the Mexican border, by way of Chouteau's Island on the Arkansas and the Lower Spring of the Cimarron. Afterwards, he ran a ferry on the Missouri River, served as a captain of militia in the Black Hawk War, and was elected to the Missouri legislature from Saline County.

Eighty-one persons made up the Marmaduke party in 1824, and twenty-five wheeled vehicles were used for the transportation of goods and travelers. Only two of the conveyances were heavy freight wagons, the others being two carts and twenty dearborns—four-wheeled carriages with curtained sides—and a small cannon mounted on wheels. The value of the trade goods was $30,000 in Missouri. In the Cimarron desert the traders suffered for water, meeting the barest needs of the men and livestock by sinking wells in the bottom of a sandy ravine. A small dog traveling with the traders died from the extreme heat and lack of water. The party arrived in Santa Fe, however, and the members were compensated for their hardships by excellent profits. They were back in Missouri by September 24, 1824, and they brought with them $180,000 in gold and silver, in addition to furs valued at $10,000.[4]

Among the adventurers who gave their energies to the Santa Fe trade, few were more persistent than Josiah Gregg, and none contributed more to the historical record of the famous wagon trail. His brothers, also, were engaged in the venturesome occupation of transporting goods by wagon from the bend of the Missouri to the capital of New Mexico; but it was Josiah who made a career of the Santa Fe Trail, as a trader and as a writer.

He was born in Overton County, Tennessee, in 1806. When he was three years old, his father moved to Illinois, and in 1812 moved to Howard County, Missouri. Perhaps the meagerness of his formal schooling was no serious handicap to the lad. He was studious

[4] William Becknell, "The Journals of Captain Thomas Becknell," loc. cit., 79–84; Billington, The Far Western Frontier, 24, 25, 26; F. A. Sampson, ed., "Santa Fe Trail: The M. M. Marmaduke Journal," Mo. Hist. Rev., Vol. VI, No. 1 (Oct., 1911), 1–10; Gregg, Commerce of the Prairies, 13; Dictionary of American Biography, II, 119–20 (article on William Becknell, by Harrison Clifford Dale); Chittenden, The American Fur Trade, II, 506–507; R. L. Duffus, The Santa Fe Trail (N.Y., 1950), 69.

—a bookworm, his associates regarded him—and he would have taken prizes for scholarship in almost any school. It must be admitted, however, that a frontier fort under threat of Indian attack —his environment from age six to nine—would not ordinarily be selected as an ideal spot for primary instruction. Josiah was known as a "puny" child; in fact, he was sick during a large part of his youth and probably would not have lived through early manhood if he had not discovered the curative effects of outdoor life as a trader on the western trails.

Josiah Gregg made his first caravan journey from Missouri to Santa Fe in 1831. Within the next ten years he traveled from the Mississippi Valley across the Great Plains four times. On the first expedition he learned the way to better health. Riding in a dearborn carriage for the first week, he became stronger each day. When he mounted his pony and took his place among the active horsemen of the party, his status as an invalid was ended. He carried his share of toil and monotonous chores, and he was accepted by the frontiersmen of the party as their equal. He helped to haul freight wagons out of the sand when teams had to be doubled; he took his turn as sentinel; he "kept his eyes peeled" for hostile Indians, hunted buffalo, and practiced marksmanship with his pistol when hundreds of rattlesnakes crawled out of their holes near the trail in the Arkansas Valley. While winning his fight over chronic dyspepsia and consumption, Gregg kept books for Jesse Sutton and studied Spanish in preparation for contacts with the people of New Mexico.

During his career as a trader, Josiah Gregg became acquainted with roads that extended far beyond Santa Fe into the interior of Mexico; and on his last expedition with trade goods marked a new trail west beginning at Van Buren, Arkansas. He traveled along the Arkansas and Canadian rivers and arrived in New Mexico more quickly than the caravans that started at Independence. Gregg noted other advantages of the southern route, chief of which was the earlier pasturage of the Canadian Valley. However, the limitations of Van Buren as a source of trade goods and a market for Santa Fe products, other than livestock, prevented the Indian Territory trail from cutting into the volume of commerce to the

Missouri, although Gregg's southern route was followed by many hundreds of wagons going overland to California.

In addition to the natural obstacles of the Santa Fe Trail, the merchants had two other major difficulties to overcome. With many grievances stored up against the European peoples who were steadily and surely forcing their way into the narrowed hunting grounds, Plains Indians were generally belligerent. Armed with good guns, well supplied with ammunition, and mounted on hardy ponies, these warriors were a definite menace to travelers, especially those who carried large supplies of goods without adequate means of defense. A peculiar type of diplomacy was required in dealing with the warlike chiefs, and some of the trading parties suffered from Indian aggression largely because of incompetence in this area.

Jedediah Smith with his two partners, David Jackson and William Sublette, entered the Santa Fe trade in 1828 after selling out their interests in the Rocky Mountain fur trade. On the first expedition along the Santa Fe Trail, Smith left his party after they had passed the Arkansas and turned due south toward the Cimarron River. Twenty-two wagons with seventy-four men made up the caravan, which included Thomas Fitzpatrick and William Sublette. Water in the Arkansas was extremely low, and the trail beyond it was hot, barren sand. Riding alone, Smith had reached the Cimarron and was engaged in scooping out a water-hole in the sand when he was attacked by a party of fifteen or twenty Comanche Indians. He had been warned by Spanish traders that the Comanches were hostile and would attack without parleying, but he had no chance to escape. Since his horse had been without water for two or three days, he decided to leave his hole in the sand to collect water while he rode up to the Indians. They "succeeded in alarming his horse," his brother Austin wrote to their father in Ohio; and, when his horse turned, they fired, wounding Smith but not knocking him down. He fired quickly, killing their leader; the Comanches returned the fire, and the great Mountain Man was dead on the Cimarron sand.

American merchants who imported European or Asian goods for the Mexican market before 1845 had to pay both the United

States tariff and the tax collected at Santa Fe. At Chihuahua and other interior towns demand for European and Oriental textiles was strong; and to meet the competition of goods imported through Mexican ports, the Missouri traders wanted a rebate on United States tariffs. For fourteen years they sought relief from the double tax until, finally, in 1845, Congress met their demands by passing the Drawback Act. The result was an immediate increase of caravan hauling.

The highest profits, relative to amount invested, were obtained by Santa Fe traders in 1824 and 1825. Above the cost of outfits, freight from the Missouri to Santa Fe at ten cents a pound, Mexican taxes, and the cost of trade goods, profits were about 300 per cent. Increasing competition gradually pulled the profits down; but when Mexican taxes were reasonable and Indian losses checked, the returns were still quite attractive. Merchants charged higher prices to the traders than to other customers, and credit for the goods usually cost an additional 20 per cent. Yet, in 1845, when the traders brought back $1,000,000 in gold, silver, and Mexican products, their net gain was approximately 40 per cent.

In the caravans of 1843, largest prior to the Drawback Act, thirty proprietors with 230 wagons paid $450,000 for goods in Missouri. In 1846, with the rebate to hold prices down, Missouri traders used 363 wagons and transported goods valued at $1,000,-000. A large part of the increase consisted of products imported from Europe for the Chihuahua and Santa Fe markets. Wagon transportation was to continue on the southwestern Plains until steam locomotives supplanted the mules and oxen of the Santa Fe Trail.[5]

A great variety of vehicles were employed in the Santa Fe caravans. Some travelers, particularly invalids who were looking for a cure in the dry climate of the Southwest, made the journey in a dearborn, the side curtains of which could be closed to shut out the bright sunlight. Wagons for heavy freight were either Cones-

[5] Gregg, *Commerce of the Prairies*, Introduction, xviii, xix, xxii, xxvii, xxix; 9–19, 22–34, 40, 46, 51–55, 61, 158–68; Gregg, *Commerce of the Prairies* (Milo Quaife, ed.; Chicago, 1926), I, chap. 8; Billington, *The Far Western Frontier*, 27–37; Chittenden, *The American Fur Trade*, II, 483–553; 519n., 508–10, summary of expeditions, 1825–34; Max L. Moorhead, *New Mexico's Royal Road*, 55–75.

togas, made in Lancaster County, Pennsylvania, or western wagons constructed on the same general model. The Pittsburgh wagon was much in demand, and the Murphy wagon manufactured in St. Louis appeared on the Santa Fe Trail in great number after 1839. The wagons used in the early trade generally had beds twelve feet long, three and one-half feet wide, and thirty inches deep, with front wheels thirty-seven inches high and rear wheels forty-nine inches high.

In 1839 a change in tariff policy at Santa Fe brought a sharp reaction on the part of traders with respect to the character of goods and the capacity of wagons. The new governor, Manuel Armijo, placed an arbitrary tax of $500 on each wagonload of freight that entered the town of Santa Fe. Since the average load for vehicles on the Santa Fe Trail between 1828 and 1839 was valued at $1,410 on the Missouri market, the new tax was a serious threat to the trade. The 760 vehicles—an average of 76 per year—carried loads during that period of approximately 1,000 pounds each; but the principal wagon maker of St. Louis, Joseph Murphy, quickly adjusted his shop to demands for larger units.

As an Irish immigrant, Joseph Murphy had come to St. Louis several years before Missouri statehood. In 1819 he was apprenticed to Daniel Caster, the proprietor of a blacksmith shop where tools and farm implements were made. He built his first vehicle for the Santa Fe trade in 1827—a small wagon which he sold to Jacob Jarrett for the sum of $27.

The Murphy wagons of 1839 were built by expert German-born workmen who, like their Irish employer, had served exacting apprenticeships. Joseph Murphy himself selected the timber for the giant wagons. The rear wheels were seven feet high, with rims eight inches in width and spokes that were described as "young oak saplings." The wagon beds were sixteen feet long, with sides as high as a tall man, and had a capacity of two and one-half tons.

Dismantled, many of the Murphy wagons were shipped by river packets to Westport Landing, where they were assembled and made ready for the Santa Fe Trail or for some other service in the Far West. It was reported that 200,000 Murphy wagons were used by emigrants from the Mississippi Valley during the "covered wagon" era. The United States Army, during and after the Mexican War, purchased ox wagons for the Santa Fe Trail and a great variety of military goods from the Murphy shops. The significance of the Santa Fe trade is fully apparent only when that commerce is viewed in its relation to other developments in Missouri: specie, and its impact upon the state's money system; merchants whose prosperity depended in part upon the business from New Mexico; and the mule that became identified with rural life.[6]

Josiah Gregg said that oxen were able to pull heavier loads through mud or deep sand than mules or horses. When the prairie grass became dry and short, however, oxen weakened rapidly; mules were definitely tougher in adjusting to rough trails and meager pasturage. Gregg accounted for the tender feet of the oxen by the comment, "Very few among the thousands who have traveled on the prairies . . . ever knew how to shoe them properly," although the moccasins made of raw buffalo hide, when skillfully fashioned, were quite effective on a dry trail. After Major Bennet Riley proved the value of oxen for baggage wagons in his military escort of 1829, many traders on the Santa Fe Trail followed his example. Gregg estimated that about half of the wagons were drawn by oxen at the time of his expeditions into the Southwest. He pointed out that the incentive for Indian attack was reduced by the use of oxen, since mules were more in demand by the raiding tribes.

Drivers devoted much care to the training of animals—mules or oxen—for use in the caravans. Loading the great wagons with a variety of goods in such a manner as to conserve space and prevent shifting of the load on the rough trail required great skill. Protection of the goods by means of compact loading and proper use of wagon-sheets was a major consideration with every trader. Drivers with experience and knowledge of the trail, stamina and toughness of character, and skill in handling livestock were sought by every proprietor as he made up his caravan.

Parties assembled at Council Grove, 150 miles along the trail

6 Emily Ann O'Neil. "Joseph Murphy's Contribution to the Development of the Great American West" (Master of Arts thesis, St. Louis University, 1947), 1, 2, 4, 9, 14, 16, 19, 21, 27, 28, 31, 72; Duffus, *The Santa Fe Trail*, 134, 135.

from Independence. Beyond this point it was desirable to maintain an organization that would enable traders to meet effectively any attack that might be made by the Plains Indians. If the caravan was large, it usually moved out in four columns, each under a "lieutenant." The entire party was under the nominal command of an elected "Captain of the Caravan"; and the practical good sense of the travelers was generally shown by their election of an experienced plainsman for the job. The caravan of 1831 with which Josiah Gregg traveled, for example, elected Elisha Stanley, a Connecticut man who had made his first caravan journey to Santa Fe at least six years earlier. The traders must have recognized certain qualities of leadership in the man, for his election was unanimous.

The organization included provisions for sentry duty and plans for maneuvering the four divisions into a hollow square in the event of an attack by Indians. The powerful urge of frontiersmen to make their own decisions and the absence of legal restrictions upon members of the caravan made the captain's position difficult. In emergencies, however, the parties frequently acted with commendable unity, thus proving their confidence in their elected leader. Other officers of the caravan might include a marshal, a clerk, a pilot, a three-member court, a commander of the guards, and a chaplain.[7]

On December 14, 1824, Benton presented to the United States Senate a petition on the subject of commerce between Missouri and New Mexico. This "beneficial trade" had been carried on for some years, he asserted, and recited in detail the articles of merchandise that were exchanged. For domestic cotton and other American goods delivered in New Mexico, "the traders brought back gold, silver, furs, and mules." Protection was needed for these pioneer merchants against the Indian tribes that occupied the

[7] Gregg, Commerce of the Prairies, 24, 25, 30–34, 73; John Onswake, The Conestoga Six-Horse Bell Teams of Eastern Pennsylvania (Cincinnati, 1930), 89, 159–60; Seymour Dunbar, A History of Travel in America (4 vols., Indianapolis, 1915), II, 445; Solon J. Buck and Elizabeth H. Buck, The Planting of Civilization in Western Pennsylvania (Pittsburgh, 1939), 239; Chittenden, The American Fur Trade, II, 523–25; Moorhead, New Mexico's Royal Road, 123–51.

territory between the Missouri and the borders of New Mexico, to prevent "a total interruption to the commercial and social intercourse so happily begun."

Three weeks later, Senator Benton presented a document containing the results of his investigations of the Santa Fe trade, featuring his questions and the specific answers of Mr. Augustus Storrs of Missouri. The latter was an active trader whom Benton described as "a gentleman of character and intelligence late of New Hampshire," incapable of giving a false picture of the caravan trade. "The fruit of these enterprises for the present year," Senator Benton declared, "amounted to $190,000 in gold and silver bullion and coin, and precious furs." This should be regarded "chiefly . . . an earnest of what might be expected from a regulated and protected trade," he added.

The Committee on Indian Affairs, of which Benton was chairman, drafted a bill which provided for a commission to mark the road and negotiate with the Indians along the route, authority for the President to negotiate for extension of the road into Mexican territory, and an appropriation of $30,000 for these purposes. The bill was signed by President James Monroe on March 3, 1825, one day before the end of his second term. The influence of Senator Benton with the incoming Adams administration was not expected to be strong, since he had favored William H. Crawford for President until it became clear that he could not win, and had then turned to the support of Andrew Jackson.

President John Quincy Adams appointed as commissioners Benjamin H. Reeves of Missouri, Pierre Menard of Illinois, and the former agent for the Osage Indians, George C. Sibley. The appropriation was to be allocated as follows: $20,000 for negotiations with the Indians and $10,000 for locating and marking the road. Missourians could find little fault with the President's choice of commissioners, since all three were well informed on the subject of Santa Fe trade and the related problems of Indian relations. Colonel Sibley was expected to have great influence with the Osage and Kansas Indians. Benjamin H. Reeves was distinguished by his service in the Kentucky legislature, the Missouri territorial legislature, and the Missouri constitutional convention, and by his election as lieutenant-governor of Missouri in 1824.

Pierre Menard, a talented Indian agent, was soon placed on another assignment, and his place on the Reeves Commission was filled by Thomas Mather. A surveyor, a clerk, two chain-bearers, six laborers, and fifteen riflemen, who were to serve as hunters and guards, were assigned to the commissioners for work on the marking and extension of the trail.[8]

Treaties were made with the Osage and Kansas Indians in which the tribes agreed to unmolested passage for the traders and the United States agreed to give the Indians $800 in money and merchandise. Between July 4 and September 11, 1825, the surveying party marked the trail to the Arkansas River and, with the consent of the Mexican government, extended it to San Fernando the following summer. The volume of business along the trail increased sharply in 1825 and 1826. President Adams appointed Augustus Storrs to serve as consul at Santa Fe and Joshua Pilcher at Chihuahua.

The Adams administration, without enthusiasm for Benton's program as a whole, responded to the most urgent public demands in Missouri. The Secretary of War, James Barbour, asked General Jacob Brown for a report on the military needs of the Missouri frontier. General Brown recommended two infantry companies, supported by two mounted companies, with a rendezvous at "some eligible position on or near the Arkansas River." Short of the entire force he had recommended, "especially . . . the cavalry arm," General Brown believed that it was "inexpedient to make the movement. With this force it is presumed that the trade might be secured and the garrison placed beyond the probable reach of disaster."

The Whig representative from Missouri, Edward Bates, cooperated with Benton in urging federal military protection along the Santa Fe Trail. The first two caravans of 1828 lost heavily in

[8] *Register of Debates in Congress*, 18 Cong., 2 sess., 6, 7, 110, Appendix, 406; F. F. Stephens, "Missouri and the Santa Fe Trade," *Mo. Hist. Rev.*, Vol. X, No. 4 (July, 1916), 233–60; Chambers, *Old Bullion*, 87–88, 127–29.

attacks by Indians. Three men were killed, and property losses were the worst suffered since the trade began. The first caravan lost nearly one thousand head of horses, and the second lost all livestock and wagons. After burying their specie, the traders and employees of this party walked to the settlements, obtained horses, and went back to recover their hidden money.

On March 23, 1830, Benton again spoke in the Senate in favor of military escort for the Santa Fe traders. The bill which he introduced was called the "mounted infantry bill." It proposed to mount and equip ten companies of the United States Army for service on the Santa Fe Trail. The five hundred horses for this project— mounts for ten companies of fifty men each—he estimated would cost $25,000. Thomas C. Jesup, quartermaster general, placed the cost of subsistence for each horse at $50, but Benton was positive that the cost would be much lower on the frontier. A safe estimate would be $20 an animal, he thought. Including equipment—saddles, bridles, and halters—the total appropriation should be about $50,000 he said. "For each subsequent year, it will probably be about fifteen thousand dollars, say ten or twelve thousand dollars for forage, and the remainder to supply the waste of horses and equipments."[9]

In 1830, the Santa Fe traders organized so effectively that Indian attacks upon outbound and return caravans were discouraged. Two years later, Congress authorized cavalry protection for the commerce; and with improved co-operation by the traders in their own defense, danger from the Plains Indians sank almost to the status of a minor annoyance. The fur trader William Ashley, as a representative from Missouri, took an active part in the debates of the Twenty-second Congress and was a powerful supporter of Benton's plans for military protection. President Jackson understood the value of mounted soldiers on the caravan route, as well as the political possibilities of military units to purchase goods from the

[9] *Register of Debates in Congress*, 21 Cong., 1 sess., Vol. VI (Mounted Infantry Bill), 272–74; *American State Papers, Military Affairs*, III (Gen. Jac. Brown to Hon. James Barbour, Jan. 10, 1827), 615; F. F. Stephens, *loc. cit.*, 251–54; *Niles' Register*, Vol. XXXV (Nov. 29, 1828), 214; Chambers, *Old Bullion*, 163–64.

merchants and lull the fears of constituents on the Missouri frontier. The President readily gave his approval to the necessary expenditures for the escort.[10]

River commerce incidental to the fur trade, and particularly the river transportation of goods for the Santa Fe caravans, served as a powerful stimulus for business in western Missouri. The Santa Fe traders generally purchased their goods, for cash or on credit, from the merchants of western Missouri towns. The James Aull store at Lexington was one of the firms that sold supplies for the Santa Fe trade. The proprietor, with his brother Robert and another partner named Samuel Owens, opened other stores at Richmond, Liberty, and Independence, all of which were conveniently located for supplying the caravans. In 1830, Aull sold over $8,000 worth of goods to the traders before the wagons started for Santa Fe in May. Meredith M. Marmaduke combined local mercantile enterprise with the Santa Fe trade, and Alex McCausland of Franklin was interested in supplying merchants and traders with goods directly from Philadelphia. Samuel C. Lamme, who ran a store at Franklin, bought goods in the East and also engaged in freighting merchandise to Santa Fe. In 1828 he lost his life in a clash with the Indians as his caravan returned from New Mexico.

Jennets, jacks, and mules, together with other livestock, were items of some importance in the contracts of Missouri River merchants for trade with Santa Fe. The importance attached to the use of mules in the caravans and the frequent references to jacks and jennets in the records of the traders give at least a clue to the later development of the Missouri mule as a farm animal.

A Mexican contract of 1828 specified the delivery at Santa Fe to Meredith M. Marmaduke or his agent of two hundred "large fine young Jennetts," four "Jennett Jacks," and twelve "broke gentle likely young mules." An account of the return caravan in 1834, which brought $200,000 in specie to Missouri, states that the 140 men gave their attention to the care of a "drove of mules and several wagonloads of wool taken in exchange for merchandise." After

[10] Stephens, *loc. cit.*, 256–59; J. D. Richardson, *Messages and Papers of the Presidents*, II, 594–95.

six or seven years in the Santa Fe trade, Marmaduke retired with a comfortable fortune.[11]

THE GOLDEN AGE OF THE MISSOURI FUR TRADE

Closely related to the Santa Fe caravan trade was the development of trapping by Americans in the West. Furs and peltries from the Oregon country, Rocky Mountains, California, Green River Valley, and the Upper Missouri joined with the peltries and furs, gold and silver, blankets and livestock from Santa Fe to break all previous records for commerce along the Missouri. The fur trade, like the commerce with Santa Fe, shaped the population of St. Louis and lesser towns of Missouri. Not only the number of inhabitants along the great rivers, but also their occupational skills, economic bonds with people of the older states, and trends in political thought, were determined by the new commerce that moved along the principal waterways, centering in the activities of promoters and organizers of St. Louis.

Trapping by American frontiersmen developed rapidly after Missouri became a state, with no pronounced decline until the decade of the Mexican War. While fur companies and related industries were shaping the commerce between St. Louis and other river ports, the mountain men and overland traders were transforming the entire West. Routes to be followed by later hordes of immigrants moving west to settle the Great Plains, to attack the forests of the Pacific slope, and to burrow for the precious metals of the mountains were discovered and marked out. Fertile valleys for cultivation and grass-covered uplands for future pasturage were noted in the accounts of traders and trappers; and the Indians were introduced to the people who were destined to replace their primitive culture with farms and ranches, factories and stores, steamboats and steam locomotives, statutes and judicial processes, the vices and virtues of civilization, Christianity, corrupt politics, and the Bill of Rights.

[11] Lewis E. Atherton, "James and Robert Aull—A Frontier Missouri Mercantile Firm," *Mo. Hist. Rev.*, Vol. XXX (Oct., 1935), 3–27.

In his descent of the river in 1806, Captain Lewis met eleven bands of fur traders—French, American, and British. Forest Hancock and Joseph Dickson, trappers from the Illinois country, met Lewis and Clark at Fort Mandan and persuaded the youngest man of the party, John Colter of Kentucky, to return to the headwaters of the Missouri on a trapping expedition. David Thompson reported that in the summer of 1807 he saw forty-two Americans in the Oregon country, who were there to settle a trading post. Two of the men, he said, had been members of the Lewis and Clark expedition.

Manuel Lisa employed Colter to guide his trappers to the Yellowstone. The stories of Colter's adventures in the land of the Blackfeet became established episodes in the pioneer tradition of the Northwest. Not all of Colter's contemporaries were convinced that his marvelous escapes were told with strict adherence to fact; but many careful students, including Hiram M. Chittenden, are inclined to give full credit to the young explorer's accounts.

The leading St. Louis competitors in the fur trade organized among themselves the Missouri Fur Company in the summer of 1808. Included in the new association were Manuel Lisa, Pierre Menard, Andrew Henry, Pierre Chouteau, William Clark, and Reuben Lewis, a brother of Meriwether Lewis. On the first expedition sent out by the Missouri Fur Company, 172 men were employed as trappers and hunters. They carried their trade goods in nine barges and reached Lisa's Fort at the mouth of the Big Horn after a profitable exchange of goods with the Arikara Indians. The Crow Indians delivered furs and pelts at Fort Manuel, and the prospect of future profits was excellent. A part of the men moved on to Three Forks, where a new fort was begun in the spring of 1810. Fur-bearing animals were plentiful in the region, particularly beaver, and the traders were confident that they were embarked upon a successful venture when an attack by the Blackfeet changed the entire outlook.

Five of the Missouri Fur Company men were killed, and the victorious Indians carried off a large amount of property—furs, traps, guns, and horses. Discouraged by the hostility of this powerful tribe and unable to meet the challenge with additional riflemen, the St. Louis associates very reluctantly withdrew down the Missouri. Andrew Henry made another attempt, on the branch of Snake River that came to be called Henry's Fork, where he built a new fort; but the Blackfeet were a constant menace, the winter was unusually severe, and game was not plentiful. In the spring of 1811 he returned to St. Louis. On the Missouri, Indian attacks continued until the traders were forced to abandon Fort Manuel. The reorganized Missouri Fur Company made a determined bid for furs, but the continued hostility of the Blackfeet and the vigorous competition of John Jacob Astor's organization reduced the St. Louis associates to a small area in the vicinity of present Omaha.[12]

In 1810, John Jacob Astor organized the Pacific Fur Company to direct the Columbia River trade. His first ship, the *Tonquin*, reached the Columbia River in March, 1811, after the long voyage from New York, with a swing west to Hawaii. This ship was lost in a fight with the Indians on the coast north of the Columbia; but in May, 1812, a cargo of trade goods reached Astoria, the American Fur Company's principal post in the Northwest.

In the meantime, Wilson Price Hunt led a party of sixty-one men from St. Louis to Astoria. To avoid the Blackfeet, Hunt exchanged his boats on the Missouri for horses and traveled across the prairies. Part of the animals were obtained from Manuel Lisa and the rest were purchased from the Arikaras. The overland journey began on July 18, 1811, with eighty-two pack horses laden with trade goods and supplies for the trappers. They traveled up Wind River, crossed the divide, and entered the upper valley of the Snake. The winter journey down to the Columbia was filled with incredible hardships, but the "Overland Astorians" finally reached the Columbia in two parties and pushed on to the post. By February, most of the original party had arrived at Astoria.

During the War of 1812, the Northwest Company of Montreal purchased all the properties of the Pacific Fur Company, including Astoria and the lesser posts. The British war ship *Raccoon*

12 Chittenden, *The American Fur Trade*, I, Preface, x; 247–61; II, 713–23, 850–51; Billington, *The Far Western Frontier*, 41; Hafen and Rister, *Western America*, 154–56, 209–14; Ewers, *The Blackfeet*, 45–50; *Adventures of Zenas Leonard, Fur Trader* (John C. Ewers, ed.; Norman, 1959), viii, ix.

came to Astoria on November 30, 1814. Captain Black, in command of twenty-six guns, had expected to bombard the fort and capture a valuable prize, and he was keenly disappointed to learn that the British firm had bought Astoria. Two weeks after his arrival, he took formal possession and gave the place a new name, Fort George. The end of the war found British fur traders in control of the Oregon region. In 1821 the Hudson's Bay Company expanded its activities over the Columbia Valley by absorbing the Northwest Company. Headquarters for the enlarged British organization were established at Fort Vancouver, built in 1824 on the north bank of the Columbia, opposite the mouth of the Willamette. Dr. John McLoughlin was chief factor for the Hudson's Bay Company in Oregon, and his control over company affairs was so firm and yet so kindly and just that he was known by the trappers and the Indians as the "King of Oregon."

By terms of the Treaty of Ghent at the end of the War of 1812, Astoria was returned to the United States; and in recognition of the growing interest of Great Britain in the Oregon fur trade, an agreement was signed between the two nations in 1818 whereby joint occupation was provided for a period of ten years. The area was open to settlement and for the trade activities of both British and United States citizens. In 1819 the United States agreed with Spain upon a boundary line that extended all the way from the mouth of the Sabine River on the Gulf of Mexico to the point on the Pacific Coast intersected by the forty-second parallel. Thus, by terms of the Adams-Onís Treaty, the claims of Spain to the Oregon country were surrendered to the United States.

Russian claims to Oregon land, as an extension of Alaska, were regarded by Secretary of State John Quincy Adams and President James Monroe as highly dangerous to American plans for expansion, and the British were equally concerned over limits to Russian territorial ambitions. A southern boundary at 54 degrees 40 minutes was agreed upon for the Alaska Panhandle, thus surrendering Russian claims to Oregon, by formal treaties in 1824 and 1825. At the end of the ten-year period of joint occupation, the United States and Great Britain renewed the agreement without setting a time limit upon it. British fur-trading interests in the area were definitely larger than American interests, and the Hudson's Bay Company pushed its trapping activities far beyond the area of joint occupation.

Missourians and other citizens of the United States who were engaged in the fur trade had for their immediate use, in addition to the remote tributaries of the Snake and the Columbia, many productive areas that were more accessible to the Mississippi, the Missouri, or the Santa Fe Trail. The fur trade in the Rocky Mountains, in Nevada and California, Minnesota, Montana, and many other parts of the West developed into an enterprise of enormous total significance. While the venerable "King of Oregon" was expanding his company's activities, the American and British trappers and traders were establishing new records for the business that centered in St. Louis. It was reported by Jedediah Smith in 1828 that beaver skins alone had been delivered at Fort Vancouver during one year that were valued at $250,000.[13] The total value of furs that came to St. Louis was estimated by Indian Agent John Dougherty for the years 1815 to 1830 at $3,750,000. Beaver skins were valued at $1,500,000, buffalo skins at $1,170,000, and miscellaneous peltries—otter, deer, muskrat, and coon skins—at $1,080,000.

William Henry Ashley and Andrew Henry became partners in the fur trade. Hostile Blackfeet, horse-trading Arikaras bent upon self-preservation, and horse-stealing Assiniboines with the same narrow design gave the partners a rough year of massacres and property losses. Colonel Henry Leavenworth, with six companies of infantry and two six-pound cannons, failed to give the traders adequate protection.

Shut out of the upper Missouri by the hostility of the Blackfeet, Arikaras, and other Indians of the area, Ashley and Henry planned an expedition overland that would take their trappers south of the belligerent tribes. While Andrew Henry and a party of thirteen men returned to the Yellowstone in the autumn of 1823, a smaller band under Jedediah Smith, which included Thomas Fitzpatrick

13 Billington, *The Far Western Frontier*, 41–43; Hafen and Rister, *Western America*, 216, 219–23, 231, 234; Chittenden, *The American Fur Trade*, I, 221–23, 227–44.

and Bill Sublette, opened the new trail. They began their journey at Fort Kiowa, below the Arikara villages on the Missouri, and pushed west across the Black Hills to the Wind River Valley of western Wyoming. This party traveled through an arid, treeless region, where two of the men were so weakened by thirst that they had to be left behind, buried in the sand with only their heads protruding, to conserve the moisture of their bodies. Smith discovered a water hole later in the day and rode back to rescue them.[14]

Because of the remarkable men who embarked upon their careers in trapping and trading, and also because of the virgin territory that was about to be opened, a great new era was beginning for the Missouri fur trade.

James Clyman and Bill Sublette, in March, 1824, crossed South Pass and reached the Big Sandy, a tributary of Green River. Other Ashley men followed them. Jedediah Smith and a small party of trappers went farther south and camped on Black's Fork; Clyman and Fitzpatrick trapped the upper Green River; and in June the two parties came back across South Pass to meet on the Sweetwater. The furs were packed for shipment in small boats down the North Platte and were carried eventually to St. Louis by Andrew Henry.

The meeting of trappers on the Sweetwater was the first of many such gatherings by the men who trapped for William Ashley and his successors. Ashley adopted the trappers' rendezvous as a regular feature of his business in furs. Jedediah Smith, David Jackson, and William Sublette operated as partners in the fur trade, and were followed by the Rocky Mountain Fur Company, which was placed on the defensive by Astor's American Fur Company.

The Western Department of the American Fur Company had been placed under the agency of Bernard Pratte and Company in 1826. Pierre Chouteau, Jr., as a member of the St. Louis firm, became the principal director of Astor's business in the Missouri Val-

---

[14] *Zenas Leonard*, x, xi, xiii; Chittenden, *The American Fur Trade*, I, 262–70; II, 589–607, 684–91; Billington, *The Far Western Frontier*, 43, 44; Hafen and Rister, *Western America*, 221–22; John E. Sunder, *Bill Sublette, Mountain Man* (Norman, 1959), 33–45; Harrison C. Dale, *The Ashley-Smith Explorations* (Cleveland, 1918), 59–85.

ley and the central Rockies. Competition between the American Fur Company and the Rocky Mountain Fur Company was chiefly a struggle for control of beaver territory, with Pierre Chouteau matching Astor's resources and his own extensive acquaintance with the fur business against the capital and knowledge of such men as Smith, Jackson, and William Sublette, Thomas Fitzpatrick, James Bridger, and Bill Williams.

Perhaps Jedediah Smith was the most remarkable person among the mountain men. He had joined with Ashley and Henry in their trade project of 1823. With Sublette and Jackson he fought against the Arikaras on June 2, and after the battle it was Smith who volunteered for the task of carrying a message to Andrew Henry at the mouth of the Yellowstone. William Ashley persuaded a French-Canadian guide to go with the young recruit. The mission was accomplished, and Smith had made an impressive start in his career as a mountain man. He was twenty-six when he became a partner in the purchase of General Ashley's fur-trading interests in 1824.

After the Weber River rendezvous of 1826, Smith explored southward with fourteen trappers, through the regions of Utah Lake, Sevier Valley, Virgin River, and the lower Colorado. With fresh horses obtained from the Mohave Indians, he crossed the desert to San Diego. In spite of the reluctance of Spanish officers to grant permission for further explorations, Smith and his men traveled northward some three hundred miles, turned toward the headwaters of the San Joaquin, and spent the winter trapping in the mountains. In May and June, 1827, Smith and two of his men crossed the Sierra Nevada Mountains and reached the Bear Lake rendezvous early in July. The little band lost two horses and one mule during the eight-day crossing of the mountains and four more horses on the journey across Salt Lake Desert, arriving with but two pack animals.[15] Smith's brief career as a Santa Fe trader and his death in a Comanche attack have been sketched above.

15 Chittenden, *The American Fur Trade*, I, 247–54, 271, 272, 281n., 282–84, 344–62; *Zenas Leonard*, xii–xv; Sunder, *Bill Sublette*, 45–49; Dale, *The Ashley-Smith Explorations*, 117–61, 186–94; Dale L. Morgan, *Jedediah Smith and the Opening of the West* (Indianapolis and N.Y., 1953), 133–74, 175–235.

Many mountain men adopted the habits of the Indians among whom they lived. It was common for the American trapper, like the French *coureur de bois* of an earlier period, to take an Indian wife. Even the language of the trapper acquired qualities of Indian speech. Sometimes the trappers fought in the Indian tribal wars, and almost inevitably their hand-to-hand combat took on the characteristics of native fighting. They habitually scalped their enemies. Along with their short-barreled rifle, pistol, knife, bullet pouch, powder horn, bullet mold, and whetstone, the mountain men carried a tomahawk. Their moccasins were decorated with the skilled beadwork of an Indian woman, and their picturesque garb—leather pants and fringed buckskin shirt—was crowned by a fur cap, adorned with braided horsehair or the tail of an animal.

Hard pressed for food, they ate horse meat with relish, and in the direst need they added insects and worms to their diet. Even in the happy periods of plentiful game, they ate portions of slaughtered animals that were ordinarily discarded by persons of less robust appetite; and, confronted by the prospect of starvation, they might even resort to cannibalism.

Men in winter camps who could read were able, sometimes, to obtain books. Examples are on record of books in the hands of mountain men that were written by authors of high rank in the literature of the English language—such as Byron, Scott, Milton, and Shakespeare. Works on chemistry or philosophy were sometimes found among their effects, and Bibles were not unknown at the rendezvous or in the winter camp. Jedediah Smith was widely known for his devotion to reading the Scriptures.

Dr. John McLoughlin of the Hudson's Bay Company was eager to compete for the beaver skins of the Snake River country, even if he had to carry on the rivalry at a loss. Captain Bonneville persistently trapped the region to the west of Great Salt Lake. Joseph Reddeford Walker, a Tennessee man who had moved to the Missouri frontier three years before statehood when he was twenty years old, and had been elected sheriff of Jackson County when he was twenty-nine, was one of the followers of Captain Bonneville in his fur-trading venture. After the summer rendezvous of 1833,

Bonneville sent Walker on an expedition to the southwest with a party of about fifty men, well equipped with horses and supplies.

Like Jedediah Smith, Walker had qualities of natural leadership for exploration in the western mountains. Quiet and good natured, he was decisive and able to command the obedience of active men. His party explored the western shore of Great Salt Lake, trapped along the Humboldt, crossed the Sierra Nevada Mountains, and spent the winter of 1833–34 in California. In the spring Walker went south to the Kern River, eastward through the notch that came to be called Walker Pass, northward along the Sierra Nevada range, through Owens Valley, across the desert, and back along the Humboldt. Like the rest of the Far West, the regions that had been explored by Captain Bonneville and Joseph Reddeford Walker were trapped out.

Nathaniel Wyeth, after a misunderstanding with the Sublettes over an agreement to transport goods out to the rendezvous in 1834—or, as Ray Allen Billington suggests, after Wyeth was deceived and cheated by William Sublette's early delivery of supplies—led his pack train to the north and built Fort Hall as a year-round trading post. His idea gradually took root in other parts of the West, and after 1840 the rendezvous as a regular feature of the fur trade was discontinued. Fort Hall on the Snake River, purchased by the Hudson's Bay Company in 1837, Fort Laramie on the upper Platte, built by the Rocky Mountain Fur Company in 1834, and Bent's Fort, planned and constructed with elaborate detail by William and Charles Bent near the junction of the Purgatory and the Arkansas in 1833, were perhaps the best known of the fortified posts.

The golden era of the Missouri fur trade ended by 1834, although the bitter competition continued for several years. The enterprise begun by Ashley and Henry, continued by Smith, Jackson and Sublette, and developed to its greatest extent by the Rocky Mountain Fur Company, had brought one thousand packs of furs into St. Louis, valued at $500,000, over a period of a dozen years. The great overland trails to the Pacific Coast and other parts of the West had been pointed out for the so-called "pathfinders" of a later day. Missouri and the entire country had become aware of

the great area west of the ninety-fifth meridian and had learned
something of its potential wealth.[16]

[16] Maximilian, Prince of Wied, *Travels in the Interior of North America* (vols.
XXII–XXIV of Thwaites' *Early Western Travels*), XXII, 312; Chittenden, *The
American Fur Trade*, I, 252–54, 438–46; II, 657–72, 820–22; Billington, *The Far
Western Frontier*, 44–68; Morgan, *Jedediah Smith*, 362–65; Sunder, *Bill Sublette*,
94–98, 107–13; Daniel Ellis Conner, *Joseph Reddeford Walker and the Arizona
Adventure* (Donald J. Berthrong and Odessa Davenport, eds.; Norman, 1956),
Introduction, xiv–xviii; Chittenden, *The American Fur Trade*, II, 820–22.

BUSINESS AND POLITICS, 1820-1840

DAVID BARTON and his brother Joshua, the sons of a Baptist minister in Tennessee, came to St. Louis in 1812. David was twenty-seven years old, with experience in the practice of law, which brought him to President James Madison's attention in his search for young Republicans of promise who might be suitable material for holding offices in the territory. David was appointed circuit judge, but the opportunities for law practice were so attractive that he soon gave up the post in order to ride the St. Louis circuit as an attorney. With a combination of legal knowledge and definite talent for good-fellowship, David Barton was immediately successful.

In 1818, David Barton was elected speaker of the House of Representatives in the last General Assembly of Missouri Territory. His election as president of the constitutional convention in 1820 was unanimous, and his choice by the General Assembly to the United States Senate was by a substantial majority. Barton's great misfortune was overindulgence in alcohol. His popularity remained strong in Missouri until after the presidential election of 1824–25, in the final phase of which he supported J. Q. Adams over Andrew Jackson. Barton had been chosen for a full six-year senatorial term in 1824; but in 1830 the General Assembly named Alexander Buckner to fill the seat. Before the end of his first term Barton had broken with his colleague, Tom Benton.

[117]

Perhaps the most sympathetic friend of Senator Barton in Missouri and the man most intimately acquainted with his personal problems was Edward Bates, to whom he presented a sharp contrast in personality and daily habits. Bates, the founder of the Missouri Temperance Society, had in his friend Senator Barton a spectacular example of the bad effects of excessive drinking. The sparkling public addresses of David Barton, his ready wit, and his scholarly attainments probably made a deeper impression upon the frontier state of Missouri than they would have made in an older, more settled society. Even his drunkenness, which proved to be a definite factor in shortening his career and reducing the effectiveness of his mature service, might have been an element in his reputation for brilliance. The contrast between Barton drunk and Barton sober must have been evident to all observers—whether or not they were qualified to pass judgment upon his intellectual efforts. Certainly his total achievement was small by comparison with that of Edward Bates or Thomas Hart Benton. Although the people of Cooper County sent David Barton to the state senate in 1834, his political influence there was small. By 1837 he was hopelessly insane, a miserable and tragic exile from society during the final months of his life.

Thomas Hart Benton, choice of the General Assembly by a bare majority for the second seat in the United States Senate, was thirty-eight years of age and had been a resident of Missouri for five years when he was elected. Like many other Missourians, he was affected by the complicated pattern of politics in St. Louis. He had left Tennessee for a fresh start in public life after a serious personal clash with Andrew Jackson; he was not a thin-skinned person, but the circumstances of his migration provided a raw, sensitive covering for a proud man.

His brother Jesse had challenged Major William Carroll to a duel. General Jackson, friendly with the Bentons and with Billy Carroll, had tried hard to persuade young Jesse Benton that it was foolish for him to fight a duel with the Major—that he had no quarrel with Carroll and no cause to challenge him. But Jackson's plea for peace had not been effective, and he had reluctantly agreed to serve as Major Carroll's second. On the day selected for the duel, Tom Benton was in Washington to present a claim to the War Department for his friend, Andrew Jackson.

Young Jesse Benton did not display cowardice when he fought Major Carroll, but he did perform badly. Obviously, the duel which he had insisted upon fighting suddenly changed from a gay, romantic game as he faced the experienced officer and became a matter of deadly possibilities. At the signal, Jesse hastily fired a shot which struck his opponent but did not disable him; then he turned his back and suddenly squatted. Major Carroll, a cool hand with a pistol, was not disconcerted by his wound or by young Benton's unorthodox stance. His bullet struck Jesse in the seat of the pants, not only inflicting a painful wound but also making him the laughingstock of Nashville.

When Tom Benton returned to Tennessee and found that Jesse had been involved in a duel with Billy Carroll and that the master of "The Hermitage" had served as the Major's second, the older brother's anger turned against Jackson, whom he charged with "superintending the shooting" of his kinsman. With rumor as his evidence of what had been said, Jackson asked in a letter whether Thomas Benton had spoken disrespectfully of him. Benton answered that he had not challenged Jackson but added, "The terror of your pistols is not to seal my lips. . . . I shall neither seek, nor decline, a duel with you."

On September 4, 1813, a chance meeting at Clayton Talbot's Tavern in Nashville brought on the inevitable fight. Conflicting evidence renders an accurate account of the affair difficult, if not impossible; but it is certain that several persons took part on each side and that Jackson was severely wounded by a pistol ball. Both of the Bentons were injured, also. Colonel John Coffee, Alexander Donelson, Stockley Hays, and Charles Hammond, all tried desperately to aid General Jackson with pistol or dagger; and James Sumner rushed to the assistance of Jesse Benton when he was in peril from the knife of Charles Hammond and the sword-cane of "the gigantic Stockley Hays." Jackson carried from the fight a bullet which surgeons were unable to extract. Both of the Bentons were stabbed repeatedly; but it was the dignified, portly, elder brother who furnished a comic touch to the affair which came so close to tragedy. Retreating from Donelson and Coffee, who were attacking him with knife and clubbed pistol, Thomas Hart Benton backed ignominiously down a flight of stairs.

After the War of 1812, when Benton arrived in Missouri to take up residence there, several rumors followed him from Tennessee—and one of earlier origin from North Carolina—each of which could be distorted by enemies into ugly, disreputable shadows upon his record. They said he had picked a fight with Jackson and his friends at Talbot's Tavern, and had fallen down the stairs in his haste to get away from the trouble he had started; that he fled from Tennessee to avoid giving his opponent the satisfaction of a duel after Jackson had begun to recover from his wound; and that he had missed his best chance for active military service in July, 1814, by feigning sickness as his regiment advanced upon the hostile Indians near Pensacola. All of these charges were false, but they were built upon a framework of fact which could be twisted to give a semblance of truth to the entire bit of gossip.

Benton did not seek a clash with Jackson, nor did he go west to avoid meeting him. The flaws in Benton's character did not include timidity; on the contrary, he was too ready to prove his courage upon the slightest provocation. Only with the passing of years and the harrowing experience of killing a man in a duel, did he achieve a more mature confidence that enabled him to ignore insults.

The North Carolina incident which Benton considered a black mark on his record was a theft of money from schoolmates at Chapel Hill, when he was sixteen. The evidence was conclusive; on three separate occasions he filched small sums from his associates—$9.00, $8.00, and $18.00—and was trapped with a new federal one-dollar bill, planted for the purpose in a roommate's pocketbook. He had been three months in the college at Chapel Hill when he was expelled for the theft. Probably his mother's removal from North Carolina to Tennessee was an attempt to give him a fresh start far away from the scene of his disgrace. The story followed him, however, all the way to Missouri, where it was polished up to serve as an offset against his views on hard money and his theories concerning the proper way to elect the American President.[1]

Early in his Missouri law practice Benton quarreled with another young attorney, the son of Judge John B. C. Lucas. "You deny the truth," Benton said to his opponent. "You assert what is not true," answered young Charles Lucas, and Benton sent a challenge. Lucas replied that he would not fight over his conduct of a case at the bar for a client. This might have ended the incident if Charles Lucas had not afterwards sought a quarrel with the man from Tennessee at a voting place. Without official authority, he demanded, "Have you paid your taxes?" Benton was ready to answer all proper questions of election judges, he said, "but I do not propose to answer charges made by any puppy who may happen to run across my path."

Lucas sent a challenge which was promptly accepted. In their first meeting, held on "Bloody Island" in the Mississippi with Luke Lawless acting as second for Benton and Joshua Barton for Lucas, both men were wounded, Benton very slightly and his opponent, with a bullet in his neck, so severely that he could not continue the fight. Again, both of the belligerent young men felt that the matter could be dropped without dishonor; but the busy tale-bearers made Benton believe that his opponent doubted his courage. Both men had been wounded, at thirty feet; would Benton dare to face Lucas at ten feet? He dared—in fact, he insisted upon the second meeting. This time, Lucas fired hastily and missed; but Benton's bullet passed through the left arm and the heart of his antagonist. Old Judge Lucas regarded Benton as his son's murderer, and Benton himself never ceased to regret his clash with Charles Lucas.

When Andrew Jackson came to the United States Senate, about the middle of Benton's first term, the two men served together on the Military Affairs Committee and found too much common po-

1 Shoemaker, "Fathers of the State," *Mo. Hist. Rev.*, Vol. X, No. 1 (October, 1915), 2–9; Houck, *Missouri*, III, 8, 10, 17, 77, 79, 121, 250, 265, 266; *The Correspondence of Andrew Jackson* (J. S. Bassett, ed.; 6 vols., Washington, 1926–33), I, 308–15 (Hynes to Jackson, July 10, 1813; Jackson to Benton, July 19, 1813; Benton to Jackson, July 25, 1813); Chambers, *Old Bullion*, 13–17, 49–56; Elbert B. Smith, *Magnificent Missourian* (Philadelphia and N.Y., 1958), 20, 21, 44–51.

litical ground to permit keeping their old personal enmity alive. As a Jacksonian Democrat in Missouri, Benton was a member of a winning team; and his contribution to party strength after 1828 was a major factor in Jackson's political triumphs.

In his early practice of law in St. Louis, however, Benton was closely bound to the interests of the Gratiot, Chouteau, Jean P. Cabanné, and Silvestre Labadie families. These aristocrats of the Spanish régime who helped to elect Benton to the Senate did not fully understand or sympathize with the American frontier settlers. Benton was closer to the backwoods farmers than he was to the holders of large Spanish land grants who employed him to defend the titles to their property. He adjusted his views readily to agrarian theories on money and banking, suffrage and apportionment, to frontier journalism and rural political customs. As Missouri's commercial interests grew and towns developed in the regions apart from the great river arteries, Benton adjusted more intelligently to the growing nationalism of America than many of his powerful patrons. Their ruling motive was to extract profit from backwoods people, laborers, small farmers, trappers, and Indians for the benefit of St. Louis liquor dealers and other merchants. Benton's view was wider; he was in sympathy with the common people who made up the great majority of the total population. Only a man of superb talent could have held together the diverse political elements in Missouri that combined to send him to the United States Senate for five consecutive terms.

On February 24, 1824, he proposed an amendment to the federal Constitution, for direct popular election of the President and Vice-President. His general scheme was to divide the country into districts, each of which would have one vote for President and Vice-President, that vote to be determined by the people "in their primary assemblies." He spoke for two days in favor of abolishing the indirect election of the chief executive by electors who might be chosen by the legislatures rather than the people. He was not upholding the interests of his own constituents, he said; for the infant, Missouri, would be one of the greatest states. "The wonderful phenomenon of thirty thousand miles of navigable water, uniting in her center, and flowing by one channel to the Gulf of Mexico, will give her advantages unequaled by any other interior part of the globe."[2]

MISSOURI POLITICS AND THE EARLY BANKS

Alexander McNair came to Missouri in 1804. A Pennsylvanian by birth, he had served in the Dauphin County militia at twenty and as an infantry officer in the regular army afterwards. He saw active service during the Whisky Insurrection of President Washington's second term. In 1805 he became judge of the court of common pleas in the St. Louis district, and held several other offices before the admission of Missouri to statehood—sheriff of St. Louis County, trustee of the St. Louis public school, inspector-general of the Missouri militia, United States marshal, and register of the land office at St. Louis. In spite of his general popularity in the territory, he was defeated as delegate to Congress in 1814 by Rufus Easton— 948 to 854.

McNair married Marguerite Susanne de Reihle, the talented and well-educated daughter of a prominent French merchant. In the campaign for governor of Missouri in 1820, McNair's principal opponent was the explorer William Clark, who enjoyed the support of Thomas Hart Benton and many other prominent Missourians. Probably most of the voters of French descent cast their ballots for the husband of the popular Marguerite Susanne; in addition, McNair had a strong following among the American settlers. The vote was 6,576 for McNair and 2,556 for Clark.[3]

The fur trade in Missouri was the element of business that most needed the convenience of banking. Among the men who took a leading part in obtaining a charter for the Bank of St. Louis in 1813 were Rufus Easton, delegate to Congress, Samuel Hammond, formerly territorial governor, and John B. C. Lucas, judge of the

[2] *Debates and Proceedings in the Congress of the United States*, 18 Cong., 1 sess., Vol. I, 165–204; Chambers, *Old Bullion*, 65, 66, 72–77.

[3] Houck, *Missouri*, III, 9, 72, 104, 248–53; *Dictionary of American Biography*, XII, 147–48 (article on Alexander McNair, by H. Edward Nettles).

district court and a man of diverse interests. Fur traders who were actively joined in the project included Manuel Lisa, Bernard Pratte, and Auguste Chouteau. Thomas Hart Benton, after his arrival at St. Louis in 1815, invested a small sum in the stock of this bank.

The Bank of Missouri was chartered on January 31, 1815, with Auguste Chouteau as president and L. W. Boggs as cashier. John B. C. Lucas, Thomas Riddick, Alexander McNair, and Thomas Hart Benton were among the stockholders. The business was conducted in the basement of Chouteau House. The deposits were large, and the temptation to speculate must have been too much to resist. The General Assembly investigated the Bank of Missouri in 1821, but did not publish its report. Upon liquidation of its assets soon afterwards, it was found that stock notes had been used to establish the bank's capital and that the directors were indebted to the institution in the amount of $75,869.86 more than the total of its capital stock. As one of its directors, Senator Benton had borrowed from the bank; and judgment against him for $7,076 was one of the forces that compelled him to be a diligent attorney, along with his duties as a public official in Washington, during the following years. In 1823, six of his St. Louis town lots were listed for sale because of nonpayment of taxes.[4]

Benton's wife was Elizabeth, daughter of Colonel James McDowell of Virginia. Elizabeth's brother, James, was to be the outstanding advocate of restrictions on slavery in Virginia through a period of twenty years. It is likely that the views of James McDowell, reaching mature development during this period, brought some modification of Benton's attitude toward slavery, extension of slave labor into the West, and the extreme Southern Rights stand adopted by John C. Calhoun during the same time.

Nancy Benton, Thomas' mother, was over sixty years of age at the time of his marriage. Although she did not live continuously

[4] John Jay Knox, A History of Banking in the United States (N.Y., 1903), 779–82; J. Ray Cable, "Some Early Missouri Bankers," Mo. Hist. Rev., Vol. XXVI, No. 2 (Jan., 1932), 117–19; Chambers, Old Bullion, 78, 79; Bray Hammond, Banks and Politics in America from the Revolution to the Civil War, 197–226, 227–250, 259, 297.

in the house with her son, she remained the object of his special care in St. Louis until her death in 1838 at the age of eighty.[5]

The speedy failure of two banks chartered by Missouri Territory—the Bank of St. Louis in 1819 and the Bank of Missouri about one year after statehood—occurred during a period of financial instability and wild speculation in many parts of the country. The Public Land Act passed by Congress in 1800, providing long-term credit for settlers, had led many purchasers to contract for acreage far beyond their capacity to make payments. Speculators had gained possession of much good land and pushed up the price of unimproved holdings to keep pace with high prices of grain, cotton, and livestock. The Bank of the United States, the one financial organization that was powerful enough to check the reckless speculation, harvested immediate profits and took no steps toward placing limits on credit. The inevitable crash came in 1819, marked by merchant failures, collapse of state banks, and thousands of foreclosures on western real estate.

The new state of Missouri issued loan certificates as a relief measure to merchants who were in distress because they could not collect for goods sold on credit and farmers whose crops could not be marketed because of the general scarcity of money. In 1829 the Bank of the United States established a branch in St. Louis, which was open for business during the struggle for recharter by Henry Clay, Nicholas Biddle, and their Whig supporters.

Congress passed the bank bill on July 3, 1832; but President Jackson vetoed it and directed Secretary of the Treasury Roger B. Taney to cease making deposits of United States funds in the bank. The citizens of Missouri were sharply divided on the issue of maintaining the Bank of the United States, with its vast powers over national currency entrusted to private interests. However, the vote of Missouri for Jackson over Clay in the election of 1832 seemed a clear indication of majority support for the President's drastic action. Many prominent citizens of St. Louis, impressed by the

[5] Chambers, *Old Bullion*, 68, 132–52; Leota Newhard, "The Beginning of the Whig Party in Missouri, 1824–40," *Mo. Hist. Rev.*, Vol. XXV, No. 2 (Jan., 1931), 254–80.

relative safety and stability of the bank's currency, protested the veto; but the larger portion of the dominant party in the state as a whole gave steady and increasing support to Jackson and his Missouri spokesman, Thomas Hart Benton. The St. Louis branch of B.U.S. ended its career in 1834 with a net loss of $125 in five years.

The Missouri constitution authorized the General Assembly to charter a single banking corporation, with capital stock limited to five million dollars and with not more than five branches. One half of the stock was to be reserved to the state. After the St. Louis branch of the Bank of the United States brought its affairs to a close in 1834, Missouri had no banking institution with authority to issue notes; consequently, many businessmen began to demand the charter of a state bank. Since paper money from other states circulated freely in Missouri, notes of various denominations from banks in Illinois, Kentucky, and other neighboring regions came to St. Louis to meet the demands of growing population and rapidly increasing trade. Many of the banks operated under laws that did not provide adequate safeguards for the public—a situation which placed all of the penalties of state banks upon Missouri without gaining any of their advantages. St. Louis had begun the upward surge which transformed the river town into the metropolis of the West. It had a population of 5,000 during the contest for statehood, 16,489 in 1840, and 77,860 in 1850. The rate of growth —four-fold in a single decade—was reduced during the years immediately preceding the opening of the Civil War; but the city still doubled its population in ten years, reaching 160,773 by 1860.

Land sales in Missouri were booming during the inflation years of Jackson's second term as President. From 52,432 acres in 1832, the sales grew to 1,655,687 acres in 1836. During the same years the population of the state increased from 176,277 to 244,208. Wages were good, demand for labor strong, and the prices of commodities and land were high. St. Louis merchants spent from $350,000 to $400,000 annually in Pittsburgh for trade goods, and commerce with New Mexico gave an impulse to prosperity in the river towns of central Missouri. Lead and tobacco produced locally, furs and buffalo hides from all parts of the western frontier, mules and other livestock from New Mexico, and the silver that came in as a result of the Santa Fe trade combined to stabilize finances in Missouri for several years after the panic had brought disaster to other sections of the country. Lead receipts at St. Louis grew from 375,000 pigs in 1839 to 584,431 in 1843; and tobacco growing, in itself a minor source of wealth, added stability to the economic structure.

Deposits of the United States government in St. Louis provided capital for conservative enterprises. The proceeds of land sales resulted in the deposit of $744,008.82 in 1832—a sum which increased to almost $2,000,000 by 1836—to supply the needs of Indian agencies and frontier military posts. Steamboats became the principal carriers on the great rivers—actually the only means of moving distant freight from 1825 to 1850—and the river trade gave a powerful impulse to the business of St. Louis.

In 1837 the General Assembly passed the bill authorizing the establishment of the Bank of the State of Missouri with a twenty-year charter. The need for this bank was increased by Missouri's connection with the vast frontier in the West that continued to funnel the growing volume of its salable goods through St. Louis. Control of the new bank by the state was guaranteed by the provision in its charter that the president and six of the twelve directors were to be elected by the General Assembly and that failure to redeem notes in specie should result in immediate receivership. The issue of notes was limited to denominations of ten dollars and higher. Banking companies not chartered by Missouri were forbidden to carry on business within the state.

In May, 1837, the Bank of the State of Missouri opened its doors, adopting the policy of specie payment from the start. For ten years it was the only bank in the state; and for twenty years, the only corporation that had the authority to issue notes. Among the banks of the Southwest it was unique for its long record of solvency—"the best example of sound banking west of Indiana," in the opinion of one able scholar in the history of banking. The Cincinnati Commercial Agency, which had maintained a conservative banking business in St. Louis for a year, sold its accounts to the new bank of the state.

The men most responsible for the conservative policy of Missouri's experiment in monopoly were John Brady Smith, president, and Henry Shurlds, cashier of the bank. Both men were rigidly honest and devoted to the principles of safe banking. They refused to issue notes on the assumption that state bonds would find purchasers and accepted deposits only in specie or the notes of specie-paying banks during a three-year period beginning with a public announcement of their new regulation on November 12, 1839. They maintained their rigid standards against the opposition of such influential businessmen as John O'Fallon and Pierre Chouteau and of disgruntled customers who withdrew their accounts when the bank refused to accept wildcat notes from Illinois banks. Henry Shurlds once sold $100,000 in specie to the United States Bank in Philadelphia at a premium of 2 per cent.

Eventually, the Bank of the State of Missouri modified its regulations by agreeing to accept the notes of other banks at their current value. Perhaps that was an inevitable development in a city with such rapidly developing need for money as St. Louis. With the general business recovery after the panic and depression had run their course—about 1843—the bank became quite prosperous; but its policy continued to reflect the cautious principles of its management. Henry Shurlds died in 1852, five years before the end of the bank's twenty-year charter, but his conservatism dominated the directors after his death. In 1856, with a stock of $1,400,-000 in specie, circulation was approximately $2,000,000 under the $4,200,000 allowed by Missouri law. At the same time, the strong demand for notes issued by the Bank of the State of Missouri extended to California, where businessmen, miners, and bankers preferred them over all other bank notes. A considerable part of the issue left the state of Missouri and the acute need of St. Louis business for currency brought a flood of wildcat notes into the state.

The unique record of Missouri banks during the first two decades of statehood has been attributed by some observers to the natural conservatism of the people. The unhappy experiences of the territorial bankers in two ventures, the Bank of St. Louis (1813–19) and the Bank of Missouri (1817–22), have been suggested frequently as the reason for later conservative practices. But some of the men who were involved in the early failures were leading opponents of the ultraconservative policies adopted by John Brady Smith and Henry Shurlds. Lilburn W. Boggs, who served as cashier of the Bank of Missouri (1817–22), became a strong advocate of state bank chartering. In his campaign for the chief executive office, Boggs explained some of his views on banks of issue, chartered by the state: "I am aware that objections numerous and weighty have been urged," he said; "but nothing better has been presented to my mind. Banking is unrepublican, but so interwoven with our business that it can't be interrupted without great inconvenience. It is an impetus to trade. Missouri is the only state without a bank, so we are at the mercy of the money of other states."

Thomas Hart Benton probably did not derive all of his opinions on money and banking from having to pay a judgment resulting from the failure of a bank. His views in regard to the place of specie in the national currency, the relation of those ideas to his personal ventures into banking, their relation to his interest in laboring men, agrarian welfare in Missouri, and business prosperity of the Crossroads State cannot be analyzed with dogmatic certainty or nutshell simplicity.[6]

CONNECTIONS OF MISSOURI WITH NATIONAL POLITICS

During James Monroe's second term as President, the new state of Missouri conducted its political affairs with a minimum of partisan alignment. Barton and Benton, John B. C. Lucas, Henry Elliott, John R. Jones, and Nathaniel Cook all ran without party affiliation for the first Missouri seats in the United States Senate. John Scott was elected for three consecutive terms in Congress, 1820–26, without being a party candidate. Alexander McNair, the first state governor, did not claim the support of any political party; nor did Frederick Bates, elected in 1824, or John Miller, chosen governor in the special election of December 8, 1825.

[6] Dorothy B. Dorsey, "The Panic and Depression of 1837–43 in Missouri," *Mo. Hist. Rev.*, Vol. XXX, No. 2 (Jan., 1936), 132–61; Cable, *loc. cit.*, 119–22; Knox, *Banking in the United States*, 782–85.

The presidential campaign of 1824–25 provided a basis for the development of party politics in Missouri, as it did in the nation at large. Four candidates received electoral votes for President: Andrew Jackson, 99; John Quincy Adams, 84; William H. Crawford, 41; and Henry Clay, 37. Since neither one of the four had an electoral majority, it became the duty of the House of Representatives to name the President, with the choice limited to Jackson, Adams, and Crawford. Missouri voters had expressed a clear preference for Henry Clay, with 1,401 votes to 987 for Andrew Jackson, 311 for John Quincy Adams, and none for William H. Crawford. In the House election, it is not remarkable that John Scott, acting for Missouri, followed Clay's advice in giving the state's vote to Adams. David Barton shifted his support from Clay to Adams, while his colleague in the Senate, Thomas Hart Benton, gave his influence in the House election to Andrew Jackson. Perhaps the trend in Missouri politics during the following years may be discerned in the defeat of Scott in his campaign for re-election in 1826 and the defeat of Barton for the Senate in 1830.

In the Presidential campaign of 1828, Jackson won the electoral support of Missouri, carrying every county in the state. The popular vote was 8,372 for Jackson to 3,407 for Adams. As the advocate of Jacksonian policies, Benton grew in political stature while David Barton declined. Perhaps defeat in the Missouri elections—for the United States Senate in 1830 and for a seat in the House of Representatives as an anti-Jackson candidate in 1832—contributed to the tragedy of Barton's mental collapse and early death. The people of Missouri became thoroughly Jacksonian in their political responses.

In their early moves toward organization, the Jackson men based their appeal upon democracy, "the cause of majority against minority." When both William Carr Lane and Spencer Pettis desired to make the race for Congress against the pro-Adams incumbent, Edward Bates, it became apparent that division of Jackson's followers between two popular candidates might have the effect of electing their opponent. Lane and Pettis submitted their contest with each other to Senator Benton; and, as umpire, he proclaimed that Spencer Pettis enjoyed greater popular support than Lane, and that the "will of the majority ought to prevail."

Edward Bates felt keenly the sting of Benton's "dictatorial" proclamation, which meant in effect that the schism in the Jackson party was healed. Bates resorted to a type of campaigning in which the moderate and mild-mannered gentleman was out of character. He would not "touch upon the indiscretions which clouded the prospects of [Benton's] early manhood," he said. The "juvenile error" at Chapel Hill might be forgotten, he suggested—and neglected to add that it would, long since, have been forgotten if political foes had not revived it in every campaign. The Bates brothers charged that Benton had defaulted in his accounts as recruiting officer in the War of 1812; borrowed money from the Bank of Missouri as one of its directors, for which he owed the state more than $7,000; and defrauded the Treasury of the United States by padding his milage accounts. Spencer Pettis defeated Bates for the seat in Congress; a new ally in Washington had been found for Senator Benton, and without doubt he had become the most influential man in Missouri public life.

The Whig party in Missouri emerged gradually between 1832 and 1836, as the opposition to President Jackson and Senator Benton took form. The party names Whig and Democrat were not used in the election of 1832. The Jackson convention that met at Baltimore in May of that year made use of the cumbersome title "Democratic Republican." General Jackson was accepted as the party candidate in a brief resolution: "That . . . we most cordially concur in the repeated nominations which he has received in various parts of the Union as a candidate for re-election to the office which he now fills with so much honor to himself and usefulness to his country." Missouri was the only state which was not represented.

Employing the unit rule, the convention gave Martin Van Buren 208 votes out of a total of 283 for Vice-President. Each state was allotted the same number of delegates as it had electors, but some states sent more and some fewer than the number agreed upon. In determining the votes of each state, an error raised the total to 283—one more than the number originally intended. No uniform method of selecting delegates had been adopted, and the unit rule was not rigidly enforced. However, the resolution proclaiming Jackson's nomination was unanimous, and Van Buren's majority was well above the two-thirds that was agreed upon as the desirable margin for nomination.[7]

The opposition to Jackson took the name "National Republican" party. The followers of Adams and Clay had lacked organization in 1828, but in 1831 they succeeded in joining with Daniel Webster of Massachusetts and John Sergeant of Pennsylvania in calling a national convention to meet at Baltimore on the second Monday of December. Eighteen of the twenty-four states and the District of Columbia were represented by 168 delegates. The convention nominated Clay for President and John Sergeant for Vice-President. Steps were taken to strengthen the state organizations, and a second convention, the young National Republicans, was called to meet at Washington in May to endorse Clay and Sergeant. The Washington convention adopted a series of resolutions which served as a party platform. Internal improvements at federal expense was the subject of one resolution which had a particular appeal for Missouri, and the principle of protective tariff was attractive to some of its people. The resolutions did not contain a statement in regard to recharter of the Bank of the United States, since that issue did not become acute until later in the summer, after the convention had adjourned.

"Old Hickory" was re-elected with a substantial popular majority and an electoral vote of 219 to 49. Benton had predicted that Missouri would vote for President Jackson two to one, and the majority in his favor was close to that figure—8,904 for Jackson to 4,760 for Clay. The vote for the opposition candidate, a respectable minority and definitely higher than the support given Adams in 1828, probably reflected Clay's personal popularity in Missouri, together with the efforts of the St. Louis County organizations, writing hundreds of letters and rallying with speeches and resolutions in favor of the "American System and Henry Clay." Both houses of the Missouri Assembly had Democratic Republican ma-

[7] Roseboom, Eugene H., *A History of Presidential Elections,* 99n.; Stanwood, Edward, *A History of the Presidency,* I, 160, 161.

jorities, and Daniel Dunklin of Washington County was elected governor by a safe margin.[8]

The character of Whig party beginnings in Missouri is reflected in the correspondence of Edward Bates, Abiel Leonard, Charles D. Drake, and other anti-Benton men during the second decade of statehood. Writing from St. Louis, Bates addressed a tentative request toward party organization to Abiel Leonard of Franklin on April 4, 1831: "There will be a Clay candidate for Congress in this part of the State, as far as I know and believe. And in Boone's Lick, you are the only man of that side, who, I suppose could run with any prospect of success. It is getting to be time that this matter should be understood. If you . . . think that you could be elected, why strike in and our friends in these parts will stand by you to a man."

In regard to the situation of the administration party in Washington, Bates confided, "All the friends of Calhoun are, in their hearts, soon will be in their mouths—openly against Jackson."

Other followers of Clay who wrote to Abiel Leonard concerning his availability as a candidate included Rufus Easton, Charles D. Drake (with a correspondence committee), and John Stapp. The Drake committee urged Leonard: "No man . . . has a right to refuse (when called upon to help). . . . Call out as candidates in your county . . . the *best* men in your ranks—*men who cannot be beaten.*" Drake added a postscript: "Jack Gordon is as drunk as a bitch, and cried out for 'Old Tom Benton by God!' He says he has cut the cord and left us. I apologize for his conduct upon the ground that when drunk he is a *loco foco* & when sober a Whig."

J. S. Rollins wrote from Jefferson City: "Benton has been here for a week previous to the meeting of the Legislature for the express purpose of aweing [sic] into submission those of his own party who might dare to oppose him. His presence had the desired effect, and our only alternative was to let the election go unanimously for him, or to make a show at once of our real strength."[9]

[8] Chambers, *Old Bullion*, 146, 149–51, 189–90; Newhard, *loc. cit.*, 265.

[9] Leonard Manuscripts, Missouri State Historical Society, Columbia, Mo. (E. Bates to A. Leonard, April 4, 1831; Rufus Easton to A. Leonard, April 7, 1831; Whig Committee at St. Louis to A. Leonard, Jan., 1838; J. S. Rollins to A. Leonard, Nov. 22, 1838).

By 1836 the party newspapers had settled upon the names Whig and Democrat for the major parties. The Whig leaders decided against holding a convention, hoping that "favorite sons" in the various sections would prevent an electoral majority for any candidate and thus throw the choice into the House of Representatives. The Democratic convention met in Baltimore and named Martin Van Buren for President, with Richard M. Johnson of Kentucky as his running mate. Van Buren was elected with 170 votes. William Henry Harrison carried seven states for the Whigs, Webster had the vote of Massachusetts, and Hugh L. White was the choice of two southern states, Georgia and Tennessee. All of the Whig candidates combined received a popular vote of 736,250, by comparison with Van Buren's total of 762,978. The results were encouraging for the Whigs, since their candidate had carried Jackson's home state and had received strong support in all major sections of the South. Richard M. Johnson, with 147 electoral votes, was one short of a majority, since all other candidates combined had exactly the same number. The United States Senate, exercising its constitutional privilege, elected Johnson Vice-President.

Martin Van Buren carried Missouri with its four electoral votes by a popular majority of 3,658 in a total of more than 18,000. The vote for Hugh L. White, 7,337, was encouraging to the followers of Henry Clay and the American System.

The Whigs embarked upon the campaign of 1840 with enthusiasm and high hopes. The national convention at Harrisburg, Pennsylvania, after a first ballot which showed a small plurality for Henry Clay, turned to William Henry Harrison, whose fame rested chiefly upon a very ordinary military record polished to brilliance by partisan diligence. The silence of Harrison upon most of the great national issues, together with his military reputation, made him an ideal Whig candidate. It was necessary to collect the anti-Jackson sentiment into one great effort, and close analysis of political doctrines would disclose too much lack of harmony to suit the purposes of the Whig managers. Hence, they wanted a platform free from specific statements and a candidate without strong political convictions. For Vice-President the Whigs named John

Tyler of Virginia—a man of strong character and positive views on the great issues of the time.

In May, 1840, the Democrats met in Baltimore and renominated Martin Van Buren for President by unanimous agreement and avoided the expected struggle over the record of Richard M. Johnson by naming no candidate for Vice-President. The Democratic platform took a stand against internal improvements at federal expense and against protective tariff, interference with slavery by Congress, and establishment of a national bank. The Democrats also regarded it as safe to take a stand for the principles of the Declaration of Independence and for strict interpretation of the Constitution, thus linking their program with Jeffersonian doctrines. They did not, on the other hand, risk the loss of the support of business interests by coming out in favor of a narrowly agrarian view of hard money.

The Whigs made a strong appeal in their 1840 campaign for the support of the common man. In Missouri the vote for Harrison (22,972), was more than double the popular support given to the winner, Van Buren, in 1836; but the Little Magician's score in 1840 was 29,760, which gave him Missouri's electors by a margin of nearly 7,000. He carried four other slave states—Virginia, South Carolina, Alabama, and Arkansas—and two free states—Illinois and New Hampshire. Harrison won the electoral votes of New York, New Jersey, Michigan, and Maine by extremely narrow pluralities; and in Pennsylvania, where the total popular vote was 287,693, his margin was only 349. The support given to James G. Birney, candidate of the Liberty party, had no decisive effect upon the outcome of the election. Harrison's margin over Van Buren in the popular vote of the nation was less than 150,000 in a total of nearly 2,500,-000 votes cast.

A notable feature of the "log-cabin hard-cider" campaign in Missouri was the sharp rise in the number of voters. Increase of population explains in part the tremendous change; but the rise from 18,332 voters in 1836 to 52,732 in 1840 must be attributed also to the efforts of Bates, Leonard, Rufus Easton, and the rest of the anti-Jackson men in behalf of the Whig candidates, and to the activities of Senator Benton and his followers in meeting the surge of Whig politics. Missouri's vote, relative to the total population in 1840, was over 13.7 per cent—definitely higher than the ratio of voters in the Deep South and well above the average of the Border States east of the Mississippi. The voters of the Deep South in 1840 (omitting South Carolina, where there was no popular vote on presidential electors), represented approximately 9.4 per cent of the total population. In the Northwest Territory area, the average ratio in 1840 was 18.3 per cent.[10]

[10] Roseboom, *Presidential Elections*, 108–23; Stanwood, *History of the Presidency*, I, 185, 188, 190–205; *Seventh Census of the United States, Appendix*, xlii, xliv, xxxvi, 645–48.

8

NEW BONDS WITH THE WEST

THE MORMONS IN MISSOURI, 1831–1839

THE MORMON MOVEMENT, based upon the claims of Joseph Smith concerning revelations at Cumorah Hill, New York, reached Missouri during the administration of Governor John Miller. Before Joseph Smith was fourteen, he had begun to see "visions," which he believed to be a part of his religious experience. The angel Moroni came to his room, Smith said, and informed him that God had work for him to do. A book written upon gold plates containing the true Gospel had been deposited along with two sacred stones in silver bows, Urim and Thummim, fastened to a breastplate, which would enable the chosen Prophet to translate the book. Young Smith related that he found later, on the hill of Cumorah near the village of Manchester, the sacred objects mentioned by Moroni.

Forbidden by God's messenger to remove the plates from their hiding place the Prophet continued his life as a farm laborer, sometimes with his father and at other periods as a hired hand, until 1827. Four visits by Moroni and annual excursions to Cumorah kept him in touch with the revelations. The story of Smith's discovery of the revelation on golden plates hidden in a hillside for more than fourteen centuries was a complicated tale presented in the style of the King James version of the Christian Bible. To many persons, the "revelation" was a ridiculous attempt by an ignoramus to link ancient religious concepts with nineteenth-century America and races of the Near East with North American Indians.

Inconsistencies in the Book of Mormon, pointed out by these critics, did not prevent Smith and his associates from obtaining followers. The Church of Jesus Christ of the Latter Day Saints was formally established at Fayette, New York, in 1830, and within a year missionaries had been sent to the Indians in Kansas. At the request of the Indian agent three Mormons were promptly expelled from the Shawnee-Delaware reservation.

Joseph Smith established headquarters at Kirtland, Ohio, but within a short time he announced a revelation which directed him to consecrate a new Mormon metropolis in western Missouri. Independence, a raw frontier village which had become the principal river port for the Santa Fe trade, was selected as the City of Zion, and elaborate preparations were made for its development. Recruits from New York and elsewhere settled in Jackson County, and by the summer of 1833 about one-third of the region's four thousand inhabitants were members of the Mormon church.

At Independence, Smith planned a compact city one mile square with fields and stables apart from the town. New members arriving from the East in small bands continued to swell the population, and the earlier settlers in western Missouri—frontiersmen who might display strong individualism in politics and at the same time a stubborn absence of religious tolerance—became alarmed over the growth of Smith's church. Peculiar views held by the Mormons set them apart from the old settlers. In some important phases of economic organization the Mormons were nonconformists. Their banking and some aspects of their retail trade were in the nature of collective production, dominated by their church. The contrast was more pronounced on the Missouri frontier than it would have been elsewhere.

On July 30, 1833, some five hundred citizens of Jackson County met at the Independence courthouse and issued a protest against the settlement of Mormons in western Missouri. The strong words of the manifesto indicated the extent of local hostility toward Smith's followers.

The charges against the Mormons included blasphemy, pretense of receiving revelations directly from God, pretense of speaking in unknown tongues "by direct inspirations," corrupting slaves, boasting that their church would take over the county, and so conducting themselves as to be a menace to public morals. The violence which broke out shortly afterwards might have been anticipated.

The old settlers demanded that the Mormons should stop immigration to Jackson County, that their newspaper, the *Morning and Evening Star*, should cease publication at once, that the Mormons already in the area should give a pledge to remove, after an opportunity to close their affairs without substantial property loss, and that the Mormon leaders should use their influence to stop further immigration of eastern members.

Upon the refusal of Smith's followers to give the desired pledges, the anti-Mormon settlers proceeded to violent action. The printing office was destroyed; a mob invaded a Mormon store, but did not damage the goods in it when the owner—Elder Sidney Gilbert—agreed to pack up and move; Bishop Edward Partridge and a member named Charles Allen were conducted to the public square, stripped of their outer clothing, and given a coat of tar and feathers.[1]

Oliver Cowdery, W. W. Phelps, and Bishop Partridge were among the leaders who agreed to move out with their families by January 1, 1834. John Corrill and Sidney Gilbert were assigned the task of winding up Mormon business, and Gilbert was given the privilege of selling out his remaining goods. The leaders agreed that all the Mormons should leave the county by April 1, 1834, and that they would use their influence to prevent further immigration of members.

After receiving a directive from Joseph Smith, however, the Jackson County Mormons sent two members to confer with Governor Daniel Dunklin at Jefferson City. The Governor's reply was definitely friendly. "No citizen or citizens," he wrote, "have a right

---

[1] Williams and Shoemaker, *Missouri*, I, 285, 520–47; Joseph and Heman C. Smith, *History of the Church of Jesus Christ of the Latter Day Saints* (B. H. Roberts, ed.; 4 vols., Salt Lake City, 1948), 1–13, 390–92; *The Book of Mormon*, trans. by Joseph Smith, Jr.; *The Sacred Book of Ancient America* (Harold I. Velt, ed.; Independence, Mo., 1952), 102–105; William A. Linn, *The Story of the Mormons* (N.Y. and London, 1902), 120, 142–52, 166–74.

to take the redress of their grievances, whether real or imaginary, into their own hands." Governor Dunklin promised support for any legal steps the Mormons might take to protect their lives and property; and thus encouraged, they retained Alexander Doniphan, David R. Atchison, and two other attorneys to advise them concerning their rights under the law. On October 20 they issued a proclamation—they would remain in Jackson County and defend their property.

Less than two weeks later a mob attacked the Mormons in the Big Blue community west of Independence. Members were roughly handled in their homes and their families mistreated. Men were whipped, women and children were driven out of their houses, and a dozen of their dwellings were destroyed. The local justice of the peace clearly took the side of the non-Mormons when the Saints attempted to begin legal action against the marauders. The net result in the courts was the seizure of four Mormons who had caught a marauder on November 1, 1833, in the act of hurling stones into a Mormon's house at Independence. When the culprit was taken before a magistrate, he became the accuser and the Mormons were charged with false imprisonment.

When it became evident that Missouri courts were unlikely to provide relief, Big Blue and other Mormon settlements determined upon armed resistance to attacks. Several skirmishes were fought in which numerical strength and the means for carrying on guerrilla warfare were clearly on the side of the anti-Mormons. After a bloody conflict on November 4, the Mormons agreed to remove from Jackson County. It was agreed that they should settle in Clay County, where there was no organized opposition to their entrance. Some fifteen hundred persons were thus driven out of their homes, leaving behind them the smoking ruins of several hundred houses. Property losses in chattels as well as buildings were heavy.

Outnumbered, under suspicion because their ideas on religion and social organization differed sharply from the accepted views and customs of older settlers, the Mormons tried various locations in western Missouri over the span of half a dozen years. In Clay County, where the population was only 5,338 in 1830, their period of welcome lasted from December, 1833, to the spring of 1836. The sparse population of Caldwell, Carroll, and Daviess counties also provided friendly climates for their settlement. Merchants and other classes of settlers wanted the population to increase, but the same kind of difficulties arose in each successive Mormon community. The disturbances at Liberty in 1836 were similar in every respect to the earlier conflicts around Independence. Caldwell, organized by the legislature as a separate county in December, 1836, at the request of the Mormons, became their particular stronghold. It was cut off from the northern part of Ray County, and its county seat, Far West, was a Mormon town built according to the plans of church leaders. Within two years, three thousand members had taken up residence there, but the attitude of Missourians in the area had become definitely unfriendly and threatening.

Dissension among Smith's followers in Ohio and conflict with the civil authorities over violations of the state banking laws caused the "Prophet" and Sidney Rigdon, his principal lieutenant, to flee from their headquarters at Kirtland and come to Far West in 1838.[2] All of the settlers in Far West at that time and the principal elected officers of Caldwell County were Mormons. The church leaders founded new settlements in Caldwell, Carroll, and Daviess counties and planned the building of a temple on the square at Far West.

On July 4, 1838, at the laying of the cornerstone for the new temple, Sidney Rigdon preached his "salt sermon," in which he announced the policy of violent resistance to aggression. Rigdon's language was intemperate, with a strong plea for a "war of extermination" against all who disturbed the Mormon settlements. The "gentiles" in western Missouri regarded this statement of Mormon policy as a declaration of war, and tension mounted.

Violence became so general that Governor Lilburn Boggs sent a militia force of four hundred mounted men into Daviess County to "protect the people" and ordered General Clark to drive the followers of Smith and Rigdon out of Missouri "or to exterminate them." Here was an official answer to Rigdon's "salt sermon," and

[2] In October, 1837, Rigdon and Smith were convicted of operating a banking business contrary to state law.

the Governor's language, like the preacher's, was inexcusably harsh and unreasonable. The Mormons of Missouri, even after they removed from the state, were particularly bitter toward Governor Boggs.

Before the end of October, Far West surrendered to a militia force under General S. D. Lucas. Six of the Mormon leaders, including Joseph Smith, were arrested and taken to Independence for trial on a variety of serious charges, and fifty were held in jail at different places—Independence, Liberty, Gallatin, and Richmond. General Lucas stripped the Mormons of their weapons and exacted promises that they would all leave Missouri. The trials began at Richmond with Judge A. A. King presiding and resulted in a large percentage of convictions. Joseph Smith and four other leaders, accused of larceny, arson, burglary, murder, and treason, obtained a change of venue and on the road to Columbia escaped from custody. They succeeded in crossing the Mississippi and on April 22, 1839, arrived in Quincy, Illinois.

Some fifteen thousand of their followers, reluctantly carrying out their promise to remove from Missouri, traveled eastward also about the time of Smith's escape and settled at Nauvoo, Illinois. Politicians of both major parties welcomed the immigrants, made strong bids for their support in the coming elections, and obtained many advantages for them—including full control of their town. Congress refused to take any action upon the Mormon claims against Missouri, which involved property losses of more than $2,000,000 in their enforced removal. In 1842, Joseph Smith was accused of instigating an attempt by O. P. Rockwell, a citizen of Nauvoo, to murder Lilburn Boggs; but it was impossible to obtain an indictment against either of the men at Nauvoo, where Smith was in virtual control of the municipal government and held a commission from the governor of Illinois as lieutenant general of the Nauvoo Legion.

The persistent tendency toward conflict between the followers of Joseph Smith and the "gentiles" resulted in more violence and still another great migration. In 1843 a "revelation" to Smith approved polygamy for leaders of the church who could afford plural marriages. He clashed with certain members who did not approve his autocratic control of Nauvoo, and particularly with Dr. R. D. Foster, whom Smith accused of theft and other crimes. The anti-Smith faction of the church maintained that the "Prophet's" interest in Foster's wife had occasioned the "revelation" and that his charges against the husband were intended to remove Dr. Foster as the woman's protector.

To meet a general uprising against the Mormon power at Nauvoo, Smith declared martial law; but the opposition to his personal control was not to be denied. Joseph Smith and his brother Hyrum were imprisoned at Carthage, charged with treason; but before they could be brought to trial, a mob broke into the jail on June 27, 1844, and killed them. Continued hostility of the "gentiles" and repeated eruptions of violence brought repeal of the Nauvoo charter, and in October, 1845, a new agreement with the Mormons to remove from their homes. This migration took them west under Brigham Young to the region of the Great Salt Lake.

The Mormon troubles in Missouri cannot be explained entirely by the intolerance of the Jackson County frontiersmen or by the Mormon opposition to slavery, as some writers have attempted. In the third volume of the *History of the Church*, edited by Brigham H. Roberts, it is pointed out that the people who lived along the Missouri River in "the early decades of the nineteenth century" were chiefly from Kentucky, Tennessee, Virginia, and the Carolinas. These Missourians, it is alleged, migrating from a slaveholding area, looked with contempt upon white persons who labored. The generalization is too inclusive for even an approximation of the true condition in Jackson County at the time. As a matter of fact, most Missourians labored with their hands. A considerable number of the immigrants who came from states of the upper South were opponents of slavery, and most of the people of Missouri were not slaveholders. Slave labor, therefore, was never sufficiently widespread to create a dominant slaveholding aristocracy. The fact that Mormons clashed with "gentiles" in New York, Ohio, and Illinois would seem to indicate the failure of the "Saints" to adjust their followers to harmonious relations with the American people, the fellow-citizens of the Mormons.

The combination of church and state practiced by the Mormons in Missouri was out of step with the development of that western commonwealth. Lack of tact, ignorance, and, in rare instances, viciousness were to be found among both the Mormons and the "gentiles." Inevitably, a new religious movement that is attractive to the masses obtains the support of some persons who are low in mentality and weak in character. Every frontier in America has attracted and produced some members of society who were inclined toward crime. It would have been remarkable indeed if the Mormons had not encountered serious trouble in western Missouri.[3]

THE MEXICAN WAR AND NEW CONTACTS WITH THE FAR WEST

Two events during the third decade of Missouri statehood affected deeply the nature of crossroads trade. First, the annexation of Texas, followed by war with Mexico and expansion over a vast area in the Southwest, transformed the international trade with Santa Fe into domestic commerce and extended the interest of western settlers all the way to the Pacific. Second, beyond the valley of the Missouri in the Northwest, the compromise upon the Oregon boundary with the British in 1846 furnished a great impulse to westward migration and began a new era in Missouri commerce.

Missouri had a peculiar interest in all questions that concerned Texas from the beginning of its settlement by people of Anglo-Saxon descent. Moses Austin, who brought his family to Mine à Breton, Missouri, in 1798, was well known through his activities in lead mining. With his son, Stephen Fuller Austin, he became identified in 1820 with a great project for colonization in the Spanish province south of the Red River. This enterprise strengthened the bond between Missouri and Texas, and the Texas Road across the Indian Territory provided a convenient means of travel for Missourians who wanted to visit friends and kinsmen in the new set-

---

[3] Williams and Shoemaker, *Missouri*, 527–29; Linn, *Story of the Mormons*, 177, 178; Thomas F. O'Dea, *The Mormons* (Cambridge, 1955), 1–10, 41, 226; Joseph Smith, "An American Prophet's Own Story," *Among the Mormons* (Wm. Mulder and A. Russell Mortensen, eds.), 16, 17—Mormonism's Creed.

tlements. A steady and growing stream of immigrants to the Texas lands moved along the road after annexation.

Senator Benton had so much interest in Texas that he provided a reservoir of material for the debates on every controversial aspect of Southwestern diplomacy. He wrote articles for the *St. Louis Beacon* in 1829 in which he accused John Quincy Adams of "throwing away a vast area" in the Florida purchase treaty of 1819. He proposed that the region be recovered from Mexico by purchase.

The Northern politicians revealed a "sinister purpose," Benton declared, "the abolition of slavery." In this strictly southern literary broadside, perhaps Benton was helping to build up sentiment in Missouri that was to prove a factor in his downfall two decades later, when his own position had changed with the growing nationalism of American thought.[4]

The Texas revolution of 1836, the attitude of many American citizens toward the conflict between Texas and Mexico, and the annexation of the Texas Republic by the United States led directly to war with Mexico. Participation of Missouri troops in considerable number was a natural development in view of the many Texas settlers from Missouri, the positive leadership of Governor John C. Edwards, and the service of Alexander W. Doniphan. A regiment of Missouri soldiers, many of whom had fought under Zachary Talor in the Seminole War, enlisted in response to General Gaines's call for volunteers and began the journey to New Orleans by river boats.

On May 11, 1846, Congress authorized the enlistment of fifty thousand soldiers and appropriated ten million dollars to carry on the war. For a proposed expedition to New Mexico, Governor Edwards of Missouri assembled his recruits at Fort Leavenworth, beyond the western border of the state. By the second week of June more than 1,350 Missourians had reported for service there.[5]

[4] *Mo. Hist. Rev.*, Vol. XXIX, No. 2, 127; Vol. XXXII, No. 4, 601–603; Vol. XXXIII, No. 2, 273, and No. 4, "Missouriana," 533–41; *Dictionary of American Biography*, I (articles on Moses Austin and Stephen F. Austin, by Eugene Barker), 435–36, 437–40; Chambers, *Old Bullion*, 158–59.

[5] Richardson, *Messages and Papers of the Presidents*, IV, 442, 480, 483; G. P. Garrison, *Westward Extension* (N.Y., 1906), 204–206; *Dictionary of American Biography*, V (articles on Alexander W. Doniphan, by Stella M. Drumm), 365–66.

Alexander W. Doniphan, who had gained professional influence by his bold leadership in defending the Mormons, was elected colonel of the First Regiment of Missouri Mounted Volunteers.

General Stephen Watts Kearny commanded the expedition to Santa Fe. By the end of July, 1846, he reached Bent's Fort on the Arkansas with about 1,800 men, and on August 18 occupied Santa Fe without a battle. Kearny's orders gave him wide discretion in New Mexico. He organized a provisional government and on September 25 started for California, where his instructions directed co-operation with Commodore Robert F. Stockton in securing possession for the United States. Kearny marched with 300 dragoons, understanding that his column would be followed by an additional company and the battalion of 500 Mormons who were to be discharged in California. Actually, Kearny's force was reduced to a single company when he learned that California was practically in the hands of United States naval forces and decided to send two hundred soldiers back to Santa Fe. On December 6, 1846, Kearny defeated a Mexican party at San Pascual, and then he marched to San Diego.

While Kearny was occupying New Mexico and moving on to the Pacific slope, General Taylor proceeded with the broad plan of conquest in northern Mexico. The army of the center, a force of 3,000 men under General J. E. Wool, was sent against Chihuahua in October, 1846. From Monclova, however, he was diverted eastward to support Taylor's force, and Colonel A. W. Doniphan marched with 850 men from Santa Fe into the province of Chihuahua. Doniphan's line of march was through Brazito, about twenty-five miles above El Paso, where he fought a sharp engagement with a Mexican force of superior numbers. At the Pass of Sacramento he won a second battle, against a party of one thousand cavalry, and on March 1, 1847, he entered the city of Chihuahua. After two months of occupation he marched some five hundred miles to the southeast, where his force was joined to the principal army of occupation at Saltillo. General Taylor, reinforced by Wool's Army of the Center, had defeated Santa Anna in the decisive battle of Buena Vista, on February 23, 1847.

The southern campaign under General Winfield Scott, from the landing of troops near Vera Cruz on March 9, 1847, to his occupation of Mexico City on September 14, six months later, need not concern us here. But in the California campaign, Missouri troops and officers played a major part. General Stephen W. Kearny had lived in the West nearly thirty years and regarded himself a citizen of Missouri. In 1830 he had married Mary Radford, the stepdaughter of General William Clark. John C. Frémont, the son-in-law of Senator Benton, was also a spectacular but not always a thoroughly creditable actor in the California drama.

American naval forces had made the initial moves toward detaching California from the Republic of Mexico immediately after Commodore John D. Sloat learned that war had been declared, in May, 1846. Sloat occupied Monterrey on July 7, and Commodore R. F. Stockton, who replaced him in command, captured Los Angeles a few weeks later. In the meantime, San Francisco was occupied by Captain J. B. Montgomery, and all of the Mexican posts in the north were quickly in American hands. For a short time the Flores revolt in the southern part of the province threatened the control established by Commodore Stockton, but Los Angeles was quickly recovered, and General Kearny arrived from New Mexico in time to convey to American officers the orders of W. L. Marcy, secretary of war, concerning the establishment of civil government in California. "It is expected that the naval forces of the United States . . . will co-operate with you in the conquest of California," Marcy had written.

After Kearny's clash with the Mexican force at San Pascual on December 6, 1846, in which eighteen Americans were killed, the United States troops regained control of Southern California and completed the conquest of the province in January, 1847. It was Commodore Stockton's purpose to install Senator Benton's son-in-law as provisional governor, and in the contest for control between General Kearny and the naval officer, Frémont displayed his tendency toward political climbing. In fact, he was so eager to promote his claim to the governorship that he refused to obey orders from the War Department, some of which must have been passed upon by the President before Secretary Marcy issued them. In August, 1847, Kearny brought Frémont back to Washington to face court-martial proceedings. The trial lasted from November until January 31, 1848.

Senator Benton defended his son-in-law and clashed bitterly with General Kearny during the trial. The court found Frémont guilty of mutiny, disobedience of orders, and conduct prejudicial to the public service. President Polk was in doubt as to the proof of mutiny, but agreed with the court, as did all the members of the cabinet, that the officer was guilty of the other charges. The President approved the sentence of the court, that Lieutenant Colonel Frémont "be dismissed from the service," but in view of the recommendation for executive clemency, restored him to his rank and command. Thereupon, Frémont resigned his commission and returned to California, where the new state legislature named him to the United States Senate.[6]

With the success of United States arms in all sectors of the Mexican War, peace negotiations, although complicated by the maneuvers of rival political factions in Washington, Mexico, and even in the American armed forces, at last resulted in a treaty. Santa Anna had abdicated, and the new government of Mexico selected commissioners in the autumn of 1847 to deal with Nicholas Trist on the basis of the instructions that had been handed to him seven months earlier. The treaty of Guadalupe-Hidalgo was signed on February 2, 1848, and ratified by the United States Senate on March 10. New Mexico, extending west from the Río Grande, and Upper California, stretching beyond it to the Pacific, were surrendered to the United States, along with Texas, from the Sabine to the Río Grande. The United States agreed to pay a nominal compensation for the vast territory west of the Río Grande.[7]

[6] Garrison, *Westward Extension*, 230–31; Rockwell D. Hunt and Nellie van de Grift Sánchez, *Short History of California* (N.Y., 1929), 361; George Lockhart Rives, *The United States and Mexico* (2 vols., N.Y., 1913), II, 368n., 369–74.

[7] 30 Cong., 1 sess., *House Ex. Doc. No. 60*, 153–55. For President Polk's war message, May 11, 1846, see *ibid.*, 4–10; Polk, *The Diary of a President* (Allan Nevins, ed.; London, N.Y., 1929), 300–303 (Feb. 5, 12, 13, 16, 1848); Chambers, *Old Bullion*, 321–23; Rives, *The United States and Mexico*, II, 177, 185, 188–89, 584–613; Chambers, *Old Bullion*, 322–23; Garrison, *Westward Extension*, 251–53.

MISSOURI AND THE PACIFIC NORTHWEST

The annexation of Texas and subsequent extension of United States territory to the Pacific, south of the forty-second parallel, was accompanied by a move to define our boundaries with Canada west of the Rocky Mountains. In the political campaign of 1844 the Democratic party had linked the Texas question with settlement of Oregon's status, and Polk was eager to obtain a satisfactory treaty with Great Britain.

The fur traders had made the Northwest particularly interesting to the people of Missouri. Men who met in the country stores and meeting-houses, as well as those who gathered in the chambers of the General Assembly, were likely to fall into conversation about the opportunities in Oregon. Lewis F. Linn, who was appointed United States Senator to fill the unexpired term of Alexander Buckner in 1834 and elected to the office in 1836 and 1842, was active in the interests of Missouri River trade and in settlement of the Northwest. After several years of preparation, Senator Linn introduced a bill in 1841 which provided for the construction of a chain of stockades and blockhouses to guard the passage from Independence, Missouri, to Astoria, on the Pacific slope. He included in the bill a land grant of 640 acres to each male settler over eighteen and the extension of American territorial government to the forty-ninth parallel. The grant of public land to emigrants was attacked by John C. Calhoun as a violation of joint-occupation with Great Britain and defended hotly by Thomas Hart Benton.

Presently George McDuffie of South Carolina injected a note of strong personal hostility into the argument, creating a chasm between two well-defined groups: the representatives of South Atlantic cotton and rice plantations supported by the employers of factory labor in New England; and those persons who spoke for the agrarian interests of the Northwest and the Southwest.[8]

Senator Linn's bill passed the Senate by a vote of twenty-four to twenty-two on February 3, 1843. The bill went to the House of

[8] *American State Papers, Foreign Affairs*, V, 553–64; VI, 641–706; *Debates of Congress*, 27 Cong., 3 sess., 240; Garrison, *Westward Extension*, 160–63; Chambers, *Old Bullion*, 85, 264–65.

Representatives, where it was defeated by a narrow margin. Emigration to Oregon steadily increased, as Congress debated the merits of legislation designed to promote settlement of the area. The greatest factor in the contest was migration—Americans to the region south of the Columbia and British subjects north of that river.

Thomas Jefferson's diplomatic aims in the exploration of Louisiana had centered upon a route to the Northwest Coast as a means of opening Oriental trade. Thomas Hart Benton's early vision of a foothold on the Pacific as an outlet to Asiatic trade, disclosed in his St. Louis *Enquirer* editorials before Missouri statehood, had been a prominent factor in Oregon diplomacy. The Columbia as a boundary, persistently offered by British negotiators, had never been acceptable to the United States because such a settlement would have cut the Americans off from the fine harbors of Juan de Fuca and Puget Sound. Although British interests also shifted from fur trade to Oriental commerce, it became clear to the diplomats of both countries that the Columbia boundary could not be established without war.

President Polk's first Annual Message, December 2, 1845, proposed to Congress the enactment of a law authorizing the year's notice to Great Britain for ending joint occupation. The President further recommended extension of United States laws over the people of Oregon, establishment of Indian agencies west of the Rocky Mountains, military installations on the road to Oregon, and overland mail to the Pacific.

Both Houses passed a resolution in April, 1846, authorizing the President at his discretion to give notice to Great Britain for terminating the agreement of 1827. President Polk signed the resolution and on May 21 notified the British government that joint occupation was to end within twelve months.

Polk's secretary of state, James Buchanan, had offered a compromise settlement of the Oregon boundary at the forty-ninth parallel, on July 12, 1845, which Sir Richard Pakenham, the British minister in Washington, had rejected on July 29, without consulting his government. The extension of the Louisiana Territory boundary beyond the Rocky Mountains had been proposed earlier by officials of the United States, coupled with free navigation of the Columbia for subjects of Great Britain. Apparently Lord Pakenham regarded the offer of the same line without navigation of the Columbia a waste of time, and his reply was peremptory. President Polk withdrew the offer a month after Pakenham's answer was received.

Probably the negotiations for a compromise line would not have been reopened by Polk's government. In his *Diary* on June 3, the President noted that a dispatch from Louis McLane, United States minister at London, contained the substance of a proposition which the British government was ready to make. "If Mr. McLane is right in the character of the proposition . . . it is certain that I cannot accept it," Polk wrote. "If I reject it absolutely and make no other proposition the probable result will be war."

On June 6, however, Secretary Buchanan handed the President a proposal "in the form of a convention" for dividing the Oregon country substantially as the United States had previously offered. It was stipulated that the Hudson's Bay Company and persons trading with that company should have free use of the Columbia River for their commerce. The proposal was submitted to the Senate in advance for the President's guidance; and by a vote of thirty-seven to twelve Polk was advised to sign the convention. Thus practically assured of ratification and of Senate support for his deviation from the "fifty-four–forty" plank in the Democratic party platform of 1844, the President ended joint occupation of Oregon by a compromise that has generally been regarded as reasonable and just.[9]

The Emigrants' Guide to Oregon and California described eight distinct routes to the Pacific Coast; but the one which most concerned Missouri was the road from Independence through South Pass to Fort Hall near the forty-third parallel in present-day Bingham County, Idaho.

The Oregon Trail beyond Fort Hall is simply described as "down

[9] Benton, *Abridgment of the Debates of Congress*, XIV, 686–89; Garrison, *Westward Extension*, 164–69; Polk, *The Diary of a President*, 109, 111–12; Norman A. Graebner, *Empire on the Pacific* (N.Y., 1955), 26–32; Chambers, *Old Bullion*, 84–85.

Lewis' river fifteen days to Fort Wallawalla; and thence down the Columbia ten days to the lower settlement in Oregon." Those settlers who elected California as their destination, beyond Fort Hall, traveled "west southwest about fifteen days to the northern pass in the California mountains; thence three days to the Sacramento; and thence seven days down the Sacramento to the Bay of San Francisco in California."

The *Emigrants' Guide* also described a more direct way from Independence to California, which would require about 120 days of travel. The twenty-one hundred miles to Oregon was also a four months' journey, "exclusive of delays."

From the earliest exploration and the beginning of settlement in Oregon, people from Missouri took a prominent part. Meriwether Lewis and William Clark, both of whom were territorial governors of Missouri, were the most distinguished among the explorers. Wilson Price Hunt, a native of New Jersey, was established in business at St. Louis before he led the Astoria overland expedition of 1810–12, and after that event he continued as a St. Louis resident. Three nephews of Alexander McNair, Missouri's first state governor, were hunters for the overland party.

Father De Smet, a native of Belgium, had been assigned to the novitiate at Florissant, near St. Louis, in 1823. His progress with the Indians of the Oregon country was a notable achievement in the civilization of native Americans from 1840 to 1846 and a definite factor in the strong position of the United States in the diplomatic discussions. For more than twenty years after the agreement upon Oregon's boundary, Father De Smet continued his work as a mediator in Indian relations, performing invaluable service on many occasions.

From the beginning of American settlement of Oregon on a large scale, the question of slavery in the region was a matter of concern to the people and to members of Congress, who were increasingly aware of sectional conflict of interests. At Champoeg on July 5, 1843, a settlers' meeting adopted a provisional territorial government, in which slavery was forbidden and the laws of Iowa Territory were extended to Oregon. In 1848, Congress linked the organization of Oregon Territory with the problem of government in the new regions obtained from Mexico. Senator John C. Calhoun and his partisan followers denied the constitutional authority of Congress to pass legislation which would "deprive the citizens of any states of this Union from emigrating, with their property, into any of the territories of the United States." Calhoun and the extreme advocates of the extension of slavery also objected to squatter sovereignty. When both houses passed a bill excluding slavery from Oregon by applying the restrictions of the Northwest Ordinance, Senator Calhoun urged President Polk to veto the measure on constitutional grounds. Polk approved it, however, with the observation that Oregon was wholly north of the Missouri Compromise line.[10]

GOLD AND WESTERN MIGRATION

The number of persons who moved along the trails to the Pacific Slope during the gold rush years is not a matter of accurate census. John Augustus Sutter, the Swiss immigrant who twice ventured to travel the Santa Fe Trail, working as a clerk in the store of Wiese and Laufkotter at St. Charles during the interval, often considered and discussed the opportunities of the great West. He operated a trading post at Westport. Bankrupted by a series of bad purchases, Sutter took the trail for California. On a large grant of land in the Sacramento Valley the Swiss-American established himself, and there James Wilson Marshall, another emigrant from Westport, made a rich discovery of gold. The strike was made in January, 1848, and the following years became a period of "Great Migration."[11]

After the gold rush became a population movement of major

10 Lansford W. Hastings, *The Emigrants' Guide to Oregon and California*, 134–38; "Missouriana," *Mo. Hist. Rev.*, Vol. XXXIII, 230–41; *Dictionary of American Biography*, 255–56 (article on Pierre-Jean De Smet by Joseph Schafer). *Cong. Globe*, 29 Cong., 2 sess., 455; 30 Cong., 1 sess., 1002–1005, 1062, 1078–80, 1081; Polk, *The Diary of a President*, 338, 339; Garrison, *Westward Extension*, 297, 301, 305.

11 Georgia Willis Read, "Women and Children on the Oregon-California Trail in the Gold Rush Years," *Mo. Hist. Rev.*, Vol. XXXIX, No. 1, 1–23; Kate L. Gregg, "Missourians in the Gold Rush," *Mo. Hist. Rev.*, Vol. XXXIX, No. 2, 137–54.

importance, catching the imagination of a widening circle of prospectors, the volume of westward travel shifted from Oregon to California. The first prospectors took nuggets and gold dust from dry gulches and the bed rock of old river courses by methods that required little knowledge of mining. Men from California and Oregon settlements, with a few Mexicans and mountain trappers, were the forerunners of a giant wave of immigrants. Perhaps two-thirds of the men in Oregon went south to try their hands at mining gold.

Prices of commodities soared as the prospectors hit pay-dirt and realized big profits. Late in the summer of 1848, newspapers in New York began to take notice of the developments on Sutter's property in California. Methods of mining improved as prospectors exchanged ideas, pushed up the streams, and expanded the diggings over an area of two million acres. President Polk, in his Fourth Annual Message, noted with great satisfaction the recent discoveries of valuable minerals.

The "4,000 persons engaged in collecting gold," mentioned by President Polk's message in December, 1848, grew to 50,000 within two years and to 100,000 by December, 1852. Probably about 25,000 prospectors reached the gold fields through San Francisco, by way of Cape Horn, or by the Panama route during 1849. The overland trails brought more than twice that number, with the heaviest traffic along the roads from Independence and St. Joseph, Missouri, to South Pass. The population of California increased more than fourfold during its first decade of statehood, from 92,597 in 1850 to 379,994 in 1860. Oregon also developed rapidly, in spite of a temporary loss of population to the California gold fields. Oregon Territory became the state of Oregon in 1859, and the census of the next year found that its inhabitants numbered 52,465.

The Overland Trail, particularly during the gold rush, brought new emphasis to the trade routes across Missouri. The sales of vehicles and supplies for the long journey across the plains and the wagon-outfitting business that developed at the head of the trails had centered in Independence for twenty years of active Santa Fe trade before the outbreak of war with Mexico. Supplies for United States armies in the Southwest during 1846, however, were generally unloaded from steamboats at the Westport landing, above Independence. This change had the advantage of avoiding the caravan ford on Big Blue and placed the head of the trail a few miles nearer to Santa Fe.

After the war, emigrants bound for Oregon and California also shifted their business to Westport landing, and the town of Kansas, adjacent to the river, developed on the basis of gold-rush emigrant trade. Forty thousand men en route to the California diggings spent five million dollars for mules, oxen, supplies for the trail, and Murphy wagons or similar vehicles. Senator Benton, observing the trend of emigrant business in 1853, was moved to an eloquent prediction of great development as he addressed an audience near the Westport landing.

Perhaps to a greater degree than any man of his time, Tom Benton understood the significance of Missouri's position at the crossing of great commercial routes; his statue in Lafayette Park, St. Louis, has on its base an engraved quotation of his prophetic vision of the Pacific movement: "There is the East; there is India!"

Independence, six miles from its landing on the Missouri River, continued as a competitor for the lucrative business of supplying the caravans. In 1849 tracks were laid for mule-cars between the town and the bank of the river; but Westport Landing continued to get the larger volume of trade. A shift in the Missouri River bed deposited a sand bar which practically cut off the lower landing from steamboat service, and the town of Kansas gained more support from the "end of the trail" business. Freight wagons began the practice of loading directly from the river boats. The opening of Kansas Territory to settlement in 1854 gave further impulse to growth of the Missouri town, which began to be called "Kansas City" at this time. Its population, constantly shifting, was variously estimated from four thousand to almost twice that number.[12]

[12] Ralph P. Bieber, "California Gold Mania," *Mississippi Valley Historical Review*, Vol. XXXV, No. 1 (June, 1948), 3–28; Billington, *The Far Western Frontier*, 218–42; Darrell Garwood, *Crossroads of America: The Story of Kansas City*, 21, 23–33; Hubert H. Bancroft, *History of California*, VI, 56; Richardson, *Messages and Papers of the Presidents*, 629–70 (Polk's Fourth Annual Message). The portion of the message that deals with California minerals is on p. 636.

THE BEGINNING OF RAILROADS IN MISSOURI

Railroad transportation has been a vital factor in the development of the United States as a whole, and particularly important in the western states, where vast distances separated the early centers of production from the main group of population. The great rivers along the eastern border of Missouri, the northwestern boundary, and through the heart of the state gave an impetus to early commerce, providing business not only for the towns along their banks but also for settlements on tributary streams and the primitive wagon roads.

Completion of the Erie Canal across central New York in 1825 and its successful operation during the following decades served as a constant reminder to the American public that cities were dependent upon good transportation facilities. When railroad construction began in Massachusetts, Pennsylvania, New York, Maryland, South Carolina, and other eastern states, Missouri had its advocates for the new means of reaching inland communities. Governor Lilburn Boggs proposed railroad building in his first message to the General Assembly in 1836; and later, after the effects of the Panic of 1837 had subsided, Governor John C. Edwards became a persistent supporter of all efforts to give better means of transportation to Missouri. The first railroad convention was held at St. Louis in 1836, and the General Assembly showed enough interest to issue charters to a great variety of corporations—none of which was ready to build in the face of national depression.

Steam locomotives had been operating in the eastern seaboard states for two decades before Missouri began its first railroad.[13] The steamboats on navigable waters had long contributed to the distribution of the inhabitants and to the mobility, occupational interests, outside contacts, cultural opportunities, and political attitudes—in short, to the character—of Missouri's people. As the feverish interest of Americans in railroad building spread to the

13 R. B. Oliver, "Missouri's First Railroad," *Mo. Hist. Rev.*, Vol. XXVI, No. 1 (Oct., 1931), 12–18. See also copy of newspaper clipping in *Mo. Hist. Rev.*, Vol. XXX, No. 2 (Jan., 1936), 170, 171.

West, promoters appeared in St. Louis with schemes for making the river town a great railroad center. Some factor of conservatism among the people and their law-makers, however, led Missourians to continue their reliance upon the navigable rivers and the clumsy, old-fashioned wagons for heavy transportation. During twenty years of ventures in canal and railroad building in the older states —experiments that were frequently accompanied by sizable losses for private investors, banks, and state governments—Missouri avoided the pitfalls of hasty construction and rash investment. The problem of better facilities for rapid and economical transportation had long since crossed the Mississippi, however, and it was only a question of time before Missouri would be involved in the railroad plans of the nation.

A railroad convention at St. Louis in 1849 considered the problem of a route from the eastern seaboard to the Pacific, and quite naturally put forward the claims of St. Louis as the most desirable point for a transcontinental line to cross the Mississippi. Governor Austin A. King at this time was in favor of state financial aid for railroad construction in Missouri. In 1851 the legislature voted a grant of $1,500,000 in bonds to the Hannibal and St. Joseph Railroad Company for aid in constructing its proposed line across the state between the two towns, and a grant of $2,000,000 to the Pacific Company for aid in building from St. Louis to the western border of the state. The bill for railroad aid in the form of state bonds was introduced in the Missouri General Assembly by Thomas Allen, who was chairman of the Senate Committee on Internal Improvements and also president of the Pacific Railroad. The roads obtained the bonds as a loan, which was secured by a first mortgage on the railroad property. Before the end of the year, construction began at the eastern terminal of the Pacific Railroad; a locomotive was brought across the Mississippi, and in 1852 transportation began, from St. Louis to Cheltenham, a distance of five miles.

During the following year, 32 miles of track were added, and by 1856 the rails had been steadily pushed westward to Jefferson City, a total distance of 125 miles. The Pacific (now a part of the St.

Louis and San Francisco properties) reached Kansas City in 1865. At that time, Missouri had 928 miles of railroad under the following managements:

Pacific (main line)	283.0 miles
Pacific (southwest branch)	77.0 miles
Hannibal and St. Joseph	207.0 miles
North Missouri	168.5 miles
St. Louis and Iron Mountain	90.0 miles
Cairo and Fulton	37.5 miles
Platte County Railroad	52.0 miles
Quincy and Palmyra	13.0 miles
Total	928.0 miles

Up to 1860, Missouri had voted bonds for railroad building in the amount of $24,950,000. Analysis of the building program shows that milage steadily increased during the nine years preceding the outbreak of the Civil War, but dropped under 25 miles a year between January 1, 1861, and the end of 1865. Construction began again in 1867, and by the end of 1870 had reached a total of 1,955 miles of track, more than double the milage of the first nine years.

During a period that was roughly comparable (since war years were almost negligible in new construction), the United States as a whole had constructed 16,500 miles of railroad (1849–57), with seven trunk lines crossing the Appalachian barrier, eight places of contact with the Ohio River, and ten with the Mississippi. In this surge of railroad building, New England and the North Central states led, building nearly 12,000 miles of new track. Municipal and county governments subscribed for bonds, towns developed keen rivalry in the location of new lines, and the question of standard gauge became a burning issue in local politics. The telegraph came into common use, and the United States postal service made use of trains in mail contracts. From the upper Mississippi and its tributaries a drastic change in direction of commerce developed, with western producers of wool, cattle, grain, and lumber discovering new markets in New York and Philadelphia and finding new resources in cash for the purchase of manufactured goods, American and European. River commerce and coastwise trade on the

Atlantic did not decline. A rising trend in exchange of goods, together with rapid growth of population, held up the tonnage of inland water transportation. The number of coastwise and Great Lakes vessels increased as immigrants moved to the West in steadily increasing numbers and new demands arose in the manufacturing centers of New England and the North Atlantic for raw products.

Missouri shared, to a moderate degree, in the prosperity that arose from the transportation of farm products by rail to the eastern cities. The relatively high price obtained by the Hannibal and St. Joseph Railroad for its public land indicates a strong demand for Missouri grain in the period of the road's construction. Shipments of wheat to England, after the repeal of the corn laws, and to the European continent, after the serious decline of Russian wheat in the period of the Crimean War, had a tendency to push the wheat-producing areas farther west into new territory. As the states of the Northwest Territory increased their acreage of small grain and American wheat production increased from 100,000,000 bushels in 1850 to 171,000,000 bushels in 1860, northern Missouri and Kansas Territory felt the impulse toward grain production.

The population of St. Louis doubled during the first decade of railroad transportation in Missouri, and the state's inhabitants increased from 682,044 in 1850 to 1,182,012 in 1860. From thirteenth among the states in 1850, Missouri moved up to eighth at the outbreak of the Civil War. The growth in population was most pronounced on the farms, with some increase in mining and lumbering areas, a considerable increase in railroad construction employees, and definite growth of the workers in river transportation. The number of farms increased sharply, and wheat production grew from 2,981,652 bushels in 1849 to 14,315,926 bushels in 1869. Corn and oats made similar gains.

River transportation had been a significant factor in the development of St. Louis during the first thirty years of Missouri statehood. In 1840 the town had 16,469 inhabitants, and ten years later, 77,860. River trade was chiefly responsible for the development, St. Louis ranking third among American cities in the registration of steamboats by 1850. Even after railroads began to tap new sources of trade, the freight and passenger transportation on the rivers continued to grow. Over five thousand steamboats arrived at St. Louis during the year 1860.

The rapid growth of Chicago as a competitor for western trade stimulated railroad building in Missouri. Before 1840, Chicago had shown little promise of the gigantic growth that came later. From a sprawling town of 4,470 in that year, the lake port had grown by 1850 to a flourishing little city of 30,000, with a remarkable record for its volume of exchange in grain, lumber, livestock, meat, hides, and wool. Between 1836 and 1848, Chicago effected a water connection with the Mississippi River by means of the Illinois and Michigan Canal, and in 1854 completed its first railroad connection with the Mississippi. St. Louis was to hold its own in the race with Chicago for middle-western leadership until the postwar period. After 1870, Chicago was to become the greatest railroad center and the second city of the United States.[14]

The Pacific Railroad obtained a land grant of 125,000 acres from the federal government in addition to the aid in bonds voted by the General Assembly of Missouri. The Hannibal and St. Joseph, which completed building from its eastern terminal on the Mississippi to St. Joseph on the Missouri in four years, received a larger grant—611,323 acres—and sold its land at a higher price than that obtained by the Pacific. For example, the northern road sold 14,301 acres at an average price of $10.24 per acre in 1859, while the Pacific sold 78,000 acres at an average price of less than $2.00 per acre. Moreover, the later sales of the Hannibal and St. Joseph were made at a substantial increase in price, and the road's bonds, based upon mortgages of its valuable land, were readily salable. John M. Forbes and other eastern railroad builders bought stock in the Hannibal and St. Joseph Railroad, along with investments in the Michigan Central and the Illinois Central. These men were inter-

14 Paul W. Gates, "The Railroads of Missouri, 1850–1870," Mo. Hist. Rev., Vol. XXVI, No. 2 (Jan., 1832), 126–41; Slason Thompson, A Short History of American Railways (Chicago, 1925), 119, 168; Henry Parker Willis, Stephen A. Douglas (Philadelphia, 1910), 108–27; Ira G. Clark, Then Came the Railroads (Norman, 1958), 12–17, 19, 25–26, 35–37, 63–64; Theodore Clarke Smith, Parties and Slavery (N.Y. and London, 1906), 59–67; Robert E. Riegel, The Story of the Western Railroads (N.Y., 1926), 49, 50, 52.

ested in the broad plan of connecting Detroit with western Michigan and with Indiana, Illinois, and Missouri. They brought prestige and added capital for the building program of the Hannibal and St. Joseph.

Completion of this railroad across the state to the Missouri River two years after the panic of 1857 descended upon the American public was a notable achievement. The Civil War stopped construction on most lines—although the Pacific Railroad did reach the western border of Missouri in 1865, six years after the Hannibal and St. Joseph. Roads in southern Missouri were retarded in conducting their regular business, and in some instances suffered losses through seizures of property by the armies that swept through the area. After the first year, railroads north of the Missouri River suffered little from military occupation. Union armies gained much training in railroad construction, since it was necessary for the Northern military forces to build track, repair bridges, and operate locomotives in the occupied territory.

Excellent prices for farm products was an added incentive for railroad construction during the war. High prices for materials and shortage of laborers, on the other hand, made road building difficult in Missouri—brought extension of lines almost to a stop, with a few exceptions. Among these were the Pacific, which constructed fourteen miles in 1861 and 1862, thirty-three miles in 1864, and fifty-five miles in 1865. The St. Louis and Iron Mountain Railroad, which had pushed its line to Pilot Knob in 1858, and the Pacific southwestern branch, which ran trains from St. Louis to Rolla, were used extensively by both armies for hauling supplies during the campaign of 1864.

The problem of safety was an important issue in early railroad development in Missouri, as elsewhere. Accidents were frequent and devices for the protection of passengers and property came slowly. Gradually the flimsy construction of the earliest roads was replaced by more substantial roadbeds and heavier rails, and the bridges became sturdier—more suited to the heavy loads they were required to carry. The worst railroad accident in Missouri resulted from the impatience of the Pacific Railroad management to open the new line to Jefferson City. On November 1, 1855, an excursion train, carrying ten cars of passengers from St. Louis in celebration of the event, fell through the unfinished bridge over the Gasconade River. A long list of killed and injured persons filled the newspapers of the time.

In 1861, Confederate military forces damaged or destroyed railroad bridges over the Gasconade, Osage, and Lamine rivers and the bridge over Gray Creek. During the same year Governor Claiborne Jackson ordered destruction of the North Missouri Railroad, and property losses of $86,310 resulted. In 1864, General Price's raid brought further destruction of bridges and buildings on the Pacific, and damages of $100,000 to the North Missouri Railroad.[15]

[15] Gates, loc. cit., Vol. XXVI, 130, 131, 134; Riegel, Story of the Western Railroads, 66–68; John W. Million, State Aid to Railways in Missouri, 81, 83, 84, 126. The average cost of building Missouri railroads (1850–60) was about $50,000 per mile (ibid., 121).

9

THE END OF AN ERA

A LARGE PART of the slaves who came into Louisiana before 1800 were sold to planters in the lower territory. However, a few hundred were sent to the Missouri lead mines, and some crossed the Mississippi into the Illinois country. Of the annual supply imported by the Company of the Indies (1717–31)—perhaps numbering between three hundred and five hundred—very few found their way up the river except as laborers on boats. Adult males brought a price of $150, and women sold for about $120.

After the War of 1812, settlers in Missouri came largely from Kentucky, Tennessee, Virginia, North Carolina, and other slave states. Many of the immigrants planned to clear bottom land and engage in tobacco or cotton planting. The ratio of slaves to free white population grew steadily from 17.5 per cent in 1810 to 21.7 per cent in 1830. During the following decades, however, immigration from states of the upper Mississippi Valley increased, and the ratio of slaves to free white population declined. Free whites numbered 1,063,489 by 1860, Negro slaves 114,901, and free Negroes 3,572. Thus the ratio of slaves to free white population decreased from 21.7 per cent in 1830 to 10.8 per cent in 1860. It is significant that the total population of Missouri grew from 383,702 in 1840 to 682,044 in 1850—an increase of 78 per cent; and to 1,182,012 by 1860, a growth of 73.3 per cent during the decade preceding the Civil War.

[163]

European immigrants helped to swell the population of Missouri, along with farmers from the Northern states. In the period of Missouri's struggle for statehood, slave property was a large factor in the wealth and social structure of the area—which accounts for her insistence upon equality with all other states in control over her labor system. However, by 1860 slavery was of less relative importance.

In the earlier period there had been five white citizens for every Negro slave, and in the later period, nine. There had never been a time when Missouri was the particular domain of the slaveholder, to control as he saw fit; and with the growth of free white population—small farmers, laborers, tradesmen, craftsmen, river and railroad workers, and the professional men to care for the legal practice, medical needs, educational problems, and religious demands of this diverse population—the region took on the character of the West rather than of the South.

Political decisions showed a strong tendency to lag behind economic growth in the state. Only after forty years of statehood, when Missouri was confronted with the issue of secession, did the character of the new population assert itself.

Relatively few large plantations producing a single money-crop were to be found in Missouri. Many of the slaves were accustomed to a variety of tasks since they had to work with livestock, the planting and harvesting of grain, and the cutting and storage of hay crops. Cotton, hemp, and tobacco were generally produced on farms that were not devoted to a single crop. A few slaves were engaged in lead mining, some in the heavy labor of loading and unloading the river boats, and a large number in the work of clearing new land.

Walter R. Lenoir, who migrated from North Carolina in 1834 and settled in Boone County, bought 360 acres of land near Columbia at six dollars an acre. After a public sale at his North Carolina plantation he brought two wagons, two carryalls, eleven horses, and twenty-three slaves to Missouri. There he engaged in general farming, with livestock a major factor. An inventory nine years after he came to Columbia listed nineteen slaves, twenty-four sheep, twenty-three cows, nine calves, and eighty head of swine. Probably some of the slaves had been given to his married sons and daughters before his death; but his widow in 1860 still owned fourteen. Steadily rising prices of slaves was a natural result of the modest prosperity enjoyed by slaveholders in the Missouri Valley. The land that Lenoir purchased at six dollars an acre in 1834 was assessed above seventeen dollars an acre in 1860.

The top price for field hands in Missouri, up to 1830, was about $500; but by 1850 adult male slaves of the best type sold for $1,300 and females for $1,000. Probably Governor Claiborne Jackson's 1860 estimate of the total value of slave property in Missouri, $100,000,000—about $870 for each slave—was too high; but certainly the slaves were still a considerable factor in the state's wealth at that time.[1]

Slave trading was an important commerce in St. Louis. The prosperity of the state was dependent upon a variety of products, but land and the chattels associated with farming were fundamental. Families of social distinction were expected to maintain a staff of house slaves. Frederic Bancroft regarded Missouri, except the northern counties and St. Louis, "not much less Southern than Maryland or Kentucky." Local slave trade was active from territorial days through forty years of statehood; and the water connection with Louisville, Natchez, and New Orleans, in addition to Missouri River towns to the west, gave St. Louis unique advantages in the business of buying and selling slaves. The planters of Maryland and Virginia, Kentucky, and South Carolina, farming

[1] The increase of 798,310 in twenty years, based on the population of 1840, was well over 200 per cent. *Eighth Census of the United States, Population*, xiii, 277, 281, 283, 285; *Sixteenth Census, Population*, I, 583; Lewis Atherton, "Life, Labor, and Society in Boone County, Missouri, 1834–1852," *Mo. Hist. Rev.*, Vol. XXXVIII, 207–304; Harrison A. Trexler, "Slavery in Missouri," *ibid.*, Vol. III, No. 3, 179–98; "The Value and the Sale of the Missouri Slave," *ibid.*, Vol. VIII, No. 2 (Jan., 1914), 69–85; Bolton and Marshall, *The Colonization of North America*, 278–79, 282; A. B. Hart, *Slavery and Abolition* (N.Y. and London, 1906), 128ff.; James Thomas Angus, "The Attitude of Missouri Toward Slavery from 1850 to 1860" (M.A. thesis, University of Missouri, 1932); Earl John Nelson, "The Passing of Slavery in Missouri" (M.A. thesis, University of Missouri, 1932).

land that was reduced in fertility by many plantings of tobacco or other crops, had a surplus of slave labor.

During the decade of the 1830's alone, Virginia exported 118,000 slaves to the Southwest; South Carolina, 67,707; and Kentucky, 23,230. Charles S. Sydnor's comment on this situation gives emphasis to the economic factor; the sale of slaves in the Southwest was "worth millions of dollars yearly to Virginians."

Missouri was a natural field for the sale of slaves who could not be employed profitably in the East, and St. Louis was the point where trading opportunities were most likely to be found. Green's *Directory* in 1850 listed thirty traders, and doubtless there were many others who engaged in the sales but did not publicly announce their connection with the slave market.

Diversity of tasks and the relative freedom of owners from the intense competition of single-crop production made agricultural slavery in Missouri mild by comparison with the Deep South. The slave trade, on the other hand, was not sufficiently regulated by either custom or statute to prevent repulsive excesses. The separation of Negro families by sale was not restricted to vicious slaves or habitual runaways. An incident in the career of trader Walker, who assembled slaves from various places in Missouri and worked them on a farm near St. Louis until he received an attractive offer from a buyer, discloses the lack of consideration which often brought tragedy to the life of a slave. This trader generally did not dispose of all his purchases in the local market, and it was his practice to ship the surplus south in gangs of one hundred. The Negroes who worked on Walker's farm were secured at night by means of chains.

Walker, mounted on a horse at the head of twenty Negroes in a coffle, with the rear guarded by his mulatto assistant, also riding a horse, marched from the interior toward St. Louis. The wailing infant of a slave woman annoyed the trader so much that he suddenly snatched it from its mother's arms as the party was moving out of St. Charles and gave it as a present to a woman who was watching the scene. Many other examples of slave family separations are on record in Missouri.

John Mattingly, a bachelor who lived in Barnum's City Hotel, advertised during the winter of 1851–52 that he would pay from $50 to $100 more per head for Negroes than any other trader. Reuben Bartlett at the same time was buying slaves in the St. Louis market for purchasers in Memphis and New Orleans. He advertised that he would travel to any community in Missouri to obtain slaves. Columbia, Marshall, Platte City, and St. Joseph provided a significant number of Negroes for the St. Louis trade. The exchange of slaves at Lexington was of sufficient volume to maintain two full-time traders, one of whom held his Negroes for the market in a three-story slave pen.

Bolton, Dickins and Company established its main office in St. Louis on Chestnut Street between Sixth and Seventh streets, near the city jail, although the partners maintained their own barracoon (or private jail for slaves). Their advertisement stated that "our Mr. Dickins" was prepared to pay the highest prices for slaves. Over the door of an office opened by this firm at No. 52 Second Street, a sign boldly proclaimed, "Negroes Bought Here." Corbin and Thompson, Bernard Lynch, and many other slave traders maintained active establishments in St. Louis. One of these, located at No. 57 South Fifth Street, specialized in sales of Negro children aged five to sixteen. This company gave "particular attention to selecting homes for polite servants." Slave mothers and their broods were purchased together and sold separately.[2]

Missouri's laws relative to the control of slaves were based principally upon the state constitution and the slave code which was adopted by the General Assembly in 1825. The original constitution of the state provided fundamental elements of protection for slaves and authorized the legislature to implement the general principles. Slaves were entitled to jury trials, the advice of counsel,

---

[2] Frederic Bancroft, *Slave Trading in the Old South* (Baltimore, 1931), 135–42; Hart, *Slavery and Abolition*, 123–25; Harrison A. Trexler, *Slavery in Missouri, 1804–1805*, 19, 109, 112, 115, 124, 125, 131, 134–72; Trexler, "The Value and Sale of Missouri Slaves," *Mo. Hist. Rev.*, Vol. VIII, No. 2 (Jan., 1914), 69–73. This account gives numerous examples of sales and prices at different periods. Alice Dana Adams, *The Neglected Period of Anti-Slavery in America* (Boston, London, 1908), 3–7, 109, 198; Charles S. Sydnor, *The Development of Southern Sectionalism, 1819–48* (Baton Rouge, 1948), 252, 258, 259.

and, upon conviction, customary punishment. In general, rules applicable to the trials of white citizens and free Negroes were employed for the trials of slaves. Insurrection or rebellion as the result of conspiracy by slaves was punishable by death. Murder, a criminal attack upon a white woman, and striking the master or one of his family were also capital crimes. Lesser offenses were punishable by whipping; and misdemeanors such as neglect of tasks, small personal injuries to other slaves, and running away or staying out in the woods for a limited time were generally punished by the master or mistress. Resistance to disciplinary measures was a serious offense, punishable by death or severe whipping by a public officer. The blacksnake or cowhide whip strongly applied to the slave's bare back was certain to leave scars that would reduce his market value; therefore, some masters preferred a rubber strap attached to a wooden handle, which inflicted pain without the bruising effects of the leather whip. The paddle, also, might be substituted for the leather whip as a means of avoiding permanent scars in the punishment of minor offenses.

Unfortunately, legal punishment was sometimes supplanted by lynch law, in which an unreasoning mob acted in the capacity of arresting officers, judge, jury, and executioners. Murder of a white person by a slave or free Negro or the rape of a white woman were the commonest incentives to mob violence. In the event a slave or free Negro was charged with a crime of particular atrocity, execution by a mob usually took the form of burning. In 1835 a mulatto named Frank McIntosh was held in the St. Louis jail, accused of murdering with a knife the police officer who attempted to arrest him. A mob entered the jail, took the prisoner out, and burned him to death.

Judge L. E. Lawless of St. Louis County instructed the grand jury to ignore the event. If the lynching "was the act . . . of the many—of the multitude, in the ordinary sense of these words . . . of congregated thousands, seized upon and impelled by . . . frenzy . . . then, I say, act not at all in the matter; the case then transcends your jurisdiction—it is beyond the reach of human law."[3]

[3] Trexler, *Slavery in Missouri, 1804–1805,* 117–19; Hart, *Slavery and Abolition,* 109–22; U. B. Phillips, *Life and Labor in the Old South* (N.Y., 1929), 85–90, 362;

Helping a slave to escape from his owner was a crime of some magnitude. In the summer of 1841, Alanson Work of Quincy, Illinois, with two theological students from Hunter's Mission Institute crossed the Mississippi River one night, intending to help Negro slaves to escape from their masters in Marion County, Missouri. The slaves who were approached by the abolitionists exposed their plans, and they were captured. Bail was set at $2,000, a sum that none of the prisoners was able to post. Threats of mob violence gave the case publicity, and newspapers in Missouri expressed freely their editorial views. The *Daily Missouri Republican* of St. Louis branded Alanson Work and his two companions, James Burr and George Thompson, "that species of character which we believe may be found in Saint Louis as well as in Illinois, who will pray for you at evening and steal your negro at midnight."

Work, Burr, and Thompson were tried in the Missouri circuit court at Palmyra on September 10. Judge P. H. McBride ruled that the testimony of the slaves, given indirectly through their masters, was admissible in spite of the statute excluding slave testimony against white persons. The jury, after an hour of deliberation, returned a verdict of guilty, and each defendant was sentenced to twelve years in the penitentiary. As an interesting aside, one of the jurors in this case was John M. Clemens, the father of Mark Twain.

Public opinion ran strongly against any person who took the side of the slave in a case of mob violence. Elijah Lovejoy, who came to Missouri from New England in 1827, held the antislavery view that was becoming common in his section of the country and had a flair for journalistic disputation. He edited the weekly newspaper, the *St. Louis Observer*, in which antislavery editorials began to appear about 1834. Writing about the assassination of the mulatto Frank McIntosh, he was critical of the mob and of the retreat from law enforcement by Judge Lawless. After the publication of this editorial he agreed with his principal St. Louis backer to remove his activities across the Mississippi River.

In 1837, Lovejoy was engaged in the publication of an anti-

F. L. Olmstead, *The Seaboard Slave States* (N.Y., 1904), 438–40; Olmstead, *The Back Country*, 82–88.

slavery newspaper in Alton, Illinois. The people of Alton, however, were no more friendly to his antislavery views than the citizens of St. Louis. He persisted in his efforts to publish the paper; and after his plant had been wrecked twice, a third mob seized his press and killed Lovejoy when he wounded one of the attackers in an attempt to protect his property.

Like Virginia, the state of Missouri had many citizens who were in favor of gradual emancipation as a program of economic betterment. Probably Thomas Hart Benton, who showed a definite interest in the movement as early as 1828, would have taken the same stand as that of his wife's kinsman, James McDowell of Virginia, with the encouragement of more popular support. But the intellectuals of the time were more inclined to agree with the theories of George Fitzhugh, whose book, *Cannibals All*, published at Richmond, Virginia, in 1857, contained the following statement: "Never were people blessed with such wise and noble institutions as we; for they combine most that was good in those of Rome and Greece, of Judea, and of Medieval England." In another passage Fitzhugh indulged his fancy in these words: "The Negro slaves of the South are the happiest, and in some sense the freest people in the world. . . . They enjoy liberty, because they are oppressed neither by care nor labor."[4]

In summary, slave property was an important factor in the history of Missouri, before and after statehood. It was so important in 1820 as to cause the entire constitutional convention to accept it as a desirable condition for the proposed state. Even Joseph Charless and the abolitionists who followed his editorials were agreed upon noninterference with slave property already in the territory. Judge Lucas denied that he was in favor of immediate emancipation, and the men who were elected to the convention were generally strong advocates of slavery as a labor system. Pierre Chouteau, Jr., as a candidate for a seat stated his position thus: "Any attempt to prevent the introduction of slaves . . . will meet my warmest opposition."

[4] Missouriana: "The Marion County Abolitionists," *Mo. Hist. Rev.*, Vol. XXIX, No. 1 (Oct., 1934); Hart, *Slavery and Abolition*, 248; Trexler, *Slavery in Missouri, 1804–65*, 121; George Fitzhugh, *Cannibals All, or Slaves Without Masters*, xv, 29.

The relative weight of slave labor in the production of wealth and in the direct interest of citizens declined after 1830—particularly after St. Louis began its rapid growth and the northern counties were being occupied by small farmers. Immigration of German, Irish, and other European settlers became so large in volume during the 1840's and 1850's that it tipped the scale in favor of a free-state population. By 1850, one-third of the 77,860 inhabitants of St. Louis were German-born, and more than 72,000 of the state's 592,004 white population were foreign-born. During the next ten years, the foreign-born population of Missouri reached a total of 160,541; and of the 588,763 white residents in 1860 who were born outside of Missouri, 319,650 came from regions, European or American, where slavery was illegal. Climate and resources, latitude and river connections, railroads and other commercial facilities were combining to nullify the hold of slave labor upon Missouri.

Conditions of slavery in Missouri provide extreme examples, good and bad. The slave trade was not a highly regarded occupation, although some reputable citizens were engaged in it. Many of the atrocities which furnished ammunition for the abolitionists were connected with the activities of the slave traders. Harrison A. Trexler, the most thorough student of slavery in Missouri, records the charge that Trader Walker "forced a beautiful mulatto slave into concubinage . . . and sold her and his four children into slavery before marrying a white woman."

Although the statutes did not give slaves in Missouri complete protection against separation of kin by sales and many examples of brutal disruption of family life are recorded, there is evidence that the practice was discouraged. For example, an advertisement in St. Louis appeared in this form: "For sale—a good Negro man, 32 years old, and not to be taken from the city."

In 1835 the merchant James Aull, of Lexington, wrote to the Quaker firm—Siter, Price and Company of Philadelphia—which refused to do business with any slave trader: "We are the owners of Slaves [but] it would gratify me exceedingly to have all our negroes removed from among us . . . but to free them and suffer them to remain with us I for one would never consent to." Concerning free Negroes, he added: "A worse population I have never seen."

Disputes over slavery led to violence many times. Generally, propaganda in favor of emancipation aroused the wildest anger on the part of proslavery men. President David Nelson of Marion College, who publicly read a mild proposal of gradual emancipation by means of purchase—the money to be provided by public subscription—was forced to flee from his home. Colonel John Muldrow, who had drafted the proposal and offered to give $10,000 toward implementing his scheme, got into a fight with a proslavery man named John Basley and injured him severely. Colonel Muldrow stood trial at St. Charles with Edward Bates as his attorney, and was acquitted.

The Platte Purchase of 1837 made an important addition to the region open to slavery, since it was situated north of 36 degrees, 30 minutes in the Louisiana Territory. Antislavery members of Congress did not put up a strong fight against this addition to Missouri, since no addition to slave-state representation in the United States Senate was involved. Governor Lilburn Boggs worked hard for the annexation, and the two senators, Benton and Lewis Linn, pushed vigorously for the measure.[5]

OPPOSITION TO THOMAS HART BENTON, 1829-45

The opposition to Senator Benton in 1844 and 1850 has been analyzed by many writers, and his defeat in the election by the Missouri Assembly in January, 1851, has been explained with some variety. Of course, the truly remarkable fact of his career is not that he was defeated in that sixth bid for a seat in the United States Senate, but that he won the place five times and represented his state with distinction for thirty years.

Benton's career was notable in two fields prior to James K. Polk's election to the presidency in 1844. First, he had been the foremost leader in Congress in Jackson's struggle against the Bank of the United States. Closely related to his support of the President in

[5] *Seventh Census of the United States, Appendix*, xlii; *Eighth Census of the United States, Population*, 301, 598-99, 601-604; Trexler, "The Value and Sale of Missouri Slaves," *Mo. Hist. Rev.*, Vol. VIII, No. 2 (Jan., 1914), 79, 84; Trexler, *Slavery in Missouri, 1804-1805*, 115, 120, 124; Lucien Carr, *Missouri, a Bone of Contention*, 186-87.

that contest and the subsequent development of a banking program by the Democratic party was Benton's confidence in "hard
money," particularly silver coins. Second, he had been the most
effective advocate of providing for the settlement of public lands
on terms that would be attractive to landless people. He regarded
filling the West with settlers as a guarantee of national prosperity
in the long view of the future. Not only would frontier farms solve
the immediate needs of poor people; their occupation of these
farms would have a tendency to create new wealth in the form of
marketable goods, and their demands would establish new markets for American manufacturers and other producers.

Senator Benton's third major interest was to prevent the slavery
question from erupting into sectional warfare. He was among the
earliest of the lawmakers to recognize the terrible danger of agitation on a subject so closely interwoven with popular concepts of
progress and reform, on one side, and with immediate economic
interests on the other. As a slaveholder and a descendant of Southern stock, Benton was in sympathy with Southern views on Negro
slavery; but as a citizen of the West he saw his adopted region
moving steadily in the direction of free-state enterprise as opposed
to the economic system of the South.

No man in Missouri Territory was more insistent than Benton
upon the right of the people to shape the domestic institutions provided by their first state constitution. The theories of young
Benton, the writer of editorials on Missouri statehood, suggested
strongly the states' rights doctrines of Beverly Tucker or the extreme views of John Randolph when that eccentric genius regarded
himself the only true Jeffersonian. But Benton had developed with
his state. Probably a strong impulse was given to the nationalism
of the mature statesman by South Carolina's extreme claims on
nullification in 1832. Certainly within a dozen years of that time,
he had grown to regard Calhoun as the focal point of a dangerous
trend toward disunion.

Senator Benton easily weathered the storm that arose over his
opposition to the Bank of the United States in 1832 and helped to
carry Missouri for Jackson, nearly two to one. The St. Louis vote,
however, favored Clay, and Benton's strength in the Missouri As-

sembly shifted to the small farmers and laboring people. During Jackson's second term as chief executive, Senator Benton demonstrated his grasp of party issues by combining the policy of scaling tariff rates downward with reduction of public-land prices. As noted above, it was in the extreme states' rights program of Hayne and Calhoun that Benton of Missouri found alliance with them impossible.

Fundamental differences between the interests of privileged classes in the Southeastern states, who spoke for the Democratic party in that section, and the interests of Missouri's small farmers and laborers were clear to Benton if they were not apparent to anti-Benton Democrats. St. Louis merchants who profited from the policies of Nicholas Biddle and his supporters found many items of conflict with the Missouri senator. Benton's efforts to adjust his thinking to the growing current of nationalism in America, to the interests of the West instead of the Southern class from which he sprang, were confusing to many observers. One newspaper writer, unable to follow the trend of national development and bewildered by the shifting relations of political leaders expressed his resentment by the sour comment: "Col. Benton has read a good deal; but his mind is like a baggage wagon, full of all kinds of lumber."[6]

The original constitution had contained this clause: "Each county shall have at least one representative but the whole number of representatives shall not exceed one hundred." Originally, fifteen counties had been represented by forty-three members. Organization of new counties during the first sixteen years of statehood brought the total number to sixty, and the Assembly had apportioned ninety-eight representatives among them. Thirty-six new counties were created during the years 1837 to 1843, for a total of ninety-six counties. The apportionment law gave each of the counties one representative, as provided in the constitution, with one additional representative for Platte County and three additional

---

[6] Chambers, *Old Bullion*, 148, 149, 177–79, 186, 189, 191, 194; C. H. McClure, "Early Opposition to Thomas Hart Benton," *Mo. Hist. Rev.*, Vol. X, No. 3 (April, 1915), 154–96. Henry Clay was married to "Uncle" Thomas Hart's daughter, Lucretia. Chambers, *Old Bullion*, 26.

representatives for St. Louis County. The population basis for one member in St. Louis County was about 12,000; in Caldwell County, 1,583; and in Boone County, 14,290.

In general, the older counties were under-represented, and as a consequence their citizens pressed for a constitutional convention to revise apportionment. The sparsely settled counties on the frontier took a stand against calling a convention, in which they would face the possibility of losing separate representation in the lower house.

In 1835 the move for a convention failed; but in 1844 the question of a convention with the senatorial district as the basis of representation was submitted to the people. The vote was 34,426 in favor of calling the convention, with 13,750 opposed. The convention of 1845 provided new legislative districts in the sparsely settled areas, with apportionment based on population; but in the general election of 1846, the people voted against the proposed change by a majority of 10,000.

District election of congressmen, as opposed to election-at-large, was considered a democratic procedure which would result in the frontier counties' electing their share of the members. In harmony with his long record for more democratic government, Senator Benton should have taken the lead in advocating district elections. His attitude toward the convention, however, was lukewarm, and his stand on districting the state for Congressional elections was noncommittal. He feared that a convention would fail to maintain constitutional restrictions on banking and that districting would deprive his political friends of their best hope of being elected to Congress. Sterling Price of Chariton County, M. M. Marmaduke and Dr. Penn of Saline County, John C. Edwards of Cole County, and Claiborne F. Jackson of Howard County were all definitely opposed to district elections—since they were sure to be grouped in a single district, from which only one person could be elected to Congress.

In the United States Senate and in speeches at St. Louis and Jefferson City, Benton declared that currency was the great question of the age. Gold and silver, the constitutional currency in the United States, had replaced bank notes since the denial of recharter to the Bank of the United States. His hope was that every state would "suppress within its own limits the circulation of all paper under $20."[7]

The Democrats of St. Louis and other Missouri commercial centers who regarded exclusion of "foreign" bank notes injurious to business were the nucleus of a "soft-money" faction which was ready to join with the Whigs against Benton. In the national capital conservative followers of Jackson were satisfied by the defeat of the charter for the Bank of the United States, but Benton was determined upon a thorough reorganization of the monetary system with specie as the basis. William L. Marcy, who was opposed to the "hard-money" theories of the "Locofoco" faction in New York City, resigned from the United States Senate in July, 1832, to become governor of his state. In the Democratic party of New York, he was identified with the faction which emphasized business opportunity. He denied the contention of workingmen's associations that paper money, subject to fluctuations in value, was merely a technique for cheating them out of their wages. Marcy served as governor of New York for six years, 1833–38, the period which saw a sharp division in the Democratic party on the issue of "hard money."

John Bell and Hugh L. White of Tennessee broke with Senator Benton on the specie issue. Judge White, as president of the State Bank of Tennessee at Knoxville from 1812 to 1827, had established a remarkable record for sound business management. John Bell was a member of the national House of Representatives from 1827 to 1841, served as Speaker for about one year, and was elected to the United States Senate in 1847. He served two full terms in the Senate. In the Congressional election of 1835, Missouri had two seats to be filled and three candidates who ran as Jackson men. Benton's newspaper organ, the *Missouri Argus*, opposed the incumbent, William H. Ashley, on the ground that he was for Hugh L. White as Jackson's successor in preference to Martin Van Buren, and that he had failed to support either Senator Benton's specie program or his public-land policy. Ashley was elected. Benton

[7] Quoted by C. H. McClure, *loc. cit.*, 164; Chambers, *Old Bullion*, 206–21, 251–70; *Missouri Constitution of 1820*, Art. 3, sec. 2.

attacked the record of George F. Strother as a Democrat so effectively that he was defeated for the second seat by Albert G. Harrison. In a speech at St. Louis, Senator Benton attempted to clarify
the political issues which were dividing the Jacksonian Democrats.
There are just two parties, he declared; one stands for the rule of
the people, the other for the rule of property. The *Missouri Argus*
printed the speech in full; and the editor of *Niles' Weekly Register*
was so much impressed that he, also, published the substance of
the address.[8]

DEFEAT OF BENTON FOR A SIXTH TERM

The record of Thomas Hart Benton in regard to slave labor and
policies concerning slavery cannot be explained by the single word
expediency. His views went through a series of stages, and can be
explained in a given period only by his background and experience
up to that time. His acquaintance with plantation labor in North
Carolina and Tennessee, with the politics of slavery in Missouri
Territory, and with the record of sectional struggle in Congress for
control of the western territories enabled him at last to see the
problems in their entirety. Other men who lived in border slave
states enjoyed the advantages of varied experience, of course; but
none of them except Benton represented in the Senate of the
United States a slave state that stood at the gateway to Santa Fe,
the great Northwest, and California—over a period of three full
decades. In a sense, the changing concept of Senator Benton in
regard to slavery ran parallel to the revised concept of the nation.

Benton the Southern expansionist condemned the shortsighted
policy of John Quincy Adams in 1819, for "throwing away Texas."
As an ardent advocate of states' rights in the discussions of Missouri's admission to statehood, Benton was among the leaders in
the fight for slave property. During his second term as senator, he
still regarded the Northern or "Federal party" as a force hostile to

---

[8] Chambers, *Old Bullion*, 185, 189, 204, 210; McClure, *loc. cit.*, 163; *Dictionary
of American Biography*, II, 157–59 (article on John Bell, by Philip M. Hamer); XX,
107–108 (article on Hugh Lawson White, by Thos. P. Abernethy); *Niles' Weekly
Register*, Vol. XLVIII, 462–64.

the agricultural South and West, bent upon public-land policies that would discourage settlement and filled with the sinister design of abolishing slavery.

In the Senate debates of 1836, on Calhoun's motion to refuse petitions praying for the abolition of slavery in the District of Columbia, Benton's chief concern seemed to be avoidance of dangerous sectional friction. He argued for postponement of the motion in order to "give an opportunity for Senators to reflect . . . and to conclude what was best to be done where all were united in wishing the same end, namely, to allay and not to produce, excitement." It is worthy of note that William C. Preston of South Carolina was demanding "peace and repose" by the process of excluding the petitions and that Benton attempted appeasement of "Southern Rights" extremists by dividing the abolitionists into two groups. "Many of them were good people," he said, "endeavoring to ameliorate the condition of one part of the human race." But another group of abolitionists he branded as "incendiaries and agitators."

After two terms in the United States Senate, Benton's attitude towards slavery and the rights of the states concerning slave property separated him from Calhoun's Southern Rights faction. Offended by the doctrine of Nullification arising on the issue of protective tariff, the Missourian was able to trace accurately the sources of agitation on the question of slavery expansion. By the end of his fourth term, Benton was not likely to underestimate the strength of the sentiment in the North against expansion of slavery, or to fail to grasp the extent of Southern attachment to the peculiar institutions of the region. His strong inclination toward national union as opposed to separatism helped him in adjusting to Missouri's changing economic position. Powerful new bonds with the Great Lakes and the Old Northwest, rapid settlement of the northern counties, new commercial ties with the Atlantic seaboard, and particularly the new importance of Missouri as the roadway between the West and the East threw traditional values in politics out of balance. It was Benton's tragedy that he could not prevent the lag in political development which bound Missouri between 1850 and 1860 to policies that Calhoun and his states' rights zealots imposed upon the South.

The opposition to Benton in Missouri took new form and acquired new potency as he debated against President Tyler's Texas annexation treaty. The fear of being led into an "unjust war" against a "peaceable neighbor" was the basis of his opposition. He explained that, while he was Southern in all of his fundamental interests, he was not willing to join in the agitation for expansion of slavery at any cost. "I am a slaveholder and shall take the fate of other slaveholders in every aggression on that species of property," he declared. But he added, with penetrating discernment of the issues, "I must see a real cause of danger before I take alarm; I am against the cry of wolf when there is no wolf."

He defined his position more completely: "I will not engage in schemes for [slavery] extension in a region where it was never known." His entire program, which included a scheme for peaceful annexation of Texas by negotiation with both republics, Mexico and Texas, would have left about half of Texas free soil. Senator George McDuffie attacked Benton's new stand on expansion of slavery as an example of disloyalty to the Democratic party and treason to his section, and Benton replied in a speech described by John Quincy Adams as "merciless and personal."

James K. Polk of Tennessee was nominated for President by the Democratic convention over Van Buren and Cass. In Missouri, Benton campaigned for Polk and had the satisfaction of helping to carry the state for him by a majority of 10,000. The Missouri Assembly re-elected Benton for a fifth term in the Senate and selected David Atchison to fill the unexpired term of Senator Linn. Benton's majority was seventy-four to fifty-seven, the opposition being composed of Whigs, advocates of paper-money issues, and perhaps a few who opposed him on personal grounds.

On Tyler's treaty for the annexation of Texas, which was defeated in the Senate by thirty-five "Nays" to sixteen "Yeas," Benton voted with the Whig majority against confirmation. Six other Democrats, all from Northern states, voted against the treaty. For the first time since his reconciliation with Jackson in 1823, Benton and the former President were on opposite sides of a live political issue. David Atchison, Benton's colleague in the Senate, voted for confirmation; and in the years that followed—an extremely critical period in the history of Missouri and in the career of her senior senator—it was Atchison who took the lead in favor of Calhoun's Southern Rights doctrine.[9]

The Wilmot Proviso, a proposal introduced by a Pennsylvania congressman in 1846 to exclude slavery from any territory that might be acquired from Mexico, passed the House of Representatives but met defeat in the Senate, and thereafter appeared many times and in many forms in the debates of both houses. Free-state legislatures generally supported the Proviso while the slave-state legislatures passed resolutions that bitterly denounced it. The people of Missouri, in the press, in public meetings, and through their representatives in the General Assembly, debated the issue with keen interest and a growing tendency toward violence.

The antislavery portion of Missouri's population, steadily growing as the subject of slavery extension became a great national issue, were quick to seize upon the changed attitude of the senior senator. Francis P. Blair, Jr., who was graduated from Princeton in 1841 and began the practice of law in St. Louis, returned from service in the Mexican War with a reputation for reckless courage and a strong hostility toward slavery extension. He was delighted by Benton's mature stand on the subject and with many other Free-Soil Democrats in St. Louis was eager to welcome "Old Bullion" to their support. Expressions of approval came to Benton from John A. Dix of New York and Gideon Welles of Connecticut. In Washington, Senator Benton called upon John Quincy Adams, who returned the call, meeting Elizabeth, three of the Senator's daughters, and his son-in-law, John C. Frémont.

The Senate debate on the Wilmot Proviso in February, 1847, found John C. Calhoun prepared with a sharp attack on restrictions that were hostile to the "structure of Southern society, economy, and culture." He declared that loss of Southern equality in the Senate would result in "political revolution, anarchy, civil war, and widespread disaster"; and proposed a set of resolutions which denied the constitutional power of Congress to exclude slave prop-

[9] *Mo. Hist. Rev.*, Vol. XXXII, 374; *ibid.*, Vol. XXXIV, 502; Chambers, *Old Bullion*, 159, 208–209, 275, 276, 277; Benton, *Abridgment of the Debates of Congress*, XVI, 341–42, 392, 443, 455, 459.

erty from the territories. Benton objected to the consideration of "such a string of abstractions." In reply, Calhoun stated: "The Constitution is an abstraction. Propriety is an abstraction. All the great rules of life are abstractions. . . . I have as little desire as any senator to obstruct public business." He had expected Benton, speaking for a slaveholding state, to be found in favor of the resolutions, he said.

"I shall be found in the right place," answered Benton. "I am on the side of my country and the Union."

On March 2, 1847, the Senate voted against the Wilmot Proviso, "Yeas," twenty-one; "Nays," thirty-one. Benton voted "Nay," thus giving support to Calhoun and his followers and denying his aid to Silas Wright, John A. Dix, John Fairfield of Maine, and other Free-Soil Democrats. But Benton's vote supported President Polk, who regarded the Proviso as unnecessary emphasis upon the slavery question—"mischievous and wicked agitation."[10]

Two Southern senators were particularly eager to clash with Benton and seemed bent upon physical combat. The debate over confirmation of Stephen W. Kearny as brevet major general was more than ordinarily acrimonious. Senator Benton opposed the appointment and complained bitterly of Kearny's "persecution" of John C. Frémont in California. Sectional views, at no time far from the surface in this period, emphasized the Missourian's departure from the leadership of the Deep South; and Senator Andrew P. Butler of South Carolina became so resentful that he sent a challenge to Benton. The Missouri statesman refused to fight, on grounds which suggest that his opinions on the subject of dueling had become more mature. The challenge had been delivered by Senator Henry S. Foote on a Sunday, under circumstances that excited and alarmed Benton's family. Certainly a younger Tom Benton would have accepted Butler's challenge and probably would have opened the way also for Foote to obtain satisfaction.

In the debates of 1850, Benton proposed to pay Texas for dis-

[10] Henry H. Simms, *A Decade of Sectional Controversy*, 47, 48; Benjamin H. Merkel, "The Slavery Issue and the Decline of Thomas Hart Benton," *Mo. Hist. Rev.*, Vol. XXXVIII, 388–407; Chambers, *Old Bullion*, 313–17; William Ernest Smith, *The Francis Preston Blair Family in Politics*, I, 158, 175, 205, 240, 249, 298ff., 323, 337; II, 134, 216; *Congressional Globe*, 29 Cong., 2 sess., 453–55, 555.

puted territory east of the Río Grande. Foote replied by launching into a violent tirade on the evil effects of adding the soil of slaveholding Texas to the public domain, where slave labor was still an open question. He objected to Benton's statement that Mexican law excluded slavery from any part of the disputed territory. Then he turned to his self-appointed task of personal assault, referring to Benton's lapse of good conduct as a schoolboy in North Carolina. Next came a comparison of the Missourian's career with that of Cataline in the Roman Senate. With as much dignity as he could muster—lacking a toga in which to wrap himself—Benton stalked out of the room.

On April 17, in the midst of the debate on Henry Clay's "Omnibus Bill," Benton mentioned the "Southern Address" of 1847, which he had refused to sign, and stated that he regarded the document a part of the unnecessary "agitation" over the slavery issue. In reply, Foote again broke into a torrent of personal abuse; but when the Missouri senator arose from his seat and walked rapidly toward him, he broke off suddenly, hastily retreated, and drew a pistol from his pocket.

Benton demanded Senate action on the incident, declaring that Foote had come into the chamber with the intention of provoking a quarrel and committing murder. A committee of investigation condemned Foote's frequent resort to verbal attacks upon the Missourian. At the same time, the committee report called attention to Benton's failure to maintain the dignified aloofness with which he had met Foote's earlier insults. No action was taken against either member.[11]

In March, 1849, the Missouri Assembly adopted the Jackson Resolutions. This series of six resolutions, reported in the upper house by the chairman of the committee on federal relations, Claiborne Fox Jackson, denied the authority of Congress to legislate on slavery in the states, the District of Columbia, or the territories. "Excluding the citizens of any part of the Union from removing to

[11] Chambers, *Old Bullion*, 356–57, 361–62; Daniel M. Grissom, "Personal Recollections of Distinguished Missourians," *Mo. Hist. Rev.*, Vol. XVIII, No. 2 (Jan., 1924), 129–45. In regard to Senator Foote's threat of Benton with a pistol, William H. Chambers comments, ". . . while Foote still held the gun he was nearer fleeing than firing" (*Old Bullion*, 361).

such territories with their property, would be an exercise of power by Congress inconsistent with the spirit upon which our federal compact was based, insulting to the sovereignty and dignity of the States thus affected, calculated to alienate one portion of the Union from another, and tending ultimately to disunion," the second resolution proclaimed. The conduct of the Northern States on the subject of slavery served to release the South from adherence to the Missouri Compromise. To the people of a territory, in the form- ing of their constitution for a state government "or in their sov- ereign capacity as an independent State" belongs exclusively the power to prohibit slavery. The fifth resolution pledged Missouri to the support of other slaveholding states; and the sixth *instructed* the Senators in Congress and *requested* the Representatives to "act in conformity with the foregoing resolutions."

The General Assembly, in passing the Jackson Resolutions, dem- onstrated its will to support the extreme proslavery doctrines of Calhoun. Twelve years later, in St. Louis, a Missouri convention refused to follow South Carolina into the overt act of secession from the Union, and the state returned, approximately, to the mod- erate view of states' rights and the practical view of living with other people in the nation that Senator Benton had been able to see earlier. In the meantime, however, the assurance in Resolution Five that Missouri would be found "in hearty co-operation with the slaveholding States" in resisting the "encroachments of North- ern fanaticism" had added confidence to the secession movement. Possibly, the belief that the Confederacy, in addition to Louisiana, Texas, and Arkansas west of the Mississippi, would have the added support of Missouri, with its population well above one million, its wealth, and its important trade routes, was a factor in determina- tion of the South upon disunion. In any event, the ten-year political alliance of Missouri with the plantation South was an unnatural coalition, resulting in stiff, stilted, states' rights documents, remi- niscent of Nathaniel Macon in the days of the Confederation or of John Randolph in his most exalted passages on local liberty.

Senator Benton refused to be bound by his instructions from the Missouri Assembly. On May 9, 1849, he issued at St. Louis an open letter addressed "To the People of Missouri." He stated that the whole body of the people should have an opportunity to consider the Resolutions and his refusal to obey them. If the voters confirmed the Assembly's instructions, then Benton would give them an opportunity to find a senator to carry their views. He added, "I cannot do anything to dissolve the Union or to array one half of it against the other."

The Senator's campaign for vindication lasted five months and carried his views on the proslavery Resolutions to most of the towns in Missouri where large crowds could be assembled. He purposely visited the strongholds of his opponents, the counties in which slaves were most numerous. His was still the most powerful single voice in Missouri, but the anti-Benton forces were too thoroughly organized. The opposition was composed of Whigs, proslavery men, "soft-money" men, and professional politicians who were pledged to oust Benton as a means of advancing their own party fortunes.

His enemies called him a "Free-Soiler," an "abolitionist," a "Barnburner," and a "scoundrel." Calhoun declared in Washington that Benton had been false to the South for ten years; and the opposition in Missouri added other titles: "renegade," "traitor," "apostate," "liar." Many pro-Benton men in Missouri, including a substantial group of newspaper editors, believed he was winning. Richard Phillips, who published the *Union* at St. Louis, gave as his judgment, "Col. Benton cannot be put down," and defended his statement by adding that Benton's opinions were those of a majority of the people. Whig leaders, too, wrote that Tom Benton had the backing of the majority.

The General Assembly meeting at Jefferson City in January, 1851, voted on the candidates for United States senator. On the first ballot, Henry S. Geyer had sixty-four, Benton fifty-five, and the anti-Benton Democrat, James S. Green, thirty-seven. Little change appeared in the voting through twenty-one ballots over a period of three days. The twenty-sixth ballot, on the eighth day, found six anti-Benton men voting for Geyer, who received seventy votes; and on the fortieth, Geyer had eighty, Benton fifty-five, and Stringfellow, eighteen. Thus the Whig who had declared, during the election, that in his opinion Congress had no authority to limit slavery in the territories, was elected to Benton's place in the Senate.[12]

Benton was sixty-nine in the year of his retirement from the Senate. He lived seven years longer, until the spring of 1858; and during that time he served a term in the lower house of Congress, failed in his bid for re-election, tried again without success for a seat in the Senate, and was defeated for the governorship of Missouri. As a member of Congress (1853–55), he opposed repeal of the Missouri Compromise and thereby lost his hold upon the voters of his district and of the state. After thirty years of political leadership in Missouri, he must have found repeated losses at the polls keenly disappointing; but his confidence in the rightness of his course was unwavering. He believed that sectional demand for expansion of slavery was the source of the rising storm, and he threw the full weight of his influence against that powerful, disruptive force. In defeat, he was truly a great statesman.

The volume of his literary effort was enormous. Most of the published works belong to the years of political decline. In 1854 and 1856 he published the two volumes of his *Thirty Years' View of the American Government*. His *Abridgement of the Debates of Congress, 1789–1850*, in sixteen large volumes, appeared between 1857 and 1861. This work was largely a matter of assembling materials, but the abridgment was no small task and the quality of the editing was creditable. His *Historical and Legal Examination of the Dred Scott Case* contains his view of the constitutional power of Congress over slavery. It is the view of Curtis rather than that of Taney. It is partisan, but remarkable for its erudite presentation of a great constitutional problem.

The apathy of the common man in Missouri, especially the recent immigrants from other states, may explain in part the failure of the voters to support Senator Benton. Political activities were on a level at which factional log-rolling was most effective. Slaveholders, in a minority among the voters of Missouri, had the advantage of knowing exactly what they wanted. Whigs and Demo-

---

[12] Elbert B. Smith, *Magnificent Missourian*, 236–39; Leonard Manuscripts, Missouri State Historical Society (Draper to Abiel Leonard, July 26, 1849); Chambers, *Old Bullion*, 344–52, 374–77.

crats among them were united on any question which affected directly their property in slaves. The acceptance of Henry Geyer by Democrats who regarded Benton as an obstacle to their prosperity is an example of the principle in operation.[13]

[13] Thomas Hart Benton, *Thirty Years View of the American Government*, 2 vols.; Benton, ed., *Abridgment of the Debates of Congress*, 16 vols.; Benton, *Historical and Legal Examination of the Dred Scott Case.*

···✦ 10 ✦···

BORDER CONFLICT AND THE
OUTBREAK OF THE CIVIL WAR

TROUBLE ON THE KANSAS BORDER, 1854–58

EVERY ELECTION in the state of Missouri between 1840 and 1860 provided unmistakable evidence of interest there in the westward expansion of slavery. Some Missourians wanted land for farming operations, and many of them were well aware of the relation between opening new territory and the rising price of slaves. The map furnished a disagreeable prospect for slaveholders when they faced the possibility of a free state on their western border. Of Missouri's neighbors, only Arkansas on the south and a small segment of Kentucky, across the Mississippi on the southeast, were committed to slave labor. Illinois, with its long boundary on the east, and Iowa on the north had taken their stand among the free states.

Stephen A. Douglas, as chairman of the committee on territories in the United States Senate, pushed a bill through Congress in 1854 which opened Kansas Territory to slavery and thus repealed the Missouri Compromise. As friends of the Kansas-Nebraska Act pointed out, the compromise measure by which Missouri was admitted to the Union as a slave state and the introduction of slaves north of 36 degrees, 30 minutes in the Louisiana Territory was forbidden was in the form of a statute and subject to repeal by Congress at any time. Opponents of the law declared that reopening the controversy over slavery in the territories was a dangerous abuse of political power and, furthermore, a violation of the solemn agreement between the North and the South in 1820.

Organization of the Republican party, with opposition to the extension of slavery its main principle, resulted directly from the passage of the Kansas-Nebraska Act. Senator Douglas lost important elements of his popular support in Illinois and his potential strength throughout the North in the event of his running for President. His fight for the bill gained for him a temporary hold upon the Democratic party in the South. Following the principle of compromise adopted for the territory acquired from Mexico, Douglas had substituted popular sovereignty for the dividing line between free and slave territory provided in the Missouri Compromise.

Opening Kansas Territory on the basis of popular sovereignty was a signal for the outbreak of sectional conflict in tangible form. The interest of Missouri in the settlement of Kansas had many important elements besides slavery extension. Employees of the Indian agencies and workers in a variety of other jobs were directly concerned with the organization of territorial government. Many Missourians were engaged in land speculation and many others in the development of such towns as Atchison, Kickapoo, Leavenworth, and Lecompton. Wholesale merchants, the owners of steamboats, Missouri promoters of railroad lines, and St. Louis financiers, all looked upon the settlement of Kansas as the peculiar concern of Missouri. Persons who were not motivated by powerful abolition sentiment—and the abolitionists constituted a very small minority of the population indeed—were likely to make common cause with fellow-Missourians who had a positive interest in the expansion of slavery.[1]

Since 1847 the Missouri General Assembly had been urging upon Congress the acquisition of Indian land titles in Kansas and Nebraska and the organization of territorial government. David Atchison in the Senate and Willard P. Hall in the House of Repre-

[1] William F. Zornow, *Kansas: A History of the Jayhawk State*, 67–69; Richard S. Brownlee, *Gray Ghosts of the Confederacy*, 6, 7; Albert Castel, *A Frontier State at War, Kansas, 1861–1865*, 1–16.

sentatives took steps toward placing an organic act before Congress, thus indicating the interest of Missourians in the region beyond their western border. In 1854, when Thomas Hart Benton made his last futile bid for a seat in the United States Senate, his campaign against Atchison was based chiefly upon the Kansas question—Atchison supporting popular sovereignty, Benton the continuance of the Missouri Compromise line. When President Pierce signed the bill for organization of Kansas, hundreds of settlers from Missouri rushed in, occupying choice land along the west bank of the Missouri River and obtaining good locations in the new river towns.

Northern settlers responded to the challenge by planting towns farther removed from the Missouri border. The New England Emigrant Aid Company sent about 1,400 settlers in the first two years after Kansas was organized. However, it was the region north of the Ohio River that provided the major portion of the territory's population. The struggle for control between the North and the South, especially between New England and Missouri, was much discussed and has perhaps been overemphasized. The real contest was one in which climate and topography were heavily on the side of Northern occupation. Antislavery towns were founded to offset the proslavery communities. Conflict between Leavenworth, Lecompton, Kickapoo, and Atchison, on one side, and Osawatomie, Lawrence, Manhattan, and Topeka, on the other, was colorful and dramatic; but the character of the Kansas population by the end of territorial days was determined by corn and wheat, hay and cattle, and a multitude of crops and animals that could be produced by free Kansas farmers.

A large part of the people settled the West to make a living for themselves and not to save Kansas for free labor or slave labor. The struggle in Kansas resulted from the agitation of extreme proslavery men, such as Senator Atchison, Benjamin F. Stringfellow, and Claiborne F. Jackson on one side, and the equally radical opponents of slave labor on the other. Henry Ward Beecher's congregation in Brooklyn raised money to buy a rifle and a Bible for each settler of the Wabaunsee colony. Even Governor Salmon P. Chase of Ohio advocated an appropriation by his legislature to aid in the arming of free-state men bound for Kansas.[2]

As immigrants from the South and the North moved into Kansas, settling for the most part in communities that were strictly sectional, suspicion and misunderstanding mounted on both sides. It was commonly supposed by the free-state settlers that all Missourians were "Border Ruffians," bent upon holding control of the new territory by any method, fair or foul, and that most of them preferred violence. Secret societies in Missouri—"Blue Lodges," "Social Bands," "Sons of the South," "Friendly Societies"—added to the confusion by issuing defiant statements boasting of their intention to drive antislavery men out of Kansas. The ardent supporters of slavery among Missouri newspapers did nothing to calm the public mind.

Wild, irrational statements, obviously arising from prejudice and emotional excess, issued regularly from such papers as the *Democratic Platform* in Liberty, the Platte City *Argus*, and the Atchison (Kansas) *Squatter Sovereign*. The Liberty newspaper was in favor of making Kansas a slave state "if it should require half the citizens of Missouri, musket in hand"; and J. H. Stringfellow's *Squatter Sovereign* openly advocated "leveling" Lawrence to the ground. After a Kansas election in which "Blue Lodges" and "Social Bands" from Missouri invaded the territory and elected the proslavery candidate, John W. Whitfield, as delegate to Congress, the *Squatter Sovereign* was practically incoherent with diabolical glee. "We can tell the impertinent scoundrels . . . that they may exhaust an ocean of ink, their Emigrant Aid Societies spend their millions and billions, their representatives in Congress spout their heretical theories till doomsday . . . yet we will continue to lynch and hang, tar and feather and drown, every white-livered abolitionist who dares to pollute our soil."[3]

[2] W. E. Smith, *Blair Family*, I, 306, 362; Zornow, *Kansas*, 67, 68; Jay Monaghan, *The Civil War on the Western Border*, 45, 46; Clement Eaton, *A History of the Southern Confederacy* (N.Y., 1954), 38; Brownlee, *Gray Ghosts*, 3–21; H. C. McDougal, "A Decade of Missouri Politics, 1860–1870," *Mo. Hist. Rev.*, Vol. III, No. 2 (Jan., 1909), 126–53; Castel, *Kansas, 1861–1865*, 3.

[3] Quoted by W. E. Smith, *Blair Family*, I, 305; Zornow, *Kansas*, 70; Monaghan, *Civil War*, 46.

During the autumn of 1855 the free-state partisans elected a constitutional convention, which met at Topeka with James H. Lane presiding, and framed a basic law. The free-state voters ratified the work of this convention by 1,731 affirmative to 46 negative votes. This Topeka state government was denounced by President Franklin Pierce; but the Kansans who recognized it elected a legislature and a full slate of officers, naming Mark W. Delahay as their congressman. When the legislature met, it chose Lane and A. H. Reeder to the United States Senate. Meantime, the House of Representatives at Washington voted an investigation of conditions in Kansas, and Speaker Banks appointed John Sherman of Ohio, William Howard, a Michigan Republican, and Mordecai Oliver, a Missouri Whig, as members of the committee to visit the new territory.

Mrs. Sherman accompanied her husband and found the town of Westport, at the border of Kansas, filled with exciting evidences of frontier life. There was a mixed population of Americans, Mexicans, and Indians—teamsters, drovers, and river men—some with knives and pistols protruding from their belts and all with picturesque, distinctive garb, such as the wide hats commonly worn on the plains, the high-heeled boots that marked the men who spent much time in the saddle, and the uniforms of regular army men. Mrs. Sherman noted the contrast between Lecompton, with its rough wooden buildings set in straggling rows on muddy streets, and Lawrence—"neat as Boston Common."

Senator Atchison of Missouri took the lead in urging the South to help in the fight to hold Kansas for slave labor. Alabama responded, on April 7, 1856, by sending a party of three hundred men under Colonel Jefferson Buford. Uninformed citizens of Missouri and the entire South were led to believe that fanatics from New England were sending armed thugs gathered from the lowest classes in the big cities of the Northeast to settle in Kansas. Buford's band, recruited chiefly from Alabama, Georgia, and South Carolina, was described by a partisan reporter at Cairo, Illinois, as "the most despicable ruffians and cut-throats." The party carried banners with such inscriptions as "Kansas the Outpost" and "Supremacy of the White Race."

Israel P. Donaldson, United States marshal, and Sheriff Samuel J. Jones were strongly proslavery in the exercise of their official duties. In attempting to arrest free-state leaders at Lawrence, the sheriff was wounded by a pistol ball fired into his tent. Judge Samuel D. Lecompte of the United States District Court instructed the grand jury at Lecompton to indict the officers of the Topeka government on the charge of treason: "men who are dubbed governors . . . men who are dubbed all the various other dubs." The jury found true bills against A. H. Reeder, "Governor" Robinson, Jim Lane, George W. Brown, Samuel N. Wood, Gaius Jenkins, Dan Anthony, and others. On the advice of John Sherman, an attempt was made by Charles Robinson to leave Kansas, carrying with him a copy of the Howard committee findings to hand over to Speaker of the House N. P. Banks in Washington. At Lexington, Missouri, a mob boarded the boat on which Robinson and his wife were traveling. A sheriff took him into custody and sent him back to Lecompton. Mrs. Robinson continued to the East, however, with the evidence collected by the committee.

Responding to the call of Marshal Donaldson, an armed band of Missourians met in Lecompton to help in the "enforcement of law" at Lawrence. Ostensibly a posse organized to help United States officers in the performance of their duties, the force actually was a proslavery army commanded by General William P. Richardson of the territorial militia. David Atchison was at the head of one battalion—the Platte County Rifles—and Colonel H. T. Titus commanded another, made up in part from Buford's Alabama party. Dr. J. H. Stringfellow, president of the proslavery territorial legislature, commanded the Kickapoo Rangers.

Fain, the deputy marshal, arrested antislavery men for whom he had warrants without encountering any resistance. Then, under the leadership of Sheriff Jones, the "posse" proceeded to sack the town. Atchison himself fired a cannon shot at the Free State Hotel but missed it. His men, dismissed from all semblance of military order, were allowed to raid the stores and carry away such goods as they fancied, plundering and destroying. The newspaper offices —the *Herald of Freedom* and the *Kansas Free Press*—were wrecked. The Free State Hotel, spared temporarily by David Atchison's poor marksmanship, was destroyed also, and the torch was applied to Charles Robinson's house.[4]

On May 4, 1856—four days after the pillaging of Lawrence—John Brown, with four of his sons, one son-in-law, and two other free-state men, rode to Dutch Henry's Crossing on Pottawatomie Creek, called five proslavery men out of their houses, and murdered them with well-sharpened sabers. There was no element of personal enmity in the killings; it was the zealous desire of Brown and his followers to strike terror to the hearts of their partisan foes. There were other cold-blooded assassinations in this preliminary war for the control of Kansas. Stringfellow, Pate, Atchison, and other "Border Ruffians" talked and wrote constantly of violent, bloody deeds—and occasionally the Kickapoo Rangers or some other irregular military band in drunken fury murdered an antislavery man. None of these crimes was more brutal than John Brown's raid. A father and two minor sons were among the slain. One of the other victims was a member of the proslavery legislature, a man who had a reputation for violence and bullying, and the fifth had engaged in raids on the homes of free-state men with the intention of frightening them out of the territory. It was reported that he had raped the daughter of one settler—a rumor that might have been an attempt by Brown's friends to justify his action. To offset the story of the John Brown raid at Dutch Henry's Crossing, Northern newspapers gave wide circulation to the worst of the Kickapoo Rangers' crimes. A free-state man from Kentucky, R. P. Brown, was waylaid and killed—his head split with a hatchet. The murderers threw the dying man down at his cabin with the terse comment to his wife, "There's Brown."[5]

The defeat of John C. Frémont by James Buchanan in the presidential election of 1856 was regarded by many proslavery men as a victory in the contest for control of Kansas. John W. Geary, the third governor appointed by President Pierce, took measures to

[4] The Howard Report, 34 Cong., 1 sess., House Report No. 200; Monaghan, Civil War, 48–50, 53–59; Zornow, Kansas, 71–77; W. L. Fleming, "Buford Expedition to Kansas," American Historical Review, Vol. VI (Oct., 1900), 38–48; Allan Nevins, The Ordeal of the Union (2 vols., N.Y., 1947), II, 434–36.

[5] Nevins, Ordeal of the Union, II, 472–75; James C. Malin, John Brown and the Legend of Fifty-Six, 81, 82; Monaghan, Civil War, 46, 61, 62.

prevent open warfare between free-state military forces and the combined parties of David Atchison, John W. Whitfield, and Colonel H. T. Titus. The proslavery legislature called a constitutional convention; but Geary was so much disturbed by the control of territorial officers by the "Border Ruffians" and by the obvious plans of the legislature to obtain the election of members who would be dominated by visiting voters from Missouri that he took a stand against immediate statehood. Geary's life was in constant danger from the criminal element in Lecompton as a result of his efforts to check the undemocratic procedure of the legislature.

Missouri men obstructed the passage of free-state immigrants to Kansas on the Missouri River. This resulted in the opening of a northern route for immigrant wagons through Iowa and Nebraska. Jim Lane's radical leadership of bands that came along this northern road was a constant threat to the precarious lull in hostilities, and Governor Geary was hard pressed to prevent open warfare. After nine turbulent months Geary resigned on March 4, 1857, the date of James Buchanan's inauguration as President. The free-state leaders in Kansas agreed among themselves to cast no votes for delegates to the constitutional convention called by the proslavery legislature.

President Buchanan appointed Robert J. Walker of Mississippi, who had served with him in the Polk cabinet, to be governor of Kansas Territory. As a young politician in Pennsylvania, Walker had taken a prominent part in Andrew Jackson's early campaigns in that state. After his removal to Mississippi, he broke with Jackson, temporarily, on the issue of the bank; but as practical politicians, both men found that they needed each other, and Walker became a powerful factor in the party of Jackson, Van Buren, and Polk. He accepted the governorship of Kansas with some reluctance and with full understanding that the job would not be easy.

Both the President and his new chief executive in Kansas Territory professed themselves advocates of popular sovereignty; but it was Walker who quickly found himself in the midst of a torrid political fight. The proslavery convention at Lecompton could not accept the leadership of a man who stood firmly on the principle of popular sovereignty. It was a great misfortune for the Missouri-

Kansas border that James Buchanan did not feel an obligation to give the support of federal authority to Walker's strict adherence to popular decisions in Kansas.

Elected by a series of frauds and determined to thwart the will of the majority in Kansas, the members of the Lecompton convention hoped to get their constitution accepted by Congress before the voters of the territory could find a means of disapproving it. The free-state residents were rapidly increasing in number, and in a convention at Grasshopper Falls on August 26, 1857, they determined to vote in the territorial elections for a delegate to Congress and members of the legislature. Governor Walker rejected all votes that were clearly fraudulent, and the people elected a legislature that was committed to a free-state constitution for Kansas. Marcus J. Parrott, free-state candidate, was elected delegate to Congress.

The Lecompton convention was presided over by John Calhoun, who posed as a moderate but was determined that Kansas should be a slave state. Calhoun was "an honest believer in popular sovereignty," in the opinion of Allan Nevins; "but his limited moral stamina had been weakened by whiskey . . . and by association with proslavery Kansas politicians."

Other, more forceful leaders of the convention included J. H. Danforth of Georgia, Lucius S. Bolling, an eloquent Georgia attorney, A. W. Jones of Virginia, Colonel W. H. Jenkins of South Carolina, and Captain J. W. Martin of the Kickapoo Rangers. Rush Elmore was a Southern gentleman who had been appointed federal judge by President Pierce. Like Calhoun, he was not among the most radical element, who advocated pushing through a proslavery constitution and getting it accepted by Congress. The basic law proposed by the Lecompton convention was in every respect a violation of the principle of popular sovereignty, to which the Democratic party leaders were pledged. Robert J. Walker, like Geary who preceded him as governor, perceived that the trend of population in Kansas was definitely toward free-state settlers. These two governors understood, too, the resentment of the majority against the fraud and trickery of the elections.

Fearing to repudiate openly the principle of popular sovereignty, the convention finally incorporated in the constitution a rigid clause of protection for slave property, a remarkable limitation upon amendment—no change before 1864—and a clause for submitting to the voters only the question of accepting the constitution "with slavery" or "without slavery." Regardless of the outcome of this vote, if Congress accepted the Lecompton constitution, Kansas would be saddled with a labor system which a majority of her citizens clearly opposed.

On December 21, 1857, with very few free-state men taking part in the "plebiscite," 6,226 votes were cast for the constitution "with" slavery, and 569 "without." But the new legislature obtained from Fred Stanton, the territorial secretary who was acting for Governor Walker while he was absent in Washington, a call for a special session. When the lawmakers met, an act was passed which gave the voters an opportunity to cast their ballots for or against the constitution as a whole.

In the election of January 4, 1858, the proslavery men did not participate, and the vote went as follows: for the constitution with slavery, 24; without slavery, 138; against the constitution, 10,226. Perhaps it is a fair assumption that the free-state men outnumbered their opponents by a ratio of approximately ten to six at the time of these two elections. Investigation of the balloting on December 21, 1857, disclosed that sizable blocks of votes were cast by proslavery visitors from Missouri who had no legal right to suffrage in Kansas. The results of the January election left no doubts in the minds of reasonable men that the people of Kansas were in favor of organizing their new state on the basis of free labor.[6]

MISSOURI PARTY DEVELOPMENTS, 1856–60

Against the advice of many friends, Francis Preston Blair, a powerful figure in party politics at the age of sixty-five, cast his lot with the new Republican party in January, 1856. In his correspondence

[6] Nevins, *Ordeal of the Union*, II, 483–86, 488–516; Allan Nevins, *The Emergence of Lincoln* (2 vols., N.Y., 1950), I, 134–46, 142, 230–34, 268, 269, 274, 289, 301–304, 453; Frank H. Hodder, "Some Aspects of the English Bill for the Admission of Kansas," *American Historical Society, Report*, Vol. I, 199–210; Zornow, *Kansas*, 73–79; Monaghan, *Civil War*, 62–94, 96–106.

with Martin Van Buren, Blair mentioned John C. Frémont as a possible candidate for President. The "Pathfinder" had discouraged Democratic leaders who were prepared to put him forward as their candidate, primarily because he was not willing to endorse the Kansas-Nebraska Act.[7]

The movement for nominating Frémont gathered support. Frank Blair (Francis P. Blair, Jr.) reported from St. Louis that Frémont was popular with the Germans of the Missouri city, and German editors of Cincinnati and elsewhere spoke well of him. The East showed less interest in his candidacy; but his youth, enthusiasm, and reputation for reckless valor would find support for him in all quarters. Bigelow proposed that Francis P. Blair should confer with Benton on the question of his support for Frémont. The position of "Old Bullion" on the controversy between his son-in-law and Stephen Kearny seemed to leave no doubt where he would stand in the event of Frémont's running for the presidency, but Benton astonished the Blairs by refusing his endorsement.

Union of the nation was Benton's greatest desire. Frémont would be a sectional candidate; if he should be elected, the South would not accept him and the Union would be broken.

To the Democratic convention at Cincinnati on June 2, 1856, Missouri Democrats sent two delegations. The Blair-Benton wing of the party sent B. Gratz Brown as the head of their delegation, while James S. Green and John S. Phelps led the anti-Benton, Calhoun faction, which was sometimes called the "Fayette Clique." At the convention hall, Blair's friends were refused admittance; but the delegates forced their way in by knocking the door-keepers down with clubs. The dominance of the South was clear, however, when the convention seated the anti-Benton delegates. John E. Ward of Georgia was elected permanent chairman.

The failure of President Franklin Pierce to keep the peace in Kansas and his obvious efforts to curry favor both North and South by his eccentric policies made his renomination inexpedient. The Democrats needed a candidate, if they were to maintain their head-in-the-sand technique, whose policies were even more obscure than those of Pierce. Maryland, Virginia, and Louisiana were

[7] Quoted (in substance) by W. E. Smith, *Blair Family*, I, 341–42.

strongly opposed to Pierce, and other Southern states were luke-warm in their approval. B. B. French of New Hampshire, at one time secretary to President Pierce, became a bitter foe after Pierce's acceptance of the Kansas-Nebraska Act. Senator Douglas was also one of Pierce's sharp critics.

Probably the men most responsible for the boom which finally resulted in the choice of James Buchanan as the party candidate were John Slidell of Louisiana, Henry A. Wise of Virginia, August Belmont, the New York millionaire who was married to Slidell's aunt, and Judah P. Benjamin of Louisiana. James A. Bayard of Delaware and the Washington banker W. W. Corcoran also gave effective aid to Buchanan's cause. The Missouri delegates moved to the support of Buchanan when Stephen A. Douglas declared that he was willing to give up his claims in favor of party harmony. Northern Democarts who could not accept the repeal of the Mis-souri Compromise turned to Buchanan as a "safe man." After the seventeenth ballot, the convention agreed upon him by noisy ac-clamation.[8]

In Washington, Tom Benton of Missouri, former senator and, to many contemporaries, the sage of the West, busied himself with studies in history—Congressional debates, law, politics, biography. On February 27, 1855, a fire in his house on C Street destroyed a large part of his notes and the manuscript of his second volume of *Thirty Years' View*. After the fire he appealed to friends and ac-quaintances for documents, talked with many men about their "recollections," and concerned himself with current politics. *Niles' National Register* reported all news of national affairs from the Whig point of view, he thought.

Benton worked from "daybreak . . . till midnight," and at the end of May, 1856, published his second volume of *Thirty Years' View*. In the opinion of his ablest critics, this volume suffered from the loss of the documents and showed "hurried, almost harried re-writing." Yet it contained a vast amount of information and re-vealed Benton's mature views on the Southern attitude toward

[8] *Ibid.*, 338–43; Nevins, *Ordeal of the Union*, II, 452–59; Chambers, *Old Bullion*, 419.

disunion in 1850. The last chapter, on nationalism and union, was rushed to the publisher only six months behind the original schedule in spite of the delay caused by the fire.

Observing with great concern the growing tendency toward violence, Benton deplored the efforts of Atchison and Stringfellow to force popular sovereignty into the proslavery mold in Kansas. He congratulated Sumner on his Kansas speech and regarded the brutal assault by Preston Brooks, which disabled the Massachusetts senator, a conspiracy. "These men hunt in couples, sir," he commented, when told of the attack.

In declining an offer to put his name forward as a possible Democratic candidate for the presidency in 1856, Benton remarked that statesmanship had become a "hurrah on one side or the other of slavery."[9]

On June 17, 1856, the Republican national convention began its sessions at the Musical Fund Hall in Philadelphia. No delegate came from any state of the lower South and very few from the border states. The Republican platform contained one central theme, opposition to the extension of slavery, and the members of the new party fixed their attention upon that theme with enthusiasm.

John C. Frémont had been the most prominent name mentioned in the conferences of Republican leaders before the convention met. In addition to the Blairs and John Bigelow, William Cullen Bryant, E. D. Morgan, Henry Wilson, N. P. Banks, and Preston King were ready to support the explorer. Thurlow Weed and William H. Seward were not opposed to him. The New York *Evening Post*, the Boston *Atlas*, the Worcester *Spy*, and the St. Louis *Democrat* all favored him. Weed and Seward probably believed that the time for a winning Republican race had not yet arrived and were willing for the young adventurer from the West to break the ice for a later contest. Seward had made a deep impression by his debates in the Senate—the "higher law" speech in 1850, denunciation of the Kansas-Nebraska Bill in 1854, and a few others. Perhaps he could have taken the leadership of combined antislavery forces in 1856 by the simple expedient of becoming an adherent of the new

---

[9] *Ibid.*, 417–20; Nevins, *Ordeal of the Union*, II, 390.

party. However, just as Benton could not forget that he was a Democrat, Seward could not rise above the party machinery of the Whigs.

Republican leaders made a bargain with influential delegates at the Know-Nothing convention to support the Republican candidate for President. The Republican convention at Philadelphia quickly disposed of the claims of Salmon P. Chase and John Mc-Lean and nominated John C. Frémont unanimously. Shortly afterward, the Know-Nothing candidate, N. P. Banks, withdrew in favor of Frémont. In Missouri, Thomas Hart Benton was nominated for governor as a Democrat. He campaigned for Buchanan in the interest of peace, law, order, and justice, he said. Benton lashed out at Pierce—"ruled by the West Point martinet, Jefferson Davis, dogmatical and . . . an avowed secessionist." Benton traveled to Hannibal, Gallatin, St. Joseph, and Springfield (where an audience of three thousand heard him), and to many other Missouri towns—a total of 1,200 miles and twenty-five speeches, by railroad, buggy, and horseback. In St. Louis, he spoke to a crowd which the *Democrat* said could be measured only in acres—and probably numbered over ten thousand.

He carried St. Louis County, but ran a bad third outside of the metropolitan area. He might have been elected to Congress in that election, but in the race for governor Trusten Polk won decisively over the Know-Nothing candidate, Robert C. Ewing, and over Benton. Frank Blair was elected to Congress in the St. Louis district over the anti-Benton and the Know-Nothing candidates. Buchanan carried the electoral vote of Missouri by a substantial majority.[10]

In the widely publicized Lincoln-Douglas debates in Illinois, Frank Blair in the *Democrat* supported Lincoln's stand. Benton had persisted in his adherence to Buchanan and the "regular" Democrats in the national campaign, but he said, "My position is that of friendly independence, wishing for the best, fearing a little."

When the Dred Scott case was argued before the Supreme Court

[10] *Ibid.*, 460–65, 469–70, 501; W. E. Smith, *Blair Family*, II, 299–307; Chambers, *Old Bullion*, 421–24.

of the United States and the decision of the court announced, Benton disagreed sharply. He took the position that Congress exercised supreme authority over the territories and that the court was beyond its jurisdiction in attempting to extend constitutional protection over slavery to the territories. He particularly denied Chief Justice Taney's *obiter dictum* against the constitutionality of the Missouri Compromise.

In March, 1858, when Benton was seventy-six, he became violently ill. The Blairs, highly pleased with the defeat of the Lecompton constitution in Congress, reported that Benton, also, was elated by the failure of the proslavery forces. Of Buchanan, Benton said, "It is too true, he is not a firm, decided man—he is too apt to be swayed by others." Lewis Cass, he thought, was "very timid"; and he said that Douglas was "driven into the Kansas-Nebraska Bill by the Southerners."

On April 9, 1858, Benton worked all day on the *Abridgment*, and on April 10, he died. Some of his contemporaries regarded him very highly and all—even his enemies, except in the heat of conflict—respected his courage, strength of will, and mental powers. The *Washington Union* praised his "gigantic intellect . . . undaunted courage . . . application . . . erudition, capacious memory, [and] direct manner of thought." Abiel Leonard, Whig opponent of Benton through many years, held "Old Bullion" 's life before his son as an example of long-continued good conduct.

Benton had said that the Dred Scott decision was "a palpable error and wrong," that the Kansas-Nebraska Act was "all fraud," and that the Lecompton constitution was worse. In a letter to Jessie Benton Frémont, cited by Senator James R. Doolittle, Benton wrote that "the sport reign of the so-called Democratic Party" had neither a "principle or a measure in common with the Democratic Party of Jefferson and Jackson's days."[11]

William Ernest Smith declares, "In the politics of 1858 Benton was more powerful in death than he could have been in life." Both wings of the Democratic party sought the strength of Benton's

[11] Leonard Manuscripts, Missouri State Historical Society, Columbia, Missouri (Abiel Leonard to Reeves Leonard, April 24, 1858); Smith, *Blair Family*, I, 431–39; Chambers, *Old Bullion*, 417, 422–44.

clear, courageous thinking. The Blairs, committed to the platform —no extension of slavery—were eager to prove that the deceased statesman had recognized the failure of Buchanan to make compromise work; William Carey Jones and other administration men were equally intent upon proving the opposite. The newspapers of the time contributed to the resulting confusion by taking strong partisan positions—for Jones or for the Blairs.[12]

In February, 1857, the Missouri Assembly elected Governor Trusten Polk to serve with James S. Green in the United States Senate. Later, on January 10, 1862, Polk was to be expelled from the Senate on the charge of disloyalty to the United States. Hancock Jackson, proslavery lieutenant-governor, became governor for a short time, and Robert M. Stewart of St. Joseph was elected in August to complete Polk's term. The election of 1860 found Claiborne Fox Jackson, maintaining what he regarded as a neutral stand on the question of slavery in the territories, running for governor against Hancock Jackson of the Southern Democrats, James B. Gardenhire, Republican, and Semple Orr, Conservative Unionist (Whig). Claiborne Jackson won with a plurality of 10,000 in a total vote of 156,579.[13]

THE SECESSION MOVEMENT IN MISSOURI

As plans for secession developed among the radical leaders of Southern proslavery men—the men who identified states' rights with protection for slave property in the territories—Missouri's attitude was carefully watched. The population and wealth of Missouri had grown until it was first among the fifteen slaveholding states in each of these essential resources for war.

Governor Robert M. Stewart, Claiborne Jackson's predecessor, was an attorney and businessman and an amateur politician. He was firmly convinced that every public question had two sides, and

[12] W. E. Smith, *Blair Family*, II, 431; 433–39; Nevins, *Ordeal of the Union*, II, 501; Smith, *Magnificent Missourian*, 238–40.

[13] Chambers, *Old Bullion*, 424, 426; Nevins, *Ordeal of the Union*, II, 501; Brownlee, *Gray Ghosts*, 12. Brownlee classifies Missouri's chief executive as follows: "Claiborne Jackson, Missouri's new governor in 1860, was a secret secessionist" (*ibid.*, 11).

at times he seemed determined to take both of them. On the subject of secession, he straddled the fence, not timidly but with a positive, aggressive tone.

"Missouri will hold to the Union so long as it is worth the effort to preserve it," he declared. "She cannot be frightened . . . by the past unfriendly legislation of the North, nor dragooned into secession by the restrictive legislation of the extreme South." As a member of the convention in 1861, he took a strong stand for the Union and a powerful position against "coercing" the seceding states—apparently with no practical recognition of the facts of national life concerning vast properties owned by the United States and enormously vital territories that would be the subject of conflicting claims by rival North American republics. Stewart said that Southern men had the right to take their slave property into Kansas, and, to offset this recognition of "Southern Rights," he spoke with scorn of nullification and secession.

From 1860 to 1863 he was editor of the *St. Joseph Journal*. After the war began, Governor Gamble commissioned him to raise a Union brigade, but from this military post he was removed by General H. W. Halleck on the charge of heavy drinking. Stewart had some desirable qualities for public service. Probably his greatest weaknesses sprang from inexperience in politics prior to his elevation to high office. His work as an attorney and railroad promoter did not give him the best background for public office, particularly in a time as difficult as the era of the Civil War. He used his position in railroad development to further his political interests, and apparently did not hold an elevated opinion of service for the state.

Another politician of the years preceding the war who rose to a high position afterwards was Thomas C. Fletcher of Herculaneum and St. Louis. Born in Missouri in 1827 of parents who came from Maryland, Fletcher had a background of the plantation and slave labor. Like many other Southern men in the West, he became an opponent of slavery and a leader in the organization of the new Republican party. As a delegate to the Chicago convention in 1860, he supported Lincoln. Like Frank Blair, he had been an active Benton Democrat. In the war he served under Lyon at St.

Louis, became colonel of the Thirty-first Missouri Regiment, was wounded and captured at Chickasaw Bayou, and exchanged. He took part in the capture of Vicksburg, in the Chattanooga campaign, and in the advance upon Atlanta, in which he was a brigade commander. In St. Louis, he recovered from a severe illness in time to organize the defenses of the city against General Price's invasion. In the decisive stand of General Thomas Ewing at Pilot Knob, Fletcher took an active part. After the war he was to enter politics again as governor of Missouri, 1865–69.[14]

The Democratic national convention meeting at Charleston, South Carolina, in April, 1860, was the final hope for party unity and electoral success. From the start, sectional harmony in that convention was destined to fail. Charleston was not well connected with Northern and Western states by any means of speedy travel. Delegates from the Northwest, supporters of Senator Douglas, were exhausted by their railroad journey. Charleston was hot, dry, and dusty. Hotel rates, raised for the convention, were exorbitant and the accommodations miserably poor.

New England delegates came by boat. New York men, including Fernando Wood's contesting delegation, came also by coastwise steamer. John A. Logan and William A. Richardson of Illinois and George E. Pugh of Ohio were among the leaders from the Northwest whose views were definitely at odds with those of the Southern Democrats.

The political atmosphere at Charleston was not one of conciliation for the Northern delegates. At a time when harmony was most desirable to those national leaders who were intent upon avoiding a sectional clash, few of the Charleston people seemed to be concerned with the efforts toward peace. Northern delegates, too, were busy with offensive tirades against Jefferson Davis, and Douglas of Illinois was being denounced by Southern Democrats as a traitor to his party.

[14] H. E. Robinson, "Two Missouri Historians," *Mo. Hist. Rev.*, Vol. V, No. 3 (1911), 129–37; Duane Mowry, "A Statesman's Letters of the Civil War Period," *Journal of the Illinois State Historical Society*, Vol. II, No. 2 (1909), 43–49 (letters of Senator Lyman Trumbull to Senator James R. Doolittle, July 26, 1858; May 16, 1861); *Dictionary of American Biography* (articles on Clement Fletcher, James S. Green, C. F. Jackson, Trusten Polk, Sterling Price, and Robert M. Stewart).

Douglas was confident of success because of his solid support in the Northwest and the probability of obtaining five of Missouri's nine votes on the early balloting. Some delegates from border states were open to reason on the question of Douglas, and some observers believed that the people of the Gulf states would vote for Douglas if he should become the choice of the convention. For the two-thirds majority ordinarily required by the Democratic party, Douglas needed 202 of the 303 votes to insure victory.

The Committee on Resolutions, supported by fifteen slave states and the administration votes from California and Oregon, reported a platform which declared that Congress had no power to abolish slavery in the territories, that the territorial legislatures had no such power, and that it was the duty of Congress to protect slave property in the territories and on the high seas. The minority report, signed by the delegates of sixteen states and presented by H. B. Payne of Ohio, was a plea for the principle of popular sovereignty.

Former governor Austin A. King of Missouri, speaking for the minority report, declared that the slave-code platform "carried the sting of death" to the Democratic party. Adoption of the proslavery resolution would lose the vote of every Northern state and of every border slave state with the possible exception of Missouri. King's plea for unity was based upon the fact that the delegates of the sixteen states supporting the minority report were the representatives of a citizen population more than double the number of citizens living in the fifteen slave states.

The votes on the majority and minority reports disclosed a clear majority of delegates against the slave code; but the victory for the Cincinnati platform of 1856 was not enough for some of the Northern majority in the convention. When they tried to add a plank declaring that the party would abide by Supreme Court decisions, the Southern delegates refused to vote. L. P. Walker of Alabama withdrew his delegation from the convention, and the schism quickly grew until party unity was entirely destroyed. On April 29, a final effort was made by moderates to get an agreement on the Cincinnati platform, to be followed by balloting for candidates. The vote on the Cincinnati platform carried by a large majority, with Missouri voting in the affirmative along with all the other border states; but some of the proslavery men insisted upon completing the platform, including the slave code, before there was any consideration of candidates.

Disruption of the Democratic party was followed by maneuvers which resulted in two candidates from that party campaigning against each other and against the Republicans. A fourth organization held a convention at Baltimore, with the avowed intention of removing sectional issues from the campaign and adhering only to the Constitution and the Union. This party nominated John Bell for President and Edward Everett for Vice-President.

The slave-code section of the Democratic party, withdrawing from the reassembled convention at Baltimore, named John C. Breckinridge of Kentucky for President and Joseph Lane of Oregon for Vice-President. Douglas was chosen by the remaining delegates—the majority of the original convention—receiving 180 votes on the second ballot, with only 32 in opposition.

In Chicago, where William H. Seward was generally conceded the best prospect for winning the Republican nomination, stubborn opposition appeared against him. Salmon P. Chase of Ohio was one nucleus of solid strength against Seward. Simon Cameron's Pennsylvania machine was another obstacle, although it was well understood that Cameron's support could be had for a political price. Border state men were inclined to look upon Bates of Missouri as the best hope for uniting antislavery Democrats, Whigs, and remnants of the American party in a winning program. By common consent the campaign would revolve around the principle, no more extension of slave labor to the West.

Chase of Ohio fondly cherished the dream that much of the backing for Seward would turn to him—that there would be a stampede to him when delegates found that their own first choice was not likely to be nominated. In one of his estimates, Chase was correct—Weed and Seward could not obtain an early majority for the New York senator; but the discouraged Seward men did not come over to Chase's camp.

Lincoln of Illinois, who had not been given much advance publicity as a candidate, did enjoy the services of some astute political managers. David Davis was the most effective of them—perhaps Weed himself was no more skilled in shaping the ambitions of office-seekers to his own main objectives. Davis was not brilliant, his biographer asserts; but he was experienced, persistent, and indefatigable. His enemies added another adjective which was often applied also to Weed: unscrupulous.

When the Chicago convention turned away from Seward, many of the delegates were seeking a man who would be firm in opposition to the extension of slavery without being an extremist on any phase of the slavery problem. Chase, the "Attorney General for Escaped Slaves," was not exactly what they had in mind. Lincoln gave the impression of moderation to all who knew him well; his decisions would be calm, unhurried, and sane. David Davis, Norman Judd, and other Illinois men, aided eventually by the Blairs and other border state leaders who began by supporting Bates of Missouri, helped delegates to move toward the nomination of Lincoln. Greeley of the New York *Tribune* was doing all that he could to prevent Seward's nomination.

The balloting began at noon in the packed hall of the Wigwam. First among the hopeful aspirants, as had been generally expected, was Seward, with 173½ votes. Second was Abraham Lincoln, with 102; Bates of Missouri was fifth, and was followed by favorite sons whose ballots were strictly complimentary. On the second ballot, Lincoln almost came up with Seward—181 to 184½; and on the third, when a small block of votes from Massachusetts suddenly switched from Seward to Lincoln, the stampede began. When the votes were tabulated, Lincoln had 231½—two short of a majority. Within minutes, four Ohio votes were transferred from Chase to Lincoln, and the huge throng became aware that the Illinois man was the choice of his party. No television cameras recorded the event for the immediate information of the American public, of course, but a large portion of that public, in St. Louis and in backwoods Missouri, in the rural South as well as the cities of New York and New England, waited eagerly for the news from Chicago.[15]

15 Nevins, *Emergence of Lincoln*, II, 203–28, 229–60, 261–86; Walter B. Stevens, "Lincoln and Missouri," *Mo. Hist. Rev.*, Vol. X, No. 2 (Jan., 1916), 69, 70; Wood-

In the four-party campaign that followed, sectional disagreement was the dominant note. Two of the candidates represented sectional parties, with rigid separation of the North and South. Lincoln had little support in the slave states and none that could be located with certainty in the Deep South. Breckinridge was the leading candidate in the Gulf states and in Arkansas, North Carolina, South Carolina, Georgia, Delaware, and Maryland. He was high in the popular vote of Oregon and California, behind Lincoln and Douglas in California, and behind Lincoln in Oregon. In no other free state, excepting Pennsylvania, did the candidate of the Deep South make a strong showing.

Stephen A. Douglas ran second to Lincoln throughout the free states, won three of seven electoral votes in New Jersey, and carried the nine electoral votes of Missouri without winning a popular majority in that state. John Bell, candidate of the Constitutional Union party, won the electoral votes of three states—Kentucky, Tennessee, and Virginia—but was hard pressed by Breckinridge in all of them. Lincoln had 180 electoral votes, a clear majority of the total, since the combined electoral count for the other candidates was only 123. Lincoln received less than 40 per cent of the popular vote in the nation, however, and just over 55 per cent of the ballots in the free states. Breckinridge was second in electoral votes, with 72, but his popular vote was only 18 per cent of the total across the country and only 45 per cent in the slave states. Stephen A. Douglas, whose electoral vote was only 12, had a popular support of 1,376,957—nearly double the vote for Breckinridge and short of Lincoln's popular vote by fewer than 500,000.

This sectional election gave emphasis to some important differences among the states in their electoral procedures. Popular voting in the Deep South was small by comparison with that of the Upper South and the border states. The popular vote of the North was considerably greater, relative to population, than that of the slave states in general. For example, the vote of New York and Pennsylvania combined was larger than the total number of votes

row Wilson, *Division and Reunion* (N.Y., 1921), 204–208; F. E. Chadwick, *Causes of the Civil War* (N.Y., London, 1906), 98–101, 113–16, 119–23.

for President in all of the eleven states that seceded to form the Confederacy.

The slave states, with their limited popular vote, did not give a majority to Breckinridge, the candidate who was generally supposed to advocate secession as a last resort. The people of the South, in the majority, were in favor of one or another of the Union candidates. Missouri's votes were for Union candidates over four to one. In no Southern state except Texas, which was somewhat cosmopolitan and definitely western in its political tendencies, was there a popular vote free from military control on the question of secession.

Six weeks after the election of Lincoln dissolution of the Union began, with the secession of South Carolina. It was no accident that the movement started in the state where John C. Calhoun had made his political contributions. Last among the states to give up the old practices of domination by the landed aristocracy, South Carolina still chose its presidential electors by vote of the state legislature. It had agreed to the Union of the states in 1781 without popular vote; and it had ratified the Constitution of 1787, which its leaders still regarded as a compact among sovereign states, through the action of a convention.

On December 20, 1860, the South Carolina convention voted to dissolve connections between the state and the United States. The plantation system of agriculture, large holdings of slaves, and a society based upon slave labor held South Carolina to the political methods of the short-lived Confederacy of 1781. Unfortunately, other Southern states were to fall under the blighting influence of decisions that belonged to an earlier generation. Like South Carolina, Georgia and the Gulf states were under the leadership of men who depended upon slave labor for their weath, social position, and political status. In rapid succession, six other states of the Deep South seceded. Eight slave states remained undecided until the overt act of war, the firing on Fort Sumter, forced a decision. Then the three states adjacent to the original seceders withdrew, by action of their conventions, and the vital state of Virginia also seceded. Later, thirty of Virginia's counties that were least interested in slave property and most exposed to the attacks of Northern armies seceded from Virginia and became a new state in the Union.

Naturally, the slave states bordering Mason and Dixon's Line hesitated to take the step that might bring large-scale military invasion. Missouri, with a long Iowa border, a longer river boundary in common with Illinois, and railroad connections with the entire Northeast, hesitated, considered secession, and finally reached the only decision she could reasonably adopt. Like Kentucky, Maryland, and Delaware, she retained her place in the Union.

Claiborne F. Jackson, running as a Douglas Democrat for governor, had strong support from Missouri voters who hoped to maintain the Union, as Douglas did. However, on the great issue of the day, Jackson quickly demonstrated his real attitude. Unlike Douglas, the Missouri governor took a stand for the Confederacy. A majority of both houses in the Missouri Assembly belonged to the Breckinridge wing of the Democratic party. Thomas C. Reynolds, lieutenant-governor, was regarded as a Douglas Democrat; but the party that demanded protection for slave property in the territories elected their man as speaker of the House of Representatives. When the problem of secession came up for solution, the Assembly took a definite stand for the step.

Jackson's inaugural address in January, 1861, made his position clear. He hoped for settlement of the controversy over slavery without resort to violence; but if the Southern states should separate from the Union, he advocated taking a stand with them, in a new Confederacy. Lieutenant-Governor Reynolds also took his place rather promptly with the Confederates.

The Assembly set February 18, the date of Jefferson Davis' inauguration as president of the Confederacy, for the election of delegates to a convention. The principal purpose of the convention was to settle the question of secession. Each senatorial district was to elect three delegates, a total of ninety-nine. The convention began its sessions at Jefferson City on February 28, 1861. A large majority of the delegates—eighty-two of ninety-nine—were from slave states, and there was much talk among them concerning their attitude toward the Union. A few were called by the newspaper

PORTRAIT BELIEVED TO BE A LIKENESS OF JOSIAH GREGG
Santa Fe trader and chronicler of the Santa Fe Trail.
From a daguerreotype made in New York, presumably in 1844.
From *The Diary and Letters of Josiah Gregg: Excursions
in Mexico and California, 1847–1850.*

George F. Green and the Native Sons of Kansas City, Missouri
MAIN STREET OF INDEPENDENCE IN 1845
after a contemporary sketch by W. L. Pynchon.
Many a Santa Fe–bound caravan outfitted here.

State Historical Society of Missouri

SKIRMISH BETWEEN MORMONS AND GENTILES AT GALLATIN, 1833

State Historical Society of Missouri

DONIPHAN'S EXPEDITION ON THE MARCH

Thomas Gilcrease Institute of History and Art
"THE CUMING AND GOING OF THE PONY EXPRESS"
from a painting by Frederic Remington.

CARONDELET, ABOUT 1846–47
From Henry Lewis, *Das Illustrirte Mississippithal* (1857).

Missouri Historical Society

St. Louis in 1854
was a rapidly growing city.

Pilot Knob
where Price's advance toward St. Louis was halted.

State Historical Society of Missouri

"ORDER No. 11"

Bingham's famous painting of an infamous Civil War incident.

STATUE OF YOUNG GEORGE WASHINGTON CARVER
at the Carver National Monument near Diamond.

reports "unconditional Union men," but the majority preferred the designation, "conditional Union men."

"Unconditional Union men" placed union ahead of all other considerations; "conditional Union men" covered a wide range of opinion. Some would make their final decision on the ground of expediency, and a few stood for the Union only if that result could be achieved by giving to the proslavery extremists all of their demands. Many political "leaders" in Missouri were watching carefully the drift of public opinion and considering through every source of information the developments in other parts of the nation. Traditional grooves of politics were shaken, and the lawmakers faced the emergency of making decisions in harmony with the voters' opinions. A decision of the convention to secede would have been submitted to the people for ratification, a procedure in sharp contrast to that of the states in the Deep South.

The pro-Confederate Assembly voted a resolution against coercion of the seceding states. Governor Claiborne Jackson invited Dan R. Russell of Mississippi, a representative of the Confederacy, to address the Assembly; and every day brought additional evidence that the fight for political control of Missouri would soon be reduced to one definite choice—Union or Confederacy.

The outstanding leader for Union was Frank Blair of St. Louis. A member of a prominent Kentucky family that counted among its older generations some famous men of Virginia, Frank Blair could not be classified as an upstart, opposed to slavery through ignorance or inexperience. After his service in the Mexican War and in the office of attorney general in New Mexico Territory, he had come back to St. Louis a strong opponent of slavery. He supported the Free-Soil candidate for President in 1848—Martin Van Buren of New York. He applauded every step in the transformation of Thomas Hart Benton in the direction of antislavery Democracy.

Young Frank Blair was elected to the Missouri legislature in 1854 and to Congress two years later. His opposition to slavery was chiefly on economic grounds. His attitude toward the Union was that of Benton and of Abraham Lincoln. He disagreed with the theory of legal secession and opposed breaking up the Union as a remedy for real or fancied injustices.[16]

Sterling Price, elected president of the Missouri convention in session at Jefferson City, was a "conditional Union man." In his case, that meant that he was ready to take Missouri out of the Union unless the federal administration should meet all the demands of the extreme proslavery men. A Virginian by birth, Price had come to Missouri at the age of twenty-two. He was Governor Claiborne Jackson's brother-in-law. He had served in the Assembly, in Congress, and in the Mexican War as commander of the regiment that was sent to reinforce Kearny at Santa Fe. His service as a soldier was distinguished. In 1852 he had been elected governor of Missouri on the anti-Benton ticket.

After the election of Price as president of the convention, an invitation was received to hold the sessions at the Mercantile Library in St. Louis. Free transportation was offered along with free use of the hall, and the invitation was accepted. On March 4, 1861, the date of Lincoln's inauguration as President, the first session was held in the new quarters. A Georgia man reported to the convention the secession of Georgia and gave his reasons for advocating the secession of Missouri. The Committee on Federal Relations, of which Hamilton Gamble was chairman, also reported to the convention. There was "no adequate cause" for separation from the federal Union, the report declared. Twelve members of the committee joined in the report, with one dissent.[17]

MANEUVERING FOR MILITARY POSITION

On April 12, Confederate military forces fired on Fort Sumter, and three days later President Lincoln called upon Missouri to supply four regiments of infantry for the volunteer Union army. Governor Jackson answered the call with a blunt refusal. The intended use

[16] W. E. Smith, *Blair Family*, I, 97, 98, 102, 158, 229, 232, 240, 249ff., 283, 297, 336, 338, 400, 410ff., 419, 430, 453–507; II, 21, 22, 27; Chadwick, *Causes of the Civil War*, 127–32; Wilson, *Division and Reunion*, 208–12; Stevens, "Lincoln and Missouri," *Mo. Hist. Rev.*, Vol. X (1916), 74–76.

[17] Thomas L. Snead, *The Fight for Missouri*, 80, 81; Smith, *Blair Family*, 26.

of such an army, he said, was "illegal, unconstitutional and revolutionary in its objects, inhuman and diabolical, and cannot be complied with. Not a man will the State of Missouri furnish to carry out such an unholy crusade."

The Jackson government at Jefferson City and the convention that was holding its sessions in the Mercantile Library were clearly not in harmony. The Gamble committee worked diligently in the interest of peace. Gamble himself was a brother-in-law of Edward Bates, whom Lincoln had placed in his cabinet as attorney general. Missouri's interests were with the Union, and the state's most useful function at this critical time was to serve as an intermediary between secession leaders and extremists in the North. A member of the convention commented, "Missouri will never furnish a regiment to coerce the South"; but William A. Hall answered that Missouri was in the Union and it was her duty to respond to federal demands for troops. James O. Broadhead of St. Louis stated firmly, "Missouri has not the power to go out of the Union if she wanted to."[18]

Frank Blair, with strong support from the German population of St. Louis, had organized a club called the "Wide-Awakes" to distribute Republican propaganda during the Lincoln campaign. The Union Clubs that grew out of this political effort he now armed and organized into companies as military units. The convention at St. Louis adjourned on March 22, 1861, setting the third Monday of December for its next meeting and leaving in the hands of a committee the power to call an earlier session.

The extreme proslavery element in Missouri, represented by Claiborne F. Jackson and a majority of the Assembly, cannot be regarded as an accurate reflection of the will of the state. The slaves in Missouri, 114,931 in number, owned by fewer than 25,000 persons, were confined to a small area, mainly along the Missouri River. It is estimated that two-thirds of all the slaves lived within twenty miles of the river. The counties of this area, with active political interests, skilled and experienced leaders, and a thorough understanding of property owners' objectives, had been chiefly responsible for the defeat of Thomas Hart Benton and the failure

18 Carr, *Missouri*, 288, 290, 313–41; Smith, *Blair Family*, II, 26, 28, 37.

of Missouri to adjust to its new commercial importance and its large new population of small free farmers.

St. Louis was rapidly approaching 200,000 population. More than half of its people were foreign born: chiefly German, Irish, Swiss, French, Scottish, and Canadian. All of these aliens had a tendency toward support of a free-labor system, and some of them were bitterly opposed to slavery. Of the native American population in the city, 56,780 were Missouri born, 21,130 came from free states, and 7,400 from slave states. Thus less than one-third had a social background that gave them an acquaintance with slave labor.

Frank Blair trained his "Wide-Awakes" secretly in such buildings as they could find—a few unoccupied halls, an old brewery, an old foundry—covering windows with blankets and posting sentries to keep out spies. Some of the European boys were experienced soldiers and some had been trained in revolutionary military units.

The St. Louis Arsenal contained an important stock of military goods: 60,000 rifles—Enfield and Springfield—1,500,000 cartridges, and 90,000 pounds of powder. The other munitions were of little value, but the total stock gave the United States forces a definite advantage during the early maneuvers in the West. Governor Jackson and his followers well understood the value of the arsenal, and their quiet steps toward obtaining possession of the military supplies leave no room for doubt concerning their intentions.

General William S. Harney, commander of the Department of the West, had been an officer in the United States Army for forty-two years. Entering the service as a second lieutenant in 1818, he rose to the rank of lieutenant-colonel during the Seminole campaign in Florida and was brevetted colonel for gallantry in action at the time of the Everglades engagement. He began the Mexican War as a colonel when he was forty-six and was made brevet brigadier general for gallantry in the charge up Telegráfo (at Cerro Gordo). He was commander in the action against the Sioux Indians in 1847 and commander in Oregon afterwards. He was placed in charge of the Department of the West in 1861.

Under normal conditions of peace, broken only by minor disorders, he was still a good officer; but after the beginning of secession in the South, he was not fit to command United States troops in Missouri. He had strong connections with the Confederacy, and he found it impossible to take the vigorous action that was necessary if the Union was to control Missouri. If Harney had been younger and more decisive, it is possible that he might have taken charge of the arsenal and moved against the hostile military force of Governor Jackson. On the other hand, he might have decided, as Sterling Price did decide, to take a military command for the Confederacy. He did, in fact, try to play a neutral role—a peculiar status for an officer in the army of the United States in time of war.

In Missouri, events moved in rapid succession after the Confederate attack on Fort Sumter, April 12, 1861. The small United States Arsenal at Liberty, northeast of Kansas City in Clay County, was seized by two hundred of Claiborne Jackson's men on April 20. Major William Bell, in command of the St. Louis Arsenal, was ready to turn it over to Governor Jackson on demand. General D. M. Frost of the Missouri State Militia worked closely with the Governor and passed on to him Bell's assurance that he regarded the arsenal as Missouri's property.

Frank Blair, following closely the military activities of Jackson, Frost, and Bell, prevailed upon General Winfield Scott to remove Major Bell and to replace him with Peter V. Hagner. Blair also obtained United States troops for the protection of the Treasury vaults in St. Louis, where $400,000 in gold was stored.

From Fort Riley, Kansas, came Captain Nathaniel Lyon with a company of regular soldiers to aid in guarding the arsenal. Lyon was known in the army as a fighter and a strict disciplinarian. He had seen active service against the Seminoles after graduating from West Point in 1841. In the Mexican War, an enterprise which he regarded an act of aggression on the part of the United States, he served with distinction—at Vera Cruz, Cerro Gordo, and Churubusco. In Kansas, where he gave impartial attention to the difficult task of maintaining order between proslavery Missourians and free-state partisans, he acquired a reputation as an antislavery man. Challenged by a hot-tempered Southern officer, Lyon refused to fight; but when he was goaded a bit, he changed his mind and accepted the challenge. Lyon named army pistols across the table as his condition for the meeting. Friends of both men then persuaded the proslavery man to withdraw the challenge.

Frank Blair obtained the removal of Major Hagner and his replacement in the arsenal by Nathaniel Lyon. Governor Jackson called the legislature into special session at Jefferson City to consider the problem of raising and arming state militia, and General Frost encamped with a force of seven hundred men at a place which he named Camp Jackson, on the western border of St. Louis. Governor Jackson appealed to President Jefferson Davis for war materials, and a boatload of munitions was sent from Baton Rouge, Louisiana, to General Frost.

On April 25, General Harney was called to Washington to explain his reluctance to act against the rapid development of military support for the Confederacy in St. Louis. During his absence Blair and Lyon decided that Camp Jackson, as a threat to Union control of the arsenal, should be taken over. On May 9, Lyon disguised himself by wearing the clothes and the heavy black veil of Mrs. Alexander, Frank Blair's mother-in-law, who was an invalid. The elderly lady frequently rode in her carriage about the streets of St. Louis, and had ridden through Camp Jackson several times. Disguised, and driven at a leisurely pace by a Negro servant, Lyon passed along "Davis Avenue" and "Beauregard Avenue," in his unauthorized inspection.

On the following day, with approval of the St. Louis Committee of Safety, Lyon moved seven thousand men against the camp. General Frost asked for an interview, but Lyon refused to talk. Frost surrendered.

The troops of Camp Jackson, disarmed, were marched to the arsenal. On the way, citizens who sympathized with secession made an angry demonstration against the Union soldiers. As the regiments of Frank Blair and Henry Bernstein, conducting the prisoners in a long column, halted to close their ranks, the mob began to pelt them with rocks and brickbats. Three of the prisoners were struck by pistol balls. When it became clear that the crowd contained men who were determined to make it a bloody encounter, the soldiers fired upon the mob. Including the three prisoners, fifteen men were killed and five wounded in the skirmish. On the following day the prisoners, after they had sworn not to take up arms against the United States, were released. One man who refused to take the oath was held.

The city was wild with excitement. Preposterous rumors of plans by German soldiers of the Union to attack Southern citizens flew about, and many people fled from the city. Clashes between secessionist mobs and bands of soldiers added new casualties and increased the fears of those who were inclined to be excitable. Some Confederate sympathizers crossed into Illinois, definitely a Union state, and others simply walked out into the country. General Harney, back from Washington, tried without much success to quiet the fears of the citizens. Two full days elapsed before the people settled down to something resembling normal behavior.[19]

The seizure of Camp Jackson brought decision to many persons who had proclaimed themselves "conditional Union men." Sterling Price announced openly his approval of secession, and was appointed by Governor Jackson to lead the Missouri troops who were being organized to support the Confederacy. It has been widely supposed that the action of Lyon in taking Camp Jackson was a blunder which drove undecided men into the party of secession. The capable historian Lucien Carr declares that "it drove . . . General Sterling Price into the ranks of the opposition and ultimately into the Confederate Army." This view, however, cannot be defended in its entirety. States and persons, faced by acts that were hostile to their interests or offensive to their feelings, hesitated before taking a step from which there was no retreat. It would be as reasonable to suppose that assembling the militia force at Camp Jackson, with its threat to the arsenal, drove Nathaniel Lyon to support Lincoln as to suppose that Price's war career was determined by the capture of Frost and his men. As a matter of fact, Lyon had long agreed with Lincoln—and with Frank Blair—on the

[19] Ibid., 32–36, 38–46; Stevens, "Lincoln and Missouri," Mo. Hist. Rev., Vol. X, No. 2 (1916), 63–120; Chadwick, Causes of the Civil War, 268; Wilson, Division and Reunion, 211–12; Snead, The Fight for Missouri, 99–138, 158–76, 177–84; McElroy, John, The Struggle for Missouri, 74; Monaghan, The Civil War on the Western Border, 169.

issues of the war; and Price had long been a partisan of the pro-slavery views that defeated Benton in 1851 and shaped the Confederacy ten years later.

The clear result of Frank Blair's shrewd political maneuvers and Lyon's prompt military action was the failure of Governor Jackson to take Missouri into the Confederacy. The resources of the state were controlled, in a large measure, by the federal government during the war years. From the point of view of the Union, that was not a blunder.

General Harney, approaching the age of retirement, disinclined to give up his place in the army and incapable of turning against his friends in the Confederacy, could not carry out the sharp protection of Union interests in Missouri that the War Department was obliged to establish. He arranged a meeting with Sterling Price on May 21 in St. Louis and reached an agreement about policy in the conduct of military affairs. Price would undertake to keep the peace in Missouri, using Governor Jackson's militia, and Harney would take no action against him as long as the militia made no aggressive move. Almost immediately, complaints from Union men in all parts of the state began coming to Blair. The peace that Jackson envisioned in Missouri was one in which the resources of the state would be organized for use of the Confederacy. Both sides, in a contest which intelligent men were beginning to recognize as a life-and-death struggle, wanted the manpower and the goods of Missouri. The idea that such a region could remain neutral was attractive to men who were devoted to peace, but Missourians had to make up their minds.

Frank Blair managed the replacement of General Harney by Nathaniel Lyon. Blair carried a letter from President Lincoln with instructions to keep its contents secret until safety demanded their use. The message provided for Harney's removal. Lyon was given the rank of brigadier-general and command of the department formerly under General Harney.

Governor Jackson immediately sought a conference, with the hope of reaching an agreement similar to the Price-Harney arrangement. The Governor, General Price, and Thomas Snead—with immunity from arrest—were to meet with Blair, Lyon, and

Major Horace L. Conant at Planters' House. Lyon would have preferred the arsenal as a meeting place, and so notified the Governor; but Jackson informed him that the conference would take place at Planters' House and no other place.[20]

Blair spoke for the administration at Washington; that is, he began the discussion. But Lyon listened to both sides for a short time with growing impatience and then took the lead by answering first Jackson and then Price. There was no middle ground for a country at war. Missouri would be called upon for materials and men and the federal government would determine the time and the need for soldiers and goods.

Lyon would not agree to such a truce as Harney had made with Price. "Rather than concede to the State of Missouri the right to demand that my Government shall not enlist troops within her limits, or bring troops into the State . . . rather than concede to the State of Missouri . . . the right to dictate to my Government in any matter . . . I would see you, and you, and you, and you, and every man, woman, and child in the State, dead and buried." The terrible earnestness of the man was impressive. The interview was ended, and Lyon well knew what the next step would be.

To the Governor, he said, "This means war. In an hour one of my officers will call for you and conduct you out of my lines."[21]

Governor Jackson and his military commander went to the Pacific Railroad depot, took charge of a locomotive and short train, and hurried away to Jefferson City. On the way, Jackson and Price did not regard it a violation of the terms of the parley to strike military blows. They cut telegraph lines and burned the bridges at the Gasconade and Osage crossings.

A secession army, hastily assembled at Boonville, tried to prepare a reception for Lyon and Blair. An order was sent by Price to General M. M. Parsons at Jefferson City to fall back along the Pacific Railroad to a point near Boonville. Colonel John S. Marmaduke's regiment and a party under General John B. Clark made up the principal strength of Jackson's troops at Boonville. News came

---

[20] Snead, *Fight for Missouri*, 198.

[21] *Ibid.*, 199–200; W. E. Smith, *Blair Family*, II, 51; Brownlee, *Gray Ghosts*, 14, 15; Monaghan, *Civil War*, 135, 139, 140.

to Price that a large Federal force threatened his militia at Lexington. He left Clark in command at Boonville, and hastened to take charge at Lexington. On the way to Lexington he became so ill that he was obliged to stop at his home in Chariton County for a few days' rest. Lacking artillery, Price was not hopeful that he could hold the Missouri River towns against the advancing Union forces.[22]

[22] Snead, *Fight for Missouri*, 203–209; Monaghan, *Civil War*, 142–48.

11

THE CIVIL WAR IN MISSOURI

WILSON'S CREEK

BRIGADIER GENERAL LYON was not acceptable to certain powerful political groups President Lincoln felt obliged to keep in line. Edward Bates considered Lyon too headstrong, too impetuous, to command the Department of the West, and General Scott had little confidence in him. Missouri came under the direct control of General George B. McClellan, and Lyon's position became subordinate. Montgomery Blair tried to have Lyon elevated in rank to major general, but Scott was in a position to persuade the President not to sanction the promotion. The Blairs then took the lead in obtaining John C. Frémont, Benton's son-in-law, for command in Missouri.

At the time Frémont reached St. Louis, July 25, 1861, the Department of the West included Kentucky, Illinois, Missouri, and the area west of the Rocky Mountains. Frémont's leisurely progress to the West from New York had been maddening to Missouri men who waited eagerly for his appearance, but the Blairs remained on good terms with him through another month. By September, however, it had become clear that the political general was not a suitable commander for the Department of the West.

He was deficient in two essential qualities, tact and military skill. The "Pathfinder" was too egotistical for self-effacement. He saw himself as a western Napoleon, ignoring the orders of incompetent superior officers and shaping the war on the basis of his own genius.

He lacked the elastic qualities necessary for give and take; his own first idea became, for him, the only tenable idea. He could not take advice and he could not take orders. His incapacity was not due to his youth—Frémont was forty-eight. In California, at thirty-three, his conduct had been that of an irresponsible boy, and in the interval he had not matured.

Jessie Benton was his mental superior in many respects when she married him at the age of sixteen, twelve years younger than he. She tried hard to mold him into a man, but the material she worked with was mediocre. Perhaps old Thomas Hart Benton understood the situation better than he ever stated in words. He tried to protect John Charles and Jessie; but he balked at lending his support for making the brash young man President of the United States.

In the second essential for waging a successful war in Missouri, Frémont was notably lacking. In military operations, he was second rate. He was prompt in his demands for supplies and correct in his estimate of chaotic conditions in St. Louis, but he was not capable of using the available men and goods and his judgment on conducting the campaign was bad. The total result was disaster on two fronts.[1]

The force with which General Lyon pursued Price and Jackson to Jefferson City numbered about 1,700 men, including the young St. Louis Germans drilled briefly by Frank Blair and Lyon in the "Wide-Awake" bands. The party traveled by river boat to Jefferson City, where they learned that Jackson and the pro-confederate members of the General Assembly had departed.

The Assembly had authorized Jackson to enlist men in the Missouri State Guard and to sell bonds in the amount of $1,000,000 for a military fund. The school fund and all other available cash was also added to the military fund. Jackson appointed nine brigadier

[1] Jared C. Lobdell, "Nathaniel Lyon and the Battle of Wilson's Creek," *Bull. Mo. Hist. Soc.*, Vol. XVII, No. 1 (Oct., 1960), 3–15; Castel, *A Frontier State at War*, 45; W. E. Smith, *Blair Family*, II, 53–89; Snead, *Fight for Missouri*, 210–11; Eaton, *Southern Confederacy*, 38, 39; *Journal of the Illinois State Historical Society*, Vol. II, 46, 47; Stevens, "Lincoln and Missouri," *Mo. Hist. Rev.*, Vol. X, No. 2 (Jan., 1916), 76, 77; Eugene M. Violette, "The Battle of Kirksville," *Mo. Hist. Rev.*, Vol. V, No. 2 (Jan., 1911), 95–97; Monaghan, *Civil War*, 142, 147.

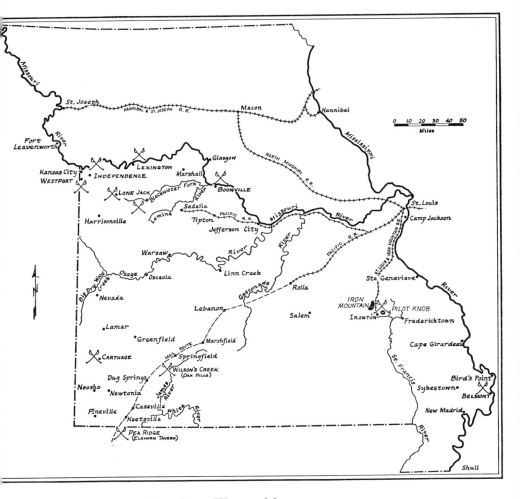

THE CIVIL WAR IN MISSOURI

generals to serve under Sterling Price and proceeded with enlistments. Colonel John S. Marmaduke, a nephew of Governor Jackson and the son of a former Missouri governor, headed a regiment which he had begun enlisting for Missouri when President Lincoln issued his first call for volunteers to serve in the Union Army. Young Marmaduke, a graduate of West Point in 1857, had resigned his commission in the United States Army to enlist his regiment for Southern service in the Missouri State Guard.[2]

Colonel Marmaduke was sent to meet Lyon's force, and the first minor clash took place about six miles east of Boonville on June 18, 1861. The battle lasted several hours before the raw Confederate troops began to fall back. Lyon issued a proclamation in which he stated his intention to observe all the rights of citizens and to protect their property, but to maintain the authority of the United States under war conditions. No man who had taken up arms against the United States would be molested, the proclamation promised, if he would go home and remain there quietly.

State Guard enlistments were checked and Lyon was free to move against Lexington, the principal center of Governor Jackson's military activities. Commanders of Union forces moving into Missouri from Kansas and Iowa were ordered to meet Lyon at Lexington. General Price retreated to the Osage, where he hoped to establish a line of defense. Since he had failed to hold the strategic Missouri River towns, this was an excellent alternative move, except for one important factor: the Union commander had anticipated it.

Evidence of General Lyon's skill in conducting a large-scale campaign is plentiful. He assigned to Colonel John D. Stevenson the task of holding control of the Missouri River across the state. Jefferson City, Boonville, and Lexington were occupied by small garrisons. At this time his immediate superior officer, General McClellan, left Lyon free to conduct his campaign in Missouri. Colonel Samuel R. Curtis with the Second Iowa Infantry had the task of upholding the Union cause north of the Missouri River. McClellan himself was concentrating a force at Cairo, Illinois, under Brigadier General B. M. Prentiss.

[2] Violette, *loc. cit.*, 98–112; Snead, *Fight for Missouri*, 33, 34, 180–84.

Before he moved west from St. Louis, Lyon had sent Franz Sigel, Frederick Salomon, and B. Gratz Brown with their regiments into southwestern Missouri. Command of the party was given to Captain Thomas W. Sweeney, who acted as brigadier general by election. The purpose was two-fold: to check the advance of General Ben McCulloch northward from Arkansas and to cut off General Price and Governor Jackson in the event Lyon was able to dislodge the State Guard from the line of the Osage.[3]

Nine miles northeast of Carthage, on July 5, 1861, Sigel led an infantry force of 950 men, supported by seven pieces of artillery, in an effort to cut off Jackson's march toward the Arkansas line. Approximately 2,600 infantry and artillery men, supported by 1,500 mounted troops, armed with shotguns and rifles, marched with Jackson. In addition, the State Guard included some 2,000 mounted men who were without arms, a motley band of untrained and partly trained citizens—lawmakers, state officials, and county officers—and a wagon train containing hastily gathered miscellaneous goods. The Governor's "army" had welcomed the militiamen from Camp Jackson recently paroled by Lyon at St. Louis.

Sigel challenged Jackson's advance, and the opposing forces engaged in an artillery duel until Jackson ordered an advance on both flanks. Then Sigel began an orderly retreat toward Carthage. He occupied the town and held it until his baggage train was several miles on the way to Springfield. Then he fell back to Sarcoxie, a distance of fifteen miles, where he arrived at three o'clock in the morning. Sigel had lost thirteen killed and thirty-one wounded; Jackson, ten killed and sixty-four wounded. The German recruits from St. Louis in their first experience under enemy fire had justified Sigel's long hours of infantry drilling.

Sterling Price was not present at Carthage. He was on a short journey into Arkansas, where he met General Ben McCulloch and made an earnest plea for his help in the Missouri campaign. Mc-Culloch was reluctant to cross the state line with his soldiers, since the Confederate policy was to avoid invasion of a state that had not seceded. The situation was difficult for a cautious man. Mc-Culloch had stationed his army at Fort Smith, and the governor

3 *Ibid.*, 210–28; Monaghan, *Civil War*, 139–42.

of Arkansas was urging Leroy P. Walker, Confederate secretary of war, to accept the services of 8,000 Arkansas soldiers for the invasion of Missouri; but Walker would not take the responsibility of ordering Southern troops into a state that had not seceded.

General McCulloch received only a suggestion from Secretary Walker that he might proceed to Fort Scott, Kansas, and at that point give some help to the followers of Governor Claiborne Jackson. When Price returned to Missouri, he carried with him a tentative agreement that McCulloch would help Jackson to recover Jefferson City.

McCulloch was relieved when weather conditions brought a change in the plan. Heavy rains in Kansas and western Missouri put the Osage and other streams out of their banks, and, without regret, McCulloch turned back into Arkansas. The Missourians, without uniforms and poorly armed, had not impressed him favorably. His own force was better equipped and better drilled as a unit. He had no way of knowing that Price's followers had among them many experienced soldiers and officers.

Price went into camp on Cowskin Prairie, near the site of present Southwest City in McDonald County. There he began the task of molding an army out of his untrained assortment of followers, using the veterans to train beginners. Fortunately for his military program, he was soon free from the presence of Governor Jackson, David Atchison, and Thomas C. Reynolds—men whose shadows in politics loomed high above their stature as field officers. These three went to Fort Smith by stagecoach, to Memphis by Arkansas River steamer, and on to consult with President Davis in Richmond concerning Missouri's position in the Confederacy.

General Lyon was in command of about 7,000 men at Springfield. On August 1 his scouts reported that Price had come up to Wilson's Creek, where General McCulloch had joined him. In the evening the campfires of the united forces, extending several miles along Wilson Creek and spaced to the width of more than one mile, gave ample evidence of Confederate strength.

To Lyon's repeated pleas for reinforcements from St. Louis, General Frémont finally sent an answer which might be regarded an order. If Lyon could not hold his ground in southwestern Missouri, he was to fall back to St. Louis.

One fact about Lyon is unquestionable—he was a fighter. He was also a clear-headed and experienced officer, skilled in estimating the strength of enemy forces and adept in maneuvering troops. His reports on Confederate numbers sent to Frémont were somewhat exaggerated, but is is possible that he enlarged his guess on McCulloch's army to give urgency to his requests for Union troops. It is certain that Lyon knew he was confronted by an experienced officer with forces roughly 60 per cent greater than his own.[4]

Combining the Southern military parties had been accomplished only with great difficulty. General Price saw clearly the opportunity for a crushing defeat of the Union force, and he was willing to yield to McCulloch in everything, provided only the Confederate officer would join the Missouri troops in an attack on Lyon. "I will put myself under your commond. . . . I must have your answer before dark, for I intend to attack Lyon tomorrow." McCulloch finally agreed, obviously with great reluctance, to Price's plan; or at least to a part of it.

When General Frémont was informed by messenger that Lyon would hold Springfield, whether or not reinforcements arrived, the "Pathfinder" exclaimed, "If he fights, he will do it upon his own responsibility."[5]

The combined forces of McCulloch, Price, and N. B. Pearce were in a position that made withdrawal by Lyon extremely hazardous; furthermore, General William J. Hardee in northern Arkansas was in position to co-operate with General Price. Perhaps the decision of Lyon to attack Price and McCulloch at Wilson's Creek was not as rash as it has been represented. It seems clear that the weakness in the Union defense of Missouri was in the commander at St. Louis rather than the fighting general at Springfield.

Lyon, with a force of about 4,200 men, marched toward Price's left wing late in the afternoon of August 9. Sigel, in command of

---

[4] *Ibid.*, 149–55, 157, 159, 160, 163; Snead, *Fight for Missouri*, 248–67.
[5] *Ibid.*, 253, 257, 264; William E. Connelley, *Quantrill and the Border Wars*, 198.

two regiments of Missouri Volunteers, with two companies of regular cavalry and six pieces of artillery, moved by a different route to attack the Confederate right wing. By one o'clock in the morning, Lyon had passed the Confederate left flank without arousing their sentries, and Sigel was on the march down the Fayetteville road. Lyon rested until dawn and then resumed his maneuver against the Confederate left flank.

The two Union forces were on opposite sides of the Southern army. McCulloch and Price were not aware of the presence of Lyon and Sigel at six o'clock in the morning. Sigel mounted four of his guns on a hill above Tyrell's Creek, left a small party of infantry to support the cannon, and took position with his main force to wait for Lyon's signal to begin the attack. When Totten's battery opened the firing and Sigel's guns signaled their readiness, the Union troops on both sides advanced.

Possibly the decision of Lyon and Sigel to divide their inadequate force for the battle had been an initial blunder. Every major element of Lyon's attacking party was confronted with overwhelming power. For example, Captain J. B. Plummer with a battalion of home guards attacked Herbert's Third Louisiana Regiment in a broomcorn field. The Confederates were in position to rake the Union line as it came into range, and Lyon took elaborate measures to dislodge the Third Louisiana.Plummer's advance was covered by Du Bois's battery, and a small unit of Iowa infantry was stationed in a position to protect the battery. Plummer, Du Bois, and the captain commanding the Iowa infantry unit lacked the power to do the job assigned to them. Colonel James McIntosh, in command of the Second Arkansas Mounted Riflemen and Louisiana troops that outnumbered Plummer's party four to one, was not pushed back in confusion by the impetuous advance of the Missouri troops. McIntosh, an able and experienced officer, coolly estimated the strength of the advancing Union battalion, rallied his men and charged.

Plummer's battalion was routed. Eighty of Lyon's men were killed or captured in this action. DuBois was wounded and carried to the rear. Totten's battery checked the McIntosh charge, but the trend of the battle was determined in this opening clash.

General Lyon was hit but not disabled. The wound was nothing, he said, and galloped to the front. Later he was hit again, in the head, and knocked off his horse. "Nothing but a wound in the head," he told Major S. D. Sturgis, who found him sitting on the ground. A fresh horse was ordered up for the General; but a short time afterward he was shot again, this time fatally, through the heart. Lyon's death occurred about nine o'clock in the morning.

Cannon smoke rolling across the field, together with the rapid maneuvers of cavalry units, caused much confusion. The First Kansas wheeled into line with one of Price's Confederate units. A Kansas soldier, dimly aware that something was wrong, suddenly recognized the former postmaster of Leavenworth, a well-known proslavery man, and shot him. General Sigel, in the path of Herbert's advancing Louisiana Infantry, supposed that they were the First Iowa and ordered his men to hold their fire. Herbert's regiment, supported by Arkansas troops, mowed Sigel's force down by the scores. Sigel himself was one of the few survivors in that sector.

With Lyon's death, command of the Union army was taken by Major S. D. Sturgis. General Sigel fell back to Springfield, and Sturgis ordered Lyon's army to retreat. There is good reason to believe that the Confederate army was badly demoralized and that the commander was about to withdraw from the field when he noticed that Union forces were falling back along all parts of their line. Major John Schofield, who was Lyon's adjutant general, believed that Sturgis missed a great victory only because he did not order a charge instead of falling back. It is quite possible that Lyon, unhurt, could have won. General Sigel's uncertainty and final retreat, the hesitancy of other officers in Lyon's command to take the lead, and possibly a failure of discipline in the Union army—to the extent of some men breaking ranks to plunder as they passed through a part of the Confederate camp—all contributed to the Federal defeat. General William T. Sherman, looking back upon the battle at Wilson's Creek long afterwards, said that Lyon's death brought four years of internal strife to Missouri.

The casualties were heavy on both sides: Federal soldiers, 1,302 killed, wounded, and missing; Confederates, 1,242. Enlistment officers for the armies of the South were kept very busy at Springfield, in Arkansas, and elsewhere after the victory of Price at Wilson's Creek. Even in the Indian country southwest of Missouri, young warriors who had hesitated to join the military forces of either section hastened to join the Confederate units of Stand Watie, Cherokee partisan of the South, or John Jumper, Seminole, or Chilly McIntosh of the Creeks. Choctaws and Chickasaws, wedged in a corner between Arkansas and Texas, had already enlisted in the Confederate ramy commanded by Douglas H. Cooper, their agent.[6]

Sterling Price reached the pinnacle of his military career at Wilson's Creek. His judgment in regard to moving against Lyon's position had proved sound. If McCulloch, adhering rigidly to the policy of avoiding a Confederate invasion of Missouri, had refused to co-operate, probably Price would have attacked Lyon with pro-Confederate Missouri troops alone. Perhaps the Confederate success in the Wilson's Creek campaign caused General Price to be overrated by contemporaries and even by present-day historians. He never again attained such military success as he did on August 10, 1861. It is true that he afterwards captured Colonel Mulligan's force at Lexington, after a hard fight with 15,000 men against Mulligan's 3,000; but at Pea Ridge, and in his campaigns east of the Mississippi, at Pilot Knob in Missouri and at Westport, he was to get repeated practice in the art of orderly retreat. Then, at the end of the war, he was to demonstrate the essential smallness of his attachment to the United States by his attempt to join Maximilian, the Austrian archduke whom Napoleon III had elevated to an imperial throne in Mexico. After the fall of Maximilian, General Price returned to St. Louis, where he died in 1867.[7]

LEXINGTON AND BELMONT

In St. Louis, General Frémont had important decisions to make, not only in regard to troop movements but also on complicated

[6] Lobdell, *loc. cit.*, 7; Williams and Shoemaker, *Missouri*, II, 73–77; Monaghan, *Civil War*, 158–69, 170–81; Snead, *Fight for Missouri*, 268–92; Edwin C. McReynolds, *Oklahoma: A History of the Sooner State* (Norman, 1954), 203–208.

[7] W. E. Smith, *Blair Family*, II, 62, 63; *Dictionary of American Biography*, XV, 216–17.

legal problems that were peculiar to this civil conflict. Constitutional questions regarding the status of slave property, issues that were the subject of much controversy even in time of peace, became doubly difficult under war conditions. Many Northern citizens, with heavy investment in war expense, felt that something should be done, and done immediately, toward eradicating slavery. These people hated the institution and considered its existence the primary cause of the war.

President Lincoln was obliged to deal with the total problem of slavery. The legal status of slave property in the Confederacy and in border states that had not seceded, the limits on executive authority in regard to slave property, and the place of Congress in executive plans for constitutional change—these were some of the questions that the President had in mind. Of greatest immediate importance, perhaps, were two related issues: first, the attitude of slaveholders in states that had not seceded; and second, the attitude of European nations that had abolished slavery toward the war in America.

The owners of slaves in Missouri, Kentucky, Maryland, and Delaware had a direct interest in decisions concerning their chattels. In 1861, the issue of secession in these border states depended upon the confidence of influential slaveholders that their property rights would be respected. In his inaugural address, Lincoln had assured these men that he did not have legal authority and had no desire to interfere with slaves in states where the law gave such property the right of protection. Union support in the border states resulted directly from the President's deliberate handling of the slavery question and his moderate stand on emancipation.

As a diplomatic issue, slavery was closely interwoven with the delicate problem of European intervention in the American Civil War. Emancipation by the President as an exercise of unique war power, applicable only to the slaves of owners who were actively engaged in rebellion, could be made a vital function in diplomacy. Governments abroad would hesitate long before intervening in North America to uphold slave labor. On the other hand, the President and Congress could not defend a shift in Lincoln's publicly expressed view on the legal status of slave property. Confiscation of property, held under state law by loyal citizens, could not be adopted as a policy by the Lincoln administration.

In Missouri, General Frémont met the disorder that followed Wilson's Creek by a declaration of martial law. He defined the territory under the Union army of occupation by an arbitrary line, from Cape Girardeau on the Mississippi River northwestward to Ironton, Rolla, Jefferson City, and thence to Leavenworth, Kansas. The property of persons who had taken up arms against the United States was subject to confiscation, Frémont proclaimed. All slaves belonging to persons in rebellion were declared free. Furthermore, men bearing arms without authority of the Union government were to be executed. This proclamation of the commanding general was not in harmony with the act of Congress dealing with the same general problem that had been signed by the President on August 8, 1861; and Lincoln immediately ordered that the confiscation clause and the provision for freeing slaves be modified. Frémont sulkily suggested that the President make the changes himself—which Lincoln did.

After Wilson's Creek, General McCulloch and N. B. Pearce took their troops back to Arkansas and Price occupied Springfield. On August 25, the Union commander at Warrensburg, Colonel Everett Peabody, sent a message to Frémont reporting that General Price was moving north from Springfield. Thereafter the reports indicated that Price's objective was not Fort Scott, as Peabody had first supposed, but a junction with Governor Claiborne Jackson's troops, particularly the force commanded by Thomas A. Harris on the Missouri River.

After he took command of Lyon's beaten army at Wilson's Creek, Major Sturgis had retreated to Rolla and from that point had transported his troops by railroad to St. Louis. Senator Jim Lane, who posed as commander of the "Army of the Western Border" in Kansas, enlisted men in a brigade which became chiefly a raiding unit. The Third Kansas Regiment under the fanatical Jim Montgomery and the Fourth under Colonel William Weer took part in the activities on the border which turned western Missouri into a region of peculiar violence, bitterness, and hatred.

Strangely, the men most responsible for the attitude of the partisans, Confederate and Union, were two United States senators. Senator David Atchison, who did not have the official sanction of war to cover his atrocities in the Territory of Kansas, was a definite contributor to the spirit of border belligerency. Senator Jim Lane, both before and after the war began, was a promoter of hatred and revenge. William C. Quantrill, "Bloody Bill" Anderson, "Little Archie" Clement, and many others who became notorious on the border during the years of civil strife which followed the attack on Fort Sumter, kept the spirit of "total war" at white heat over a span of years.

Many prominent men on both sides were guilty of inhuman practices and bad judgment in the acceptance of irregular military aid. Even Sterling Price was not above reproach in his attitude toward the use of raiders, and John C. Frémont's bombastic threats were invitations to chaos. The effect, may be seen in the announcement by M. Jeff Thompson, well-known Confederate leader in southeastern Missouri, that for every person executed by Frémont's order, he would "hang, draw, and quarter a minion of . . . Abraham Lincoln."

The President was prompt in measures to control John C. Frémont, but he was strangely vague in regard to Jim Lane, who undoubtedly wielded great political strength. It was the atmosphere of suspicion and hatred that made the region of the western border uncontrollable during the war.[8]

As commander at St. Louis, Frémont ordered Colonel James A. Mulligan to march his regiment of regular soldiers—the "Irish Brigade," the Illinois Twenty-third—from Jefferson City up the Missouri River to Lexington. The town was an important commercial center, particularly in Missouri's trade with Santa Fe. Of greater importance to the Union command was the fact that recruiting in western Missouri could be dominated by occupation of Lexington. Mulligan's effective troops numbered 2,800, while General Price, advancing northward from the scene of his victory at Wilson's Creek, had a potential strength of 15,000, of whom about 10,000 were well armed and ready for front-line service.

[8] Williams and Shoemaker, *Missouri*, II, 77–79; Monaghan, *Civil War*, 182–85; Snead, *Fight for Missouri*, 296; Brownlee, *Gray Ghosts*, 22–41.

From St. Louis, Frémont sent information to Brigadier General John Pope on the Hannibal and St. Joseph Railroad in regard to Price's march toward the Missouri River. Major John M. Schofield had recently joined Pope with a regiment of Lyon's army, and the combined Union forces in northern Missouri could have spared a regiment for the defense of Lexington. Certainly Jim Lane was in a position to divert Price, or to fall upon his advancing army from the rear as the long supply train moved slowly up to Lexington. A Union battalion of 3,300 men occupied a position only one day's march from the commercial center that Colonel Mulligan had been ordered to occupy and hold. General Sturgis with a regiment rested across the river, actually within sound of Mulligan's guns at Lexington.

Between the date of Colonel Peabody's warning and Price's assault upon Lexington, the Union commander in St. Louis had three full weeks, with 20,000 Union soldiers available for Mulligan's reinforcement. Perhaps Pope, Sturgis, and Lane had a share in the negligence, but Frémont alone had the unquestioned authority to send ample aid to the commander of the "Irish Brigade."[9]

Mulligan selected the Masonic College Hill near the banks of the Missouri as the best position for his defense. He prepared earthworks and studied the natural advantages of the hill. In the meantime, he sent messages to St. Louis describing his situation and urging Frémont to make haste in sending reinforcements. Mulligan became aware of the overwhelming strength of Price's army, but decided against withdrawal to the north bank, where he could unite with Sturgis; his orders were to hold Lexington until relief arrived.

The first clash of arms occurred on September 12, when a party of six Union companies came out to meet Price's advance guard. After a short but bloody battle, in which Mulligan's men used gravestones and other solid obstacles as breastworks, the Federals fell back to the Hill and a truce was agreed upon in order to bury the dead.

---

[9] *Ibid.*, 17; Williams and Shoemaker, *Missouri*, II, 79–81; Eaton, *Southern Confederacy*, 156; Monaghan, *Civil War*, 185–87; Ella Lonn, *Foreigners in the Union Army and Navy* (Baton Rouge, 1951), 227–28; Billington, *The Far Western Frontier*, 273–74; Zornow, *Kansas*, 64, 65.

Price was deliberate. His army came up slowly, six more days elapsing before he was in position to open a general bombardment. On September 17 the ammunition wagons came up, and by the following day the attacking force had occupied all the land area around College Hill. Mulligan's steamboat was captured and the possibility of retreat cut off. The qualities in Price which endeared him to the pro-Confederate Missourians and earned the respect of people of all factions, were obvious in his conduct at Lexington. He ordered the evacuation of all private houses in the line of artillery fire. Among the civilians thus removed was the young wife of Colonel Mulligan.

General Price's superior personal qualities did not make him a great commander, however. He had no way of knowing that General Frémont would be so irresponsible as to fail Mulligan in his great need for help. An attack from the rear by any one of four possible Union forces could have given time for assembling a powerful army against Price, whose slow, cautious approach to College Hill was evidence of military mediocrity.

After the bombardment began, a brick hospital standing at a distance of two hundred yards from the Union earthworks became the center of hard fighting. Colonel Mulligan stationed a small party of sharpshooters in the building to pick off Confederate officers and advancing troops. Price's men took the place in a determined charge. A company of Chicago Irish, the "Montgomery Guards," with a party of Germans from the Eleventh Missouri volunteered to recapture the brick building. With heavy losses, they took it, and at similar cost the Confederates occupied it a second time.

The fighting continued through September 18, 19, and 20. The weather was hot. Mulligan's water supply was cut off; men and horses were dying from the heavy exertion and lack of water. The Union commander put before his officers the question of surrender. The Confederates were advancing up the hill behind a moving wall of dampened bales of hemp—an ingenious device which apparently gave effective protection against small arms. The Federal store of ammunition was low. Mulligan's officers voted to surrender, and on September 21 the courageous defense ended.

Price's terms were generous. Officers were allowed to keep their side arms, personal belongings, and horses. When the Union commander surrendered his sword, the General asked for the scabbard. "I threw it away," said Mulligan. With a smile of appreciation for a brave enemy, Price then gave the sword back to its owner. Including Colonels Mulligan, Marshall, Peabody, and White, 2,700 officers and men were captured. Mulligan and Peabody were wounded. Price captured five pieces of artillery, 3,000 muskets, 100 wagons, and 1,000 horses. The small arms were useful in supplying recruits who had joined Price on his way north. He reported, also, that he had recovered $900,000 in money, "of which the bank at this place had been robbed."

On September 26, Governor Claiborne Jackson called a special session of the Missouri legislature to meet at Neosho, in Newton County. In the view of secessionists, this was the "third and special session of the Twenty-First General Assembly." The state convention had deposed Governor Jackson more than two months prior to his call for the special session. Without a quorum in either house this "rump" Assembly passed an act of secession and an act ratifying the constitution of the provisional government of the Confederate States of America. Representative George Graham Vest was the author of the "act of secession" that passed both houses. On October 31 at Cassville, Governor Jackson signed both bills, and the secession government at Richmond accepted Missouri as a member of the Confederacy.

The "General Assembly" adjourned on November 7 at Cassville, following a resolution to assemble again at New Madrid on the first Monday of March, 1862; but the meeting was never held, owing to the fortunes of war.[10]

In recognition of growing strength of the Union military forces in Missouri and perhaps because Frémont was displaying some evidence of decisive energy, Price marched his army out of Lexington just nine days after the Union surrender on College Hill. The victorious troops, who were officially joined to the Confederate

[10] Walter B. Stevens, *Missouri the Center State* (4 vols., St. Louis, 1915), I, 290; Brownlee, *Gray Ghosts*, 38; Monaghan, *Civil War*, 187–94; L. Snyder, "The Capture of Lexington," *Mo. Hist. Rev.*, Vol. VII, No. 1, 1–9; Williams and Shoemaker, *Missouri*, II, 83–86.

Army after the Neosho Assembly completed the gesture of secession, were on their way to join the Southern forces in Arkansas.

Meantime, General Frémont had gathered a force of 20,000 with which he marched toward Lexington. He followed Price south, occupying Springfield early in November. Frémont's plans were ambitious. He would drive the Confederate forces out of northern Arkansas, take Little Rock, and move a great army against New Orleans.

His conduct of the campaign against Price in southwestern Missouri was typical of the "Pathfinder's" military career—full of "tall talk" and devoid of results. The Hungarian cavalry officer, Charles Zagonyi, commanding the "Jessie Frémont Guard," charged a small party of Confederates in a woods at the western border of Springfield. Three days later Frémont entered the town without further opposition. His report of Confederate casualties in their brush with Zagonyi was an absurd exaggeration. Frémont called it a great victory—"atonement for Bull Run, Wilson's Creek, Lexington, and Ball's Bluff."

The government at Washington had made many blunders in its early conduct of military operations; but support for the bombastic son-in-law of Tom Benton was too much to expect, even from Simon Cameron. The ridiculous claims and grandiose schemes of the "Pathfinder," immediately after his failure to reinforce Lyon at Wilson's Creek and Mulligan at Lexington, deceived no one but himself. Frank Blair's charges against Frémont in the Missouri campaign, placed before the President by Adjutant General Lorenzo Thomas, included the following: "neglect of duty, disobedience to orders, gross extravagance, mis-management, mis-application of public funds, and of despotic and tyrannical conduct." After a brief investigation in Missouri by the War Department, the President decided upon Frémont's removal and the appointment of Henry W. Halleck.

The new commander was methodical and thorough, but it must be admitted that he was not brilliant as a planner nor bold as a performer. Williams and Shoemaker characterize Halleck in eight words: "He lacked only military instinct and soldierly intuition." He was easy to caricature and has been generally underestimated;

but no sympathetic treatment can make him a great field commander. His judgment was frequently at fault. When William T. Sherman, on a tour of inspection in Missouri, warned of further danger from General Price, "Old Brains" Halleck was not impressed. In fact, he gave weight to the current report that Sherman was insane.

On the other hand, he made some excellent decisions on personnel, including the appointment of Brigadier General Samuel R. Curtis to conduct the campaign in southwestern Missouri and other appointments that indicated competence. Curtis was a product of West Point, an able engineer, and at fifty-seven he was not soft. He held a seat in Congress as a representative from Iowa.[11]

General Halleck, confronted by an epidemic of pillaging by Confederate sympathizers and theft of livestock by raiders without party allegiance, put martial law into effect. Certain acts of vandalism, including burning railroad bridges, were punishable by death. General John Pope, south of the Missouri River, and Benjamin M. Prentiss, north of the river, put steady pressure upon the bushwhackers, and the worst of the outrages were stopped.

On November 1, U. S. Grant, recently promoted to the rank of brigadier general and stationed at Cairo, Illinois, was directed by General Frémont to stop reinforcement of Price from Kentucky. Grant sent Colonel Oglesby with 3,000 men to pursue M. Jeff Thompson's band of guerrillas in southeastern Missouri, and with a force of 3,100 landed on the western bank of the Mississippi about three miles below Columbus. Without waiting for Frémont's approval, Grant also occupied Paducah, Kentucky, to prevent Leonidas Polk from gaining control of the lower Ohio River.

General Polk had fortified Columbus, erecting earthworks on the bluff above the Mississippi and mounting 142 heavy guns to command the river approaches and the village of Belmont on the Missouri bank. Polk sent General Pillow to Belmont with a force of 2,500 to cut off Colonel Oglesby; and on November 7, Grant attacked Pillow's camp. The skirmish lasted four hours, and the

[11] *Ibid.*, 81; W. E. Smith, *Blair Family*, II, 53–89; W. E. Smith, "The Blairs and Frémont," *Mo. Hist. Rev.*, Vol. XXIII, No. 2 (Jan., 1929); Monaghan, *Civil War*, 198–206; Brownlee, *Gray Ghosts*, 20, 21.

casualties were heavy. Pillow retreated in some disorder, and Grant would have done well to pursue him closely, since Belmont was within range of Polk's big guns across the river.

Unfortunately, however, the raw Federal recruits stopped to plunder Pillow's camp. To bring the soldiers back to their senses, Grant ordered the Confederate tents to be burned; and when Pillow's men were out of range, the guns on the Kentucky shore opened fire upon Belmont. Grant's party fell back hastily and headed for the boats. However, General Pillow rallied his soldiers, reinforced by additional men who crossed from Columbus, and formed a battle line to cut Grant's men off from the river. The Union commander ordered a charge, and Pillow was routed a second time. Grant himself boarded the last steamer that left the shore. Confederate losses were 641 killed and wounded; Union losses, 485.

In his *Memoirs*, Grant answered the critics who later condemned his judgment in the attack on General Pillow at Belmont. If the battle at Belmont had not been fought, he wrote, "Colonel Oglesby would probably have been captured or destroyed, with his 3,000 men. Then I should have been culpable indeed." It should be noted, too, that the main purpose of Grant's commander—prevention of reinforcements for Price's army being sent from Columbus—was accomplished.[12]

THE PEA RIDGE CAMPAIGN

By the end of 1861, Union forces under the direction of "Old Brains" Halleck were in possession of Missouri's war resources except for a precarious Confederate foothold upon an area in the southwest, perhaps less than one-fourth of the state. Urged forward by Halleck, General Samuel R. Curtis marched toward Greene County with a strong force and drove Price out of Spring-

[12] Eaton, *Southern Confederacy*, 34, 35; Williams and Shoemaker, *Missouri*, II, 82, 83; *Dictionary of American Biography*, V, 131 (article on Gen. Jefferson S. Davis, by Thomas M. Spaulding); VII, 492–501 (article on U. S. Grant, by Frederic L. Paxson); *Official Records, War of the Rebellion*, Series I, Vol. III, 273–75, 277–83, 287–89, 304, 310–11, 317; Vol. VIII, 379.

field on February 11, 1862. The Federal advance was made under the handicap of severe winter weather. Curtis was remarkably durable. He had commanded Fort Gibson in the Indian Territory and led the Third Ohio Infantry in Mexico. He was highly rated as an engineer, with experience in road-building, river-control projects, and as city engineer in St. Louis. Two terms in the House of Representatives at Washington had not dulled his grasp of military problems or modified his soldierly bearing. He was one of the best Civil War officers in Missouri, Union or Confederate.

From Cassville, the Confederates retreated across the Arkansas line, through Fayetteville and to Cross Hollows. Curtis sent Colonel Grenville M. Dodge in close pursuit of Price's rear guard. A surprise attack forced Price to retreat to the Boston Mountains, where he set up camp in a strong position. General Curtis went into camp at Cross Hollows.

The Indians who occupied territory west of Arkansas had been forced from their neutral position, generally adopted at the beginning of the war, and had aligned themselves with one or the other of the belligerents. Choctaws and Chickasaws were allied with the Confederacy by the necessity of their geographic position; Creeks, Cherokees, and Seminoles were nominally tribal allies of the Confederacy, but actually were divided into bitter partisan groups. Before the end of the war, the Creeks furnished 1,575 soldiers for the Confederacy and 1,675 for the Union. The Cherokees supplied over 1,600 men for the Confederacy and 2,240 for the Union. The Seminole tribe was almost equally divided, with a majority supporting the Union before the end of the war.[13]

General Ben McCulloch joined his troops to Price's army, and Albert Pike, commanding an Indian force of 3,600—Choctaws and Chickasaws under Douglas Cooper, Cherokees under Stand Watie, a regiment of "pin-Indians" under Colonel John Drew, and 600 Seminoles under Colonel John Jumper—marched his reluctant men

[13] Annie Heloise Abel, The American Indian as a Slaveholder and Secessionist (Cleveland, 1915), 75ff.; M. L. Wardell, A Political History of the Cherokee Nation (Norman, 1938), 125ff.; Angie Debo, The Rise and Fall of the Choctaw Republic (Norman, 1934), 8off.; Edwin C. McReynolds, The Seminoles (Norman, 1957), 289–312; McReynolds, Oklahoma: A History of the Sooner State, 201; Cong. Record, 23 Cong., 1 sess., Sen. Doc. No. 512, III, 149.

across the border into Arkansas. President Jefferson Davis, fully aware of the campaign's importance, sent General Earl Van Dorn, Confederate commander of the Trans-Mississippi Department, to take personal charge of operations in northwestern Arkansas.

Between Sugar Creek and Pea Ridge, General Curtis selected a place to wait for the expected attack. Defenses were prepared, the big guns placed, and battle orders were sent to General Sigel, who had met some opposition from a Confederate cavalry force on his way to Sugar Creek.

General Van Dorn marched his men fifty-five miles in three days, on the way to join Price and McCulloch. The weather was bad, the roads muddy, and the rations not the best. Altogether, the long march took its toll. During the night after his arrival Van Dorn made a furtive flanking movement around the north side of Pea Ridge, to attack the left rear of Curtis' army at Elk Horn Tavern. Van Dorn was an officer of unusual talent, but perhaps his judgment was not the best when he added that night march to the demands upon his exhausted men. Van Dorn's total effective troops numbered 16,000, while Curtis had under his command about 12,000 men.[14]

The Confederate commander was handicapped by serious illness during the battle; he had not fully recovered after a fall from his horse on the way to Pea Ridge, and he attempted to maneuver his forces while riding in an ambulance. Perhaps Brigadier General James McIntosh could have won this engagement, using the available Confederate troops; but he was outranked by McCulloch and Price, neither one of whom was the equal of General Curtis. The hardest fighting of the three-day battle (March 6, 7, and 8, 1862) took place as Van Dorn completed his costly flanking movement only to find Curtis facing him on Pea Ridge.

Generals Ben McCulloch and James McIntosh were killed, and the sectors under their command were left to Albert Pike, who was not an effective leader of troops. General William Y. Slack was killed. Colonel McCulloch, nephew of the General, and Captain Churchill Clark, son of Major Meriwether Clark and grandson of

14 Williams and Shoemaker, *Missouri*, II, 88, 89; *Official Records*, Series I, Vol. VIII, 190, 191, 748–49.

William Clark, were among the Confederate dead. Colonel Louis Herbert of the Third Louisiana Rifles was captured. General Price was struck in the arm by a musket ball but refused to retire from the field.

One of Curtis' "political" officers who distinguished himself was Colonel John S. Phelps of Springfield, Missouri. The son of a former Connecticut congressman and a member of the House of Representatives himself for eighteen years, Phelps gave a definite partisan flavor to his command of the Springfield regiment. He was a strong Union Democrat and would have been acceptable to the Lincoln government if he had been devoid of military talent. Fortunately, he had the instincts of a soldier. His Union Missourians stopped a determined charge by Price's cavalry, and their stand enabled General Carr, who had been wounded, to hold his ground until he was relieved by Brigadier General Alexander S. Asboth, the Hungarian refugee who was in the process of becoming a military legend.

The Springfield regiment lost 175 men killed or wounded, and Colonel Phelps had three horses shot from under him. At home, his wife turned their Springfield residence into an army hospital, and probably the service of Colonel Phelps lost nothing in the telling when his grateful men gave their version of his heroism. Later, Congress voted $20,000 to Mrs. Mary Whitney Phelps, which she used to establish an orphanage for the children of Union and Confederate soldiers.

The Union army was vastly superior to the Confederate in artillery fire. In the late stages of the battle, General Curtis ordered a charge, and the Union cavalry swept everything before it. One Confederate column under Captain Jo Shelby withdrew in good order to the north. Stand Watie's Cherokees retreated to the west, under effective military discipline until they passed the Arkansas border, when their leader ordered them to scatter to their homes. On March 11, three days after the battle at Pea Ridge, General Van Dorn had collected 3,000 of his defeated troops. Both Price and Van Dorn were transferred to Albert Sidney Johnston's army east of the Mississippi.

General Curtis gave 1,351 as the total number of Union casualties at Pea Ridge—killed, wounded, and missing in action. Van Dorn reported about 1,000 killed and wounded and 300 captured. The figures are incomplete, for Curtis' army took more than 700 prisoners. Also, because of irregular recruiting among the Indians, their indifference to the issues of the war, and their inclination to withdraw from a losing cause in which they were not directly concerned, Indian casualties cannot be determined accurately. Certainly the battle of Pea Ridge was one of the bloodiest of the war on the western border, and one of the most decisive. With the brief exception of General Price's later raid into Missouri, that state was dominated by the Union during the rest of the war. Kansas, the Indian country, and Arkansas also were largely subject to the uses of Lincoln's government.[15]

FINAL PHASES OF THE WAR

Confederate recruiting in Missouri was always stimulated by success on the battlefield. After the Confederate failure at Pea Ridge, however, enlistments in the Southern armies were promoted by the return of many veteran officers from Price's army to their homes in Missouri. It has been said, and repeated many times even by historians of the present generation, that men were eager to enlist because they were shocked by the brutality of Halleck's military occupation, by excessive demands, suppression of free speech, assessments upon Southern sympathizers, and similar unreasonable activities on the part of Federal officials.

It cannot be denied, certainly, that small-minded men, assigned to important work for the Union government in a most difficult situation, sometimes abused their power. That they should do so was inevitable in the military occupation of a region inhabited by partisans of both sides in a desperate struggle for control of vital resources. It may be supposed, with reason, that followers of the North and of the South were about equal in percentages of average men, villains, and great men who could rise above the passions of

---

15 *Ibid.*, 192, 193, 195–206; *Dictionary of American Biography*, IV, 619–20 (article on Samuel Ryan Curtis, by Ruth A. Gallaher); XIV, 530 (article on John Smith Phelps, by H. Edward Nettles); Monaghan, *Civil War*, 239–51.

conflict. Men finally enlisted as soldiers, after some delay, because the climate of Missouri was not conducive to neutrality; but it is to be doubted that strong Union supporters enlisted in the Confederate Army because of Halleck's suppression of the people's rights. War necessarily causes a great transformation in the rights of citizens. Southern men resented suppression of free speech by Union military authority because it was a restriction upon freedom to speak for the South.

In northeastern Missouri, Colonel John McNeil undertook to stop Confederate recruiting by Colonel Joseph C. Porter. At Kirksville the Southern force, swelled to 2,000 by poorly armed recruits, made a stand. After heavy artillery fire, McNeil's regular soldiers routed the Confederates and drove them across the Chariton River. McNeil lost ten killed and forty-two wounded, while Confederate losses were about sixty killed and eighty wounded.

Later, on August 11, 1862, Colonel Odon Guitar came upon a party of Porter's men at a ferry crossing on the Grand River in Carroll County. Guitar attacked, and in their haste to cross the river many of the Confederates abandoned their guns and other impediments to swimming.

General John T. Hughes surprised and defeated a Union force of 450 at Independence, finally capturing all who were not killed. The Union recruits fought with great vigor before they finally surrendered, and many men on both sides were killed or wounded. General Hughes was among the dead.

Five days later, three Confederate battalions under Colonels Upton Hays, Gideon Thompson, and John T. Coffee routed Major Emory Foster's state militia unit at Lone Jack, south of Westport Landing. Foster was wounded and captured.

On September 25, 1862, ten Confederate prisoners were executed at Macon, on the Hannibal and St. Joseph Railroad, by order of Union military authority. The charges against the ten were treason, perjury, and murder. One of the condemned men, actually just a boy of twenty, sent to General Prentiss the following appeal: "general for god sake spare my life for i am a boy i was perswaded ... and forse ... i wood ben fighting for the Union if it had [not] been for others." Signed, "J. A. Wysong."

At Palmyra, General McNeil ordered the execution of ten Confederate prisoners after Colonel Joseph C. Porter had failed to release or to report on a Union citizen seized in a raid on the town. The assumption was that Porter's soldiers had killed their prisoner, an elderly man who had made himself hated by the Confederates in his zeal for service to the Federal government. McNeil received petitions urging retraction of the order to execute the ten men; but he refused, and the "massacre of Palmyra" took place on October 18.

In December, 1862, General Blunt defeated the combined Southern forces of General Hindman and John S. Marmaduke at Cane Hill, near Fayetteville, Arkansas. A month later, Marmaduke attacked General E. B. Brown at Springfield. The Confederates had the advantage of superior numbers, but Brown's veteran troops held a strong position and were able to beat off two attacks. Effective artillery fire was the decisive factor. Marmaduke was beaten again at Cape Girardeau on April 26, 1863, by General McNeil; and in August, Colonel R. G. Woodson of the Missouri State Militia captured General M. Jeff Thompson, the Confederate "Swamp Fox," and his entire band at Pocahontas, Arkansas. Thompson and the officers of his command were taken to St. Louis and confined in the Gratiot Prison.[16]

During 1863, many outrages were committed by Confederate and Union men on the western border of Missouri under the guise of military action. Worst of the Federal raiders in that year, perhaps, were Senator Jim Lane and Charles R. "Doc" Jennison. Frequent atrocities of these leaders had been reported to the War Department, but the counterclaims by their supporters made the problem of dealing with them somewhat complicated. Their political influence, particularly Lane's, was much needed by the administration.

Most widely known of the Confederate raiders on the border was William C. Quantrill. Like Jim Lane and old John Brown, Quantrill was mentally unbalanced—as were many partisans on both sides of the conflict, particularly after harrowing combat ex-

[16] *Official Records*, Series I, Vol. XIII, 119–28; Brownlee, *Gray Ghosts*, 97–99; Williams and Shoemaker, *Missouri*, II, 90–95; Monaghan, *Civil War*, 252–56.

periences. There is some evidence that Quantrill was willing to take either side of the sectional war. There is ample evidence that high-ranking military officers of the Confederacy refused, on occasion, to accept his services; but he held military commissions under the Jefferson Davis administration. Among his followers, "Bloody Bill" Anderson, "Little Archie" Clement, William Gregg, David Pool, and others were notorious in the violence and confusion on the border.[17]

General John M. Schofield replaced General Curtis as head of the Department of Missouri in May, 1863. The new commander gave particular attention to the Confederate guerrillas, placing Brigadier General Thomas Ewing, Jr., in charge of the District of the Border. The area of Ewing's command included Jackson, Cass, Bates, St. Clair, Henry, Johnson, and LaFayette counties, south of the river in western Missouri, and the adjacent portions of Kansas.

South of the District of the Border was the District of the Frontier, which was assigned to Brigadier General James G. Blunt, a physician who was developed by two years of border military service into an effective fighting commander. Blunt's reputation suffered because of his personal hostility to General Schofield and the necessity of his political alliance with Jim Lane. There were groundless rumors of excesses in Blunt's private life, the vague but expanding gossip that was inevitable in the case of an army man who was known as an abolitionist. The insanity which clouded Blunt's later years has been seized upon by unthinking critics as proof of his dissolute private life. In fact, four years of savage warfare provided ample basis for his mental instability three decades later.

Thomas Ewing, Jr., new commander of the District of the Border, was a young attorney who had practiced law at Leavenworth, Kansas, in partnership with his brother, Hugh Boyle Ewing, and

[17] *Official Records*, Series I, Vol. XIII, 33, 286–87; Vol. XXII, Part I, 55; Vol. XXXIV, Part II, 957. William E. Connelley's *Quantrill and the Border Wars* is the most complete and accurate account of Quantrill's activities. The guerrilla warfare is treated in a lively fashion and with scholarly attention to facts, by Richard S. Brownlee in *Gray Ghosts of the Confederacy*, cited above.

his brother-in-law, William Tecumseh Sherman. Young Ewing's father was an Ohio Whig who had held various offices before the Civil War—United States senator, secretary of the treasury, and secretary of the interior. Thomas Ewing, Jr., was the first chief justice of the Kansas Supreme Court in 1861. He resigned to enlist men for the Eleventh Kansas Volunteers and saw active service in Arkansas. He was advanced to the rank of brigadier general and assigned to command the District of the Border in June, 1863.

On August 14, women prisoners of war belonging to the families of Confederate guerrilla leaders were the victims of a prison tragedy which had far-reaching effects. The women had been involved, as relatives of Quantrill's men, in carrying information, supplying horses, guns, and supplies, and giving aid and comfort to these irregular fighters, who hid behind the guise of civilian garb to carry on brutal and bloody warfare against their neighbors and small parties of soldiers. Murder from ambush was their favorite technique, and they were a constant menace to citizens who supported the Federal government.

The building in which women prisoners were kept in Kansas City was a dilapidated three-story structure on Grand Avenue, between Fourteenth and Fifteenth streets. The building collapsed on August 14, killing four of the women prisoners and injuring others. One of "Bloody Bill" Anderson's sisters was killed and another, only sixteen years old, seriously injured. Since most of Bill's vicious killings came after this accident, they are often attributed to his desire for revenge. Before the war, however, he had been involved in such serious crimes as robbery with firearms with his father and brother, at no great distance from his home. Bill Anderson—like the savage, illiterate killer George Todd and the evil assassin Quantrill—embarked early upon a criminal career and conditions on the border gave him opportunity for full development.

General Ewing's "Order Number Ten" on August 18, 1863, directed the arrest of all men and all women "not heads of families" who gave assistance to the irregular Confederate fighters. Wives and children of known guerrillas were to be warned to get out of Missouri and the District of the Border. Failure to comply with the request would be followed by their removal, "with their clothes and such . . . provisions as may be worth removing."[18]

Quantrill and his "cabinet" had often considered a raid on Lawrence, and the border events after General Ewing's appointment renewed their interest in the project. On August 19, 1863, the band of approximately 300 bushwhackers started west from their rendezvous on Blackwater Creek, south of Lexington. They crossed the Kansas line at a point near the village of Aubry, after being joined by two other parties—about 100 Confederate recruits under Colonel John D. Holt, and some 50 bushwhackers from the Osage area. The total number of Quantrill's command was thus about 450, the largest guerrilla force that operated in the District of the Border.[19]

The Quantrill raiders reached Lawrence at dawn on August 21. On the march through eastern Kansas they had killed ten of their guides, whom they identified as Union men. George Todd, desiring to kill a farmer on the outskirts of town without sounding an alarm, simply beat him to death with a musket. The town was caught by surprise, and the bushwhackers rode through the streets shooting down citizens in their yards or doorways and pushing into houses to continue the slaughter. Seventeen recruits in the camp of the Second Kansas Colored Regiment were killed, and Lieutenant S. S. Snyder of the same unit was shot to death as he milked a cow in his yard. The bushwhackers broke into saloons, and many of them drank freely as they continued the massacre of unarmed citizens. "Kill every man big enough to carry a gun," Quantrill had ordered; and the drunken estimates of ability to lift a weapon were probably somewhat blurred, for young children were among the 150 dead.

[18] *Official Records*, Series I, Vol. XIII, 127, 128; *Dictionary of American Biography*, VI, 237–38 (articles on Thomas Ewing and Thomas Ewing, Jr., by Reginald C. McGrane); XVII, 93–97 (article on William T. Sherman, by Oliver L. Spaulding, Jr.); Castel, *Frontier State at War*, 82, 97–98, 111, 126–27, 154–58; Brownlee, *Gray Ghosts*, 98, 99, 115, 119–22, 134. See also *History of Vernon County, Missouri* (St. Louis, 1887).

[19] Stand Watie commanded larger parties in the Indian Territory, using the same technique as the Missouri guerrillas, scattering to avoid contact with a strong Union force. *Official Records*, Series I, Vol. XXII, Part I, 580–83; McReynolds, *Oklahoma*, 216.

The business district of Lawrence was attacked, and a total of 185 buildings were burned—some with fugitives in them. The three newspapers were destroyed—buildings wrecked and equipment broken up. Colonel John Holt took no personal part in the massacre and apparently made some effort to control his recruits, but soldierly discipline and restraint were unpopular in Quantrill's command that day. Larkin Skaggs was the one raider who was killed. Too drunk to ride, he remained behind and was shot and mutilated by a furious mob.

Senator Jim Lane was prevented from taking "military" revenge upon Missouri only by the prompt and decisive orders of General Ewing. Lane was instrumental, however, in the issue of "Order Number Eleven," the drastic measure which he helped Ewing draft. It was sent out from headquarters at Kansas City on August 25, 1863, just four days after the sack of Lawrence. By its terms, all residents of Jackson, Cass, and Bates counties and the northern half of Vernon county, with certain exceptions, were ordered to leave their homes. The exceptions were persons living within a mile of military posts that were listed in order: Independence, Hickman's Mills, Pleasant Hill, Harrisonville, Kansas City, and Westport. Persons who could give satisfactory evidence of their loyalty to the United States were permitted to move to any military station within the district or to any part of Kansas other than counties on the eastern boundary. All others were required to remove beyond the limits of the District of the Border.

No phase of the war in the West has been less understood than "Order Number Eleven." Enforcement of Ewing's removal order became the subject of a well-known painting by George Caleb Bingham. The grief and suffering of the exiles, the dejection of people suddenly torn from their homes by crude enforcers of the hard decree, the tragedy and despair of war are all presented in one flash by the skill of the artist. The factors not included are as important for a complete understanding of the order as the persons and action of the great painting. The nights of terror in which other citizens on the opposite side from Bingham's fugitives, dragged from their houses and murdered for their stand in favor of the Union, cannot be pictured. Raids of the bushwhackers, rendering futile the military control of garrisoned towns and making the war an endless nightmare of confusion and grief cannot be shown. Personal enmity between the painter and General Ewing may account for the artist's choice of his subject. The dramatic incident which brought sudden death to women prisoners in Kansas City would have been a war theme of great interest, perhaps; but Bingham was not the man to use that one since his wife was the owner of the wretched building which collapsed and killed the Rebel women.

General Ewing's position may be stated briefly. The civilian population of the border counties encompassed some thousands of persons who were eager to fight for the Confederacy. Although they did not, ordinarily, wear uniforms and fight in regular military units, many were bold and resourceful; and they were skilled in taking advantage of the credulity and other weaknesses of officers who were given the job of keeping them in order. Without sufficient cavalry to police the country roads and backwoods communities, unable to descend suddenly upon remote places that were used for refuge by the bushwhackers, the commander could not bring the District under control as long as Southern sympathizers lived unmolested in their homes and worked secretly with the guerrilla bands.

The women spies, scouts, and auxiliaries must have known that they were engaging in warlike acts when they aided Quantrill, Anderson, Todd, and other wholesale killers. If the bushwhackers and their families, and the friends who aided them, expected to engage in war without suffering any of its penalties, "Order Number Eleven" must have been a shock. In any event, it was war at its worst.

Perhaps a considerable share of the blame should rest with the Confederate officers who made use of irregular soldiers. Certainly the guerrilla chiefs who permitted their women to take an active part in the dangerous game of war were culpable. The justification for General Price and other officers who accepted the aid of bushwhackers is that they were trying desperately to win a war, and they welcomed aid from any quarter. The same reasoning explains Ewing's harsh order on the opposite side.

The leaders of irregular Confederate troops were, in many cases, poor, misguided youths whose ignorance made it impossible for them to solve rationally the complicated problems of loyalty which confronted them. Once in the struggle, they gave to it the courage, effectiveness, and tough persistence of frontier fighters; but their heroism, gallantry, and devotion to their cause have been over-emphasized by sentimentalists for nearly a century.[20]

The war in 1864 was given unique character by the daring raid of Sterling Price into Missouri. Earlier raids into the region north of 36 degrees, 30 minutes had been turned back. Probably Douglas H. Cooper planned a drive toward Fort Scott and Kansas City in the fall of 1862, before General Blunt met his army at Fort Wayne and changed the direction of its movement from north to south. A year later Colonel Jo Shelby with a force of 2,500 retreated after plundering Boonville.

General Price, as Confederate commander of the District of Arkansas, took full advantage of Federal troop withdrawals to the east. The success of Quantrill and other leaders of guerrillas in striking spectacular blows on the Missouri border and afterwards eluding Union pursuit, led Price to believe that invasion of the state by a well-organized army would result in its recovery for the Confederacy.

On September 19, 1864, Price moved toward Missouri with an army of twelve thousand mounted veterans, supported by fourteen pieces of artillery. General William S. Rosecrans, who had replaced John M. Schofield as Union commander at St. Louis on January 30, 1864, was expecting the invasion and had planned a defense with such forces as he had in the state. General Curtis, victor over Van Dorn, McCulloch, and Price at Pea Ridge, had been named commander of the new Department of Kansas and Thomas Ewing transferred to St. Louis, where he came under the command of Rosecrans.

Jo Shelby and John S. Marmaduke rode north with Price in command of separate units, and General James Fagan led a third column composed of Arkansas troops.

[20] Brownlee, *Gray Ghosts*, 110–27; Castel, *Frontier State at War*, 124–41; Williams and Shoemaker, *Missouri*, II, 96, 97.

General Price approved the device of using guerrilla troops in northern Missouri to divert the attention and resources of Rosecrans from the invasion. In fact, before the march to Missouri began, he sent Captain John Chestnut to confer with Quantrill, Bill Anderson, and George Todd. The plan was to keep the 17,000 available Union troops busy in northern Missouri, thus clearing the way for Price's march toward St. Louis. The outbreak of guerrilla activities north of the Missouri River supports the evidence of Confederate officers, including Shelby's adjutant, Major John M. Edwards, who reported Price's contacts with Quantrill and "Bloody Bill" Anderson.

On September 24, General Rosecrans received word that Price's army was south of Pilot Knob. The Union commander ordered Tom Ewing to learn Price's objective and to delay any movement toward St. Louis. Ewing went to Pilot Knob, the terminus of the St. Louis and Iron Mountain Railroad, and with the one thousand men assigned to his command occupied a strong position that had previously been selected and fortified. The little force worked diligently on the defenses of their stronghold, Fort Davidson—building up the earthworks and placing the big guns to cover the pass through which Price's army would move. Within twenty-four hours after Ewing's arrival the Confederates attacked, under Price, Fagan, and Marmaduke.

Union guns took a heavy toll as Price's cavalry came within range and advanced toward Fort Davidson. The Confederates bombarded Ewing's position, and the cavalry, dismounted, charged the breastworks again and again. Through a day of slaughter the veteran Union troops stubbornly held their position, using their big guns effectively and beating off charges of dismounted dragoons with small arms at point-blank range. Before dark Ewing became aware that fresh troops were arriving to bolster Price's attack and that the Confederates were hauling artillery pieces to high ground, from which it would be possible to drop shells into Fort Davidson. By effective use of earthworks and superior artillery, General Ewing's little party had held at bay a force that outnumbered them six or seven times. With depleted strength and diminishing ammunition, however, the course of another day's battle could easily be predicted. Ewing decided to withdraw during the night.

The Confederates had wrecked the track of the St. Louis and Iron Mountain, effectively cutting off use of the locomotives for Federal reinforcements or for escape. General Ewing spiked his guns, destroyed his ammunition and other supplies that could not be readily carried away, and slipped out of Fort Davidson during the night. Explosion of the Union magazine was the first intimation Price had of the retreat. A Confederate cavalry force, hastily organized, followed and attacked Ewing's rear guard, but the main body of Union troops beat off the pursuers and marched to Rolla.

A message sent from St. Louis to General Ewing during the retreat from Pilot Knob serves as a connecting link between the tragic business of war and the normal affairs of life, even in the case of commanders. The U. S. military telegraph message was as follows: "Gen'l Ewing *via* Mooney's Bridge. You've got Twins." Signed, "G. V. DuBois, Col. and Chf. of staff."[21]

The plan of General Price's raid in the swing through southern Missouri toward St. Louis was not centered upon a single objective other than inflicting damage upon the cause of the Union. Probably he was confident that his little army could take St. Louis until he met the unexpected resistance of Ewing's stand at Pilot Knob. He had estimated carefully the withdrawal of Union soldiers to fight in the campaigns of the East.

Withdrawal of Missouri troops for service in Virginia, Georgia, and Tennessee had left Rosecrans a hard task in dealing with irregular Confederate forces. Price had counted heavily upon the diverting actions of Quantrill, Anderson, and Todd to keep the limited Federal army of Missouri occupied. He had not estimated correctly, however, the defensive power of Ewing's artillery in the narrow passage at Pilot Knob or the persistence and skill of Union

---

21 Papers of the Ewing Family, Library of Congress, Manuscript Division; *Official Records*, Series I, Vol. XLI, Part I, 445–52, 625–40; Part II, 238–40, 505, 786, 838, 855, 892; Brownlee, *Gray Ghosts*, 181, 182; Castel, *Frontier State at War*, 184–202; Williams and Shoemaker, *Missouri*, II, 103–105.

officers in preparing defenses. The action at Pilot Knob changed Price's immediate objective from St. Louis to Jefferson City.[22]

Union military forces under John McNeil, by this time a brigadier general, in a strong position at Jefferson City with reinforcements under Brigadier General John B. Sanborn, made Price's prospect for an attack at that point very dim. A series of engagements, beginning at the capital and culminating in the battle of Westport, brought an end to the campaign.

As Price and his army moved west, General Curtis and James Blunt in northwestern Missouri prepared to receive them. Kansas militia, supported by a large part of the new state's newspapers, assumed that the campaign was over and demanded release from military service. On October 16, at Hickman Mills, Lieutenant Colonel James D. Snoddy sent a request to General Blunt that his militia regiment be permitted to return to Linn County. Blunt refused, and Snoddy attempted to march the troops home on his own authority. Blunt stopped the mutiny and placed under arrest the officers most responsible for it—including Brigadier General William H. Fishback. Before the showdown battle with Price at Westport, however, there were many desertions from the militia along the Kansas border.

A Union division under General Blunt moved east to Lexington, where Price's advance guard under Joseph O. Shelby met them. Blunt retreated toward Independence, and Price followed him.

At the crossing of Little Blue, nine miles east of Independence, Blunt assigned to Colonel Thomas Moonlight the task of delaying Price's advance. Probably Blunt would have begun the main contest here if General Curtis had not ordered him to fall back to a point nearer the Kansas border. This order was given because the Kansas militia resented any movement that would take them more than a few miles beyond the state line.

General Rosecrans sent the cavalry division of Alfred Pleasonton in pursuit of Price's army. At Boonville, Price was joined by "Bloody Bill" Anderson with more than 1,200 men, including many

[22] *Official Records*, Series I, Vol. XXXIV, Part IV, 523; Brownlee, *Gray Ghosts*, 221–22; Williams and Shoemaker, *Missouri*, II, 104; Zornow, *Kansas*, 116–17; Castel, *Frontier State at War*, 185–86.

veteran bushwhackers. The Confederate general ordered Quantrill to operate along the Hannibal and St. Joseph Railroad and assigned to Anderson the task of destroying the North Missouri Railroad.

General Curtis established his battle line on Big Blue, with some protection in the form of trenches and breastworks. He hoped to stop Price's army at that line and squeeze the Confederates by means of Pleasonton's advance. On October 22, General Shelby came up to this line and broke through it. He crossed the river, pushed Jennison's brigade back, and turned Curtis' right flank. General Curtis rallied his tired soldiers, and as darkness came on, he was able to stop Shelby's advance.

Pleasonton on the night of October 21 had learned that Curtis would make a stand on Big Blue. The next afternoon his cavalry division reached Independence and there attacked Price's rear guard, commanded by John S. Marmaduke. The bushwhacker George Todd was killed in the running fight as Marmaduke fell back to Big Blue. General Price ordered Shelby to join Marmaduke. At Byram's Ford on Big Blue, Pleasonton drove Marmaduke back, and Shelby, attempting to carry out Price's order, was savagely attacked by Curtis and Blunt.

Marmaduke cut his way through the Union lines and retreated south. Ten miles out of Westport, Curtis, Blunt, and Pleasonton met in a farmhouse for a conference. Price's entire army was in flight some five miles farther south near the Kansas border. As Curtis moved south, his advance guard found evidence from time to time of atrocities committed by Price's auxiliaries, the bushwhackers serving under General Shelby. At Trading Post, Kansas, for example, the body of a preacher, too old for military service, was found lying near his burned house. His family, stunned by the sudden descent of the war upon their home, were huddled together near the scene of disaster.[23]

[23] Quoted by Castel, *Frontier State at War*, 186–96; *Official Records*, Series I, Vol. XLI, Part I, 371–79; Part IV, 22–23, 57–58, 97, 190, 194, 206, 354; Brownlee, *Gray Ghosts*, 323–31; Williams and Shoemaker, *Missouri*, II, 105–109; Zornow, *Kansas*, 116–17; Wiley Britton, *The Civil War on the Border* (2 vols., N.Y., 1890–99), II, 437, 446–49, 544–45; Connelley, *Quantrill and the Border Wars*, 435–50, 451–53, 454–59; Borland, "General Jo O. Shelby," *Mo. Hist. Rev.*, Vol. VII, No. 1 (Oct., 1912), 2–19.

General Blunt believed that a rapid flanking movement, to stop Price's retreat and force him into a general engagement, would result in the capture of his entire army; but Curtis vetoed the suggestion. Instead of a quick move through Kansas to get in front of Price, the Union commander brought up Pleasonton's cavalry division to harrass the Confederate rear guard. Price made a brief stand on the Marais des Cygnes and then resumed his flight toward the Arkansas River. At Mine Creek, Kansas, the Confederate baggage train had trouble in the ford, and Price ordered Fagan and Marmaduke to check the Federal advance.

As the two Confederate divisions were wheeling into position, Pleasonton's cavalry charged into them. Shelby came to Marmaduke's relief and probably saved his division from being completely wiped out. As it was, Pleasonton captured General Marmaduke and 500 of his men. Because of his men's exhaustion, Pleasonton was forced to withdraw from the pursuit at this time.

General Blunt, impatient to come into contact with the retreating Confederates, moved with a party of 1,000 men too far in advance of the main Union army and caught up with Shelby at Newtonia. Blunt attacked and Shelby quickly saw his advantage. The Confederates turned suddenly upon Blunt's little force, which was hard pressed to hold its position until reinforcements hurried forward. John B. Sanborn joined Blunt with a brigade of fresh troops, and Price retreated again. General Grant sent orders for the Federal troops to follow Price to the Arkansas River. Curtis rested until he was rejoined by 1,800 of Pleasonton's soldiers and resumed the pursuit.

General Price's raid and the retreat from Westport ended the war in Missouri. Curtis reached the Arkansas River on November 8, 1864. Five months later Lee surrendered at Appomattox, and within another month President Jefferson Davis of the Southern Confederacy was a prisoner.

Missouri, with greater population and wealth than any other state west of the Mississippi River, sent approximately 60 per cent of her men of military age into the armed services. Over 30,000, in addition to irregular fighters who were not enlisted, fought under the Confederate flag; and 109,000 Missourians were enrolled in the Union armies. The percentage of enlistments relative to total population was among the highest of the states, and the casualties were tragically large. Over 14,000 Missourians in the Union Army and 4,000 Confederates were killed in battle.[24]

Perhaps in no other slave state that did not secede was support for the Confederacy so determined and so costly in lives and property as in Missouri. Military tradition, particularly from the Mexican War, gave Missourians a strong impulse toward participation in the greatest conflict of all time in the Western Hemisphere. The political fight for control of Kansas, characterized by violence and bitterness, had made Missourians excessively partisan.

[24] Castel, *Frontier State at War*, 197–99; Williams and Shoemaker, *Missouri*, II, 109–10.

⁓⊰ **12** ⊱⁓

ADJUSTMENT TO REVOLUTION

THE PROVISIONAL GOVERNMENT, 1861–65

THE DECADE of the American Civil War was a period of basic change in government—a revolution. The war itself was the most spectacular phase of the revolution, but the changes in the Constitution were fundamental; the federal Republic was transformed in the direction of national authority. In the amending of the Constitution, a semblance of legal forms was maintained; but abnormal conditions of war and large-scale disorder made possible the changes.

The Union was preserved, but the several states emerged from the great war with new restrictions on their authority, and the people came through the contest with a new concept of national unity. Some of the changes were simply transfer of power to the nation—such as the abolition of slavery and all forms of involuntary servitude by the Thirteenth Amendment to the Constitution. Others were new developments which resulted in gradual, almost imperceptible growth of national authority. Pacific railroad legislation, speeded by secession of the Southern states, was directly connected with settlement of the Great West—and less directly the cause of increased nationalism.

The Civil War amendments, XIII, XIV, and XV, were inseparably connected with Union victory on the battlefields. Under normal conditions of peace between the North and South, neither of the three amendments could have been adopted during the decade following 1860. The possibilities of emancipation by action of the border states are interesting as a field of speculation, and many historians have declared that the war could have been avoided. In fact, most wars could have been avoided if the leaders and people had shown enough wisdom. But to single out the American Civil War as a needless conflict, to the exclusion of other wars, is to demonstrate a shallow concept of history and a failure to grasp the trends in American politics from 1820 to 1860. The fundamental changes in basic law were inevitable, and their achievement under normal conditions impossible.

While the Congress and President of the United States were struggling with the issues of reconstruction in the former Confederate states, Missouri was working out within its borders a series of related problems. At Washington, settlement was complicated on one side by the vested interests of some Northern men who were willing to extend the period of abnormal wartime government, and on the other side by the determination of some Southern leaders to defeat the achievements of the costly war. The conflict between President Johnson and the Fortieth Congress over the process of reconstruction did not bring order out of the confusion.

In Missouri, hatred sprang from four years of desperate warfare preceded by an equal period of border strife in which killing became common and the bitterness of armed conflict was intensified by personal acquaintance. Here, there was no problem of regaining the state's place in Congress. Frank Blair and Nathaniel Lyon had held Missouri in the Union during the short period of greatest danger in 1861, when the General Assembly and Governor Jackson were ready to join the Confederacy.

The convention of 1861, elected on February 18 to consider the question of secession, was guided by a most important restriction. Section ten of the statute provided: "No act, or ordinance, or resolution of said convention shall be deemed to be valid to change . . . the political relations of this state to the Government of the United States . . . until a majority of the qualified voters of the state, voting on the question, shall ratify the same."

The election of Sterling Price as president of the convention and the change in its meeting place from Jefferson City to St. Louis was followed by the significant resolution: "At present there is no adequate cause to impel Missouri to dissolve her connection with the Federal Union."

Between the first and second sessions of the convention, which was called to reassemble in Jefferson City on July 22, 1861, Governor Claiborne Jackson and nineteen of the ninety-nine members, including Sterling Price, joined the movement for secession. Vice President Robert Wilson became president of the convention, and that body met the necessities of the time by exercise of revolutionary powers. The offices of governor, lieutenant governor, and secretary of state were declared vacant. The convention made provisional appointments and set a time for elections.

In the selection of Hamilton R. Gamble for governor, the convention gave Missouri a leader of great vigor and determination, a statesman who was able to exercise revolutionary power without losing his sense of democratic direction. He was moderate, willing to accept the guidance of men elected to perform the unique function of providing emergency regulations, and ready to surrender his authority as chief executive. President Lincoln recognized the validity of the convention's work and co-operated with Governor Gamble. The convention authorized bonds, increased taxes, issued warrants in denominations ranging from five dollars to one thousand dollars, and made provisions for a loyal state militia.

The convention attempted to deal with two major problems: emancipation of slaves, and the complicated question of loyalty to the United States and to the provisional government. Former political ties with people of the Confederacy, personal friendships with Southerners, and many other factors added difficulty to the loyalty question. On March 3, 1862, a military order by General Halleck required voters, attorneys, and jurors to take an oath of loyalty to the United States. During the war period and for five years afterward, the loyalty oath in various forms was required for suffrage and as a test for engaging in many professions and even business functions.

Two groups of Union men in Missouri advocated emancipation of Negro slaves. The "Claybanks" were in favor of gradual emancipation; the "Charcoals" demanded immediate freedom for all. On

June 7, 1862, the convention debated a proposal to abrogate clauses of the Missouri Constitution which forbade freeing slaves without compensation or without consent of the owners.

In the elections of November, 1862, the "Claybanks" won in four Congressional races, the "Charcoals" in five. During 1863 the great problems of Governor Gamble and the Assembly revolved around financing the war. The Governor was authorized to use "Union Military Bonds" for militia expenses up to $3,000,000, and to negotiate for a loan of $3,000,000 from the federal government.

Although Governor Gamble was born in a slave state, Virginia, and lived there until he came to Missouri Territory at the age of twenty, he was known as an advocate of emancipation. His forty years' acquaintance with slavery in Missouri—in Howard County, where he was prosecuting attorney, in St. Louis, where he practiced law, and in other parts of the state—had convinced him that slavery was not economically sound in that part of the West.

On June 15, 1863, Gamble called the fifth and final session of the convention. His principal topic was freedom for the Negro slaves, and he announced his resignation as governor, to date from the last day of the session. President Lincoln's Special Message of March 6, 1862, had recommended federal aid to any state that might adopt gradual emancipation. The Missouri convention debated and passed an ordinance freeing the slaves, which was approved by Governor Gamble on July 1, 1863. The constitutional stumbling blocks to emancipation were abrogated. All slavery in Missouri was to cease on July 4, 1870; provided, however, that freedmen over forty years of age were to remain with their masters as servants and those under twelve were to remain until they were twenty-three. All other freedmen were to remain with their masters as servants until July 4, 1876. No Negroes were to be sold to nonresidents after July 4, 1870. After the passage of this ordinance, slaves were not taxable property.

Upon formal request of the convention, Governor Gamble remained in office, and he was still chief executive at the time of his death, January 31, 1864. Willard P. Hall, lieutenant governor, succeeded to the office and held it until the next elected governor, Thomas C. Fletcher, was inaugurated in January, 1865. In the meantime, the Assembly had chosen B. Gratz Brown and John B. Henderson to represent Missouri in the United States Senate. The *Missouri Statesman* (November 20, 1863) characterized the two men thus: "Henderson is a conservative; Brown is a radical of the worst sort. Henderson supported Lincoln, Schofield, and Gamble; Brown goes for Chase, Butler, and the Devil." The estimate was picturesque but not accurate in either case. Both of the senators were men who rose, on occasion, to the stature of statesmen—far above the level of the ordinary politician of this period.

Brown was a Kentuckian who had come to Missouri at the age of twenty-three in 1849. He was the grandson of one of Kentucky's first United States senators and was no beginner in politics, himself. He had been a member of the Missouri Assembly in 1853 and 1854, and was elected again in 1856. He was known as a Free-Soiler and a Benton Democrat. Like Frank Blair, he supported Lincoln for President in 1860. He was an advocate of gradual emancipation with compensation for the owners of slaves.

John B. Henderson was a Virginian who came to Missouri as a small child in 1832. Before his twenty-third birthday he had been admitted to the bar and had begun his law practice at Louisiana, Pike County. He was elected to the General Assembly as a Democrat in 1848. He was elected again in 1856, but was defeated for Congress by James S. Rollins. He ran as a Union Democrat for a seat in the convention of 1861 and was elected by a substantial majority. His choice by the Assembly for the United States Senate was essentially a reflection of Missouri's position relative to the Lincoln administration in 1863. Furthermore, his introduction of the joint resolution on January 13, 1864, in the United States Senate for the abolition of slavery by constitutional amendment, was a recognition of Missouri's new position on a great national problem.

On January 26, 1864, five days before Governor Gamble's death, the Missouri Assembly passed an act providing for the election of a constitutional convention. Each senatorial district was authorized to elect two delegates for each of its state senators.

The Missouri Radicals, offended by President Lincoln's refusal to support Charles D. Drake's extreme demands—removal of General Schofield, replacement of the enrolled militia by units from the regular army, and federal enforcement of the election laws—tried to defeat his nomination for President by the National Union convention at Baltimore, in June, 1864. After a stiff contest between rival delegations in the convention hall, the Radicals won the Missouri seats; but on the first ballot for presidential candidate, Lincoln had a large majority. Before the count was finished, the Missouri delegates voted with the overwhelming majority to make it a unanimous choice.[1]

CHARLES DANIEL DRAKE, TOP RADICAL

In the presidential election of 1864, Missourians cast 71,676 votes for Lincoln to 31,626 for McClellan. For state officers the trend was definitely Radical. Thomas C. Fletcher had a majority of 42,536 over the Conservative candidate, Thomas L. Price. For seats in the convention, the Radicals were far in the lead with 50 of 66 members, and held a majority in both houses of the General Assembly. Officers in 80 of the 114 counties were also Radicals, generally elected without vigorous opposition.

The convention met at the Mercantile Library in St. Louis on January 6, 1865. Arnold Krekel of St. Charles was elected president, but the most powerful member from the first day was the vice-president, Charles D. Drake. The influence of this Radical policy-maker from 1865 to 1870 was truly remarkable, especially when his personality is considered. Egotism, without a trace of humor or realistic self-analysis, placed a barrier between Drake and that large portion of the public which follows a leader with warmth and affection as well as respect. He was opinionated and

---

1 Williams and Shoemaker, *Missouri*, II, 52–54, 55, 142–63; *The Lincoln Papers* (David C. Mearns, ed.), I, 42; Richardson, *Messages and Papers of the Presidents*, VI, 68, 69; W. E. Smith, *Blair Family*, I, 292, 294, 328, 400, 416ff., 454, 460, 467, 474, 504–505; II, 22, 216, 221, 252, 262–64, 266, 276, 294, 348, 432ff., 448ff.; J. K. Hosmer, *The Outcome of the Civil War*, 125ff.; *Dictionary of American Biography*, III (article on Benjamin Gratz Brown, by P. Orman Ray); *Complete Works of Abraham Lincoln* (Nicolay and Hay, eds.), IX, 155–64.

dogmatic, and he regarded with contempt all views that differed from his own. He bristled with hostility in verbal battles and won forensic contests by the intensity of his convictions.

Unfortunately, Drake's grasp of democratic government was limited and his shallow ideas of political reconstruction had little permanent value. Yet his program of revenge appealed strongly to certain Union men who were embittered by losses of the war and intent upon tangible evidence of their recent victories. To the Missouri Confederates, on the other hand, his Radical policies were obstacles to recovery of citizens' rights; and to Union men of moderate views they represented an unreasonable extension of wartime partisanship. It required five years of adjustment for the Missouri electorate to overcome the worst features of Radical legislation passed in 1865—the hate-inspired "Draconian Code."

The man who dominated the era was a peculiar person in every respect. Charles D. Drake was the son of a Cincinnati, Ohio, physician, whose ancestors migrated from England to Boston in 1630. His grandfather, Isaac Drake, who came to Kentucky by way of New Jersey, was married to a Quaker maid named Elizabeth Shotwell. Their second son, Daniel, was fifteen when they moved to Cincinnati. The family background contained no direct acquaintance with slave labor, either in New Jersey, where slaves were in the process of gradual emancipation, or in Kentucky, where the family kept no slaves. Although the Drake family had not become noted as abolitionists, it is probable that there was a pronounced aversion to slavery among them.

After he was fifteen, Daniel Drake's schooling was in Cincinnati. In 1807 he was married to Harriet Sisson of New Haven, and he gradually established his medical practice in the Ohio River town. The doctor's first child died in infancy; but Charles Daniel, born in 1811, the second of five children, lived to become prominent. Another of Dr. Drake's sons died before he was three, but the two youngest children grew up in the Cincinnati household.

Some evidence of mental instability appears in Dr. Daniel Drake's record; but in the case of his son, Charles Daniel, abnormal behavior was so persistent as to make his recovery seem almost miraculous.

[264]

The house in which Charles was born—a small, two-story frame dwelling—stood on the east side of Sycamore Street about one hundred feet south of Fourth; but when the child was in his second year, Dr. Drake built a new brick house which overlooked the Ohio River and the Kentucky hills beyond. Although his medical practice did not provide enough income for an elaborate force of domestic servants, Dr. Drake did employ some housekeeping help. The home that he provided for his wife, son, and two daughters was spacious, comfortable, and beautiful.[2]

Everyone who knew little Charles agreed that he was a "wild, harum-scarum" boy—even Charles himself in an autobiography that was begun when he was almost seventy years of age. Much disagreement appears, however, regarding the reasons for the child's wayward tendencies. His mother wrote to her sister when the lad was two: "Charles is so extremely active and mischievous that it is sufficient employment for one person to look after him." At four, with a broken leg, he was a "very bad patient." At six, seven, eight, and later, Charles ran away from a variety of schools, public and private. His father described him, when he was six: "He is not wicked, but as volatile, restless, pugnacious, and changeful as Will Weathercock in the farce. I have seen him personate a whole flock of wild ducks, at the same time."[3]

In all of this, there is nothing indicative of mental aberration except, perhaps, the youth's tendency to run away from all forms of restriction upon his behavior. It was his later refusal to accept responsibility and his persistent tendency toward placing the blame for failure upon some other person that mark him as a border-line mental case.

In the part of his "Autobiography" that was written when he was sixty-eight, Drake suggested that his mother, after the loss of her first-born, gave him too much attention and indulgence while he was the only child in the household—that is, before he was two years old. He also blames his father and the influence of boyhood

2 "Autobiography of Charles D. Drake" (MS in the Missouri State Historical Society, Columbia), 1–13; David De Armand March, "The Life and Times of Charles Daniel Drake," 1–20 (unpublished Ph.D. dissertation, University of Missouri, 1949).

3 Drake, "Autobiography," 23.

companions on Third Street and the Ohio River, transient residents of a "lower order." In commenting on his childhood environment, Drake wrote: "Our beautiful home was an unfortunate one for me"; and in the same passage stated that every associate he had from the age of five to ten was "hurtful and degrading."

During his elementary schooling, Charles ran away from or was expelled from such schools as that conducted by Moses Dawson at Cincinnati, Bishop Chase's boarding school at Worthington, Ohio, Walnut Hill day school, and others. For six years after he was withdrawn from Bishop Philander Chase's school at the age of ten, little Charles attended at least one other institution of learning each year. According to his own account, he fell upon a strange cat with sticks and stones and beat it to death. He destroyed toys, threw rocks through the windows of vacant houses, and kept up such an uninterrupted chain of minor offenses as to injure his father's medical practice and cut off years from his devoted mother's life.

Charles placed a thorn on the kitchen floor for the servant girl, Betsey Schermerhorn, to step on with bare feet. Later he forgot about it and stepped on it himself. Served him right, he admitted. He was not malicious, he says in the "Autobiography"—and readers must have been expected to suppose that all of his "pranks" were just good clean fun. He was not sure when he was sixty-eight that the severity of Dr. Daniel Drake was not a contributing factor in his delinquency. Furthermore, neither of his parents was an active church member, and lack of religious training might be blamed for his conduct.[4]

At ten, he was deeply offended by his reception at Worthington by Bishop Chase. When Charles was nearly eleven, Dr. Drake wrote to him, ". . . after the fatigues of the day it is killing to us to be kept awake all night by the distress of mind occasioned by your idle and dishonorable conduct!"

Drake's estimate of Bishop Chase and the other persons in authority at the school, after many years of consideration, was that they were unfit to manage boys. No criticism is included of their

[4] *Ibid.*, 18, 36, 42, 44, 45, 48, 49, 52–55, 58.

lack of religious emphasis, as in the case of his delinquent parents; the Chases and their employees simply did not understand pedagogy and the discipline of growing boys—subjects in which young Drake had observed many and varied systems, most of which were entirely futile when applied to him.

At the age of thirteen, Charles was in school at Lexington, Kentucky. He spent the money he was to have used for stage fare home, borrowed more, and lied to his father about the origin of the debt. Bad companions at Lexington caused this deviation from rectitude, Charles thought.

His mother died when he was fourteen. Dr. Drake tried, in vain, to teach Charles at home. Then he was sent to a military school in Connecticut, where the "poor discipline" of Captain Partridge and the "unfairness" of the other cadets were serious handicaps to Master Drake.

Through his cousin, Postmaster General John McLean, Dr. Drake obtained for Charles an appointment as midshipman in the navy. For a time, the discipline of the *Delaware* seemed to fill a need in his life; but the officers and crew of the *Porpoise*, to which he was transferred, did not understand the young man and he was court-martialed. There were several charges against him: He had cursed and abused one of the crew, after Lieutenant Goldsborough had repeatedly ordered midshipmen not to curse any more on board; he had also struck Lawrence Hoose "repeatedly" with a billet of wood, disobeyed orders, and habitually conducted himself in an unofficer-like manner. Charles resigned under the charges. Dr. Drake refused to pay Charles's debts, and he borrowed from the United States consul at Malta to return home. The former midshipman was nearly eighteen at this time.

Through the influence of John McLean, Charles D. Drake obtained another chance in the navy. His resignation simply was not accepted, and he was ordered back to duty. On the *Hornet*, at New York and in the West Indies, Charles was detested by officers and members of the crew. He decided to get out of the navy for good, and resigned. Again, he was restored to his place in the navy. He was assigned to the *Grampus*, where he had trouble with Lieutenant Broughan, among others. Commodore Ridgeley's report to the Navy Department finally brought his dismissal from the service for "general insubordination."

At nineteen, it must be admitted, Charles Daniel Drake showed little promise of becoming a good naval officer, and the navy cannot be charged with failure to give him a fair chance. His father shed tears when he met the young man in their Cincinnati home and welcomed him back to a new opportunity for a career in civil life.[5]

Stormy scenes with his father at home, study of law with his lenient Uncle Ben, who didn't have to live with him, writing poetry for publication—these were the young man's activities during the following years. The literary critic on the staff of the New York *Mirror* summarized his comments on Drake's poetry in a single word, "Mediocre!" The estimate was not erroneous in the least; but perhaps for the reader who is trying to understand the influence of Drake the attorney in Missouri politics, it will be helpful to know that his literary work showed steady improvement—in diction, style, and maturity.

Eventually he was admitted to the practice of law. Finding some difficulty in building up a practice in Cincinnati, where his income during the first six months was not enough to pay the office rent, he decided to remove to St. Louis. He spent a short time in Jacksonville, Illinois, where he met and almost came to blows with Stephen A. Douglas. After six weeks, Drake came back to St. Louis, where he was fortunate enough to gain the support of Hamilton R. Gamble. This acquaintance, which began in 1834, resulted in a close friendship that lasted until the two men disagreed over Reconstruction policies thirty years later.

Drake's law practice grew steadily. In 1835 he proposed marriage to Martha Ella Blow, who was twenty-two, two years younger than he. Old Dr. Drake wrote the young woman, in care of Charles, advising postponement of the marriage until the attorney should be more firmly established. Perhaps the advice was not called for; but it should be remembered that the father had known many disappointments in his son, and he could hardly accept the idea of

[5] *Ibid.*, 84–86, 98, 122–72. (For experience in the navy, chap. VII through XII.)

his being ready for the responsibilities of marriage. At the time of his autobiography, more than forty years afterwards, the son still resented his father's letter.

At twenty-four, the young attorney proved his maturity by a dignified and determined insistence upon his right to marry Miss Martha Ella Blow, who agreed with him completely. Not only the opposition of his father, but also the hostility of Ella's sister Elizabeth had to be overcome. A third sister was the wife of Joseph Charless. Charles Drake made it clear to all concerned that he would be glad to have the good-will of the relatives—and that Ella and he were determined to settle the important question of marriage for themselves.

St. Louis was probably the best field in the United States for a young attorney. In rapid succession, young Drake became city attorney, public administrator of St. Louis County, and a member of the Presbyterian church. A son was born in 1836 and a daughter in 1838. A second daughter was born two years later but died in infancy. Ella lost the use of an arm after an accident and later became paralyzed. Charles consulted specialists in Chillicothe, Ohio, and Louisville, Kentucky, but six months later Ella died. The children went to live with Mr. and Mrs. Peter Blow, and still later, Charles also took board and room with the same family. In 1843, Drake married a second time, a widow named Margaret Emily Brown.[6]

In politics he generally supported Whig candidates. He served as city attorney and as federal solicitor for the Treasury. After a brief residence in New York, he was back in St. Louis in 1850 with John F. Darby as a law partner. Drake was elected to Congress. His law practice became prosperous again, and he took a house at 502 South Fifth Street, where he lived for fifteen years, 1852–67.

In 1855 the disaster on the Pacific Railroad, the collapse of the Gasconade River bridge, made a deep impression upon Drake. The bridge gave way under the weight of a locomotive and tourist train, killing or seriously injuring a large number of passengers. The St. Louis attorney had planned to make the trip but had decided instead to prepare a brief for a Supreme Court case that was about to be called. He felt that his life had been saved by the

[6] *Ibid.*, chap. XIII through XVII (403–572).

intervention of Divine Providence. This sanctimonious tendency to identify his personal safety or his private interest with matters that were in the realm of Universal Good was characteristic of the new Charles Daniel Drake. Instead of a young hellion ready at all times to rebel against authority, with or without good reason, we have now an ultra-pious middle-aged hypocrite who fancies himself protected by God's special care—denied to other humans—and whose opinions immediately acquire the weight of divine ratification.

Reasonably intelligent but poorly educated by reason of a wasted youth, Drake became a confused, boresome dispenser of platitudes in prewar St. Louis. At the dedication of the first public high school in the city, he delivered an oration which touched upon topics in the field of education that were far beyond his depth. The effort was probably almost harmless, because it had no appeal as a constructive program. But during and immediately after the war, he was to give a demonstration of confused thinking in a position of power. As the dominant leader of Radical thought in the convention of 1865, he set back recovery in Missouri by at least five years—perhaps in some fields of politics by a full generation.

His main interest as a member of the General Assembly had been to obtain the passage of a series of Sunday closing laws. Christian Kribbeu of St. Louis, representing the German voters, gave strong opposition, but Drake's proposal passed the House by a vote of sixty-nine to forty-five. The Senate did not act upon it in that session. "Though I failed in my purpose, I thank God I did not fail in my duty," he wrote. More and more, he was becoming the zealot, the crusader, the bigot.[7]

During his political career, Drake had been a Whig, a Know-Nothing, and a Democrat. Later, he was to be the most radical of the Radical Republicans. In 1856 he voted for Buchanan in preference to Fillmore or Frémont; and in 1860 he gave his support to Douglas in preference to Lincoln or Bell, who were out of the running, in his estimation. The program of John Breckinridge he branded as treason to his party and treason to the nation—the culmination of "unhallowed schemes" to destroy the Union. He said

[7] *Ibid.*, 573–640; March, "Life and Times . . . Drake," 63–72.

that Southern men were trying to elect Lincoln by splitting the Democratic party. Drake modestly admitted that he carried Missouri for Stephen A. Douglas.

THE WORK OF THE DRAKE CONVENTION

In the political battles of 1866, Frank Blair was to charge Drake with being a Rebel at the start of the war, which the latter flatly denied. Many men who supported Douglas in 1860 did later become Confederates; but it is quite possible that Drake's stand for Douglas, followed by support for Claiborne Jackson and other secessionists of the Assembly, was the result of his confusion. In the "Autobiography" he claimed that he was at all times an Unconditional Union man. "My time, in the orderings of Providence, had not yet come," he said later. The disunionists of St. Louis favored Daniel G. Taylor for mayor in April, 1861, and he was elected over the Republican candidate, Oliver D. Filley. As a Douglas Democrat, Drake voted for Taylor, and the Mayor nominated Drake for city attorney. The St. Louis City Council refused to confirm the appointment—Blair said on account of Drake's sympathy with Rebels in the administration.

By his support of Taylor and Claiborne Jackson, Drake gave Blair a valid argument to the effect that he was a Rebel at the start of the war; however, it is more likely that he was ignorant of the views held by the candidates, as many other voters were. Drake was never a leader in planning a party program; he was effective mainly through his mastery of harangue.[8]

Only three members of the convention of 1865 had been delegates in 1861. Except for a few men, such as Henry A. Clover and Charles D. Drake of St. Louis, the members were obscure before the election, and most of them sank into obscurity afterwards. Local Radical leaders, particularly from the northern and southern border counties where unqualified radicalism had taken a firm hold, were much impressed by Drake's glib speeches. He expressed his opinion of the members thus: "Almost without exception they

[8] Drake, "Autobiography," 664–75, 690–93, 698–709, 710a, 710b, 710c; Williams and Shoemaker, *Missouri*, II, 167–68; W. E. Smith, *Blair Family*, II, 348.

were sensible, upright, worthy men; but only a very small number . . . had experience in lawmaking, and only thirteen belonged to the legal profession."

An ordinance reported by George P. Strong on January 11, 1865, provided for the immediate emancipation of slaves. The measure passed with only four negative votes. Governor Fletcher immediately proclaimed the slaves free, without compensation to their owners. Thus, Missouri formally abolished slavery eleven months before the Thirteenth Amendment to the federal Constitution was ratified.

Drake wanted the convention to undertake a general revision of the constitution of Missouri, and he had his way. He became chairman of the committee on suffrage, which included, among other members, David Bonham and W. H. Folmsbee. It was Folmsbee who said that he "hated rebels and hated all conservatives worse than rebels." A sharp debate arose over Drake's new loyalty oath. The Germans came to the support of Conservatives, and for a time it seemed to be a real contest, but the Radicals won.

A "severe and searching" oath was required for voters, officers, attorneys, jurors, priests, and clergymen. A statewide system of registration was provided, and local registration officials had the responsibility of deciding who could vote. Not only participation in Confederate activities but expressions of sympathy for the views of secessionists constituted grounds for disqualification from the vote. Eighty-six different acts had to be denied, under oath, to make a citizen eligible to cast a ballot. Conservative leaders such as William F. Switzler of Boone County and John Harris of Callaway, supported by Isidor Bush, William D'Oench, George Husmann, and Arnold Krekel, president of the convention, and other spokesmen for the German vote were unable to muster enough votes to defeat the Drake measure.

Governor Gamble had promised, as a recognition of the confusion and uncertainty of the first war year, amnesty to all who supported the Confederacy before December 17, 1861, provided they would join the Union side. The Conservatives demanded that no exclusion should extend farther back than Gamble's date, but the Radical majority wanted all persons disqualified "who had *ever* given aid or comfort" to enemies of the Provisional government.

The convention expelled Harris of Callaway County on the ground of disloyalty. Drake proposed reorganization of the judiciary "in the interest of the people." An ordinance was passed vacating all judgeships and offices of clerks, recorders, and attorneys—for the Supreme Court, circuit courts, county courts, and special courts of record. The Governor was directed to fill these vacancies. Bush proposed an amendment which would have made members of the convention ineligible for appointment as judges, but it was voted down, forty-three to five. This ordinance involved the removal of some eight hundred officers. Henry A. Clover, chairman of the judiciary committee, an able St. Louis attorney who had been a Benton Democrat, opposed Drake's oath of loyalty and refused Governor Fletcher's offer of a judgeship under the new order. By February 15, 1865, Drake had established his control of the convention and begun the composition of a new, Radical constitution. Leading the opposition to Drake's revision and to many items of the new constitution was Emil Preetorius, a German newspaper editor. The Conservatives pointed out that many loyal citizens were disfranchised. Frank Blair, outside of the convention, declared that the Radicals were trying to "build up a party upon a spirit of exasperation, retaliation, and revenge." He then asked his hearers to consider the question, "Can peace, prosperity, and tranquility be expected from those who act with such motives?"

The work of the convention was submitted to the people for their approval on June 6, 1865. Voting was limited to persons who were eligible under the proposed constitution. Since the suffrage law and the test for engaging in the professions were the most disputed clauses, a large segment of those opposed to Drake's new law was excluded from taking part in the plebiscite. Even so, there were men of moderate views in sufficient numbers to make the contest close.

Governor Thomas Fletcher, Senator Gratz Brown, and Senator John B. Henderson all had the hard problem of deciding between party solidarity and their own personal opinions, and in each case they decided to go along with the Radical party. The German Radical vote was divided. In central Missouri, James S. Rollins,

Austin A. King, former Democratic governor, and William F. Switzler fought hard against the "Draconian Code." Edward Bates, Lincoln's first attorney-general, gave all the help to the Conservative opposition that his failing strength would permit. Frank Blair, in active command of the Seventeenth Corps of Sherman's army, wrote a letter urging the people of Missouri to defeat Drake's unreasonable restrictions upon the public will.

St. Louis voted against the reactionary document, 11,248 to 5,322. Edward Bates issued a statement regarding the legality of restricting the vote on the constitution to those persons who could meet the qualifications set by that instrument. Refusal to take the oath was not a legal bar to voting. But the old Attorney-General added that Radical election officials would probably require the oath as a test for voting.

The country districts overcame the Conservative lead in St. Louis, and Drake's Law was adopted by a vote of 43,802 to 41,967. Governor Fletcher declared the new constitution in force, July 4, 1865.[9]

RETURN TO SANITY

The period of Radical domination, 1865 to 1870, was marked by definite limits. It began with the election of the convention and its opening session in the Mercantile Library on January 6, 1865, and ended with the repeal of the loyalty oath in the election of 1870.

In October, 1865, the Missouri Supreme Court considered the appeal of Father Cummings, a parish priest from Louisiana, Missouri, who had been indicted for preaching without taking the oath provided by Drake's constitution. In the circuit court Father Cummings had acted as his own attorney and attempted to establish before Radical judges that his arrest and trial were in violation of the Missouri Bill of Rights. His opponent in the trial was Senator Henderson, and the priest found himself at a great disadvantage because he was not acquainted with court procedure. Actually, however, the outcome of the trial was not affected by his lack of

[9] *Ibid.*, II, 350; Williams and Shoemaker, *Missouri*, II, 166–83; Drake, "Autobiography," 1056.

skill as an attorney. The Radical court found him guilty and assessed a fine of $500.

Father Cummings refused to pay the fine and was sent to jail, where he proceeded to make the most of his martyrdom. He appealed the case to the Missouri Supreme Court. His attorney, J. P. Garresche, added a second important objection to the test oath for preachers: it was a violation of the United States Constitution, in that it was an *ex post facto* law, contrary to the provision of the tenth section of Article I, in which states are prohibited from passing such acts. The three Radical judges appointed by Governor Fletcher ruled unanimously against the priest. The case now had the attention of the entire nation. Father Cummings appealed to the United States Supreme Court.

Frank Blair wrote to his brother, Montgomery, who had served as President Lincoln's postmaster-general, asking that he offer his services to Father Cummings free of charge. David Dudley Field agreed to work with Montgomery Blair, and that was the team that argued the case against Senator John B. Henderson and George P. Strong, acting for the state of Missouri. Blair and Field adopted the line used by Garresche in his appeal to the Missouri Supreme Court. The requirement that Cummings should take a test oath before preaching as a Christian minister on penalty of imprisonment was in effect a punishment for an act which was not a crime when it was done—clearly *ex post facto* legislation, the attorneys for Cummings argued.

Strong said that the state of Missouri had the power to set requirements for persons who were in a position to mold the character of her people. The oath of loyalty was not punishment, but a measure of protection for the citizens of Missouri. The Court reached a decision and announced it on January 14, 1867. As applied to preachers, teachers, and lawyers, the test oath was retroactive and *ex post facto*. The decision was by a bare majority, five to four. In the Court's opinion Justice Stephen Field said, "There can be no connection between the fact that Mr. Cummings entered or left the state of Missouri to avoid enrollment or draft in the military service of the United States and his fitness to teach the doctrines or administer the sacraments of his church; nor can a fact of this kind or the expression of words of sympathy with some of the persons drawn into the Rebellion constitute any evidence of the unfitness of an attorney or counselor to practice his profession, or of the professor to teach the ordinary branches of education." Thus the test oath was a violation of Article I, section X of the federal Constitution, in that it was in effect an *ex post facto* law and a form of attainder.[10]

The Cummings case was an important step in restoring the right of citizens to disagree. War had created a powerful backward movement, in which the partisans in power were eager to stamp out organized opposition by force. Americans had not seen reactionary factions, faced with popular demands for change, clinging to office with such desperate tenacity since the Federalists of 1798 passed the Alien and Sedition Acts. The objective in both cases was the same: the holders of office wanted to perpetuate their control by laws against opposition.

Frank Blair regarded the appointees of Governor Fletcher as men who were "perfectly desperate in their struggle to retain power." State troops were used to "keep the people subdued" and to "prevent the Democrats from voting." Perhaps the registrars, appointed through the influence of local Radicals, were generally unfit for public office—"insolent men selected because of their desperate fortunes and for a desperate service." In some counties, however, the Governor reappointed incumbents to executive offices and obviously made some effort to win permanent support from the people as a whole.

Fletcher's career, up to the time of his election to the governorship at the age of thirty-seven, does not suggest that he was devoid of liberal ideas. Born in Missouri and reared in the vicinity of St. Louis, he began the practice of law in 1856 and immediately considered the possibility of holding public office. His early voting indicates that he was a Benton Democrat. As a delegate to the Republican national convention in 1860, he supported Lincoln.

His Civil War record was excellent. He served under Lyon at

[10] *Cummings* v. *Missouri*, 4 Wall. 277; Thomas S. Barclay, "The Test Oath for the Clergy in Missouri," *Mo. Hist. Rev.*, Vol. XVIII, No. 3 (1924); W. E. Smith, *Blair Family*, II, 350–53.

St. Louis, saw active service at Chickasaw Bayou, where he was wounded and captured, and, after being exchanged, took part in Grant's campaign at Vicksburg. He commanded a regiment in the battle of Chattanooga and a brigade in the Atlanta campaign. Back in St. Louis to recover from sickness, he helped to organize the defense against General Price in 1864. He served with Ewing at Pilot Knob and was made brevet brigadier general by the President.

He was nominated for governor over Charles D. Drake, probably because the voters—even the restricted electorate provided by Radical suffrage laws—were not ready for Drake's narrow program of ultra-radicalism. Fletcher was elected by a large majority and re-elected two years later. The problems of the period 1865 to 1869 were difficult, and it may be assumed that every day of Fletcher's administration was filled with tension and strife. The Governor was ready for an end to the test oath before the Radical party was willing to accept that progressive move; and he tried, unsuccessfully, before the Court's decision in *Cummings* versus *Missouri*, to obtain constitutional repeal of the test oath for ministers and lawyers.

Governor Fletcher also had to face the difficult problem of railroad bankruptcy in Missouri. All the roads had financial troubles during the war, and one Missouri railroad only—the Hannibal and St. Joseph—was able to meet the interest payments on its bonds. With easy credit supplied by the state, the roads had been constructed at inflated prices. Their land grants were generally slow in providing revenue, and bad financial management had contributed to their troubles. Only the Hannibal and St. Joseph had completed the building of its line across the state. The Pacific had constructed 168 miles of track by 1860, the Iron Mountain had built from St. Louis to Pilot Knob, and the North Missouri had succeeded in extending its line northwest from St. Charles to an intersection with the Hannibal and St. Joseph at Macon City.

Since Missouri had authorized the bonds for railroad construction, it was necessary for the state government to assume the interest payments on the indebtedness of defaulting companies for which it had provided credit. With funds obtained by loans on first mortgages, the Pacific extended its track to Kansas City and ran a passenger train entirely across the state in September, 1865. The North Missouri, also, made an immediate start on new construction. During Governor Fletcher's two terms, railroad mileage in the state was practically doubled. In spite of building stoppage during the war years, the increase between January 1, 1860 and January 1, 1870, was from 817 miles to 2,000 miles.

As in the financing and building of the first railroad to the Pacific, chartered by Congress during the war and constructed immediately afterward, the roads built with state aid in Missouri provided many examples of political corruption. By 1866 the state railroad debt amounted to $31,375,340. In that year and in 1868 the state foreclosed and sold at public auction the roads that were unable to pay the interest on their bonds, at a net loss of $25,000,-000 to Missouri. Purchasers of the unfinished roads agreed to complete them within a time limit stipulated in each of the contracts. The state's loss on the sales of railroad property and the personal interest of some members of the legislature in the transactions gave Missouri a political scandal that matched in brazen dishonesty, if not in total amount obtained by fraud, the gigantic swindles of *Crédit Mobilier*.

Governor Fletcher's record in public school reorganization was creditable. He was interested in obtaining adequate support for the University of Missouri and gave special attention to the problem of teacher training and to the study of agriculture.[11]

Benjamin Gratz Brown, who represented Missouri in the United States Senate from December 14, 1863 to March 4, 1867, was another Radical whose acceptance of liberal views was a factor in recovery from the harsh laws of Drake's constitution. Brown's support of Benton in the Missouri Assembly, his support of Lincoln in the presidential election of 1860, and his stand in favor of gradual emancipation with compensation have been pointed out. His adherence to the Radical party in Missouri injected into that group an element of liberal thought from the time he joined it, and as the events of Radical Reconstruction unfolded, Brown grew more

[11] Williams and Shoemaker, *Missouri*, I, 561; II, 366–72; *Dictionary of American Biography*, VI, 468 (article on Thomas C. Fletcher, by Clarence H. McClure).

inclined toward the moderate point of view. His acceptance of Frémont in 1864 was inconsistent, a definite example of his occasional faulty judgment of contemporaries. But his stand for universal suffrage for both men and women was early recognition of a democratic trend—a position which gives Gratz Brown stature as a leader and shows he was not merely an opportunist.

He was sometimes erratic and often so outspoken as to invite personal resentment. His duel with Thomas C. Reynolds in 1856 over Brown's editorials on the Know-Nothing movement resulted in permanent lameness when he was hit in the knee by a pistol ball. Brown's lameness was a lasting reminder to all who knew him of his quick resentment and his willingness to fight. He was gullible in regard to Rebel prison atrocities and even suggested retaliation. By the end of his term in the United States Senate, however, he had taken a stand for so many liberal principles as to make him a leader against extreme Radicals. In addition to suffrage as a natural right, he advocated the merit system for federal Civil Service, an eight-hour day for government employees, and national ownership of telegraph lines.[12]

In many respects, the most remarkable Radical who became a Liberal in Missouri was the German-born editor and statesman Carl Schurz. After participation in the revolutionary activities of students at the University of Bonn in 1848 and residence in Switzerland, France, and England, Schurz had come to America in 1852. He lived in Watertown, Wisconsin, and served as chairman of the Republican delegation from that state to the Chicago convention in 1860. He was a supporter of William H. Seward for the nomination to the presidency. After Lincoln's election he was minister to Spain in 1861, but returned to serve as brigadier general of volunteers in the Union Army.

As a new American citizen, Schurz was interested in political methods and every phase of public life both in Washington and in the West. His first impression of William H. Seward, during a visit to the United States Senate is recorded in his *Reminiscences*: "There was to me something mysterious in the slim, wiry figure,

[12] *Congressional Globe*, 38 Cong., 1 sess., Part II, 984–90; 39 Cong., 2 sess., Part I, 76.

the thin, sallow face, the overhanging eyebrows, and the muffled voice. . . . He made upon me . . . the impression of a man who controlled hidden occult powers . . . a sort of political wizard who . . . commanded political forces unknown to all the world, except himself and his bosom friend, Thurlow Weed, the most astute, skillful, and indefatigable political manager ever known."

Schurz commanded a division under Frémont, fought under Sigel at the Second Battle of Bull Run, at Chancellorsville under General O. O. Howard, and under Meade at Gettysburg. He was promoted to the rank of major general in March, 1863. He fought at Chattanooga and became commander of the Corps of Instruction at Nashville. At the end of the war he was on active duty with Sherman's army in North Carolina.

The mild influence of President Lincoln probably had some effect upon Schurz's political views and his transition from Radicalism to Liberal Republicanism. During the war the German-American officer wrote many letters to the President with critical suggestions on military appointments. "You must forgive something to the sincerity of my zeal," Schurz wrote; but he offered further opinions in regard to McClellan, Buell, Halleck, and other officers, and ventured to dissect the President's view of the political situation.

This time Lincoln's long reply, although courteous and considerate in tone, contained sharp rebuttal. "If I must discard my own judgment and take yours, I must also take that of others; and by the time I should reject all I should be advised to reject, I should have none left, republicans or others—not even yourself. . . . I wish to disparage no one—certainly not those who sympathize with me; but I must say I need success more than I need sympathy."[13]

Schurz's mission to the South as the agent of President Andrew Johnson in the summer of 1865 shows evidence of internal conflict between Radical hostility to the defeated Confederacy and

[13] The Carl Schurz Papers, Vol. III (Library of Congress, Manuscript Division); Schurz, *Reminiscences* (3 vols., N.Y., 1907–1908), II, 34. In the Schurz Papers, Lincoln to Schurz, Nov. 10, 1862, and Nov. 24, 1862, are originals; Schurz to Lincoln, Jan. 25, 1863, is a photostat copy made in 1912.

enlightened desire for "healing the wounds of war." One of the most progressive suggestions in his report was readmission of the states with full political rights and further investigation of Southern conditions by a committee of Congress.

At the age of thirty-eight, in 1867 he became editor and joint proprietor with Emil Preetorius of the St. Louis *Westliche Post*, and in the following year was chosen to the United States Senate for a full term. He denounced the reactionary policies of the Grant administration, including relations with the Southern states and much of its foreign policy. Schurz was instrumental in the choice of B. Gratz Brown in 1870 as Liberal Republican governor of Missouri and in the abandonment of the worst Radical Reconstruction measures.

Perhaps the indispensable man in Missouri's recovery of her prewar liberal trend was Frank Blair. From the time of the Verandah Hall convention at St. Louis on October 26, 1865, he took the lead in uniting Lincoln men, Johnson men, war Democrats, former Whigs, discharged Union soldiers, and pro-Southern men of 1860 who wanted union. The convention accepted abolition of slavery as a final decision and took a stand for President Johnson's views on the Constitution.

The Radicals, complacent behind their fortification—the "ironclad oath" and the registry act for voters—watched with little concern Blair's revival of the Democratic party. President Johnson's use of the patronage in Missouri to build up conservative support was thwarted by the power of the Radical United States Senate to approve or reject appointments.

Among the "honorable seven" who could not be persuaded or cajoled into a vote for conviction of President Johnson during his impeachment trial was John B. Henderson of Missouri. Senator Drake, on the other hand, was prominent among those who were striving for Johnson's removal.

Chief Justice Salmon P. Chase, presiding over the impeachment trial, gave the dignity of judicial process to that partisan action. President Johnson's eminent counsel added weight to his cause, and the support of Seward and Welles gave further strength to the

defense. But in the final analysis it was the "honorable seven"—
Henderson, Trumbull, Fessenden, and the others—who prevented
the national disgrace of a false conviction for crime.

It was Senator Drake who challenged the decision of the Chief
Justice to admit evidence showing cabinet opinion on the Tenure
of Office Act. The Senate overruled Justice Chase on the question
of evidence by a vote of twenty-six to twenty-two; but the real outcome took form in the court of public opinion. A partisan Senate
was held in check by the good sense of its thoughtful minority.[14]

In the elections of 1868, Missouri voted for Grant and Colfax by
a majority of 25,883. Joseph W. McClurg, Radical candidate for
governor, was elected by a majority of about 20,000 in a total vote
of 150,000, the Democrats claiming that 100,000 persons were disfranchised. Carl Schurz won a seat in the United States Senate,
where he served with distinction for a full term, 1869–75. In 1871,
President Grant appointed Charles D. Drake a judge in the United
States Court of Claims at Washington, and the Radical leader resigned from the Senate to accept the appointment. The trend of
Missouri politics may be discerned in the election of Frank Blair
to Drake's seat in the Senate.

In the meantime, Missouri's Assembly had ratified the Fifteenth
Amendment to the federal Constitution, and the voters repealed
the law requiring an oath of loyalty by all who exercised the right
of suffrage. Repeal of the test oath was by a convincing majority—
127,643 to 16,283. Gratz Brown was the new governor by a majority of more than 41,000 over McClurg. The new Democratic party
carried four Congressional districts, the Liberals two, and the
Radicals, three. The Democrats also elected a majority in the lower
house of the Assembly.[15]

[14] William A. Dunning, *Reconstruction, Political and Economic* (N.Y. and London, 1907), 101–108; W. E. Smith, *Blair Family*, II, 297, 354.

[15] *Ibid.*, II, 401–30; Williams and Shoemaker, *Missouri*, 212–25.

⚜ **13** ⚜

DEMOCRATIC RECOVERY AND CONTROL, 1872-1900

AGRICULTURAL DISCONTENT: RISE OF THE GRANGERS

THE GRANGER MOVEMENT, beginning with the efforts of a young government clerk in 1867, effected a revolution in American farm life. President Andrew Johnson authorized an investigator to obtain "statistical and other information" in the Southern states which might be used to improve the condition of farmers. The man selected for the job was Oliver H. Kelley, who traveled through the South and observed economic developments at the beginning of a new era. His attention was fixed upon agricultural production, mainly; but the efforts of the four million freedmen to fit themselves into their new status, the system of credit that grew up for landless white and black farmers, and many related problems of the rural people came under his observation.

Kelley went back to his home in New England with the germ of an idea in mind for a great union of farmers. His niece, Miss Carrie Hall of Boston, suggested to him the inclusion of farm women in his proposed organization, and the Patrons of Husbandry began to take shape.

After February, 1868, Kelley devoted full time to the task of organizing local granges and welding the separate groups into a national order. The farmers were hard to organize, and the work moved with discouraging slowness; but in the year 1872 a sharp upward trend gave new significance to the farmers' movement. Kelley had helped to establish local and state granges in South

[283]

Carolina, Mississippi, Minnesota, and Iowa before that time, and in 1870 had moved the headquarters of the Patrons of Husbandry to Washington, D. C. By the end of the year, Wisconsin, Illinois, and Indiana had been added to the active states and a beginning had been made in New Jersey and Vermont.

The decline of prices on farm products in Missouri was an important factor in the growth of interest in the Patrons of Husbandry. From the boom period, 1865 to 1870, the early 1870's witnessed a sharp drop in land values and the prices of livestock and grains. The enormous increase in production, particularly in wheat, corn, and oats, without a parallel increase in demand, provides ample explanation for the decline of farm prices.

All the factors which made farmers of the Middle West eager to organize to better farm conditions, along with certain factors peculiar to the South, were present in Missouri. The increase of acreage in cultivation, the reduction of soil fertility because of repeated plantings of a single grain crop, and the competition of new farms in the western territories, all hastened the decline of farm prosperity in Missouri. In the cotton-producing section of the state the slave labor of prewar days had contributed to one-crop farming. Missouri farmers needed diversification of crops, better and more scientific farming methods, relief from abuses in the cost of transportation, farm machinery, grain storage, and credit; and they needed improvement in their facilities for spreading information to the rural dwellers. The Granger movement promised advantages in all these areas.

In 1870, Oliver H. Kelley visited Missouri. He found the farmers of the state—in widely separated regions—peculiarly conservative. He presented the Granger program with his usual confidence and assumption of ultimate success. In gatherings of farmers and their wives he discussed the social, economic, and political aims of the Patrons of Husbandry. He stated the objectives in plain and convincing language.

The Grange would bring to every farm community a healthier and fuller social life, since co-operation would involve frequent meetings and promote easy communication. The organization would attempt to provide each member with reliable statistics on prices and markets. It would undertake to obtain more reasonable terms for transportation, factory prices for implements, and mutual insurance rates. Kelley regarded the Grange as a vehicle for testing newly invented farm machinery and as a basic organization for co-operative retailing and manufacturing. Low interest rates, which would enable the farmers to hold their crops for higher prices when the need arose, were promised through the medium of co-operative banking or reform in the nation's banking program.

Agricultural fairs for the promotion of better farming became a favorite theme of the Grange leaders. The exact relationship between the Grange organization and the growth of interest in scientific farming is difficult to measure. Before the Morrill Act of 1862, little attention had been given to education as a means of developing better agricultural methods. The Hatch Act of 1887, introduced by Representative William H. Hatch of Marion County, Missouri, provided for federal experiment stations in the land-grant colleges. The connection between interest in scientific farming, advocated by the Patrons of Husbandry, and the enactment of federal laws for educating better farmers seems clear enough.[1]

In Missouri, the increase in use of machinery for farming was especially rapid during the 1870's. Even before the end of the war, loss of man power on farms brought a sharp demand for labor-saving machines. The cash value of farm machinery in the state was $8,711,508 in 1860, and by 1880 it had more than doubled, to $18,103,074. During the same period the acreage of improved farmland also increased in a similar ratio—from 6,246,871 to 16,745,030 acres.

By 1872 the Patrons of Husbandry, on the basis of Kelley's effective work as an organizer, together with the farmers' peculiar need for the reforms he proposed, had taken a firm hold in Missouri. From that year on, the growth of the organization was phenomenal, and in 1875 there were more local granges—though not a greater total membership—than in any other state. Outstanding leaders

[1] Solon J. Buck, *The Agrarian Crusade* (New Haven, 1920), 1–10, 14, 15, 24–42; Williams and Shoemaker, *Missouri*, II, 260–64, 330, 331; A. E. Paine, *The Granger Movement in Illinois* (*University of Illinois Studies*, I, No. 8 [1904]); Dunning, *Reconstruction*, 225–27.

from the start were Norman J. Colman, editor of the *Rural World* in St. Louis, and Thomas R. Allen, who became master of the state grange. Both of these men tried without success to keep the grange from participating in politics, except as a "balance of power" between the major parties.

Colonel William Henry Hatch, who was called the "father of agricultural experiment stations" because of his introduction of the bill discussed above, represented his district in Congress from 1878 to 1894, and spent his last years in Hannibal, where his principal occupation was the breeding of fine horses and cattle. President Grover Cleveland approved the famous Hatch Act on March 2, 1887.

In the case of *Munn* versus *Illinois* (1876), the United States Supreme Court ruled favorably upon the Granger law that set maximum rates for the storing of grain in Illinois. The law was not, said the court, a violation of that clause of the Fourteenth Amendment which provides that no state shall "deprive any person of life, liberty, or property without due process of law." Chief Justice Waite, writing the Supreme Court's opinion, cited the two-century-old principle that when private property is "affected with a public interest, it ceases to be *juris privati* only." Common carriers and grain elevators the court regarded as being so "affected with public interest." In regard to statutes regulating rates of "ferries, common carriers, hackmen, bakers, millers, wharfingers, innkeepers," and other public services, the opinion declared: "We think it has never yet been successfully contended that such legislation came within any of the constitutional prohibitions against interference with private property."

Granger laws providing maximum rates for freight hauling encountered a temporary check in a case involving the Wabash, St. Louis and Pacific Railroad Company. The exclusive power of Congress over interstate commerce, established by the Constitution and recognized by the courts, rendered state regulation of rates—even for transportation wholly within the state—a violation of the Constitution. The result, however, was the establishment of the Interstate Commerce Commission by an act of Congress in 1887, with authority to enforce a limited regulation of the great common carriers. The full force of the principle established by *Munn* versus *Illinois* did not serve as an effective check on railroads until the passage of the Hepburn Act in 1906; but that law and subsequent rate legislation had the effect of extending Granger reforms to the country as a whole.[2]

PARTY POLITICS: BEGINNING OF DEMOCRATIC CONTROL

The People's party in Missouri grew directly out of the grievances of farmers. In September, 1874, its first state convention of 450 delegates at Jefferson City contained more than 100 active members of the state grange. For governor the convention chose Major William Gentry of Pettis County, a man with an independent political background. In the period of Abiel Leonard's prominence, he had been a Whig; he was a conservative in opposition to C. D. Drake's radical program; and he joined the Independent Democrats in their alliance with the Liberals in 1870 and 1872. Gentry was acceptable to the grangers, since he was a farmer and keenly interested in agricultural problems.

The platform of the People's party in 1874 included planks for strict limitation upon the state debt, rigid control of railroads, improvement of public education, development of waterways, economy in government, limitation of regular legislative sessions to one every four years, and steps to check contraction of the currency.

The emergence of the People's party was seized upon by the Republicans as an opportunity for recovery. Instead of putting a third slate of candidates before the voters, the Republican Central Committee took steps toward union with the new party as a practical means of opposing the united Democrats. Silas Woodson, who held the office of governor from 1873 to 1875, had been a compromise candidate of the Democratic convention. Deadlocked on four strong men—James S. Rollins, Joseph L. Stephens, R. P. C. Wilson, and John S. Phelps—the convention had nominated Woodson, who defeated the liberal and able Republican candidate,

2 *Ibid.*, 228, 229; Williams and Shoemaker, *Missouri*, II, 264, 325–54; *Munn v. Illinois*, 94 U. S. 113; *Wabash, St. Louis and Pacific Railroad Co.* v. *Illinois*, 118 U. S. 557.

John B. Henderson, by a majority of 35,443 votes. The union of former Confederate voters with the heirs of the Benton and Blair Union Democrats, supplemented by reinforcements from the Liberal Republicans, was practically unbeatable.

The first step toward gathering fragments of opposition to the triumphant Democrats was a statement by the Republican Central Committee—the party would support any movement "for peace, prosperity, and good government." Nobody could find fault with that.

In another resolution the committee made direct reference to the candidates of the People's party: they were "immeasurably superior" to the Democratic candidates. Finally, the Republicans made no nominations but left their members free to choose. The implication was strong enough to suggest support for the slate of the People's party, which included, in addition to Gentry for governor, L. W. Headlee of Springfield for lieutenant-governor, John H. Fisse of St. Louis for state treasurer, and E. T. Howell of Princeton and Louis Houck of Cape Girardeau for judges of the Supreme Court. Houck was known in southeastern Missouri as a rising attorney and railroad builder and was later to receive recognition as the author of excellent books on Missouri history. His *Law of Mechanics Lien* gave him prestige in the legal profession.

Senator Carl Schurz took a positive stand for the candidates of the People's party. The Democratic convention nominated Charles H. Hardin of Mexico, Audrain County, for governor, and Senator Schurz declared that he saw no prospect of reform in the Democratic party program. He had transferred his support from the Radicals to the Liberal Republicans to help in the contest for the restoration of suffrage to Missouri citizens. He had been a party to alliance with the Democrats to give weight to moderate and just reforms. He expected personal abuse to arise from his new independent stand—he would be accused of disloyalty to his party.

What has the Democratic party done with its power in Missouri? he asked. Let the attacks upon his record come; let each one be "as much of a gentleman as he pleases." He charged that the acrimony of Civil War had been revived. In some counties, Union men had been made uncomfortable on account of their support of the Union, the Democratic administration had failed to suppress crime, and Missouri's record for disorder was an obstacle to migration of new settlers, hence a hindrance to prosperity. Schurz urged the Republicans and Democrats to lay aside partisan hostility and "join hands" in a common effort.

The Democrats replied to Missouri's independent-minded senator. And although the answers to his questions were not in every way satisfactory, they were politically effective. In two years, Silas Woodson's Democratic administration had lowered the public debt by $1,012,000. The remaining debt was the result of Civil War expense and the extravagance of railroad aid measures. Crime and mob violence were no more the fault of the Democrats than of members of other parties. The administration could not maintain a large military force to control criminals.

The total vote of the state was 16,000 less than Missouri's vote in 1872, when the Democrats combined with Liberal Republicans to elect Silas Woodson over Henderson and to give its electoral vote for President to Horace Greeley over Grant. Again the Democrats won a decisive victory, Hardin receiving a majority of 37,462 over Gentry. In St. Louis and St. Charles counties, where Schurz's influence was strong, the total vote was high. Gentry actually carried thirty-four counties and ran a close race in thirty-two more. Perhaps some Missouri Republicans were reluctant to support candidates of the People's party, and perhaps some Grangers could not see their way clear to co-operate with the Republicans.

The Assembly elected Francis M. Cockrell over Schurz for the United States Senate. The Republicans were divided in this balloting and the Democrats united in the choice of a former Confederate general. The influence of Carl Schurz is not to be measured by the immediate reaction of the electorate to his political maneuvers. Certain principles that he stood for had little appeal until men's mature thoughts shaped themselves to his advanced views. Gradual development of public opinion in favor of the merit system for administrative services is a good example of what he advocated. Many times, too, men who were vaguely disturbed by abuses in public offices became articulate when they read his sharp criticisms or listened to his eloquent speeches. He could not make independent thinkers of all the Missouri voters, but he did inject a spirit of critical judgment into the elections of his time and afterward.[3]

THE CONSTITUTION OF 1875

Edward Bates, the mild and sensible Missouri statesman who served as attorney-general for Abraham Lincoln, looked forward hopefully and worked for the constitutional changes that took place in 1870. Unfortunately, Bates died in 1869, and was not among those Missourians who rejoiced in the defeat of the reactionaries by the Liberal Republicans and Democrats in 1870. Bates would have been delighted by the huge margin of victory for repeal of the loyalty oath and by the election of Gratz Brown as governor over Joseph McClurg.

In his inaugural address, Governor Brown had proposed a constitutional convention, and although his Democratic successor, Silas Woodson, was reluctant to risk a general revision of the basic law, the leaders of his party were able to overcome his objections. According to the evidence of his associates, Woodson feared partisanship, and he mentioned expense as a reason for postponing the convention. On March 24, 1874, however, he approved the bill which authorized a popular test, and a majority of 283 voted for the convention.

The election of delegates was set by Governor Woodson for January 26, 1875. Each senatorial district was entitled to elect two delegates to the convention, which was to begin its sessions on May 5 at Jefferson City. As in the first Missouri constitutional convention, a majority of the members had come to Missouri from border states of the Old South. In 1820, Virginia, Kentucky, and

[3] Carl Schurz Papers, III; Schurz, *Reminiscences*, II, 34; Buck, *The Agrarian Crusade*, 19; Dunning, *Reconstruction*, 47–49, 191–96; W. E. Smith, *Blair Family*, II, 199, 208, 372, 400, 418, 419, 432, 437, 448, 452; William T. Doherty, Jr., *Louis Houck, Missouri Historian and Entrepreneur* (Columbia, 1960), 1–51, 106–22; Williams and Shoemaker, *Missouri*, II, 251, 265, 268–75, 553, 555; *Dictionary of American Biography*, XVI, 466–70 (article on Carl Schurz, by Oswald Garrison Villard).

Maryland provided over three-fifths of the delegates. In 1875, Kentucky, Missouri, Virginia, and Tennessee were the native states of forty-four delegates, nearly 65 per cent of the total. Seven of the delegates had been born in foreign countries.

Certainly the sixty-eight men did not include all who had made significant contributions to the return of Missouri's electorate to political sanity. Joseph Pulitzer was among the St. Louis delegates, along with the Liberal Louis Gottschalk and the Democrats, Henry Brockmeyer, Albert Todd, Amos Taylor, and James O. Broadhead. Of the six Republicans in the convention, Horace B. Johnson of Jefferson City and George Shields of St. Louis were probably best known. John Ray was a Democrat and a substantial citizen from Cassville; Benjamin F. Massey of Neosho, John H. Taylor of Joplin, Henry C. Wallace of Lexington, William F. Switzler of Columbia, Louis F. Cottey of Edina, Samuel R. Crockett of Nevada, Charles B. McAfee of Springfield, and Neil C. Hardin of Louisiana were among the Democrats. Waldo P. Johnson of Osceola was elected president of the convention.

The task of writing a new constitution required almost three months. Then, on August 2, it was adopted by the vote of sixty delegates and signed eventually by all who took part in the convention. A special popular election for ratification resulted in a large affirmative majority in a light vote.[4]

The constitution of 1875 was longer than either of the basic laws of Missouri that had preceded it. Limitations on legislative authority, concerned primarily with restricting grants to railroads by the state or by local units of government, were lengthy. That these restrictions were popular was indicated by the wide majority who voted in favor of the new constitution.

A formula was included for apportionment of members in the lower house. Each county, regardless of population, was to have one member. The population of the state was to be divided by two hundred to obtain a ratio for determining additional members.

[4] Loeb, Isidor, "Constitutions and Constitutional Conventions in Missouri," *Mo. Hist. Rev.*, Vol. XVI (1922), 189–217; Williams and Shoemaker, *Missouri*, II, 223, 289–99.

Counties containing two and one-half ratios of population were given two members. Four ratios entitled the county to three members; six ratios, four members; and in counties of larger population, there was to be one additional representative for every two and one-half ratios above six. These provisions were more nearly equitable for the city population and for the counties of large population in general than the apportionment of 1865. St. Louis County, the area of most pronounced growth in population, would receive three additional members, and other urban developments across the state with increased population would be entitled to a total of nine additional members.

Cities with more than 100,000 inhabitants, under the "home rule charter provision," were authorized to draft a charter, subject to limitations of the constitution, which would become the city's organic law when ratified by a majority of the voters. The city of St. Louis was authorized to separate its government from that of St. Louis County, and in 1876 the city adopted a municipal charter which gave it a great degree of independence.

The peculiar character of Reconstruction politics in Missouri, the large element of Southern population—a postwar group that added sectional dissent to the independent thinking of minority factions—and the unique leadership of a talented group of journalists in St. Louis and elsewhere in the state give the period a strong appeal for students of American history. Developments in Missouri throw light upon political reconstruction of the former Confederate states and help to explain many phenomena in the free states in the same period. Certainly Kentucky, West Virginia, Maryland, and Delaware had many adjustments to make that were similar to those in Missouri.

The constitutional amendments of 1870, the moderate reforms of 1875, and the ascendancy of the Democratic party during the last quarter of the century are traceable to factors that can be readily understood. The influence of Southern sectional interest and a tradition of loyalty to the South may be seen in the personnel of the constitutional convention of 1875. All the members had been old enough between 1860 and 1865 for military service. Fifteen had served in the Union Army, and eighteen had been soldiers in the Confederate Army or officers of the Confederate government. Of the members who did not serve under either government, probably a majority sympathized with the Confederacy.[5]

THE INFLUENCE OF THE PRESS

From the beginning of newspaper publication in Missouri, the press was a powerful factor in the intellectual and social life of the region. Newspapers also were important in the elections. The Irish-born printer Joseph Charless, who published the laws of Missouri Territory by a contract with Governor Meriwether Lewis, did not acquire suddenly the ability to create a sheet that was filled with dynamic news stories. The *Gazette* was short on current events and carried little advertising. During his best year of government contracts, Charless collected $1418.75. From readers of the *Gazette* he frequently accepted flour, pork, vegetables, and even old copper and brass in payment for subscriptions. Collection of money was difficult even from persons of prominence. Charless recalled that he once collected $47.00 of a $62.00 bill against John B. C. Lucas, and in 1816, Pierre Chouteau paid him $10.50 when the bill was actually $14.00.

Charless was opposed to Negro slavery and took a strong stand in the *Missouri Gazette* against the unmistakable current of public opinion favoring making Missouri a slave state. It was a losing fight; but the columns of the *Gazette* were always open to any person who wanted to express his views against slavery. It is interesting to note that Peter Blow, who became Charless' partner in the drug business, shared his unpopular opinion of slavery, and that Henry Taylor Blow, son of the druggist, president of the Iron Mountain Railroad, and head of an important lead and zinc business, joined Frank Blair in his attack upon slavery and became a leading partisan of Abraham Lincoln in St. Louis.

Most important of the contributions of Joseph Charless to the development of the American newspaper was his insistence upon

[5] *Ibid.*, 293–95; Loeb, *loc. cit.*, 209, 211, 212, 214, 217.

freedom of the press. He was not the kind of person to submit tamely to any restriction upon his liberties.[6]

One of the journalists who came to Missouri after the end of the Civil War and immediately became a force to be reckoned with in politics was William M. Grosvenor. His ancestors were Massachusetts immigrants one hundred years before the American Revolution. His father, Rev. Mason Grosvenor, was a graduate of Yale University and a professor of moral philosophy at Illinois College for many years. William spent the years 1851 to 1854 in Yale and at the age of twenty-four became editor of the New Haven *Palladium*. In 1861 he joined the Union Army and served as adjutant, captain, and finally colonel of the Louisiana Native Guards, Second Regiment, colored.

Back in New Haven, he became editor of the *Journal-Courier*, and in 1866 went to the St. Louis *Democrat*. For about seven of the nine years between 1866 and 1875, Grosvenor held the position of editor. He wielded strong influence in the repeal of Radical suffrage laws, the election of Carl Schurz to the United States Senate, and the election of Gratz Brown as governor. More than any other person, Grosvenor was responsible for exposing the tax frauds in connection with the St. Louis Whisky Ring. The prosecution of one hundred federal inspectors and distillers in 1875 and the many convictions that resulted from Grosvenor's investigations broke up the Whisky Ring.

In 1875 he became economic editor of the *New York Tribune* and continued in that position for twenty-five years, to the time of his death. His biographer describes him as a man of great physical strength, with "magnificent head and shoulders."[7]

Perhaps enough has been told of Carl Schurz to indicate his connection with reform politics in Missouri. He was one of the great journalists who found it impossible to remain entirely aloof from party campaigns. His versatility in languages gave him a great

[6] William H. Lyon, "Joseph Charless, Father of Missouri Journalism," *Mo. Hist. Soc. Bull.*, Vol. XVII, No. 2, Part I, 132–45; Williams and Shoemaker, *Missouri*, I, 114, 345, 346; *Dictionary of American Biography*, II, 391–92 (article on Henry Taylor Blow, by Thomas S. Barclay).

[7] *Ibid.*, VII, 26, 27 (article on William M. Grosvenor, by Walter Williams); Williams and Shoemaker, *Missouri*, II, 205, 206, 560.

advantage as a campaign speaker, and the fact that he was equally eloquent in German and English made him indispensable in gaining the support of new German citizens. He was also the author of a number of books, including a two-volume *Life of Henry Clay* and three volumes of *Reminiscences.*

Schurz was humorous, gay, good-natured, and hard to discourage. His charming manners and his complete lack of bitterness in political campaigns made many friends for him, even among persons who were unable to keep up with the rapidly shifting opinions reached by his independent mind. The versatility of the journalist-politician, who could do so many things well in the generally accepted group of related interests—public addresses, campaign organization, and administration—is shown by his reputation as an amateur pianist.

He was distinguished in almost everything that he attempted. As secretary of the interior, he introduced civil service examinations and merit promotions in his department well in advance of requirements of the law. He gained recognition for his enlightened treatment of the American Indians, who had been assigned to his department. He was interested in the protection of the public domain, and his administration of the department gave impulse to the movement for establishing national parks.

Emil Preetorius, editor of the *Westliche Post*, George Knapp, born in New York and transplanted to Missouri as a child in 1819, and Walter Barlow Stevens, editor of the *Globe-Democrat* for twenty years, were among the great journalists who worked in the state during the generation after the Civil War. Stevens was one of the most influential of the Washington correspondents after 1884, and in 1901 became secretary of the Louisiana Purchase Exposition Company.

Hungarian-born Joseph Pulitzer, the son of a prosperous merchant of Magyar-Jewish descent and an Austro-German mother—a beautiful and intelligent woman whose maiden name was Louise Berger—came to America in 1864, when he was seventeen years old, to fight in the Union Army. He had been rejected in England for military service in India and in France for service in the Foreign Legion because of defective eyesight. In New York harbor

Pulitzer and his companion on the voyage entered without going through the regular routine for immigrants, by dropping into the water and swimming ashore.

Young Pulitzer succeeded in enlisting as a soldier for one year. Company "L" of the Lincoln Cavalry was recruited largely from boys of German descent, but in this unit he was not an immediate success. Perhaps because of his youth or his scrawny physique he became the object of many practical jokes in the company. On one occasion he struck a corporal who was involved in the hazing, and was saved from punishment by the action of Captain Ramsey, who enjoyed playing chess with him. The young Hungarian saw action at Antioch, Liberty Mills, Waynesboro, and Beaver Dam Flats.

By October, 1865, he had been mustered out of the army and was supporting himself by means of various jobs—mostly rough manual labor. He paid five dollars for passage on a steamer down the Mississippi River, to a job with "good pay." Forty miles below St. Louis, he and the other men, who had been deceived about obtaining employment, were put ashore. They walked back to St. Louis.

Joseph Pulitzer wrote the story of this adventure and succeeded in having it published in the *Westliche Post*. A farmer who gave the young man food and shelter for a night offered him whisky, chewing tobacco, and smoking tobacco, all of which he declined. Next morning as he departed, the farmer said: "Young feller, you seem to be right smart and able, for a furriner. But let me tell you, you'll never make a successful American until yer learn to drink, chew, and smoke."

In 1867, Pulitzer received a certificate of naturalization and became a notary public. Afterwards he was admitted to the bar, but did not practice law. At the Mercantile Library he met many prominent men, and he joined a chess club, of which Emil Preetorius and Carl Schurz were members. As a reporter on the staff of the *Westliche Post*, Pulitzer found himself. One of his associates was Henry M. Stanley. Schurz and Preetorius were joint editors, and Louis Willich was city editor. In this company of newspapermen, some of whom were potentially great, the young Hungarian was outstanding for his dynamic energy and his devotion to work.

In 1870 he ran for the state assembly as a Republican, in a district that had regularly returned Democratic members, and was elected. In the legislature as in his editorial writing, Pulitzer was independent and outspoken against corrupt politics. "The *Post* and *Dispatch* will serve no party," he declared, in his first issue of the merged newspapers, and he based his career upon that independent slogan. His service in the Missouri constitutional convention of 1875 gave to that body a strong impulse toward thoughtful liberalism.

By 1881, Pulitzer was the sole owner of the St. Louis *Post-Dispatch*. In the previous year he had supported Hancock as the Democratic candidate for President and worked diligently in the campaign. James A. Garfield was elected by a narrow popular margin—9,464 in a total of 8,898,968 votes—but by a substantial majority in the electoral college. The Democratic candidate carried all former slave states, and in Missouri his popular majority was over 55,000.[8]

MISSOURI POLITICS, 1876–96

The high prices, large profits, and good wages that were characteristics of the period 1865 to 1870, in Missouri as elsewhere in the United States, were not generally recognized as elements of an artificial prosperity which was to prove transient. Missouri farmers produced more food for the market than ever before, but the prices they were compelled to pay for manufactured articles needed for effective farming were excessive. It was discontent among the rural people, as has been pointed out, that led to the rapid growth of Oliver H. Kelley's granger movement.

To meet the financial pressure of the Civil War, the government of the United States had issued greenback currency in large amounts—a total of nearly half a billion dollars. This paper money, which was not redeemable in specie, was made legal tender by act

[8] *Ibid.*, 208–10, 267–72, 318; George S. Johns, "Joseph Pulitzer," *Mo. Hist. Rev.*, XXV (1930–31), 201, 404, 563; XXVI (1931–32), 54, 163, 267; *Dictionary of American Biography*, XV, 260–63 (article on Joseph Pulitzer, by Oswald Garrison Villard); XVI, 466–70 (article on Carl Schurz, by Villard); Edward Stanwood, *A History of the Presidency from 1788 to 1897*, 417.

of Congress; and in two cases the Supreme Court upheld the power of Congress to make these treasury notes legal tender for the payment of all obligations, "as applied to contracts made either before or after" the passage of the laws.[9]

Before the end of Hugh McCulloch's term as secretary of the treasury, Congress had passed an act (April 12, 1866) authorizing the gradual retirement of legal-tender notes. By 1878, the total amount of the greenbacks in circulation had fallen below $350,000,000. Further contraction of the legal-tender notes was generally opposed in the West, where farmers had purchased machinery at high prices on credit supplied by eastern bankers. The act of Congress that provided for specie payment on all legal-tender notes, debated for several months and finally passed and signed by President Grant, had set the date, January 1, 1879, for the full return to a specie basis.

To debtors in Missouri, contraction of the currency resulted in reduction of the demand for and prices of their products. To farmers who were in debt for the new machinery that had revolutionized farming methods since the war, this meant that they would have to pay their obligation in dollars that had a higher purchasing value than the dollars they had borrowed. These debtors, and their representatives in Congress, hoped to repeal the Sherman Act, which provided for resumption of specie payments on January 1, 1879. Gradually, too, the men who reasoned that expansion of the currency was a good thing for the debtor class, hence for the West and the South as sections, developed an organization that came out boldly for more legal-tender notes instead of contraction.

Senator Lewis V. Bogy of Missouri and Thomas T. Crittenden, congressman from the Seventh District, were emphatic in their demand for expansion of the currency. In 1876, Missouri gave 203,077 votes to Samuel J. Tilden, 145,029 to Rutherford B. Hayes, and only 3,498 to the Greenback candidate, Peter Cooper. Four years later, however, when the state gave its electoral support to General Hancock, Missouri cast over 35,000 votes for James B.

---

[9] *Hepburn* v. *Griswold*, 8 Wall. 603; Legal Tender Cases (*Knox* v. *Lee*, and *Parker* v. *Davis*), 12 Wall. 457; Williams and Shoemaker, *Missouri*, II, 300, 301; Woodrow Wilson, *Division and Reunion*, 280, 281.

Weaver, Greenbacker. Furthermore, Missouri elected four congressmen who strongly favored Greenback expansion.

Perhaps even more significant was the vote for Weaver in 1892 when he ran as a Populist. Since his following, organized as the People's party, demanded "free and unlimited coinage of silver and gold at the present legal ratio of sixteen to one" and "that the amount of circulating medium be speedily increased to not less than fifty dollars per capita," the idea of currency expansion was still a clear desire of these Western voters.

Weaver drew over one million votes in a total of twelve million. Missouri gave the Democratic candidate 268,308 votes to 226,918 for the Republican and 41,213 for James B. Weaver.[10]

The majority in Missouri for Samuel J. Tilden over Rutherford B. Hayes in the election of 1876 was matched by the Democratic vote for John S. Phelps for governor. Phelps had served Missouri in a variety of public offices. In 1839, two years after he came to Missouri from Connecticut, he was one of five commissioners who selected the site for the University of Missouri. He was twenty-five years of age at that time. He had represented Missouri in the lower house of Congress for eighteen years, 1845–63. During the Civil War his service as an officer in the Union Army was outstanding; yet a large fraction of his political support was disqualified by the Drake loyalty oath in the campaign for governor in 1868. The moderate attitude of the Springfield attorney did not appeal to the Radicals, who elected Joseph McClurg by a majority of more than 20,000. By 1876, however, Union Democrats and former Confederates had been restored to suffrage rights. It is quite possible that sectional opposition prevented the election of Phelps to the U. S. Senate in 1872, when former Confederates gave their support to Louis Bogy; but four years later the "hero of Pea Ridge" had succeeded in uniting the Northern and Southern factions of the Democratic party. Phelps's majority over the Republican candidate, Gustavus A. Finkelnburg, was decisive—199,580 to 147,694.

The moderate attitude of Governor Phelps in labor disputes, his

---

[10] Dunning, *Reconstruction*, 137, 138, 252, 253; E. E. Sparks, *National Development* (N.Y., London, 1907), 143, 144; Stanwood, *History of the Presidency*, 383, 417, 508–13, 517; Williams and Shoemaker, *Missouri*, II, 301–309.

vigorous steps to settle the railroad strikes, and the quiet efficiency of his administration strengthened his party in Missouri.

Thomas T. Crittenden received the Democratic nomination for governor in 1880. Like Governor Phelps, Crittenden had been an officer in the Union Army and had gained distinction as acting commander of a regiment at the battle of Westport. In politics he was a follower of Frank Blair and a member of that able group who inherited the Democratic philosophy of Thomas Hart Benton. At Warrensburg after the war, he was the law partner of Francis M. Cockrell, who had been one of Missouri's ablest officers in the Confederate Army. Born in Kentucky, Crittenden was the nephew and protegé of Senator John J. Crittenden. He had lived in Missouri since 1857, had served as attorney-general, and had been elected twice to represent his district in Congress.

Crittenden was elected governor over Dyer, the Republican candidate, by a vote of 207,670 to 153,636. His administration was characterized by generally prosperous conditions, full employment, increase of railroad building, and the satisfactory settlement of the Hannibal and St. Joseph Railroad tax case, in which the state was awarded $3,000,000 in back taxes. Crittenden's interest in public education is shown by his recommendation of a permanent endowment for the University of Missouri. His administration made some progress toward answering the sharp rebuke of Senator Carl Schurz when he was justifying his shift from the Democratic party to the new People's party. Schurz had asked, "What have you done to suppress crime?" Crittenden's vigorous stand for the apprehension and conviction of bandits brought definite results—notably the breaking up of the James gang.

In the presidential campaign of 1884, Carl Schurz turned the full power of his independent eloquence against James G. Blaine. The contest was so closely fought and the victory of Grover Cleveland so barely won that the claim of Schurz's admirers that he was responsible for Blaine's defeat cannot be regarded as an idle exaggeration. The election turned upon New York's vote, and Cleveland carried New York by a plurality of 1,149. Missouri's sixteen electors voted for Cleveland.

John S. Marmaduke, a well-known Confederate military officer, was nominated for governor of Missouri by the Democrats. Nicholas Ford ran against him, and in some respects was an abler campaigner than his opponent. The Democratic candidate was the son of a former governor, M. M. Marmaduke, who had served briefly in 1844 upon the death of Governor Thomas Reynolds during the last year of his term. General Marmaduke had distinguished ancestry on both sides of his family—his mother was a daughter of the famous physician, Dr. John Sappington of Saline County. Marmaduke was not in good health during the campaign of 1884 and died in the third year of his term. He handled a railroad strike with vigor and fairness, and he made practical use of his five years of experience on the Missouri Railway Commission by pushing through the legislature a law for the regulation of common carriers. His successor was Lieutenant-Governor Albert P. Morehouse, who was governor from 1887 to 1889.[11]

In the presidential campaign of 1888, Missouri again supported Grover Cleveland, by a vote of 261,943 to 236,252 for Benjamin Harrison. The Republicans carried New York, Pennsylvania, Ohio, and Illinois—along with sixteen less populous states—and won the electoral vote, 233 to 168. Cleveland had a popular plurality over Harrison, however, of more than 100,000 votes. Cleveland's courageous stand for tariff revision in his annual message of 1887 cost him the vote of New York and probably cut off some support in other important Eastern states. The electoral vote of New York alone, added to the "Solid South" and Cleveland's two Northern states—Connecticut and New Jersey—would have given him a majority in the electoral college.

The Democratic candidate for governor of Missouri in 1888 was David R. Francis of St. Louis. The decline of party vigor in Missouri was evident in the failure of Francis to obtain a majority of

---

11 *Ibid.*, I, 309, 310; II, 94, 110, 212, 251, 259, 304–307, 316–20; *Dictionary of American Biography*, II, 410, 411 (article on Louis Bogy, by Thomas S. Barclay); XII, 290–91 (article on John S. Marmaduke, by H. Edward Nettles); XIV, 530 (article on John S. Phelps, by H. Edward Nettles); Stanwood, *History of the Presidency*, 448.

the popular vote. His plurality over the Republican candidate was 13,233; but the combined ballots for Republican, Prohibitionist, and Union Labor candidates totaled 6,594 more than the winner's vote. Francis had commanding strength in St. Louis, where he was mayor, and enjoyed a reputation as a "business executive" in public office. Only thirty-eight years old at the time of his election as governor, he belonged to a new group of political leaders. He was to achieve greater distinction in his later years, in a variety of public services—Cleveland's secretary of the interior, president of the Louisiana Purchase Exposition Corporation, and ambassador to Russia in the troubled period of World War I.

Missouri established a state textbook commission and adopted uniform textbooks for the public schools during the Francis administration. Also, the Australian secret ballot, which was generally accepted by reformers in the American states, was adopted by Missouri.[12]

In 1892 the People's party in Missouri held its state convention in Sedalia and nominated a full slate of candidates. Leverett Leonard of Saline County, the most widely known leader of the Farmers and Laborers Union in the state, was nominated for governor. Sixty-eight delegates were sent from Missouri to the national nominating convention which was held at Omaha, Nebraska.

The Missouri Democrats nominated William Joel Stone, of Nevada, for governor, and emphasized economy. On the tariff question, Grover Cleveland's policy of moderate reduction was accepted. This policy was set forth in the platform of the Democratic party at Chicago, which contained the following arraignment of Republican protective tariff: "We denounce the McKinley tariff law enacted by the Fifty-first Congress as the culminating atrocity of class legislation."

The Missouri Republicans nominated William Warner of Kansas City for governor. On its first ballot, the Republican national convention at Minneapolis nominated President Benjamin Harrison, and set forth in its platform a general approval of his "able, patri-

[12] *Ibid.*, 483; Williams and Shoemaker, *Missouri*, II, 320–24, 437, 593; *Dictionary of American Biography*, VI, 577–78 (article on David R. Francis, by W. B. Stevens).

otic, and thoroughly American administration." Sharp competition between the two major parties in Missouri served as a check upon the People's party vote, and all of its candidates were defeated. In the race for governor, Stone defeated Warner by a plurality of 29,661—slightly higher than the margin obtained by David R. Francis in 1888 but still short of a majority. Leonard, candidate of the People's party, received 37,262 votes.

In the presidential race, Missouri gave its electoral support to Cleveland, who had 268,400 popular votes to 227,646 for Harrison. Weaver, the Populist candidate for President, with 41,204 votes, held the balance between the two major parties. He probably took more voting strength from Cleveland than from the Republicans.

Like his predecessor, Governor William Joel Stone belonged to the younger generation of politicians. He was born in Kentucky only twelve years before the beginning of secession, and at the end of the Civil War was a sophomore at the University of Missouri. After graduation he studied law in the office of Squire Turner at Columbia, and was admitted to the bar in 1867. Two years later he settled at Nevada, Missouri, and began a law practice which lasted nearly fifty years.

In 1872, at the age of twenty-four, he was elected prosecuting attorney of Vernon County. In his growing practice he was in partnership with other distinguished lawyers—C. R. Scott, for several years, then with D. P. Stratton, and later with Granville S. Hoss. He was one of the delegates from Missouri to the Democratic convention of 1876 which nominated Samuel J. Tilden for President. He made his first race for Congress at the time of Cleveland's election to the presidency in 1884. Stone won the seat for his district—the old Twelfth—and held the office for three terms, 1885–91. Before the end of Cleveland's first term as President, Stone was known as a supporter of the growing trend toward conservation of natural resources and as a sharp opponent of graft in public office—particularly the frauds connected with land grants to the Pacific railroads.

Stone's term as governor of Missouri came almost exactly in the middle of his public career, which extended over a period of forty-six years. Fifteen years in the United States Senate was to be his final official service. No man since Thomas Hart Benton had made so deep an impression upon the political life of his generation.

The panic of 1893, which placed a heavy strain upon the finances of Missouri, was weathered by Stone's rigid economy and his intelligent adjustment to reduced revenues. Essential state expenditures were met promptly, purchases were made on a strictly competitive basis, and unnecessary expenses were slashed from the budget. A careful analysis of the Governor's program serves to explain its financial success. With revenues reduced more than 20 per cent, the state actually retired a part of its bonded indebtedness and met expenditures that could not have been anticipated. The main building of the University of Missouri had been destroyed by fire toward the end of Governor Francis' term, and fire damage on the campus of another state-supported college demanded immediate attention. Governor Stone met these emergencies with the skill of an expert financier, and he must be given chief credit for a splendid administrative record. In certain respects his moderate, common-sense liberalism is related to the deliberate and carefully progressive tendency of Missouri's people.

Among Stone's achievements, settlement of a difficult strike of the American Railway Union workers and settlement of miner's strikes, without resort to martial law for keeping order, should be mentioned. The use of state militia was common in other Middle Western states during the industrial unrest that accompanied the panic of 1893 and the widespread unemployment that was marked by such episodes as the march of Coxey's Army and the Pullman strike in Chicago. Governor Stone found time to wage a successful war against lobbies for special interests, in particular the well-trained and highly-paid railroad lobby.

In the Congressional elections of 1892, the year in which Stone was chosen governor, thirteen of Missouri's fifteen representatives were Democrats. Francis M. Cockrell, elected in that year for his fourth term in the United States Senate, and George Graham Vest, who had begun his fourth term, were also Democrats. In the state convention of 1894, however, the Democrats found a sharp division among their members on the question of money issues. David R. Francis became the leader of a faction in opposition to Representative Richard P. Bland, who was serving his eleventh term in Congress. Bland had proposed, in a House bill of 1877, the free and unlimited coinage of silver dollars—371.25 grains of pure silver in standard alloy with a total weight of 412.5 grains. The bill as passed by the House, made Bland's silver dollar legal tender for all debts except private contracts which stipulated other forms of payment.

The Senate revision of the bill, however, the Bland-Allison Act of 1878, in its final form provided for the coinage of silver in an amount not less than $2,000,000 per month and not more than $4,000,000 per month. Under Presidents Hayes, Garfield, Arthur, Cleveland, and Harrison, over a period of twelve years, the minimum amount under the law was coined each month; and in 1890 the continued agitation for silver coinage led to the passage of the Sherman Silver Purchase Act. With a majority in both houses of Congress, the Republicans assumed principal responsibility for this measure, which directed the purchase each month of 4,500,000 ounces of silver at the market price. Payment for the silver was to be made in legal-tender treasury notes, redeemable by the United States Treasury in gold or silver at the discretion of the Secretary. A special session of Congress called by President Cleveland in 1893 repealed the Silver Purchase Act.

Disagreement over the silver coinage issue cost the Democratic party heavily in the Missouri state elections of 1894. Seizing the opportunity provided by Democratic schism, the Republicans elected ten of the fifteen congressmen, a railroad and warehouse commissioner, and a justice of the Supreme Court.[13]

FREE SILVER AND FOREIGN WAR, 1896–1900

The demand for greenback issues and other moves designed to

[13] *Ibid.*, XVIII, 88–89 (article on William Joel Stone, by H. Edward Nettles); Williams and Shoemaker, *Missouri*, II, 430, 431, 449, 483; Stanwood, *History of the Presidency*, 486–518.

expand the currency were never dominant party policies in Missouri, as they were in some other Western states. Perhaps the conservative character of Missouri farmers and other citizens who were directly concerned with agricultural prosperity, kept these voters in the older, more firmly established parties. As stated above, however, Richard Parks Bland had based his career chiefly upon free coinage of silver.

The Republican convention at St. Louis in 1896, with a large part of its delegates convinced (or bargained into agreement) on William McKinley of Ohio as the candidate for President, approached the subject of currency with some hesitation. Marcus A. Hanna, Ohio industrialist with wide political interests, had been the sponsor of McKinley in a deliberate campaign for political advancement for several years. Hanna supported McKinley in the campaign which elected him governor of Ohio in 1891, and he probably looked upon his protegé as a reserve candidate for President at the Minneapolis convention in 1892. He had raised funds to save McKinley from bankruptcy in 1893—an enterprise that required more than $100,000.

McKinley was nominated for President on the first ballot at St. Louis, with 661½ votes—more than 200 above the majority required. The platform condemned the "incapacity, dishonor, and disaster" of the Cleveland administration. Protection and reciprocity were linked together as the key to tariff policy. On currency the position of the party was brief, if not clear: "The Republican party is unreservedly for sound money." Definite opposition to the free coinage of silver, "except by international agreement," gave a clue to the platform makers' idea of sound money, and the "gold plank" appeared in short terms—"The existing gold standard must be preserved. All our silver and paper currency must be maintained at parity with gold."

Senator Henry M. Teller of Colorado protested in vain against the statement concerning currency and, when he was voted down, walked out of the convention with thirty-three other delegates. Two representatives and four United States senators were included in Teller's group.

The Democratic convention was held in Chicago about three

weeks after the Republicans met in St. Louis. The free-silver men demonstrated their control from the first day. William J. Bryan of Nebraska made the principal speech for silver in opposition to the conciliatory "goldbug" address of Senator David B. Hill of New York. Bryan's address had an eloquent appeal to consideration of the wage earner, rural doctor, country lawyer, crossroads merchant, farmer, miner, and woodsman—the little people. "You shall not press down upon the brow of labor this crown of thorns, you shall not crucify mankind upon a cross of gold," Bryan said, as a climax to his dramatic address.

This speech carried the silver issue for the Democratic campaign and made Bryan the candidate of his party. By comparison with Richard P. Bland, Bryan was dynamic, forceful, eloquent, and inspiring. Bland was sixty-one years of age and a dull speaker; Bryan was thirty-six and the most effective orator of his generation. On the first ballot for presidential candidate, Bland had 235 votes, Bryan, 119; and on the fifth ballot, Bland had faded to 106, while Bryan's vote had increased to 500. Since 512 votes (a two-thirds majority) were necessary for the choice, 78 delegates transferred their votes from other candidates to Bryan to give him the nomination.

Missouri voted for Bryan by a large majority over McKinley, giving Bryan 363,652 votes; McKinley, 304,940; and all minor candidates combined, 5,416.

Bryan carried all the former slave states except Delaware, Kentucky, and Maryland. He also gained the electoral votes of Colorado, Idaho, Montana, Nebraska, Nevada, South Dakota, Utah, Washington, and Wyoming. One California elector and one from Kentucky cast their votes for Bryan. His total was 176 to 271 for McKinley. The East, the Pacific states, and large parts of the farm area in the Middle West carried the election for McKinley.

For governor, the Missouri Democrats nominated Lon V. Stephens and the Republicans selected Robert E. Lewis. Stephens won by a plurality of 43,333—somewhat under Bryan's margin in the state.[14]

[14] Eugene H. Roseboom, *A History of Presidential Elections*, 293–320; Stanwood, *History of the Presidency*, 519–69; *Dictionary of American Biography*, II,

In 1898 the United States drifted into war with Spain over disagreements concerning provincial government and revolution in Cuba. American investments of $50,000,000 in the island, annual trade that totaled twice as much, and potential interests enormously greater made it easy for United States citizens to become outraged by Spanish atrocities in the West India neighbor to Florida. Newspapers in the United States, particularly William Randolph Hearst's New York *Journal*, fanned the flame of national hatred against Spain. The diplomatic ineptitude of President McKinley's early administration was matched by the slow-moving processes of Spanish provincial decisions, and the United States declared war in April. Apparently, both President McKinley and the Spanish prime minister, Praxedes Mateo Sagasta, were sincere in their desire for peace; but the coming of war was welcomed by Americans.

Missouri was directly interested in Cuban affairs and all diplomatic questions relating to Spanish rule of the province. St. Louis and Kansas City distributors of Cuban tobacco, coffee, sugar, and other island products made their interests known to Congress.

Spain was defeated in land and naval engagements that left no doubt about the relative power of the two nations. Missouri sent five regiments of volunteer infantry into the national service upon President McKinley's first call for volunteers, and another regiment when a second request for troops was issued on May 25, 1898. The Sixth Missouri Infantry saw active service at Havana, under Colonel Letcher Hardeman. The Treaty of Paris, following an armistice on August 10, gave Puerto Rico and Guam to the United States and provided that Spain should surrender the Philippine Islands for the sum of $20,000,000.

The Philippine Insurrection, which broke out almost immediately over the character of the government to be set up there after the islands were "freed" from Spanish control, lasted much longer than the war with Spain. The Philippine leader, Emilio Aguinaldo, was captured in March, 1901, and most of the people were ready to accept United States rule by July, 1902.

355–56 (article on Richard P. Bland, by Jonas Viles); Williams and Shoemaker, *Missouri*, II, 432–35; Wilson, *Division and Reunion*, 314–20.

A young Missouri lieutenant from Linn County who took part in these two wars was to become a famous soldier. His name was John J. Pershing. His later service as commander of American troops on the Mexican border and his effective leadership of the American Expeditionary Force to France in 1917 entitle him to a position among the great military officers of modern times. Not possessed of a flair for publicity and lacking the affability which might have made him a candidate for President, the great Missouri general's reputation must rest almost entirely upon generalship.

Of the 200,000 volunteer soldiers called for in McKinley's two proclamations, Missouri provided 8,109. By comparison with the American Civil War, there were few casualties in the short conflict with Spain.

Governor Stephens, supported by many former Populists and by Democrats who advocated parity of silver at the ratio of 16 to 1, was regarded a conservative on the question of money. He was a successful banker and had served brilliantly as state treasurer. He had the confidence of businessmen, based upon his skillful management of a large St. Louis bank after it had fallen into serious difficulties in other hands. His administration was marked by progressive measures: establishment of the state board of charities and corrections, the state hospital at Farmington, a colony for the feebleminded at Marshall, and the first major appropriation for the World's Fair at St. Louis. The state historical society was organized at Columbia; the fruit experiment station was established at Mountain Grove; and at Sedalia, Missouri farmers and livestock men, as well as miners, artisans, and many other citizens, were given an opportunity to display their choice products in a great state fair.

By 1900, Missouri was one of six states in the Union with a population of more than 3,000,000. Its two leading cities, St. Louis and Kansas City, stood at 575,238 and 163,752 respectively. The major part of its people were still rural dwellers, but a wide range of occupations gave them a strong tendency toward diversity. Farming and related livestock production were still most important, followed by manufacturing, mining, and a varied group of employments connected with common carriers. Railroad and river transportation kept Missouri in its long-established position as the Crossroads State.[15]

[15] *Ibid.*, 328–38; Williams and Shoemaker, *Missouri*, II, 440–42; Thomas A. Bailey, *The American Pageant* (Boston, 1956), 615–28; James Warren Nelson, "Congressional Opinion in Missouri on the Spanish-American War," *Mo. Hist. Rev.*, Vol. LI (1957), 245–56; Ruby Waldeck, "Missouri in the Spanish-American War," *ibid.*, Vol. XXX, 365–400.

14

REFORM, POLITICAL UPHEAVAL,
AND WORLD WAR

END OF THE ALL-DEMOCRATIC REGIME

BETWEEN 1873 AND 1909 all of Missouri's chief executives were Democrats. From the election of Frank Blair to the United States Senate in 1871 and the election of Francis M. Cockrell as Carl Schurz's successor in 1875, first one and then both of Missouri's senators, also, had been Democrats. The first break in the long period of one-party domination took place in the election of state officers and presidential electors in 1904. Again the governor was a Democrat, chosen to serve from 1905 to 1909; but the Republicans elected all the other executive officers and a supreme court justice and the railroad and warehouse commissioner.

The state House of Representatives had a Republican majority after the elections of 1904, and the Assembly chose the Kansas City Republican, William Warner, as the successor of Francis Cockrell in the United States Senate. The single success of the Democrats in the race for the governorship is to be explained by the character and recent activities of their candidate.

On January 10, 1899, at the invitation of Governor Lon V. Stephens of Missouri, the governors of states that had been formed from the Louisiana Purchase sent delegates to a convention at St. Louis to consider the organization of a fitting exposition in honor of the hundredth anniversary of the great expansion of territory. Former Governor David R. Francis became the personal director of the movement, and the convention agreed upon St. Louis as the place for the Louisiana Purchase Exposition.

Congress recognized the national character of the proposed celebration by advancing money to aid the project, and funds were obtained also from the states and territories. Space was reserved on the exposition grounds by sixty-two foreign nations. Separate American cities also constructed buildings, and a number of industries provided interesting exhibits.

The St. Louis world's fair developed into the largest, most elaborate, and finest exposition that had ever been provided in any city. Almost 20,000,000 visitors came to the exposition grounds—a tract of 1,142 acres in Forest Park—between April 30 and December 1, 1904. On the average more than 100,000 new visitors came to the fair each day, and, of course, many thousands of them repeated their visits again and again.

Architectural design, railroad and locomotive development, new machines, marvelous displays of agricultural production—in fact, all the many phases of progress in the states of the Union—were presented along with the most extensive foreign exhibits that had yet been attempted in any American fair. The Philippines, obtained as a possession by the United States after the brief Spanish war of 1898 and the longer war in the Islands, occupied thirty-five acres on the exposition grounds. Population and products of the Holy Land, all the well-known parts of Europe, the Near East, and the Orient, and strange native peoples and goods from remote regions of the earth found their way to St. Louis.

The fifteen great exposition buildings, in fan-shape arrangement, were impressive. The Palace of Electricity, designed by Walker and Kimball; the Palace of Machinery, designed by Widman; and the Palace of Forestry, Fish, and Game, designed by E. L. Masqueray, were outstanding. Among the structures of foreign nations the French Building, modeled upon the Grand Trianon of Versailles, probably had the strongest appeal for visitors to the exposition grounds.

The lack of harmony in architectural design was increased by the great variety of the foreign buildings, of course—"an astonishing pattern of elaborate and universal chaos," as one American critic described the Exposition. Perhaps the mechanical exhibit of greatest interest was the automobile, a machine that was to revolutionize transportation in America during the generation that followed. One hundred automobiles were on display—one of which had made the trip from New York to St. Louis "on its own power."

Structures of permanent value were erected. Washington University, which provided a part of the exposition grounds, acquired three fine buildings. The city of St. Louis and probably many other cities received a vigorous impulse toward distinctive public buildings in the architectural displays of the fair.[1]

Alexander Dockery was elected governor of Missouri in 1900 over the Republican candidate, Joseph Flory, by a plurality of 32,400 in a vote that totaled nearly 700,000. Since Missouri voted for Bryan over William McKinley by a margin of 38,000, elected a full slate of Democratic candidates to the administrative offices, and elected Democrats to positions in the Supreme Court, the office of railroad and warehouse commissioner, and to thirteen of the fifteen seats in the national House of Representatives, the results might have been regarded a great party victory. But certain aspects of the campaign were matters of serious concern for the Democrats.

Bryan's plurality was 20,000 less than it had been against the same opponent in 1896, and Dockery's margin over Flory was similarly reduced when compared with the plurality of Lon Stephens over Lewis. The Republican vote was steadily rising while the Democratic electorate was shrinking.

Thomas S. Barclay calls the early years of the new century a "period of political uncertainty" in Missouri. The rapid shifting of party balances, the upheavals resulting from exposure of graft, and the stampede of voters to become identified with reform movements make the description broadly revealing.

Governor Dockery had been a successful physician at Chilicothe and later a banker at Gallatin before entering politics. He had

---

[1] Williams and Shoemaker, *Missouri*, II, 260–78, 300–324, 422–23; article in the *Encyclopedia Americana* on "Louisiana Purchase Exposition"; article in *Dictionary of American History* on "Louisiana Purchase Exposition," by Frank Monaghan, III, 309–10.

been elected to Congress for eight consecutive terms in the district in which he was born. He had distinguished himself by diligent committee service, particularly as chairman of the Committee on Post Offices and Post Roads. Fast mail service between Kansas City and New York was one of the tangible results of his activity.

Representative Dockery was known also for his revisions in government accounting. The Treasury Department adopted the "Dockery accounting system" with excellent results. He proposed the substitution of salaries for fees in certain offices of the United States courts, and the annual savings effected by the change amounted to an estimated $2,500,000.

As governor from 1901 to 1905, Dockery did not emphasize rigid economy; on the contrary, he recognized the prosperity of the period by taking the lead in favor of substantial improvements. School appropriations were definitely generous. At the same time, the entire indebtedness of the state, with the exception of long-term school bonds, was extinguished before the end of his administration.

In the election that resulted in Dockery's choice as governor, the city of St. Louis made Joseph W. Folk circuit attorney. Under its home-rule charter, established in 1876 on the basis of a provision in the new Missouri constitution, St. Louis was governed by a two-house legislature and an elected mayor. The upper house, or Council, was composed of thirteen members, each elected for a term of four years with staggered terminal dates. The House of Delegates had one member from each of twenty-eight wards, elected for two-year terms. The Assembly of St. Louis had the power to fix tax rates, grant franchises, and pass upon all public improvements.[2]

JOSEPH W. FOLK AND MISSOURI'S REFORM WAVE

Joseph W. Folk was a native of Tennessee. He graduated in law at Vanderbilt University and came to St. Louis in 1893 to practice his profession. By 1900 he was a well-known member of the powerful Jefferson Club and was accepted by the Democratic party ma-

[2] Thomas S. Barclay, "A Period of Political Uncertainty, 1900–1912," in Williams and Shoemaker, *Missouri*, II, 444–50. In the same volume, see also pp. 442–43.

chine as its candidate for circuit attorney. He was popular among
the laboring classes for his part in a dispute between the Amal-
gamated Association of Street Railway Employees and the St.
Louis Transit Company. The union, struggling for a twenty cents
an hour minimum wage, a ten-hour day, recognition of the organization, and reinstatement of employees discharged for Union activity, had recently voted a resolution of thanks to Folk for his
energetic service in their behalf.

He was elected circuit attorney by a small plurality. He was
thirty-one years of age in 1900, when the city boss, Edward Butler,
and the city Democratic machine accepted him as prosecutor for
the city of St. Louis. He was quiet, affable, good-natured, scrupu-
lously honest, and personally well liked; but the intensity of his
pursuit, when he caught the scent of rumored bribery or perjury
and glimpsed the possibility of a conviction, quickly made for him
the reputation of a single-minded prosecutor.

William M. Reedy, the talented editor of the St. Louis *Mirror*,
gave Folk credit for ability and rigid honesty, but could not support him with enthusiasm because of the young attorney's "avidity
for power." Reedy called Folk an "ambitious genius" with a technique as "mercilessly cruel . . . as any logic that marks the philosophy of Nicholas Machiavelli."

Regular party men in Missouri, even those who had no political
"skeletons" to hide, were less comfortable in their contacts with
Folk than they were with associates who placed loyalty higher
among the virtues of officeholders. William Joel Stone, whose long
record was peculiarly free from scandal, once found himself on the
defensive in a Folk investigation. No evidence was found on which
a prosecution could be based; but Stone acquired the title "Gum-
shoe Bill," which was applied to him by friends and enemies alike.
Many cynical observers of the time and afterward regarded Senator Stone's immunity to prosecution a tribute to his cleverness
rather than his honesty.

Edward Butler was the Irish-born city boss of St. Louis during
Folk's early practice there. Migrating to the Missouri town before
the Civil War, Butler had become prosperous as a blacksmith. He
was interested in city politics and was elected to the House of Dele-

gates under the new home-rule charter in the late 1870's. Generally, he avoided public office for himself, but he was active in obtaining the election of men whom he could depend upon for support of his financial interests. In his practice as a blacksmith, for example, he had obtained a lucrative contract to shoe the mules of the street railway company. At the outset of his career in politics he was affiliated with the Democratic party, but in time he became known as the city's bipartisan boss. In the meantime, his real estate and other investments were shrewdly managed and he became a multimillionaire.

In 1897, one of the candidates for mayor of St. Louis, Lee Meriwether, made the charge that the street railways of the city, equipped with 1,480 cars, paid taxes on fewer than half of them, 714 cars. It was also publicly charged at that time, in regard to the railroad properties of the state, that assessments were made on a basis of 25 per cent of the property values, whereas home owners paid at rates varying from 75 per cent to 100 per cent of actual values.

Like many other St. Louis Democrats, Edward Butler was not in agreement with William Jennings Bryan on the silver issue. The political strength of the "Boss" was based upon his reputation for loyalty and his record of fulfilling personal agreements to the letter. An anti-Butler Democrat, Edwin Harrison, ran for mayor in 1897, and the "Boss" beat him by splitting the Democratic vote. Butler deliberately built up the strength of the Republican leader, Henry Ziegenheim; and when the election returns were in, he had been elected mayor, along with a solidly Republican council and a twenty-five to three Republican majority in the House of Delegates.

The coalition government, headed nominally by the Republican mayor but controlled in fact by Edward Butler, was utterly corrupt. After the "Boss" accepted Joseph W. Folk as the machine candidate for circuit attorney in 1900, he complained bitterly of the young lawyer's failure in the test of personal loyalty. On one occasion Butler said, "He spent four years tryin' to put me in the penitentiary."

When Folk began his investigations in St. Louis, with assistants chosen by himself—not Butler—he obtained thirty-two indictments of election officials. Seventeen of the accused men were Democrats and fifteen were Republicans. The circuit attorney followed these attacks by diligent research into the activities of Butler and other wealthy men whom he charged with corrupting these "little city officials."

He brought evidence before the grand jury in regard to Robert M. Snyder of Kansas City, who had agreed to pay the city of St. Louis $1,000,000 over a period of fifty years in return for a Central Traction Company franchise. Folk charged that Snyder had bribed twenty-five delegates at the rate of $3,000 apiece and seven councilmen, paying the latter sums ranging from $10,000 to $17,000, and then had sold his franchise to a rival transportation company for $1,250,000—all without having "paid a cent or constructed a foot of track."

Many prominent Missourians were prosecuted for perjury, bribery, or for accepting bribes. Some of the men who came under the fire of Folk's big reform guns were able and popular leaders. Some whom he expected to prosecute were never indicted. Folk was the only Democrat who won a major office in the state elections of 1904. His race was made on his record as a prosecutor of corrupt officials and businessmen. His investigation of the street railway franchise granted by the municipal assembly had resulted in the disclosure of a complicated pattern of fraud. He had actually obtained possession of a sum of money held in escrow as a bribe fund for members of the Council and the House of Delegates.

Folk had followed his exposure of graft in the street railway franchise by other dramatic indictments of prominent citizens—bribery and perjury in contracts involving Central Traction, Garbage Disposal, and City Lighting. Twenty-four indictments for bribery had been obtained and thirteen for perjury. Boss Edward Butler had been indicted on four counts. Nine defendants sentenced to serve terms in the state penitentiary and four who had become fugitives to escape prosecution had been added to Folk's impressive record for detecting and punishing dishonest public servants.

The circuit attorney became a candidate for governor well in advance of the active campaign in the summer of 1904. Nomination by the Democratic party depended upon the composition of the state convention, and Folk's first task was to obtain delegates who would give him a majority in the early balloting. He was fortunate in having two strong opponents who divided the support of the state central committee—James A. Reed of Kansas City and Harry B. Hawes, formerly president of the board of police commissioners in St. Louis. Since a majority of the convention delegates represented farm population, Folk devoted his attention mainly to the rural counties. The convention had to settle many disputes between rival delegations, and eventually Folk won most of the contests. He was nominated for governor on the first ballot.

The Republicans nominated Cyrus P. Walbridge, formerly mayor of St. Louis, to make the race against Folk. The Republican candidate for President of the United States, Theodore Roosevelt, was popular in Missouri. His policies had a strong appeal for the followers of William Jennings Bryan, many of whom were more favorably impressed by Roosevelt, the Liberal Republican, than by Alton B. Parker, the "safe and sane" candidate put forward by conservative eastern Democrats to lead their party.

Missouri elected Folk over Walbridge by a majority of thirty thousand, and at the same time returned Roosevelt electors by a majority of twenty-five thousand. By his record for convictions as circuit attorney in St. Louis, Folk had made a deep impression upon the rural Democrats, who were not dominated by political machines of the two cities. Personally popular, Theodore Roosevelt won the first presidential campaign in Missouri for the Republicans since the state gave its electoral vote to Grant in 1868—before former Confederate Democrats had been readmitted to the vote.

The upper house of the Assembly continued with a small Democratic majority; but the House had enough margin of Republicans to guarantee the defeat of old Senator Cockrell for re-election to the United States Senate. By a small majority of the joint session in 1905, the Assembly elected William Warner of Kansas City.

In the country at large, Theodore Roosevelt defeated Judge Parker, with more than 60 per cent of the total popular vote and 336 electoral votes to Parker's 140. In addition to Missouri, Roose-

Reproduced from Walter Williams, The State of Missouri

RAILROADS IN MISSOURI, 1904

[319]

velt won the support of West Virginia, Delaware, and Maryland, on the border of the Old South, and had the satisfaction of entering office with a Republican majority in both houses of Congress.[3]

During Folk's administration as governor, Missouri passed new legislation of a type generally regarded as progressive throughout the nation. In some instances better enforcement of old laws achieved the desired reform. A law was enacted which restricted the activities of lobbyists by providing compulsory registration and publicity. Enforcement of the anti-pass law for railroads reduced the direct influence of the common carriers over state officers.

Gambling was reduced, Sunday closing laws in St. Louis, St. Joseph, and Kansas City were enforced rigidly, child labor was restricted, and compulsory education laws were better enforced. Reformers among Folk's backers were disappointed by his failure to check vice and crime more effectively in the cities through the governor's control over police and excise commissioners, but perhaps he achieved all that could be reasonably expected in the field of law enforcement.

After a struggle that lasted two years, the Missouri Assembly passed a law that abolished the convention system for the nomination of state and local officers and for congressmen. The "open" primary became mandatory, with state election officers in charge of all elections. Joseph W. Folk had been the foremost advocate of the direct primary law for Missouri.

The initiative and referendum, devices for obtaining more direct participation by the voters in lawmaking, had been proposed by the People's party of Missouri as early as 1896. By 1900 the Democratic party was willing to submit the question to the voters in the form of a constitutional amendment. The first vote on the proposal resulted in defeat, but in 1908 the measure was again placed before the voters and passed by a majority of some thirty thousand.

In 1908, Governor Folk announced that he would enter the con-

[3] John T. Flanagan, "Reedy of the Mirror." *Mo. Hist. Rev.*, Vol. XLIII, 128–44; *Dictionary of American Biography*, VI (article on Joseph Wingate Folk, by Thomas S. Barclay), 489–91; Louis G. Geiger, *Joseph W. Folk of Missouri, University of Missouri Studies*, XXV, No. 2 (1953), 1–61, 98; Williams and Shoemaker, *Missouri*, II, 451–54; Roseboom, *Presidential Elections*, 338–45.

test for the United States Senate. Since Stone was a candidate for re-election, the test of popular support in the Democratic primary was certain to be a memorable political fight. The Governor and the Senator were not congenial party associates. Sharply different in personal traits, the two men provided contrasts also in political methods, elements of strength, and regions of popular support.

The campaign of 1908 was the first political contest in Missouri in which the automobile was an important factor. Both Democratic candidates toured the state and spoke to hundreds of audiences. Stone, who was sixty years of age, delivered 250 addresses, gradually becoming more vehement in his denunciation of the Governor. He declared that Folk was a reformer who had always carefully adjusted his clean-up campaigns to the promotion of his own political fortunes. Before Senator Stone's tour ended, he was hoarse and visibly exhausted.

Folk, more than twenty years younger than his opponent, spoke three hundred times. He, too, became abusive before the campaign ended. St. Louis and Kansas City gave Stone a wide margin over Folk—a majority large enough to overcome a small deficit for the Senator in the rural areas. Folk carried fifty-seven counties to Stone's forty-seven; but the vote of the cities was decisive. Folk had a total support of 144,718 votes, while Stone was the choice of 159,512. Under Missouri law the Assembly was bound, in the election of the United States senator, by the popular vote in the primary election. Hence the victory of Stone in the Democratic primary was a guarantee of his election by the Democratic Assembly.

The presidential campaign in Missouri was another contest that remained in doubt until the last returns were counted. William Howard Taft, President Roosevelt's choice as the Republican candidate, was not yet revealed as a conservative. Particularly, his confusion in regard to tariff issues did not become a burden of contradictions to carry through the political campaigns of the middle western states until later, after he was forced to take a stand on the Payne-Aldrich bill. During the campaign of 1908, Taft had the advantage of Roosevelt's blessing, since the retiring President regarded him as a liberal and the most desirable person to carry on the reform measures already begun.

In Missouri the Republicans won the eighteen electors by a small margin over Bryan's faithful followers. Taft's plurality in the state was under one thousand votes.

Across the nation at large, Taft received 7,675,320 votes to 6,412,294 for Bryan. With population substantially increased over 1896 and 1900, Bryan's numerical count was higher but his percentage lower than it had been in those earlier elections. His electoral support was roughly one-third of the total—162 votes to Taft's 321. The regions that voted for Bryan were the "Solid South," the border state, Kentucky, Oklahoma, Colorado, Nevada, and Nebraska; in addition, he garnered six of Maryland's eight votes. Missouri, West Virginia, and Delaware were border states carried by the Republicans.[4]

After a bitter fight in the primary election, the Missouri Democrats nominated William S. Cowherd for governor. The Republican candidate, Herbert S. Hadley, with the support of a united party defeated him in the general election by a plurality of fifteen thousand. Hadley's running mate, J. F. Gmelich, was elected lieutenant-governor by a much smaller margin; and the Democrats won all the other administrative offices. The justice of the Supreme Court, also, and ten of the sixteen congressmen were elected by the Democrats.

HERBERT S. HADLEY, LIBERAL REPUBLICAN

As attorney-general of the state during Governor Folk's administration, Herbert Spencer Hadley of Kansas City had compiled a notable record of convictions against "malefactors of great wealth." In addition to violators of Missouri's laws restricting common carriers, Hadley prosecuted the Standard Oil Company and won his case. He was particularly successful in extracting evidence from

4 *Official Manual, State of Missouri* (1947–48), 782; Roseboom, *Presidential Elections*, 347–55; Williams and Shoemaker, *Missouri*, II, 455–59; Geiger, *Folk*, 126, 129.

reluctant witnesses, including John D. Archbold, one of Standard Oil's powerful officials.

Hadley was described by a contemporary as "tall, slender, dignified, courteous [and] . . . fluent." He was definitely a liberal and an admirer of Theodore Roosevelt. He worked well with men of diverse political views and was generally accepted as a leader who earned the right to independent action by his personal honesty and the sincerity of his convictions.

His administration as governor began with a hopeful announcement of policies, including reform of the revenue laws and increased home rule for St. Louis, Kansas City, and St. Joseph. Specifically, Hadley proposed a new tax on the capital stock of corporations, inheritance duties, petroleum inspection taxes, and a license fee for wholesale liquor dealers. The Governor regarded his recommendations on the revenue system as the remedy for an acute need, since the state tax collections had fallen short of appropriations by $1,500,000 during the two years that preceded his administration.

The General Assembly of 1909, with a Democratic majority in the Senate and membership almost equally divided between the two parties in the lower house, did not prove co-operative in Hadley's major proposals. In the log-rolling schemes of the lawmakers, home rule for the cities became a partisan issue not always closely related to the democratic principle on which local self-government rests. The home-rule bills were defeated, and Hadley's tax program received only half-hearted support. He was able to prevent a deficit only by use of his authority to increase the saloon license tax by executive order.[5]

Liberal Republicans in the West became increasingly discontented with the leadership of President Taft. The Payne-Aldrich tariff was one factor in his decline of influence in Missouri. The support given by Taft to R. A. Ballinger in his contest with Gifford

[5] Tyrrell Williams, article on Herbert Spencer Hadley, in *Dictionary of American Biography*, VIII, 80, 81; Williams and Shoemaker, *Missouri*, II, 460; George E. Mowry, *Theodore Roosevelt and the Progressive Movement* (N.Y., 1960), 250 (short description of Hadley in 1912).

Pinchot, a powerful advocate of Roosevelt's conservation policies, was condemned by many liberal-minded men in all parts of the country. The Western Insurgents who combined with Democrats in the House to curtail the powers of Speaker Joseph G. Cannon in 1910 identified "Cannonism" with the policies of the Taft administration which they labeled ultraconservative.

When Theodore Roosevelt returned to the United States on June 18, 1910, from his travels in Africa and elsewhere, the grounds for his break with President Taft had already been prepared. At the outset of the new administration in 1909, Roosevelt had been surprised and perhaps shocked by Taft's failure to continue James R. Garfield, Luke Wright, and Henry White among his advisers. Roosevelt was convinced that the President-elect had given him an "unqualified declaration of intention," that he would retain these three men—Wright as secretary of war, Garfield as secretary of the interior, and White as minister to France—and the quick dismissal of all three had been an indication of Taft's purposes. In time the new President revealed more clearly his intention to shake off the liberal impulses that had on them the peculiar stamp of Theodore Roosevelt.

In Missouri the Republican state convention of 1910 was obliged to take a stand on Taft's policies in general and the Payne-Aldrich tariff in particular. Both were given half-hearted endorsement. Probably the loss of support that resulted from Taft's policies was offset by Governor Hadley's moderately progressive administration. In the elections of 1910, Republican candidates won important positions, including those of railroad and warehouse commissioner and the state superintendent of public schools. The Democrats captured thirteen of the seats in the lower house of Congress, however, and emerged from the election with a majority in both houses of the General Assembly.

The old state capitol, erected at Jefferson City in 1838 and remodeled fifty years later, caught fire on February 5, 1911, and was destroyed. The Assembly voted a bond issue for a new structure in the amount of $3,500,000, and the voters ratified the expenditure in a special election of August 1, 1911. The popular vote on the bond issue was 144,664 yes, 45,468 no. Joseph C. A. Hiller of

Glencoe, Theodore Lacaff of Nevada, Alfred A. Speer of Chamois, and Edwin W. Stephens of Columbia were appointed members of the State Capitol Commission. The building of the new capitol was a commendable example of honest, efficient, economical administration.

The seat in the United States Senate held for one term by William Warner of Kansas City was due to be filled in 1911. In the Democratic primary election of August, 1910, the voters expressed their preference for James A. Reed, also of Kansas City, and the General Assembly officially named Reed for the position. Since this was the last election of a Missouri senator prior to the adoption of the Seventeenth Amendment to the federal Constitution, Reed was the last to be elected by the Assembly. A prohibition amendment to the Missouri Constitution was submitted to the voters and defeated by a decisive margin. The negative vote was particularly large in Kansas City, St. Louis, St. Joseph, and other large towns.[6]

The presidential election of 1912 brought Theodore Roosevelt back to the center of the political show ring. As Elihu Root had foreseen, Roosevelt's efforts to organize his support for the Republican nomination led to an open break with President Taft and a serious split in the party. Nicholas Longworth and Andrew Carnegie were among the intimate friends of Roosevelt who urged him to ignore the call of ambition and the liberal governors that he should permit himself to be put forward for the Republican nomination. Hadley of Missouri was one of the prominent middle western leaders who gave support to the Roosevelt boom.

Eventually Taft became the regular Republican candidate, Roosevelt accepted the Progressive nomination, and the Democrats selected a man of little political experience but vast knowledge of government to take advantage of the uncertainty thus created among their opponents. Woodrow Wilson of New Jersey, formerly president of Princeton University and a capable scholar in the fields of government and history, was victorious in the Democratic convention at Baltimore after Champ Clark of Missouri had held the lead through twenty-seven ballots. After the

6 *Ibid.*, 120–27; Allan Nevins, article on Henry White in *Dictionary of American Biography*, XX, 102–103; Williams and Shoemaker, *Missouri*, II, 460–64.

tenth roll call, Clark had actually received a majority of the votes for a time and the Missouri delegation assumed that the swing toward the Speaker of the House could not be stopped.

But William Jennings Bryan of Nebraska, definitely a man of long experience and some skill in the ways of political conventions, threw the weight of his influence to Wilson. After a long and bitter struggle, the college president on the forty-sixth ballot received the necessary two-thirds majority for the Democratic party's nomination. It was Senator Stone of Missouri who moved that the convention vote for Wilson be made unanimous.

In the three-party campaign, Taft and Roosevelt were left far behind. Wilson led in popular votes, with 6,296,547 to 4,126,020 for Roosevelt and 3,486,720 for Taft. The electoral vote was an overwhelming victory for the Democratic candidate, since he carried forty states with a combined strength of 435 ballots, to 88 electoral votes for Roosevelt and 8 for Taft. Wilson's popular vote was far short of a majority and smaller than Bryan had received in any of his three losing campaigns.

Missouri voted for Democratic electors by a substantial margin. Wilson and Tom Marshall received 330,746 votes, to 124,341 for Roosevelt and Johnson and 207,821 for Taft and Sherman. Governor Hadley, refusing to follow Roosevelt in the "Bull Moose" revolt against the regular Republican organization, no doubt influenced many Missourians in favor of Taft. In the campaign for governor, Elliott W. Major, Democrat, defeated the conservative Republican, John C. McKinley, by a large plurality. The Democrats also elected a majority in both houses of the Assembly, fourteen of sixteen congressmen, and three justices of the Supreme Court.[7]

ELLIOTT W. MAJOR AND FREDERICK D. GARDNER

Governor Major, who entered his duties as chief executive in 1913 at the age of forty-eight, was a native Missourian. He had studied

[7] *Ibid.*, 466, 467; Mowry, *Roosevelt*, 210, 211, 243, 251, 256, 288, 289, 340; Stanwood, *History of the Presidency*, I, 567; II, 208, 302; Roseboom, *Presidential Elections*, 356–74.

law under the guidance of Champ Clark, and had been admitted to the bar in 1885. His public service was varied, including four years in the Missouri Senate and a term of four years as attorney general of the state. His record as a prosecutor gave him a reputation for vigor and fairness.

Hadley, the moderate Republican, was not an easy man to follow as governor. Major's association with him in the office of attorney-general probably developed both men in the direction of freedom from partisanship. The program which Major planned for his administration might have been Hadley's—in fact, was Hadley's—in some of its broad features. Perhaps that was a natural consequence of Major's close acquaintance with his predecessor's activities and aims as governor of Missouri.

More effective home rule for the cities, a State Highway Commission, a Missouri Public Service Commission, a board to pass upon pardons and paroles, and a commission to deal with care of the blind were high upon Major's list of state needs. He planned many improvements in public education, particularly in the establishment of rural high schools. He was in favor of higher pay for teachers, and recommended the creation of a commission to study the problems of public schools. He was a firm believer in careful preliminary investigation and analysis of each field of proposed reform before any great outlay of public money was made upon it. He asked for commissions on land reclamation, control of insurance rates, charities and corrections, tax equalization, reforms in the penal code, reforms in court procedure, and state aid for counties in road building.

He took a stand for making full use of federal funds available under the Smith-Lever Act—an agricultural extension program. He supported ratification of the Seventeenth Amendment to the United States Constitution, which provided for direct popular election of senators. This law went into effect on May 31, 1913, three months after the amendment legalizing federal income taxes. Missouri abolished the contract system for the labor of convicts in the penitentiary, with provision for continuing contracts already in operation to the end of 1916.

In the state elections of 1914 the Democrats recovered the office of state superintendent of schools when Howard A. Gass defeated the incumbent, William P. Evans. Both houses of the Assembly also were captured by the Democratic party, with 76 of 142 members in the House and 26 of 34 in the Senate.

William Joel Stone campaigned for re-election to the United States Senate and obtained a clear popular majority. All the votes cast for Republican, Progressive, Socialist, Prohibitionist, and Socialist Labor candidates, totaled 306,611; Stone received 311,576.

The presidential election of 1916 found the Republican party united again. The Progressive movement as a separate political organization had faded, as Roosevelt's friends had warned him it would do. By accepting the nomination of the third party in 1912, he had lost his chance to lead a united Republican party in a liberal revival in 1916.

The Republican convention named Charles Evans Hughes, with Charles W. Fairbanks as candidate for Vice-President. Hughes had for some months been the choice of party leaders, who were impressed by the vigor of his reforms as governor of New York. They believed that he might be acceptable to both wings of the Republican party, except members of the Old Guard who feared all measures of reform on the ground that change is bad for business.

The Democratic convention put Wilson and Marshall at the head of their ticket again. In Wilson and his opponent, Charles Evans Hughes, the voters were offered a choice between men of outstanding ability. The items of strongest appeal in both party platforms hinged upon foreign affairs.

The European war which flamed into sudden activity in 1914 and spread to alarming proportions within a year provided the United States with its most difficult problems of diplomacy in the history of the nation. The rapidly growing wealth of the American Republic, its enormous resources for war—especially the vital necessities of world-wide conflict, shipping and manufacturing —turned the pressure of European diplomacy upon the United States. Germany and England, by shrewd maneuvering and persistent assaults upon American public opinion, struggled for the prize of alliance with the great power of the Western Hemisphere.

The British won the contest by reason of many advantages: common language with the North Americans, a common tradition of political and legal development, and superior vehicles for propaganda—among others. The United States, through investments in war materials for the Allies, was in the war on the side of Germany's opponents before any declaration of hostilities. Loans to meet the war needs of Britain and France and the resulting purchases of American goods enlisted the support of the United States on the side of the Allies. The huge demand for American products turned the scale of prices upward, brought wide employment of laborers, and checked the previous trend toward hard times.

Woodrow Wilson gained the verdict in popular and electoral votes by an extremely narrow margin. In the total vote of the major parties, Wilson received 51.68 per cent, and the electoral vote was 277 for Wilson to 254 for Hughes. The thirteen votes of California, which had been carried by the Republicans in 1908 and the Progressives in 1912, went for Wilson. The Republican candidate would have been elected President if he had carried that state.[8]

In Missouri the two major parties were nearly equal in strength, as they were across the nation. The minor parties received meager backing. The popular support for Wilson was 51.8 per cent of the entire major party vote—397,016 in a total of 766,183.

For governor the Democrats nominated Frederick D. Gardner of St. Louis and the Republicans chose Judge Henry Lamm of Sedalia. The plurality of Gardner over Lamm was 2,263 in a total of 785,052 votes. James A. Reed was re-elected to the United States Senate in a close race against Walter S. Dickey. The Democrats also elected fourteen of the sixteen congressmen and seated a majority in both houses of the General Assembly.

The United States declared war against Germany by a vote of 82 to 6 in the Senate and 373 to 50 in the House of Representatives. Diplomatic relations had been broken off by President Wilson on February 3, and the war resolution was passed on April 6, 1917. For nineteen months thereafter, the United States was actively engaged in the Allied effort to crush the military and naval power of the German Empire.

8 *Ibid.*, 379–88; Williams and Shoemaker, *Missouri*, II, 468–74; *Mo. Hist. Rev.*, Vol. XLIV, No. 1 (Oct., 1949), 91; *Official Manual* (1947–48), 782.

Frederick D. Gardner, the war governor in Missouri, was forty-eight years old when he assumed his duties at the new state capitol in Jefferson City in 1917. Kentucky born, Gardner had lived in St. Louis more than thirty years. He was a Harvard University graduate. He was the owner of the St. Louis Coffin Company, a firm in which he had been employed before going into business for himself. His political experience was limited to brief local service—as a member of the St. Louis Board of Freeholders, he had helped to draft the city charter.

The principal recommendations of his inaugural address, other than threadbare platitudes derived from recent statements of general principles of good government by Woodrow Wilson, were concerned with Missouri taxes. Gardner recognized the need for more revenue to meet the rising expense of state government. Specifically, he proposed increases in the inheritance tax, a franchise tax on the capital and surplus of corporations, a state income tax, a flat rate of $500 for saloon licenses, a mortgage-recording tax, a secured debt tax, a tax for the inspection of soft drinks, and a tax for the inspection of spirituous liquors. The Governor estimated that state revenues would be increased by $4,500,000 as a result of his tax program.

The Assembly was impressed by Gardner's sensible summary of the state's needs, and a considerable part of his plan was put into effect. The State Tax Commission, created as a part of the Governor's program, was an indispensable factor in the administration of the new revenue laws. Full advantage was taken of the federal aid offered to the states for highway construction, by the enactment of the Hawes Road Law.

In common with the other states, Missouri of necessity gave major attention to problems created by United States participation in the world war. The first military unit from Missouri was ready to start for France on June 28, 1917—less than three months after the declaration of war. This unit, the Twelfth Engineers of St. Louis, began the work of preparing transportation routes for later American forces serving in France.

The Missouri National Guard, almost 15,000 in number, promptly became a part of the great training program by which the United

States met the challenge of the German Empire and her allies. For about five months the Guard was assembled and drilled at Camp Clark, near the town of Nevada in Vernon County. Then it was sent to Camp Doniphan, Oklahoma, one of the eight large cantonments for National Guard troops in the Southwest. The greater part of the Thirty-fifth Division, which went to France in the spring of 1918, was composed of Missouri and Kansas soldiers of the National Guard.

The Forty-second Division (the Rainbow), which was assembled at Camp Mills, sent directly to France, and trained there for early participation in combat, contained the First Missouri Field Signal Battalion under Major Ruby D. Garrett. The Rainbow Division, made up of select National Guard units from twenty-six different states, was on the battle line of the Western Front during 164 days—125 in quiet sectors, 39 in active sectors. Only the First and the Twenty-sixth divisions put in longer front-line service, and only the Second, First, Third, and Twenty-Eighth suffered greater casualties.

The Thirty-fifth Division, composed largely of Missouri and Kansas National Guard troops of whom about two-thirds were Missourians, served on the Meuse-Argonne sector for ninety-seven days, and suffered 7,283 casualties. The Eighty-ninth Division, in which most of the selective service troops from Missouri were enlisted, received eight months of training at Camp Funston, Kansas, under General Leonard Wood before they embarked for France. In combat, they were in a quiet sector for fifty-five days and an active sector for twenty-eight days. This division had 1,433 men killed in battle and 5,858 wounded. As a result of its effectiveness during the Meuse-Argonne offensive, the unit became known as the "Fighting Eighty-ninth." The battle of the Meuse-Argonne in the autumn of 1918 was the climax of the desperate, four-year struggle for existence. The object of the offensive, in the words of General Pershing's report, was "to draw the best German divisions to our front and to consume them." American troops engaged in the battle numbered 1,200,000. The German Army met the great offensive with every available division, and at the end of a battle that lasted forty-seven days, the German divisions had been crushed. Starting on September 26, the battle ended with the Armistice of November 11, 1918.

Missouri men who were enlisted in the armed forces were divided among the various services as follows: National Guard, 14,756; selective service, 92,843; volunteers in the Regular Army, 30,780; Navy, 14,132; and Marine Corps, 3,721. Total officers and men, 156,232.

General John J. Pershing of Missouri, commander of the American Expeditionary Army, was one of the distinguished military leaders of his generation. Pershing was born in Linn County, where he worked on his father's farm and attended the local public school. He received an appointment to the United States Military Academy, from which he was graduated in 1886. His service in the army included Indian campaigns in Arizona, New Mexico, and Dakota territories; a term as instructor at West Point; combat duty in Cuba and the Philippines, where his effective control of the turbulent Moros won high praise from President Theodore Roosevelt.

In recommending promotion for Captain Pershing, the President launched a typical Rooseveltian attack upon "mere seniority" as the basis for determining military rank. This practice Roosevelt characterized as the "triumph of mediocrity over excellence." The outcome of the controversy begun by the blast from the chief executive was Pershing's promotion to the rank of brigadier general over the heads of 862 officers.

From 1906 to 1914, he served in the Philippines again. In 1915 he commanded the El Paso patrol on the Mexican border, and in 1916, President Wilson appointed him commander of the punitive expedition into Mexico in search of Francisco Villa. A great personal tragedy for Pershing during that year was the loss of his wife and three small daughters in a fire at his home in California. A maid was able to save the life of one child, Pershing's son, in this catastrophe.

President Wilson's policy in Mexico, referred to as "watchful waiting" by his friends and called "deadly drifting" and various other less complimentary names by his opponents, was a program adopted at the beginning of his administration and continued through the troubled years of our neutrality in the European war.

General Huerta, a member of the clique that murdered President Madero two weeks before Wilson's inauguration in 1913, tried in vain to get official recognition from the United States. New York investors in Mexican properties condemned Wilson because he refused to adopt armed intervention at the time of greatest confusion and later denied official recognition to the inhuman Huerta—who apparently had the best prospect of restoring order.

Eventually President Wilson felt obliged to seize the Mexican port, Vera Cruz, as a means of preventing a German ship from landing supplies for Huerta. Nineteen Americans were killed in the action at Vera Cruz and more than one hundred Mexicans.

Still determined to avoid war with Mexico, Wilson accepted an offer of mediation by Argentina, Brazil, and Chile. The meeting at Niagara Falls, to which the ABC powers sent representatives to meet with American and Mexican delegates, made no final decisions; but Wilson's determination to "add no territory by conquest" was clearly demonstrated to all the world.

Huerta, denied recognition by the United States—and by Latin-American countries that were influenced by Wilson's policy—and challenged by other strong revolutionary leaders, was forced to resign. In July, 1915, President Wilson was ready to recognize the partisan chief whom he had favored from the start, Venustiano Carranza, as president of Mexico.

In January, 1916, Francisco Villa took a belligerent stand against the shipment of American military supplies to Carranza. As tangible evidence of his disapproval, his soldiers took sixteen American citizens from a train at Santa Ysabel and murdered them. Villa followed this outrage two months later by an armed invasion of United States territory. The town of Columbus, New Mexico, lying just north of the border, was raided and seventeen American citizens were killed.

President Wilson demanded of Carranza that permission be given for an expedition into Mexico by American troops as a means of preventing further border massacres. National Guard troops were mobilized and General Pershing was sent into Mexico with six thousand regulars. He pursued Villa to Parral, deep in the state of Chihuahua; and here the chase ended, despite the fact that

Villa had not been caught. Carranza felt obliged, because of deep Mexican resentment against the presence of American troops, to place many obstacles in the way of Pershing's search for the bandit. The diplomatic situation in Europe had become steadily more threatening, and the President decided upon withdrawal of the Mexican expedition in preference to an open break with Carranza.

Wilson's policy in Mexico had resulted in the establishment of relatively good order and safety for American citizens near the border. The Central Powers in Europe had failed to get a foothold or to obtain the alliance of a strong Mexican chief. A good beginning had been made in the gigantic task of creating an effective army—a force large enough and with sufficiently thorough training —to take a creditable part in the war to restrict the imperial ambitions of the German Empire. Mexico had been provided with excellent grounds for reversing her hostile, suspicious attitude, based upon resentment as old as the Mexican War of 1846–48.

General Enoch H. Crowder, who had charge of the selective service program; Brigadier General Edgar Russell, chief signal officer of the American Army in France; Rear Admiral Robert E. Coontz and Rear Admiral Leigh C. Palmer are among the distinguished Missourians who saw active duty as leaders of the armed forces. Admiral Coontz, a native of Hannibal, Missouri, was a veteran officer of the Spanish-American War, who became chief of naval operations at the age of fifty-four, in 1918.

Edward D. Taussig, born of an Austrian immigrant family at St. Louis in 1847, served in the Civil War as a teen-age lad, graduated from the United States Naval Academy in 1867, and after a long and distinguished naval career retired in 1909. He returned to active duty in 1918 and added a chapter to the credit of his well-known family by his valuable service in naval training.

Gregory C. Davison of Jefferson City, who graduated with honors from the Naval Academy in 1892, made his most valuable contributions in the field of mechanical inventions. His "balanced turbine torpedo" and his "Y" gun, used in firing depth bombs to check the German submarine threat, gave him a high place among those men who contrived implements of destruction. In 1933 he invented the "Davison all-purpose gun," a combination fieldpiece and anti-aircraft gun.

Frank W. Taussig, son of the St. Louis immigrant, William Taussig, had gained distinction as a scholar and was able to use his great talents in civilian activities during the war. He was born in 1859, and at the time of Woodrow Wilson's first campaign for the presidency, had become recognized as the foremost American authority on tariff. His preparation included youthful studies at Smith Academy in St. Louis, two years at Washington University, completion of his undergraduate studies at Harvard University, a year of study in Berlin, Germany, and two graduate degrees at Harvard. He was the author of a number of books, including *Principles of Economics* and *Tariff History of the United States*. During the war he served as chairman of the United States Tariff Commission and at the Conference of Versailles as an advisory delegate on economic problems.

The director of food production during the war was David F. Houston, secretary of agriculture. Houston was a native of North Carolina, a graduate of Harvard University, and for ten years a resident of Texas. After teaching at the University of Texas, he went to the Texas Agricultural and Mechanical College as president in 1902, and back to the University of Texas at Austin as president, in 1905. He came to Missouri as chancellor of Washington University at St. Louis, and was in that position when President Wilson appointed him secretary of agriculture. In 1920, when Carter Glass resigned as secretary of the treasury, the versatile Houston filled the place until President Wilson's term ended in 1921.

Civilian organization in Missouri during the war against Germany was ably directed by Governor Gardner. He took the lead among state governors in calling a food conference and was active in the work of the Missouri Council of Defense, which was directed by Dean F. B. Mumford of the College of Agriculture of the University of Missouri. The attention of the council, with its membership of 12,000, was devoted largely to food production—a natural development, perhaps, since Dean Mumford held the office of state food administrator. Missouri's rank among the states in value of agricultural products moved up from fourteenth place in 1916 to fifth in 1917.

The Women's Committee of the Council of Defense, under the chairmanship of Mrs. B. F. Bush of St. Louis, was notably active in providing refreshments for traveling soldiers and a multitude of incidental services. The fashioning of surgical dressings and hospital garments; toilet necessities, smoking supplies, dinners for departing soldiers; knitting; the mailing of letters—these were among the services rendered by Mrs. Bush's committee.

No small part of the civilian work in Missouri was done by the Red Cross, Y.M.C.A., K.C., and other voluntary groups. Men and women who delivered short speeches in connection with war bond sales were doing a task that was indispensable. Such civilian activities provide the unity—the wartime solidarity—in a democratic state that is supplied by enforced obedience among the people of a country which enjoys no tradition of liberty and popular voice in government.[9]

With the defeat of Germany and the beginning of the Peace Conference at Versailles in January, 1919, a strong isolationist movement took form in the United States. Led by Senator Henry Cabot Lodge, opponents of the League of Nations—President Wilson's design for keeping the peace among nations—obtained the signatures of thirty-nine United States senators to a manifesto denouncing the League. Since the negative votes of thirty-three senators would be enough to defeat Wilson's treaty, this proclamation amounted to legislative denial of his leadership.

Prominent among the "irreconcilable" senators was James A. Reed of Missouri, who based his arguments against the League upon a view of nationalism that was almost a denial of his twentieth-century environment. With Norris of Nebraska and La Follette of Wisconsin objecting to the injustices of the League, while rabble-rousers such as Borah of Idaho appealed to every current anti-foreign prejudice and demagogues such as Johnson of Cali-

[9] Roseboom, *Presidential Elections*, 379–90; Col. Leonard P. Ayres, *The War With Germany*, 13–23, 26, 29, 57, 114, 117, 139; *Official Manual* (1947–48), 782; Williams and Shoemaker, *Missouri*, II, 474–76, 482–85, 583–96.

fornia added to the confusion of voters by eloquent appeals to their ignorance, the league to keep the peace did not have a chance in America.

President Wilson, trying vainly to take the issue to the people on a speaking tour, collapsed and suffered a paralytic stroke. For several months he was wholly or partially unable to attend to his duties as President. Lodge and his followers completed the ruin of Wilson's efforts to give the United States a leading place in world organization. That defeat of President Wilson in his final great political contest was the prelude to the election of 1920.[10]

[10] Thomas A. Bailey, A *Diplomatic History of the United States* (N.Y., 1940), 664, 667–77; Julius W. Pratt, A *History of United States Foreign Policy* (Englewood, N.J., 1958), 495–506, 512–23.

-·≼ **15** ≽·-

MISSOURI AND THE ISOLATIONISTS,
1920-1933

THE ELECTION OF 1920

THE POLITICAL EVENTS OF 1904, when Missouri voters elected a long list of Republican officers, had removed the "one-party" label from the state. If any doubts remained, election of the Republican candidate for governor in 1908 by a plurality of 15,000 helped to dispel them. The evidence of the national elections provided more of the same two-party pattern, since Republican electors were chosen in 1904 and 1908. In later campaigns, too, the party of Theodore Roosevelt and Herbert S. Hadley displayed persistent vitality in Missouri through two Democratic administrations.

For the space of twelve years, 1921 to 1933, Republican chief executives were at the controls in Jefferson City, in the persons of Arthur M. Hyde, Sam Baker, and Henry S. Caulfield. During the same period, when Republican presidents were in office, Missouri gave its electoral support in turn to Harding, Coolidge, and Herbert Hoover.

The Wilson administration had not taken full advantage of Missouri's facilities for transportation and of its industrial development when the wartime projects were distributed among the states. Sixteen cantonments for the training of Regular Army troops and sixteen National Guard camps were established. Also, more than five hundred other military projects were undertaken by the federal government. Factories for the making of explosives, plants for the manufacture of a great variety of war materials, warehouses for

[338]

the storage of enormous stocks of goods, and many other expensive installations were made. The total expenditure for these construction projects was about $800,000,000—as Colonel Leonard P. Ayres has pointed out, about "twice the cost of the Panama Canal."

Only two of the 541 military establishments were situated in Missouri. The Democratic party leaders of the state found themselves in a weak position with respect to pressure for party favors at the beginning of the war; and it may be assumed that many Missouri citizens, at the end of the conflict, were not satisfied with the Wilson administration's conduct of the gigantic operations. Americans have always taken a strong stand in favor of substantial profits as a by-product of taking up arms. President Wilson himself was not a leader of wide experience in dealing with intra-party conflict. Missouri's claims to preference in the location of federal projects were neglected; and, as a result, the Democratic organization for a decade worked under a serious handicap.

In April, 1917, to be sure, one of Missouri's two Republican congressmen had voted for the declaration of war and the other had recorded no vote. Four Missouri Democrats in the lower house, however, had voted against the proposal of President Wilson in his war message; and one of the senators, William Joel Stone, had thrown the weight of his great influence against the President. The other Missouri senator, James A. Reed, was a party recalcitrant who later became an outright supporter of extreme Republican isolationism.

In 1917, the major political plans of the Democratic President were not warmly supported in Missouri. The partisans of Lodge and Taft, Root and George Norris, Hiram Johnson and Frank B. Brandegee were in no position to obtain war industries and troop concentrations for Missouri; and the leaders of the President's party found the competition from surrounding states unbeatable.

Iowa and Illinois had voted for Charles Evans Hughes in 1916, while Missouri had cast its eighteen electoral votes for Wilson. Yet Iowa and Illinois obtained Camp Dodge and Camp Grant, while Missouri was not favored by the location of any large—and expensive—concentration of troops. Oklahoma with Camp Doniphan, Arkansas with Camp Pike, Texas with three National Guard camps and the Regular Army cantonment, Camp Travis, all fared well with regard to military training expenditures. Kansas had Camp Funston and Kentucky, Camp Taylor.

A glance at the independent record of Missouri's leaders in both houses of Congress will serve to explain more fully the distribution of army posts. William Joel Stone had been a member of the United States Senate since 1903. As chairman of the Foreign Relations Committee he had great influence with members of both houses; and his substantial record for honesty and party regularity added to his weight in the Senate and with the voters of Missouri.

On April 4, 1917, Senator Stone addressed his colleagues in words that have generally been regarded the most effective statement that was made against the declaration of war. In the course of the short speech, he said: "I fear that Congress is about to involve the United States in this war, and when you do that . . . you will commit the greatest national blunder in history. I will vote against this mistake, to prevent which, God helping me, I would gladly lay down my life." In the same speech, Stone declared: "While we may differ . . . about the policy of entering the war, once in, all differences must cease." An obvious conflict was going on in Stone's mind, with party harmony opposed to his sincere personal dislike for war. It must be apparent, too, that the large number of pro-German Missourians among his constituents bolstered his stand against the declaration of war. He pledged full support, however, for such policies in the conduct of the war as might be agreed upon by Congress and the President.[1]

The attitude of some Missouri congressmen during the war was related to partisan bitterness that grew out of Woodrow Wilson's first nomination for President in 1912. Speaker Champ Clark himself, smarting over his defeat by Wilson five years after the event, could not make the transition in his thinking from volunteer armies to the selective draft. On April 25, 1917, he spoke in the House against the conscript system.

"I regret exceedingly that I cannot agree with the President . . . on everything in this bill," Clark said. He could not refrain from

[1] Ayres, *The War With Germany*, 28, 49–54, 58, 72–84, 85–100; *Congressional Record*, 65 Cong., 1 sess., Vol. 55, Part I, 210.

pointing out that the President of the United States is a powerful official. "He has his functions to perform, and, as far as I am able to observe, he is not bashful about performing them." Clark was still fighting the convention battle, after the voters had sent Wilson of Princeton back for a second term as President. The professional politician who was Speaker was still contesting the right of the upstart to exercise the high functions of his office, still trying to show that Wilson was not at home in the chief executive post, still maintaining the factional view, still fretting because Champ Clark had not been elected President.

The problem on which Speaker Clark had chosen to break with administration policies was a matter of vital concern to the nation, and the narrowly partisan view of the Missouri man was scarcely concealed by his bluff, good-natured manner. His factional tendency was obvious in his appeal to Missouri's pride in her truly great military record and her prejudice in favor of volunteer troops.

Henry Watterson of the Louisville *Courier-Journal* sent a letter to Speaker Clark, with a duplicate to Representative Sherley Swager of Kentucky, in which the great editor gave his views on selective service: "The volunteer system, like the stagecoach, served its purpose in primitive times; but like that stagecoach, it proved unequal to the expanding needs of modern times. The selective draft system is the contribution which experience offers to intelligence." With the experience of large-scale war, most thoughtful Americans have accepted the Watterson view, as Wilson's administration did.[2]

James A. Reed, the junior Democratic senator from Missouri during the war, was a man whose personal characteristics brought him into sharp conflict with Woodrow Wilson. In 1913, Reed had been sufficiently impressed by his party's program to avoid sharp conflict with the new President. He did, however, adopt a technique of deliberate insistence upon long debate on the Federal Reserve Bank Bill, with the obvious intention of slowing Wilson's schedule of reform. By comparison with Carter Glass, Robert

[2] *Congressional Record*, 65 Cong., 1 sess., Vol. 55, Part II, 1119–23; *Dictionary of American Biography*, XIX, 552–55 (article on Henry Watterson, by Arthur Krock).

Owen, and McAdoo, Reed was a novice in public finance. His insistence upon extended hearings on the banking and currency legislation gave the impression of stubborn resistance without valid reasons. His career as a prosecutor in Kansas City had not fitted him for deep analysis of the proposed Federal Reserve system; but as a member of the Senate Committee on Banking and Currency, he was in a position to obstruct a key measure of Wilsonian reform.

The bill was amended 563 times before it was reported by the Senate committee. Reed was still not satisfied with it, but the President's friends finally put it over. Secretary McAdoo attributed Reed's stand on the bill to the "antagonistic and controversial quality of his character." President Wilson, who studied the Federal Reserve Act with its principal authors in long, exhaustive night conferences at the White House, recalled in 1922 that Senator Reed, in committee, had "interposed every possible objection to the completion and adoption of the bill." The President also remembered that Reed's objections were "varied and inconsistent with one another."

Repeal of toll exemptions on the new Panama Canal, as a gesture of friendship to Great Britain and strictly honest treaty enforcement, was another of Wilson's measures that Reed opposed, unsuccessfully. On the appointment of Thomas D. Jones of Chicago as a member of the Federal Reserve Board, however, the junior senator from Missouri made his weight felt. His opposition to Jones, he said, was that he was a director in the "Harvester Trust created by Pierpont Morgan." The President explained that Jones held one share in the corporation, to qualify him for membership on the board of directors, and that his purpose in gaining that membership was to help in the fight against monopoly. But Reed had made the headlines as a great independent, and he held persistently to his original stand. Jones was not confirmed by the Senate.

William Joel Stone had voted against the declaration of war because he was an advocate of peace and believed sincerely that continued neutrality was America's best policy. He understood and had sympathy for the attitude of first and second generation Germans, who had political strength in the city districts that gave him substantial backing. His conduct as a regular party man, after his original gesture against the declaration of war, was co-operative. Before the end of the war, President Wilson had complete confidence in Stone's loyal support on Democratic party measures.

Reed, on the other hand, understood little of the complicated problems on which he took an "independent" stand. He was not a thinker but a political opportunist, who discovered that belligerent opposition to the President was a means of attracting the attention of many voters. He was not accustomed to defeat. As prosecuting attorney in Jackson County, he had obtained 285 convictions in 287 cases. "He hunted in leash . . . for law-defying corporations," George Creel wrote of him; "and there is no record of a single disinterested service in behalf of humanity."

Senator Reed had supported the Underwood-Simmons tariff. His original acceptance of Democratic party doctrines had been based chiefly upon his conversion to lower tariff rates; and the 10 per cent reduction provided in the new law could not fail to meet his approval. He also gave his support, generally, to the President's Mexican policy. In later years, after the end of his third and final term as senator, he was to write a timely book on repeal of the Eighteenth Amendment. This book, *The Rape of Temperance*, was an extravagant but fairly effective statement of his opinions on Prohibition.

Like Champ Clark, Senator Reed was a vehement opponent of the selective draft. In an editorial, the Kansas City *Star* said of the Senator: "He has not inspired confidence. He is a spoils politician of the old-fashioned sort." On April 20, 1917, the *Star* gave a more complete character sketch of Jim Reed, in two sentences: "He is fighting the President's selective conscription measure. After he is bowled over by the Senate and finds how popular the measure is in the state, he will come home and tell how he and the President got through the democratic bill for universal service." Perhaps Reed took his cue from this bit of sarcasm; for he finally voted for conscription and later mentioned the vote as a reason for pride in his war record.[3]

[3] *The Kansas City Star*, April 20, 1917; *Mo. Hist. Rev.*, Vol. XXXIX, 281–82; *National Cyclopedia of American Biography*, XXXIV, 8–11; James A. Reed, *The*

The junior senator hated Herbert Hoover and opposed his appointment as food administrator. His persistent attacks upon Hoover, the Food Control Bill, and the administration of the bill, his savage, perverse, unjust thrusts at the man who was working at a war job with no apparent partisanship brought general condemnation from fair-minded editors and other persons. In his choice of Hoover as food administrator, President Wilson was undoubtedly trying to de-emphasize party politics. Hoover did the work with energy and effectiveness—one of the best examples of nonpartisan administration in the entire war period.

Perhaps it was no coincidence that Reed repeatedly assumed the task of violent attack upon decisions of the President. It was Reed who had named Champ Clark as the choice of the Missouri delegation in 1912 at Baltimore. It was Missouri's misfortune that two of her most influential Democratic leaders were nursing grievances against Woodrow Wilson at the beginning of the preparations for war. Clark could not forget how close he had been to success at the Baltimore convention; and Reed, as the floor manager for Speaker Clark, could not forget that his candidate had been beaten by an amateur—Professor Wilson.

It was the misfortune of the Democratic party, too, that Woodrow Wilson could not start with a clean blackboard and take better care of the distribution of war orders during his second administration. Probably Missouri would not have voted Republican in three consecutive campaigns for President and for state officers if the state had received its full quota of war business.[4]

In 1920 the issues growing out of the war provided most of the party debates in Missouri. The Republican national convention met in Chicago from the eighth to the twelfth of June and announced a platform in opposition to the League of Nations. The candidates selected by the convention were hostile toward Wood-

---

Rape of Temperance (N.Y., 1931), 274–84; Lee Meriwether, Jim Reed: "Senatorial Immortal," 216–21; Bert A. Smith, "The Senatorial Career of James A. Reed" (M.A. thesis, University of Missouri, 1950), 6, 9, 10, 11, 13, 16, 19–29, 30, 32, 35–38); Congressional Record, 65 Cong., 1 sess., 2457.

[4] Smith, "James A. Reed," 39–44; Meriwether, Jim Reed, 233–34; Roseboom, Presidential Elections, 356–74.

row Wilson, "entanglement in European affairs," and Wilson's domestic reforms, including reduction of tariff rates.

The Republican candidate, Senator Warren G. Harding, was an Ohio newspaperman who had married a banker's daughter, prospered in the publication of the Marion *Star*, and built for himself a reputation as a conservative. Among his close political associates were Joseph B. Foraker and Henry N. Daugherty. He was on excellent terms with George B. Cox, whom he regarded a "peerless leader," but whom Allan Nevins—with the judgment of unbiased historical perspective—has described as "the notorious Cincinnati boss."

Probably Jess Smith of Washington Court House, Ohio, had been most helpful to the editor of the Marion *Star* in his climb to a seat in the United States Senate. Smith, as a close personal friend of the lobbyist Harry M. Daugherty, was a strong factor also in Harding's nomination for President by the Chicago convention.

The Democratic convention met in San Francisco, and passed over the Secretary of the Treasury, William G. McAdoo, who was married to President Wilson's daughter and had been referred to derisively as the "Crown Prince." Some of the state delegations paraded "favorite sons" before the convention, which also considered, along with McAdoo, several other members of Wilson's cabinet. A. Mitchell Palmer, the attorney-general who had made a ridiculous bid for publicity and the support of reactionary, antiforeign sentiment by his crusade against Red Russian Radicals, was much in the news but had little tangible support from liberal Democrats. Leadership of the party, wavering between support of Wilson's best ideas and withdrawal to a vague, evasive concept of isolationism, was definitely mediocre. In some instances, statements coming from local party committees amounted to a pusillanimous retreat.

Finally, on the forty-fourth ballot, it was Governor James M. Cox of Ohio who obtained the necessary two-thirds majority for the nomination. Cox was not identified with the diplomatic program of the Wilson administration, which left him in a position to avoid commitments on some of the questions that divided the Democrats.

Unfortunately, however, he could not make a strong bid for the support of liberals. His dependence upon state bosses of his party —such as Tom Taggart of Indiana, George Brennan of Illinois, and Charles Murphy of New York—alienated party strength that Wilson had built up. Since the Democratic platform approved Wilson's stand on the League of Nations and his conduct of the war and the peace negotiations, it is probable that McAdoo, Baker, Meredith, or some other member of the cabinet could have run a stronger race than Cox. Probably not one of them could have been elected President in 1920. Cox was particularly weak because his connection with boss-ridden electorates offset an effective Democratic argument against Warren G. Harding.

The Democrats conducted their campaign with meager funds. The Republican National Committee spent $5,417,000; their opponents spent $1,470,000. In reviewing these figures, Professor Eugene H. Roseboom remarked that "no amount of money could have saved Cox." Certainly, Cox's lack of enthusiasm for his party's platform and the lack of personal enthusiasm among Democratic voters for their candidate were serious obstacles.

Missouri, like most other states, did not like Cox and found many flaws in the Democratic platform. Many of the voters were strongly impressed by the early opposition of William Joel Stone to the declaration of war by the United States and by the persistent sniping at the President's war program by Senator Reed and Speaker Champ Clark.

When the time came for Missouri voters to choose between Cox and Harding for President, the count was 727,521 for the Republican to 574,924 for his opponent. Arthur M. Hyde, Republican candidate for governor, defeated John M. Atkinson of Ripley County by a plurality of more than 140,000. Atkinson was an experienced Democratic leader who had served three terms in the Assembly, had been speaker of the lower house, assistant attorney-general of Missouri, and chairman of the Missouri Public Service Commission.

Warren G. Harding and his running mate, Calvin Coolidge, carried the popular vote of the United States by a margin well over five million. The electoral count was decisive, 404 votes for Harding to 127 for Cox. Support for the Republican candidate was strong in all the border states of the Old South, Kentucky alone remaining in the Democratic ranks by a narrow margin. Tennessee, one of the former Confederate states and a factor in the Solid Democratic South since 1872, voted for Harding by a substantial majority.[5]

THE HYDE ADMINISTRATION, 1921–25

Arthur M. Hyde was a native Missourian, in his forty-fourth year at the time of his inauguration as governor, January 10, 1921. His father was a native of New York who had moved to Ohio, enlisted in the Union Army during the Civil War, and removed to Princeton, Missouri, after the war was over.

Arthur attended the public school at Princeton, an academy at Oberlin, Ohio, and the University of Michigan at Ann Arbor. He graduated in law at the University of Iowa and was admitted to the Missouri bar in 1900. After fifteen years as his father's partner at Princeton, he removed to Trenton in Grundy County. In politics he was a liberal Republican, a strong supporter of Theodore Roosevelt, and a losing Progressive candidate for the office of attorney-general in 1912. Prior to his election as governor in 1920, he had held no public office.

Hyde announced five main objectives in his inaugural address, pledging his administration to improvement of public schools and a policy of economy. Other promises were: "clean and efficient police administration"; "non-political . . . humanitarian control of the charitable institutions"; and "a fair redistricting of the state upon a population and not a partisan basis."[6]

As a measure of economy, Governor Hyde decided to use existing surveys of state governments as a basis for reform. "The results of the studies made by expert commissions in other states are available," he pointed out. He called attention to the similarity of activ-

---

[5] *Ibid.*, 391–97, 402; *Dictionary of American Biography*, VIII, 252–57 (article on Warren G. Harding, by Allan Nevins); *Official Manual, State of Missouri* (1955–56), 945; Williams and Shoemaker, *Missouri*, II, 585–86; Stanwood, *History of the Presidency*, II, 423.

[6] *The Messages and Proclamations of the Governors of Missouri* (Sarah Guitar and Floyd C. Shoemaker, eds.), XII, 3–10; *Mo. Hist. Rev.*, Vol. XXVIII, 323–24.

ities studied, and proposed concentration of responsibility in the office of governor as a means of increasing efficiency.

On the subject of corrupt elections, Hyde spoke plainly. He recommended changes that had proved useful in other states—the blanket ballot, voters' signatures at the time of casting ballots, and "teeth in the primary election law." He recommended support for consolidated rural schools, equal facilities for Negro children, better support for the state normal schools, and increased attention to the needs of the state university.

The Republicans held a working majority—19 to 15—in the Missouri Senate, and in the lower house a majority of 104 to 38. Fourteen of Missouri's sixteen congressmen were Republicans, and all three of the new judges in the Missouri Supreme Court were Republicans. Upon the death of William Joel Stone in 1918, the voters chose Selden P. Spencer, St. Louis Republican, by a majority of 35,283 over Joseph W. Folk to fill the vacancy in the United States Senate. Two years later, Spencer was re-elected over Breckenridge Long by a margin of 121,663 votes.

Governor Hyde's principle of executive responsibility was accepted by the Assembly for a referendum vote on the new departments of agriculture, budget, finance, labor, and public welfare. In the popular vote of 1922, however, all were defeated except the consolidated department of finance.

The state road bond election of November, 1920, had resulted in the passage of the "Centennial Road Law." Bonds in the amount of $60,000,000, approved by the voters after a spirited campaign, made possible the greatest road-building campaign yet attempted in Missouri. The State Highway Board appointed by Hyde's predecessor, Frederick D. Gardner, met in December, 1920, and awarded contracts on state and federal-aid projects that covered 402 miles of road building. By paying freight charges, Missouri received from the federal government heavy equipment for road construction valued at $3,249,903.75.

The Hawes Act of the Gardner administration, providing for extensive co-operation in President Wilson's grant-in-aid highway program, had furnished a basis for modern expansion in the roads of Missouri. The number of registered vehicles in the state was nearly 300,000 and increasing rapidly. The license-tag fees added over $2,000,000 to the state highway funds each year.

Governor Hyde placed four strong men on the State Highway Board. Theodore Gary of Macon and Kansas City was chairman. The members were S. S. Connant of Faucett, Murray Carleton of St. Louis, and C. D. Matthews of Sikeston. The state geologist, H. A. Buehler of Rolla, sat with the commission as an adviser but did not vote.

On August 2, 1921, the voters authorized, by a majority of 48,225, a convention "to revise and amend the constitution." In the same election a provision was added to the constitution making women eligible for state offices. The delegates to the convention were elected on January 31, 1922, and the eighty-three members convened at Jefferson City four months later. Of the twenty-one amendments proposed by this convention, only six were adopted by the voters. An additional bond issue for meeting a deficiency in payment of the soldiers' bonus and changes in the laws concerning suffrage, registration of voters, impeachment, and nepotism were among the amendments ratified. Kansas City was authorized to issue bonds for specified public improvements.[7]

The Missouri Democrats displayed great energy in the mid-term campaign of 1922 and won back many offices. James A. Reed, still running as a Democrat, was re-elected to the United States Senate over R. R. Brewster by a majority of 44,258. Charles A. Lee defeated Sam Baker, Joplin and Jefferson City Republican, for the office of state superintendent of schools by the slim margin of 6,045 votes. Three Democratic judges were elected to the Supreme Court, and twelve Democratic candidates for Congress, along with four Republicans. The Democrats also emerged from the campaign with majorities in both houses of the Assembly—nineteen to fifteen in the Senate and eighty-three to sixty-seven in the House.[8]

[7] *Official Manual, State of Missouri*, (1923–24), "Constitutional Convention of Missouri, 1922–23," 489–552; Williams and Shoemaker, *Missouri*, II, 486–89; *Congressional Directory*, 66 Cong., 3 sess., 1920, p. 56 (article on Selden Palmer Spencer).

[8] Williams and Shoemaker, *Missouri*, II, 489.

THE ELECTION OF 1924: SAM BAKER'S ADMINISTRATION

On August 2, 1923, President Harding was stricken with bronchial pneumonia at the end of a trip to Alaska, and died. Most of the financial scandals of his administration had not yet come to light, but the suddenness of his death, coupled with certain dramatic exposures of officers high in the executive branch of the government, started a wave of wild rumors.

Charles R. Forbes, head of the Veterans' Bureau, had resigned six months earlier under charges of corrupt administration. Charles F. Cramer had committed suicide; and Jess Smith of Washington Court House, Ohio, regarded by many observers of current politics the most intimate friend of the President and certainly a member of the inner circle that managed patronage in the form of contracts and appointments, killed himself in the apartment of Attorney-General Daugherty.

Two men who were definitely not of the scandal-monger group, eager to pounce upon the President's sudden death as material for sensational rumors, were William Allen White of Kansas and Nicholas Murray Butler of Columbia University. Both men talked with the President before his trip to Alaska, and both reported that he appeared to be much troubled—burdened by a weight of information which he could not discuss with party friends. Perhaps it was not remarkable that men in quest of bizarre news bits should find the President's death an item of consuming interest, or that the possibility of suicide or murder should be linked with the rumors that flew about.

Vice-President Coolidge, who promptly assumed the office of chief executive, provided a refreshing change from the irresponsible, "good fellow" atmosphere surrounding Harding's tenure as President. The mid-term elections to Congress had already furnished evidence that the voters were dissatisfied and that the party of isolation and high tariff would have to guard more closely against corruption. The elections of 1922 reduced the Republican majority in the House from a two-to-one position of control to a bare margin of 15—225 Republicans, 207 Democrats, and 3 Independents. In the Senate, the 51 Republicans did not enjoy a comfortable superiority because of the independent trend of the Norris-La Follette group, who sometimes gave their support to the 45 members of the opposition.

The new President was not so rigidly upright as to refuse political favors from corrupt party machines and Republican state bosses, such as W. Murray Crane of Massachusetts, Boies Penrose of Pennsylvania, and James E. Watson of Indiana. But he was a politician of too much skill to wreck his party by such personal appointments as Harry M. Daugherty, Jess Smith, Charles R. Forbes, and Albert Fall. Harlan F. Stone, a man of outstanding ability and integrity, replaced Daugherty as attorney-general in 1924; and gradually the worst of Harding's appointees lost their posts.

The Republican convention met at Cleveland on June 10, 1924. Coolidge placed his aspirations for a full term as President in the hands of William M. Butler, a textile manufacturer of Massachusetts. Butler was an experienced campaign organizer—a leader of the old Murray Crane machine. Coolidge was nominated on the first ballot by an overwhelming majority. After Governor Lowden of Illinois had refused to make the race for Vice-President, the Convention named Charles G. Dawes, also of Illinois.

The Democratic convention, in session at New York from June 24 to July 9, displayed a lack of harmony and general ineptitude in its struggle over platform and candidates that were reminiscent of 1920. The Ku Klux Klan was an issue which could not be settled satisfactorily by a national Democratic organization. The Klan flourished in the South, where it was looked upon as a revival of the old, post–Civil War organization that first used the name. The new Klan lacked the screen of justification that sheltered the hooded night-riders of Reconstruction days, when Radical dominance in Washington and carpetbaggers in the Southern states made conditions intolerable for men accustomed to political rights.

The new organization added to the unlawful violence of its forerunner all the prejudices of the old Know-Nothing, Native American movements. The Klan advocated a positive stand for white, Protestant supremacy, and cultivated suspicion and hatred for foreigners, Catholics, Jews, and Negroes.

Oscar Underwood of Alabama was a possible compromise candidate for the presidency until he lost the support of his own state and a large part of the entire South by revealing that he was not pro-Klan. Governor Smith of New York was placed before the convention by Franklin D. Roosevelt, in a speech that marked him for future notice by his party. William G. McAdoo had the support of many rural Democrats, particularly the "drys"; but he could not get enthusiastic support from the Klan, since he had never given it his approval. Alfred E. Smith could not expect support from delegates who came from Klan-dominated states or from sections that voted for dry laws, since he advocated repeal of the Prohibition amendment and was the son of immigrant Irish Catholics and the product of the most widely known big-city political machine in America, Tammany Hall. No one of the strong men among the Democrats was able to gain the full approval of the convention.

After 100 ballots, a conservative judge from West Virginia, John W. Davis, took the lead over Smith, McAdoo, and Underwood; and on the 103d ballot, was given the necessary two-thirds majority. Charles W. Bryan of Nebraska was chosen to make the race with Davis. Rising prices, even on farm commodities, forced the Democratic leaders to alter their campaign support of Davis and Bryan. They could not charge the Republicans with economic disaster. Their issues were not strong or clear cut and their candidates were weak.

Calvin Coolidge was popular and shrewd enough to remain silent on public questions of which he was ignorant. It was natural that as the successor of Warren G. Harding he should create an impression of statesmanlike virtue. He swept the country with a margin of seven and one-third million votes over Davis, and nearly ten million over La Follette, who ran as a Progressive. Coolidge received 2,500,314 more votes than his two opponents combined. The electoral college stood 382 for Coolidge, 136 for Davis, and 13 for La Follette. Only the "Solid South" voted Democratic, along with the adjacent Southwestern state, Oklahoma. The states on the border of the Old South—West Virginia, Maryland, Delaware, Kentucky, and Missouri—voted for Coolidge.[9]

[9] Roseboom, *Presidential Elections,* 403–17; *Official Manual, State of Missouri* (1925–26), 193–94.

[352]

The Missouri Republicans took a stand against the Ku Klux Klan and harped on the familiar refrains: economy and reduction of taxes. The road-building program was emphasized. Sam Baker of Jefferson City was nominated for governor, and he spoke at length on the subject of just administration for eleemosynary institutions.

The Democrats condemned the high-tariff views of President Coolidge and advocated lower taxes, reduction of railroad rates, and promotion of co-operative marketing. For governor the Democrats nominated A. W. Nelson of Bunceton.

The Missouri vote for Coolidge was 648,486, and for Davis, 572,753. In the great wave of isolationism in 1920, Harding had received 78,676 more votes than Coolidge four years later; and Governor Cox had received a Democratic vote approximately equal to that of Judge Davis. Robert M. La Follette, running as a National Liberal in 1924, with the support of the American Federation of Labor and the railway brotherhoods, received 81,160 votes in Missouri. Jackson County gave Davis a slight plurality; but Kansas City voted for Coolidge by a majority of 15,506. St. Louis County gave Coolidge a majority of 10,000; and the city of St. Louis recorded 139,433 votes for Coolidge to 95,888 for Davis. Sam Baker ran behind the national Republican ticket, finally edging out A. W. Nelson by a plurality of 5,872.

The Republicans elected all of the major state officials and gained control of the lower house, seventy-nine to seventy-one. The Democrats strengthened their hold upon the upper house, however, electing eleven of the seventeen members for whom votes were taken. After the election the Senate had twenty-three Democrats to eleven Republicans. For the national House of Representatives, the Democrats placed nine, the Republicans, seven. On May 25, 1925, Senator Selden Spencer died, and Governor Baker appointed George H. Williams of Clayton to fill the office until the end of the term. In the election of 1926, Williams became the Republican candidate for the full senatorial term, but he was defeated by Harry B. Hawes, St. Louis Democrat. In this mid-term election, too, the Democrats elected twelve of the sixteen members of Congress.

In his biennial message, Governor Baker admitted, in effect, that economies practiced by his administration had not resulted in sharp reduction of state expenses. He pointed out, however, that increased spending was, in every instance, the result of popular votes for special activities.

Governor Baker recommended and the Assembly passed a law authorizing local boards of education to add two years of college work to their offering. Municipal junior colleges, it was predicted, would help to solve the problem of rising costs in higher education.[10]

By 1920 the population of Kansas City had grown to 324,410 and was steadily climbing. Political methods and political results in Kansas City were becoming increasingly important to the state. The Pendergast family, particularly James and his two brothers, Michael and Thomas J., had become very powerful in Kansas City since James first came to the West Bottoms in 1880. Their rise to power had been rapid since 1892, when James was elected to the City Council, where he served for eighteen years with Michael and Tom as his loyal adherents.

Three Jackson County men who were associated with the Pendergast organization in the 1920's were destined to expand their influence far beyond the limits of Kansas City. One was Jim Reed, whom the Pendergasts supported for mayor in 1900 and for other positions of public trust later. He served as city counselor, Jackson County attorney, mayor of Kansas City, and United States senator for three terms, 1911 to 1929. Up to the age of eighteen, Reed was a Republican. As a Democratic politician, he broke sharply with President Wilson on foreign relations; and during the first term of Franklin D. Roosevelt became so bitter against the new Democratic President's policies that he frankly gave his support to the Republican campaigns in 1936 and 1940.[11]

A second Kansas City man who grew to the stature of national

[10] Williams and Shoemaker, *Missouri*, II, 494–501; *Official Manual* (1925–26), 243–44; *Mo. Hist. Rev.*, Vol. XXVIII, 163.

[11] *Dictionary of American Biography*, IV, 121–22; VI, 489–91; XVIII, 88–89 (articles on Clark, Folk, and Stone); Louis G. Geiger, *Joseph W. Folk of Missouri* (Columbia, 1953), 126–29, 156–68; Smith, "James A. Reed," 9, 22, 23; Garwood, *The Crossroads of America*, 175, 311–12; *Official Manual* (1945–46), 12–20; William P. Helm, *Harry Truman*, 3–27; William M. Reddig, *Tom's Town*, 7, 8, 28–38.

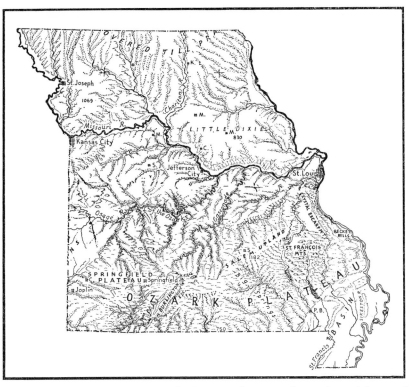

*From landform outline map drawn (copyright 1954)
by Erwin Raisz; used by permission*

Landform Map of Missouri

importance was Joseph B. Shannon. Born in 1867 in St. Louis, Shannon was five years older than Tom Pendergast. While the Pendergast brothers were building up their political following in the West Bottoms, Shannon was attending business college, studying law, serving as constable, and becoming in 1892, market master of Kansas City. He was chairman of the Democratic State Committee in 1910 and delegate to the Democratic national convention seven times during the years 1908 to 1940. He was a member of the Missouri constitutional convention in 1922 and 1923. He was a member of Congress from 1931 to 1943.

As a political leader in Kansas City, Shannon was a supporter of the Pendergast organization on some occasions; but he made his greatest reputation as boss of the "Rabbits," a rival faction which contested Pendergast's "Goats" in political campaigns that were colorful—to say the least.

Another of the Jackson County politicians who began his ascent in public office as a protégé of the Pendergasts was Harry S. Truman of Independence. Of the three—Reed, Shannon, and Truman —only the third achieved the eminence of statesmanship. If Truman's career had ended after his senatorial investigation of war contracts and before his election as Vice-President of the United States in 1944, he would be entitled to high rank among Missouri leaders. However, his achievements as President, which will be considered in a later chapter, provide the final test of his stature.

As judge of the Jackson County Court—an office to which he was elected in 1922, 1926, and 1930—Truman earned the right to be considered for a higher post. He was promoted for election by the Pendergast organization, which was exposed, in the course of years, as a corrupt political machine. Every other man elected in Jackson County, and in many other centers of American political activity, was put in office during the same period by similar forces —Democratic, Republican, or nonpartisan.

Woodrow Wilson, who proved to be a leader of exceptional purity of motive, was carried into the office of governor of New Jersey by a state boss who needed an honest man for a candidate. Many partisan critics have spoken with scorn of Truman's connection with the Pendergast organization of Kansas City, without taking the trouble to analyze that relationship. Many distinguished men in public life who have left unblemished personal records were as close to corrupt deals as Truman. Calvin Coolidge needed the approval of the Murray Crane organization for his rise in office; yet Coolidge is generally regarded, even by political opponents, as personally honest. Truman's record certainly entitles him to the same respect—even if his political opponents did find him a determined, aggressive, resourceful fighter.[12]

Another man who wielded outstanding influence in Jackson County and a much wider area, who never held high office but was a potent force in the choice of officers, was William Rockhill Nelson. He was born in Indiana from wealthy families on both sides— the Rockhills and Nelsons. He was one generation away from the uncritical grasp of Jeffersonian principles that held both Jim Reed and Joe Shannon back from a thorough understanding of Missouri in the twentieth century; that is, Nelson's father as a farmer was an ardent Jeffersonian, but he made no great contribution to the Democracy of his own time.

From his home in Indiana young William R. Nelson was sent to Notre Dame College. He was too much the individualist to adjust himself to Notre Dame discipline. Before he removed from Indiana, he had become interested in newspaper work through his connection with the Fort Wayne *Sentinel*. His experience was wide enough to make him believe, at the age of thirty-nine, that he had "already made most of his mistakes" when he came to Kansas City. The year was 1880, the time that also marked the arrival of Jim Pendergast from St. Joseph.

Nelson met and became acquainted with Eugene Field, founded the Kansas City *Star*, and continued the building of a great career in journalism. In his own peculiar way the editor of the *Star* was worthy of taking his place along with Joseph Charless, William Grosvenor, Carl Schurz, Emil Preetorius, Joseph Pulitzer, and the other great newspapermen of Missouri. Nelson built his career on a long fight against bossism. He fought the Pendergasts and forces that were allied with them—including Jim Reed and Joe Shannon

[12] *Ibid.*, 33ff., 108, 168–72, 174–84; Garwood, *The Crossroads of America*, 174, 183–84, 295–98; Helm, *Harry Truman*, 27–30; *Official Manual* (1945–46), 12–20.

—without assuming the posture of "other-worldliness" that characterized so many of the reformers. Nelson admitted raising money "for the workers" in a campaign for amending the charter of Kansas City.

Wilson, Coolidge, Truman, and Nelson the publisher rose above the sordid background that was a part of the American political scene during their active years. Daugherty, Fall, Doheny, George B. Cox, and Warren G. Harding did not. Tom Pendergast was not able to keep clear of the evils of Kansas City politics; as a party boss, in spite of his unquestioned generosity and sympathy for the unfortunate people who came to his attention, he contributed largely to corruption and crime in the region of his influence.

To censure every man, however, who was in any degree connected with political machines in boss-ridden states is to display a complete absence of political understanding. To single out a successful politician and condemn him without evidence of personal guilt, is worse; it is an example of injustice and partisan bias that is inexcusable.[13]

ELECTION OF 1928: HENRY STEWART CAULFIELD

In 1928, Republican plans definitely included a second full-term election for Coolidge; but the President announced that he would not run, and he stuck to the decision. The Secretary of Commerce, Herbert Hoover of California, who had also served in the Democratic administration of Woodrow Wilson, hoped for the Republican nomination and worked diligently to get it. Coolidge did not want Hoover as the next President, but Hoover was active and determined. Republican leaders compared the claims of Secretary Hoover with those of various "favorite sons," and usually came out with many factors in favor of Hoover.

Governor Lowden of Illinois was the strongest competitor, but he did not work effectively at the job of lining up delegates. In the first ballot for President at the Republican convention, Hoover had

---

[13] Garwood, *The Crossroads of America*, 146–49, 153; Helm, *Harry Truman*, 26, 42, 56; Reddig, *Tom's Town*, 37, 38, 323, 361–62; *Dictionary of American Biography*, XIII, 427–28 (article on Wm. R. Nelson by Victor Rosewater).

837 votes against a combined opposition of 221. A motion to make the choice unanimous was quickly passed, and the Republican delegates had selected their strongest man to run for President. Charles Curtis of Kansas was nominated for Vice-President.

Foremost among the Democratic aspirants for the nomination was Alfred E. Smith, the "Happy Warrior" whom Franklin Roosevelt had tried to make the party candidate in 1924. Smith had a strong appeal for laborers and for a wide range of "little people" who had confidence in this son of humble, sturdy parentage. He was a boss truckman's son, who had been elected governor of New York four times—in 1918, 1922, 1924, and 1926. Smith had the backing of Tammany, in spite of his disposition to limit its selfish aims to New York City. The Governor was without doubt the head of his party in the state. Urban labor organizations the country over would give Smith strong support, and there were many eastern businessmen who were aware of his careful, economical management of state business as governor. He also had the approval of social reformers who discovered his interest in, and his effective help for the solution of, urban social problems. Smith was a professional politician who knew how to conduct a campaign, whose reputation had not suffered greatly by contact with Tammany. He had outgrown the city machine and proved his honesty in many tests—as New York assemblyman, sheriff, member of the New York State constitutional convention, and chief executive of the state.

Al Smith's name was placed before the Democratic convention at Houston by Franklin D. Roosevelt. This was actually the third time Smith had been proposed as the presidential candidate by his fellow New Yorker. On the first ballot at Houston, the two-thirds majority was missed by a narrow margin. It was so close that the ballot was simply revised by changed votes, and the result without a second ballot was as follows: Smith, 849 2/3; George of Georgia, 55½; Reed of Missouri, 52; Hull of Tennessee, 50 5/6; Jesse Jones of Texas, 43; and smaller votes for some other "favorite sons."

Reed of Missouri had ruined his chances for more favorable Democratic backing by his unreasoning support of isolationism, his extreme hostility toward Herbert Hoover, and his factional contests with Woodrow Wilson. Reed could not find any favor

[359]

among the "drys"—those who opposed Al Smith because he was in favor of repealing the Eighteenth Amendment—for the Missouri senator was an ardent worker for repeal.

The greatest handicap of Al Smith as a candidate was the fact that he was a Roman Catholic. In some sections of the rural South, where the Democratic party was ordinarily certain of a majority, "Protestant supremacy" was almost as strongly entrenched as "white supremacy." The same important electorates were generally inclined toward "dry" voting, and contained many citizens who were suspicious of city dwellers, particularly if they bore the stamp of big city political machines.

Selection of the candidate for Vice-President demonstrated some skill in party management, definitely above the blundering choices of 1924 for both President and Vice-President and far better politics than the nomination of Cox for President in 1920. Senator Joseph T. Robinson, as an Arkansas Protestant and a "dry," was a man to inspire confidence in the South, and he had a respectable following of Democratic voters in the North and East.

The Democratic platform pledged the party to "an honest effort to enforce the Eighteenth Amendment." But Al Smith lost the "dry" support that this statement might have gained by his positive stand for repeal. One newspaper, the organ of a southern Protestant church that was making a vigorous fight against election of a "wet" candidate, published a brief news item that was obviously designed to be misleading. Without comment on the large number of Smiths in New York or identification of the subject of the item, a single sentence was printed: "Al Smith was arrested in New York last night, and charged with drunk driving."

In the United States, Hoover received approximately 59 per cent of the popular vote—over 21,000,000—to 15,000,000 for Smith. The electoral count was Hoover, 444; Smith, 87. The Republicans carried the West, nearly all of the North, and all of the former border slave states. Six states of the Old South voted for Smith: Arkansas, where the voters would not turn against Senator Robinson; Mississippi, Louisiana, Alabama, Georgia, and South Carolina. In Massachusetts and Rhode Island, where Smith's religious connection and his preference for repeal of prohibition were marks in his favor, the vote was Democratic.

Missouri voted for Hoover by a margin of more than 140,000. The percentage of Democratic votes was over 45, by comparison with 41 per cent in the nation at large. Jackson County voted for Hoover; but the City of St. Louis went for Smith, 176,438 to 101,701.[14]

For governor the Missouri Republicans named Henry S. Caulfield, and for Reed's seat in the Senate, Roscoe C. Patterson. The victory of Caulfield over his Democratic opponent, Francis Murray Wilson, was decisive—784,293 to 731,783. Patterson won the Senate race over Hay by a wider margin—787,499 to 726,322. The minor-party vote was negligible.

Governor Caulfield was fifty-five years of age when he took the oath of office at Jefferson City in January, 1929. Born in St. Louis near the end of Silas Woodson's administration, he received his elementary schooling there, was graduated in law from Washington University in 1895, and began the practice of law at the age of twenty-two. He had been elected to many offices: to Congress, from the Eleventh District, 1907–1909; St. Louis Excise Commission, 1909–10; judge, St. Louis Court of Appeals, 1910–12; and city counselor, 1921–22. After his term as governor, he was to meet defeat in 1938 at the hands of Bennett Champ Clark in a race for a seat in the United States Senate.

In his inaugural address on January 3, 1929, Governor Caulfield called sharp attention to violations of the federal Constitution in Missouri's segregated schools. He said there was no provision for equal educational facilities. Districts with fewer than fifteen Negro children had no separate schools, which denied all "school facilities whatever" to four thousand Negro children of school age. Exclusion of Negroes from the University of Missouri, Caulfield said, was "unjust and unconstitutional." The new Governor was pointing out clearly the bases on which the later struggle over integration would be fought. He recommended adequate transportation for Negro children in districts where no schooling was provided.

[14] *Official Manual* (1929–30), 206–209; Roseboom, *Presidential Elections*, 418–25.

He stated that Lincoln University might be developed "into a university in fact." He must have known that the cost of full-scale equality in separate schools would be prohibitive and that the state would retreat with sullen awkwardness from its violation of the Fourteenth Amendment.

No Missouri Democrat in high office took an equally progressive stand on the Negro problem until Harry Truman made his bid for the Negro and liberal Democratic votes in his 1940 campaign for the United States Senate. In a later section of this book Truman's stand on civil rights under the Constitution will be discussed more fully.

The Caulfield administration was a time of positive effort toward economy. The Assembly appropriated $26,526,739.65 for the years 1931 and 1932. The cost of government in 1931 was $10,646,537.58; and in 1932, $7,482,941.04. Thus the total expended was $8,397,-261.03 less than the appropriation.

Among the most notable of Caulfield's achievements, in addition to economical administration, were his steps toward support for the budgetary system, the Highway Patrol, and the Administrative Survey Commission. In recommending the survey, the Governor did not condemn the former chief executives of his party, Hyde and Baker, for omitting it. He simply called attention to the state's increasing need for information on the conduct of its business. Caulfield upheld the authority of Missouri to reduce insurance rates, and, upon affirmation of the principle in the United States Supreme Court, took the necessary measures to obtain refunds to policy-holders.

His attitude toward executive responsibility was revealed in a speech that has often been quoted. Five executive officers in Missouri, he said, were elected by the people and not responsive to direction by the governor. The auditor, treasurer, secretary of state, attorney-general, and superintendent of schools, together with the chief executive, give Missouri, in effect, six governors.

Governor Caulfield's veto of a redistricting bill, late in his administration, was probably the result of a blunder in party strategy. He refused to call a special session of the Assembly to consider a new bill, and in the next election the Democrats won all the

Congressional races. The high point of Tom Pendergast's power, outside of Kansas City, was probably a by-product of Caulfield's decision on the special session.

The Assembly granted his request for a commission to survey the needs of Missouri and make recommendations. The chairman of his commission was Theodore Gary of Kansas City, and the Governor himself took an active part in the survey. One of the recommendations was a bond issue of $15,000,000 for improvements in state eleemosynary and penal institutions. The voters approved the bond issue, thus clearing the way for a much-needed program of permanent improvement.[15]

15 *Messages and Proclamations*, XIII, 4–10; *Official Manual* (1929–30), 237–38; (1939–40), 39, 116–18.

-⋙ 16 ⋘-

THE RISE OF HARRY TRUMAN, 1933-1940

PRESIDENT HERBERT HOOVER regarded the financial panic of October, 1929, as a crisis for speculators but not a matter of vital concern for other Americans. He held firmly to his original view that economic conditions were basically sound and joined Secretary Mellon in predicting rapid recovery. The Smoot-Hawley Tariff Act, which passed the Senate by a bare majority in 1930, was signed by President Hoover against the advice of the country's leading economists, who joined in protesting the excessively high rates of the measure.

Many prominent businessmen, including the American Bankers Association as a group, took a stand against the bill before it became law on the ground that its protective features would serve as a barrier to foreign trade and thus retard an upward trend in American prices and employment. Economic conditions did not become better but grew steadily worse, and President Hoover was included in the resentment of voters toward his party.

The Smoot-Hawley Tariff was an object of attack not only because of its contents but by reason of the manner in which it was pushed through Congress. Joseph R. Grundy, prominent as a Republican agent for raising campaign funds in Pennsylvania and president of the Pennsylvania Manufacturers Association, had made the influence of the group he represented quite apparent by means of an ardent lobbying schedule in Washington. Governor Fisher seized the opportunity of a vacancy in the United States Senate to appoint Grundy as the second Pennsylvania member while the debates on the tariff bill were still unfinished.

It was natural that opponents of the high protective tariff policy should call attention to Grundy's position and that the public should refer to the revenue measure as the "Grundy Tariff." The President's approval of the bill in its final form linked him inseparably with a most unfortunate and reprehensible law. Hoover's efforts to improve the situation by means of an inadequate public works program, drought relief, and establishment of the Reconstruction Finance Corporation to bolster private credit did little to restore public confidence in the administration.

The Republican convention met on June 14 in Chicago. An ambiguous resolution on repeal of the Eighteenth Amendment was included in the party platform; but by the summer of 1932 a positive stand on either side of the prohibition question probably would have won more votes than the attempt at evasion. On the all-important subject of measures to stop the depression, the Republican resolutions were quickly branded by the Democrats as a "whitewash" job. President Hoover's record was praised in his party's platform, and blame for the lack of demand for American products was fixed upon world trade conditions.

The more conservative platform-makers succeeded in putting into the document some vague references to avoidance of "burdensome bureaucracy." Little was included that was satisfactory to such Republican progressives as Norris and La Follette. The Hoover veto of Senator Norris' plan for federal operation of Muscle Shoals had established a climate of hostility between the Republican administration and the liberals of both parties.

Little effective opposition to renomination of Hoover was found in the Republican convention and he received a large majority on the first ballot. His support of Charles Curtis for Vice-President was enough to gain a majority for him also.[1]

[1] *Official Manual, State of Missouri* (1933–34), 491–98; Roseboom, *Presidential Elections*, 430–34.

Charles Michelson, Democratic publicity director, by cleverly designed hints, made Hoover's errors in judgment appear more execrable than they were, in fact. A large part of the American public, impressed by the sarcasm and sly suggestions of Michelson's propaganda, came to regard Hoover as a weaker President than either of his immediate predecessors. Actually, he was far more intelligent than Coolidge and a vast improvement over Harding in every quality of executive competence during a most trying time.

The Democratic national convention opened its sessions two weeks later than the Republicans, also in Chicago. One candidate was far above all others in pre-convention forecasts—Governor Franklin D. Roosevelt. Probably the New York Governor would have been nominated on the first ballot if Alfred E. Smith had not suddenly decided to enter his name as a candidate. On the first three tests Roosevelt stood far above Smith of New York and Garner of Texas, but was nearly one hundred votes short of the two-thirds majority. Then James A. Farley, Roosevelt's manager, made a trade with the Garner support and received the promise of California and Texas votes in exchange for the nomination of Garner to the vice-presidency without opposition.

The Democratic platform advocated repeal of the Eighteenth Amendment, tariff rates based upon the needs of the Treasury and at competitive levels, federal credit to the states for relief of the unemployed, expansion of Herbert Hoover's public works program, and old-age insurance. Co-operative marketing, liberal terms on farm-mortgage loans, and control of surplus farm products were offered as the best solutions for rural problems. The Democratic resolutions also included a guarantee of antitrust law enforcement, a promise that appealed strongly to farmers.

Labor organizations and liberals of many occupations and regions approved the stand for reducing the hours of labor and for insurance against unemployment. The Democratic platform contained many items that stood in sharp contrast to the views of Harding, Coolidge, and Hoover relative to individualism in the age of giant machinery.

The Democratic candidates were in general harmony with the work of the Resolutions Committee. James A. Farley as head of the National Committee continued Charles Michelson as director of publicity and employed experts in various fields to help in the campaign for Roosevelt. Perhaps the most effective assistance in planning was from Justice Samuel I. Rosenman, who has been credited with some of the best ideas in Roosevelt's speeches. The candidate himself, in the opinion of Charles Michelson, was better as a "phrasemaker" than any of his assistants.

In the November election Roosevelt carried all but six states— Maine, New Hampshire, Vermont, Connecticut, Delaware, and Pennsylvania. The electoral vote was 472 for Roosevelt to 59 for Hoover; and the winner's popular margin over President Hoover was more than 7,000,000.[2]

Missouri voted for Roosevelt and Garner by the largest majority ever recorded in a national election in the state up to that time. The votes for Hoover and all the minor candidates combined were 584,488. Roosevelt's vote was over one million. In the Republican landslide of 1920, Harding had received a majority that was approximately one-third as large. Jackson County gave its support to Roosevelt by a margin of 70,000, and the vote in the city of St. Louis was 226,338 for Roosevelt to 123,448 for Hoover. Ozark County, on the border of Arkansas, and Douglas County immediately north of it were carried by the Republicans, as they were to be during the entire period of Franklin D. Roosevelt's four campaigns; but the state as a whole had returned decisively to the Democrats.[3]

For governor of Missouri in 1932, President Hoover's party nominated Edward H. Winter and Roosevelt's party chose Francis M. Wilson. Winter was completing his term as lieutenant-governor. A month before the election, Wilson died. The Central Democratic Committee immediately named Guy Brasfield Park, circuit judge in the Fifth District, to make the race as a substitute for Wilson.

2 *Official Manual* (1933–34), 451–52; Roseboom, *Presidential Elections*, 434–42.
3 *Official Manual* (1933–34), 212, 213; Edgar Eugene Robinson, *They Voted for Roosevelt, 1932–44*, (Stanford, 1947), 116–21.

Park was elected by the largest majority ever given to a candidate for governor of Missouri. The support for minor candidates was negligible. Park received 968,551 votes and Winter, 629,408. Kansas City's vote was 147,995 for Park to 71,957 for Winter, and the city of St. Louis gave Park a majority of 44,218.

THE PARK ADMINISTRATION

The new Governor was sixty years of age. His party background was Democratic, since his father had been a Confederate soldier under General Sterling Price and a factor in the Missouri counterpart of the "Solid South." Guy Park had attended the University of Missouri, graduating in law at the age of twenty-four, and had served in a succession of political offices in Platte County. In 1922 he was elected delegate to the state constitutional convention after serving as a city attorney in Platte City and prosecuting attorney for Platte County. He became a circuit judge in 1922 and was re-elected six years later, resigning from this office in 1932 to make the race for governor.

Park's inaugural address provided a glimpse of the difficult problems of 1933. More than three years had passed since the stock-market crash of President Hoover's first year in office, with no substantial recovery of prosperity in Missouri. Most important to the Missouri rural population was the long-continued decline in farm prices, reaching back to the beginning of Calvin Coolidge's first year as President. Perhaps the lowest point was reached in the early days of 1933, when Missouri poultry farmers sold eggs at ninety cents per case—three cents a dozen.

The need of relief for people in distress and the urgent necessity of reduction in governmental expenses challenged new state officials at the outset of the administration. "Drastic reduction of expenses—state, county, and municipality—is an implied pledge that must be kept," Park said. "Now, at the very beginning is the time for action."

His basic principle of democratic organization was stated in brief form: "It is the function of government to aid and protect, to relieve distress, and to promote happiness and prosperity." These ends must be achieved without a "yoke of oppressive taxation," without requiring people to "give more than they receive," he declared. The view on reduction of taxes might have been borrowed from Calvin Coolidge himself; but the statement in regard to the "function of government" marked the new Missouri governor as an apostle of the New Deal.

Park took steps at once to cut the number of state employees, and every department of the Missouri government began operating at a reduced cost. The Department of Agriculture absorbed some functions formerly belonging to separate agencies. Other instances of consolidation appeared in the economy program, which allowed Park to recommend stronger support for the educational institutions than his original estimate. He called attention to the figures published by the State Tax Commission which indicated that 58 per cent of all Missouri revenue was devoted to public education.

The state co-operated fully with the federal government in Public Works, Civilian Conservation Corps, and direct relief. A state bond issue of $10,000,000 for construction and repair of penal and eleemosynary buildings was supplemented by $7,000,000 in aid from the federal government. A sales tax of 1 per cent was passed in 1935, a rate that was doubled two years later.

Congress had proposed a Constitutional amendment to eliminate the "lame duck" session. Governor Park recommended ratification of the proposed change, which became the Twentieth Amendment upon passage by three-fourths of the states. The governor also recommended steps to guarantee "speedy justice" in the courts of Missouri by "returning to the courts the right to promulgate rules of pleading, practice and procedure."[4]

Revision of Missouri's liquor laws was made necessary by the adoption of the Twenty-first Amendment to the federal Constitution. The Department of State announced ratification of the amendment by conventions in three-fourths of the states on December 5, 1933. Removal of Constitutional restrictions on the manufacture and sale of alcoholic beverages brought drastic revision of the state laws in Missouri, as in most other states. A few

[4] *Official Manual* (1933-34), 13, 216-17; *Messages and Proclamations of the Governors of the State of Missouri*, XIII, 307-20, 333-39, 535-37.

states were still "dry" by provision of their own constitutions or by statutory restrictions. Prohibition was not to be repealed in the last state, Oklahoma, until 1959.

GOVERNOR LLOYD STARK AND THE PENDERGASTS

In the mid-term elections of 1934, Missouri Democrats had an opportunity to make a determined bid for recovery of Roscoe C. Patterson's seat in the United States Senate. The candidate who won the Democratic nomination, Harry S. Truman of Independence, was acceptable to the Pendergasts of Kansas City and the party organizations in other cities of the state. It must be added, too, that he was accepted with enthusiasm by the voters of Jackson County, where he was best known.

Probably Tom Pendergast would have preferred James A. Reed above all other Democrats to put forward for the Senate seat. Reed had been out of office since 1929, however, and he was seventy-three years old. Many voters of Missouri, with the perspective of six additional years, had lost confidence in Reed's judgment as a senator. A hard campaign was not a pleasant prospect for the old politician, and he discouraged the draft as a means of getting him into the race.

Pendergast called upon Joseph B. Shannon as his second choice to unseat the Republican, Senator Patterson. Shannon was sixty-seven, six years younger than Reed, and an experienced campaigner. He was firmly settled in his own district, ready to run for his third term as representative in Congress, with an excellent prospect of winning. He was armed with a briefcase full of devices for holding the attention of unthinking voters—tricks that had proved effective over the years.

He was prone to harp on the idea of Jeffersonian Democracy with little depth of understanding but with the zeal of a Crusader. Without the warning of a moment's notice, he could launch into a declamation on free enterprise, governmental abstinence from engaging in business, or any related topic. He could even afford the luxury of wild, melodramatic statements, such as: "I fear that Roosevelt and his clan are trying to set up a dynasty in this coun-

State Historical Society of Missouri

HARRY S. TRUMAN
as President of the United States.

THE TRUMAN LIBRARY AT INDEPENDENCE

MAIN HALL OF COTTEY COLLEGE AT NEVADA

Massie photograph, Missouri Commerce and Industrial Development Division
PRESENT-DAY KANSAS CITY INDUSTRIAL AREA

Massie photograph, Missouri Commerce and Industrial Development Division
MISSISSIPPI LIME COMPANY PLANT AT STE GENEVIEVE

Massie photograph, Missouri Commerce and Industrial Development Division
EAGLE-PICHER PLANT AT JOPLIN

Walker photograph, Missouri Commerce and Industrial Development Division
A KANSAS CITY GRAIN ELEVATOR

Massie photograph, Missouri Commerce and Industrial Development Division
THE MERAMEC MINING COMPANY'S PEA RIDGE
iron-mining project near Sullivan.

SENATOR THOMAS HART BENTON

Massie photograph, Missouri Commerce and Industrial Development Division
ARTIST THOMAS HART BENTON, HIS GREAT-NEPHEW

Massie photograph, Missouri Commerce and Industrial Development Division

SEGMENT OF THE CONTROVERSIAL MURALS
by Thomas Hart Benton in the Capitol at Jefferson City.

Walker photograph, Missouri Commerce and Industrial Development Division
THE CAPITOL OF MISSOURI, JEFFERSON CITY

try. The King, the Queen, and the Crown Prince Jimmy." Shannon preferred the relative certainty of election in his own district to the untried state-wide campaign for the Senate.

He objected to Tom Pendergast's third choice, Harry Truman. Shannon was inclined to measure men by the relative importance of the job they held or by their financial standing. He said that Truman lacked political stature for the Senate post. Six years later Shannon was to support Truman's campaign for the same office with great vigor. Truman the incumbent United States Senator was very different from Truman the county judge.

On November 6, 1934, Truman defeated Patterson by a count of 787,110 to 524,954. The winner's margin over all other candidates combined, in a vote that totaled 1,321,876, was more than a quarter of a million. Jackson County gave its favorite son a vote of four to one; and Kansas City, where the Pendergast organization was most potent, gave him five to one. The city of St. Louis voted for Truman by a margin of 50,000, and nearly all of the more populous counties gave him a majority. However, St. Louis County outside of the city voted for Patterson by a narrow plurality, and Greene County also went Republican, 14,010 votes to 13,848.[5]

Bennett Champ Clark, as senior United States senator from Missouri in 1936, was recognized as head of the state's delegation at the Democratic national convention in Philadelphia. Acting upon Clark's resolution, the delegates voted to abandon the century-old two-thirds rule for nomination. Clark was still full of resentment for the defeat of his father after he had carried a simple majority time after time in the balloting at Baltimore in 1912. Adoption of the more democratic rule in 1936 was too late to give the Clarks a personal advantage. It was to aid Roosevelt, however, in the nominations of 1940 and 1944, when the South probably would have taken a determined stand against his Civil Rights program; and it was to serve as a boon to Truman in his bid for the office of Vice-President in 1944.

[5] *Official Manual* (1945–46), 12–20; (1935–36), 298–99; Helm, *Harry Truman,* 3, 27–33; *Biographical Directory of the American Congress,* article on Joseph B. Shannon (speeches on Thomas Jefferson—"Certain Principles of Thomas Jefferson," etc.).

Democratic delegates at Philadelphia in 1936 made no important decisions in addition to dropping the two-thirds rule. The candidates and platform had been determined in advance. Roosevelt and Garner were nominated without effective opposition, and the predetermined resolutions were adopted with equal facility. Three radical movements, controlled in each case by such adolescent singleness of purpose as to prevent union, gained wide attention but had small effect upon election results. Senator Huey Long of Louisiana had become political boss of that state on the basis of strong opposition to the New Deal. He hoped to make himself a threat as presidential candidate through his fantastic "Share-the-Wealth" movement.

The other leaders of schemes that provided diversion from main political currents were Father Charles Coughlin and Dr. Francis Townsend. Each employed sensational claims and startling methods to compensate for lack of information and ability to think constructively. Coughlin was sufficiently vague for adjustment to any specific program, but he found it impossible to work with men who were not interested in simultaneous attacks upon Communists and international bankers.

Dr. Townsend stood for an unworkable old-age pension—$200 a month for all persons over sixty—based principally upon the stipulation that the money must be spent during the month of its payment to the pensioner. Dr. Townsend's ignorance of economics, public finance, and the incentives for thrift inherent in human nature did not prevent Townsend Clubs from taking money from the meager funds of elderly persons who were hard-pressed to pay for food and shelter.

The Republican convention at Cleveland labored over platform and candidates from June 9 to June 23, 1936. The New Deal had failed to solve the great national problem of unemployment, and the Republicans proposed to attack the blight by encouragement of private business. Economy was emphasized along with promises of old-age pensions, relief for the unemployed, and a thirteen-point farm-aid program—all of which suggested the opposite of an economy drive.

Governor Alfred M. Landon of Kansas was nominated for President over Senators Vandenberg of Michigan and McNary of Oregon. It was supposed that Landon as an oil producer would appeal strongly to American business. An attempt was made to put him forward as a liberal, a former supporter of Theodore Roosevelt, and at the same time a middle western businessman who would revive the "normalcy" of the Coolidge regime. Thus, to match the platform, the stand of the candidate was made to appear as a distortion. Landon accepted the nomination in a speech at Topeka, Kansas, approved the resolutions, and organized his campaign.

In selecting a candidate who would be recognized by many Americans as an ordinary man, the Republicans made an error which is almost inevitable in the popular choice of a great number of officials. The fact that a candidate is able to make people comfortable by reason of an obviously mediocre intellect and unobtrusive virtues does not mean that he is capable of performing well as President. Governor Landon probably would have been a second-rate chief executive, and he certainly proved to be a dull campaigner.

James A. Reed of Missouri, out of harmony with New Deal policies, joined with other disgruntled Democrats to support Landon's cause. The group was clearly conservative in the political appeal of its best-known names. In addition to Reed, the seceders were joined by Bainbridge Colby and by John W. Davis, Democratic candidate for President in 1924. Al Smith also thought he saw a chance to strike back at Roosevelt, who had been so inconsiderate —after years of support for Smith—as to rise above him in the political pattern of the Empire State. The Jim Reed faction called themselves "Jeffersonian Democrats," a clear indication of their lack of unity and their muddled thinking. If they had called themselves the "Patrick Henry Patriots" or the "Paul Revere Puritans," their influence in the election would have been the same as it was —negligible.

The Republican campaign, led vigorously but without expert political knowledge and without acumen by John D. M. Hamilton of Kansas, had the advantage of a $9,000,000 campaign fund and support of the nation's major newspapers. The Democrats were able to raise $5,194,000 by various means, including Jackson Day dinners on January 8 at $100 a plate. Jim Farley demonstrated his grasp of campaign finances by quietly accepting less than $100 a plate from deserving Democrats who found that amount above the limits of their personal budgets. Both parties had the support of organizations whose expenditures did not appear on the published records of the campaign committees.

Roosevelt's effectiveness in his speeches, including frequent radio addresses, served as an offset to Landon's newspaper support. The colorless personality of the Republican candidate was obvious in his public appearances. Perhaps the most important single item in the campaign was the fact that economic conditions in the nation had improved during Roosevelt's four years in office. Employment, real wages, and agricultural net income had all increased, and this fact resulted in a remarkable demonstration of confidence in the New Deal. The popular approval was reflected in the large number of ballots cast. The Democratic vote was 62.2 per cent of the total; all other parties combined had 37.8 per cent. Roosevelt received nearly eleven million more votes than Landon and nearly ten million more than all others combined. In the electoral college, the count was 523 for Roosevelt to 8 for Landon.[6]

Lloyd Crow Stark of Pike County was the Democratic choice for governor of Missouri. The Republicans named Jesse W. Barrett of St. Louis as their candidate, and he ran well ahead of his party's candidate for President in the Missouri vote. Stark was elected governor by a plurality of 264,199; but Stark's Republican opponent received 75,000 more votes than Missouri gave to Landon for President. Barrett was able to carry St. Louis County, but Stark had a majority of nearly 60,000 in the city of St. Louis.

The Democrats carried twelve of the thirteen Congressional elections. Only Dewey Short in the Seventh District was able to win a seat in the national House of Representatives for Missouri Republicans.

At the time of his election as governor, Stark was fifty years old. Although he was a graduate of the United States Naval Academy,

[6] *Official Manual* (1937–38), 7, 9, 11, 222–25, 336–38, 393–96, 434–37; Helm, *Harry Truman*, 35–37; Roseboom, *Presidential Elections*, 446–59.

he had entered the army during World War I and had been promoted to the rank of major at the time of his discharge. His principal civilian occupation had been management of the famous Stark Nurseries at Louisiana, Missouri. As president of the Missouri-Illinois Bridge Company he had taken a major part in the promotion and building of the Champ Clark Bridge across the Mississippi at Louisiana. He had been chairman of the Citizens' Road Bond Committee in 1928, in a drive which resulted in a bond issue of $75,000,000.

Stark's principal rival for the Democratic nomination had been William Hirth of Columbia, president of the Missouri Farmers' Association and a close personal friend of the winning candidate. Jesse W. Barrett, whom Stark defeated in the general election, also became a firm friend of the Governor. The new Missouri Senate in 1937 contained 31 Democrats and 3 Republicans; the House, 105 Democrats and 45 Republicans.

Governor Stark's inaugural address on January 11, 1937, emphasized the following objectives: administration of the state's business in an economical, efficient manner; co-operation with the humane policies of relief undertaken by the national government; expansion of Missouri's program of social security, including old-age assistance; permanent registration and honest elections; and an adequate program of highway expansion.

The Governor's chief concern in the field of education was elimination of waste through co-ordination. He was in favor of immediate action on teachers' retirement, authorized by popular vote in the latest election. He took a positive stand in favor of increased pay for members of the Assembly, state-use system for prison-made goods, improvement of the workingmen's compensation law, more effective inspection of mines for safety, liquor legislation to protect minors, and laws to implement the conservation of wild life.

Governor Stark gave special attention to the problems of farmers. Direct help for the victims of drought, relief from excessive taxation, and co-operation with the federal government for control of insect pests all met with his approval. He also had words of praise for the federal program of rural electrification and for the

program of land use through attention to forestry. Soil conservation under the federal plan was dependent upon state co-operation,
which meant to Stark that Missouri should give full support.

The Stark administration was outstanding in its major objectives.
For example, his financial management alone was enough to give
him high rank among the state executives of his time. The records
of his vetoes provide evidence of determination to hold the line on
expenditures. The executive vetoes of items in an appropriation
bill (House Bill No. 583) on July 8, 1939, provide an example of
thoughtful and determined economy. The largest item vetoed was
$100,000 from an appropriation of $800,000 to be devoted to administration of the Sales Tax Law. The total of all items vetoed on
that day was $553,000. The largest percentage of veto on any item
was $10,000 from an appropriation of $15,000 "for administration
of intoxicating liquor laws, Subdivision A."

The public debt of Missouri was reduced during two years, 1939
and 1940, from $114,341,839 to $100,881,839. On January 9, 1941,
the Governor estimated that the debt would be further reduced
during the biennium 1941–42 by an additional sum of $13,475,000.[7]

Tom Pendergast's organization had supported the election of
Stark, with the result that he received approximately three-fourths
of Kansas City's vote. In pursuance of his determination to fight
for clean elections, however, Stark found it necessary to take action against the Democratic machine in Kansas City. The city
manager, H. F. McElroy, was making a very bad record, which
included corrupt police officers in partnership with criminals and
a resulting prevalence of vice, burglary, robbery, and violence of
many kinds.

Election frauds, including a great variety of abuses practiced by
officials, coupled with the interference of gangsters in the casting
of ballots by citizens, brought intervention by the Governor and
the federal authorities. A woman preacher, Mrs. Dahlby, made a
public attack upon the evils of the gambling rackets and the Rabbi
Samuel Mayerberg boldly denounced the criminals who operated
with official protection. Mrs. Dahlby's children were threatened

---

[7] *Official Manual* (1937–38), 224, 228, 236–335; *Messages and Proclamations of
the Governors of Missouri*, XIV, 3–14, 159–63, 315–26.

in anonymous telephone calls that came to her home in an ominous campaign of terrorism. She was forced to leave the city; but Rabbi Mayerberg remained to see the beginning of a great reform movement.

On January 1, 1939, three officials took a significant stand in regard to cleaning up the shameful coalition of criminals and public servants in Kansas City. Governor Stark, Judge Allen C. Southern of the Sixteenth Missouri Circuit and federal Judge Albert L. Reeves were ready to take simultaneous action. Judge Southern ordered the Jackson County sheriff, Jim Williams, to make surprise raids on "protected gambling" places and called a grand jury to investigate crimes in Kansas City. The sessions of the grand jury were held in secret.

The boss of the north-side gamblers, John Lazia, had been shot to death by rival gangsters in 1934; but his successor, "Big Charley" Carollo, became the object of grand jury attention. He was indicted and eventually sentenced to a term in the penitentiary. The prosecutor and the sheriff of Jackson County were ousted. The grand jury indicted over two hundred persons, of whom seventy-eight served terms in jail or in prison. In the course of Carollo's trial, he stated that he had collected sums of money from gamblers and turned a fixed ratio of such collections over to Tom Pendergast.

The investigations also extended to the question of insurance rates in Missouri. Beginning some years earlier with the inaugural address of Elliott W. Major in 1913, the insurance companies had been more or less under fire by thoughtful citizens whose first concern was public welfare. Governor Major had recommended investigation, and a long struggle began over the state's authority to control insurance rates. Eventually the sum of $10,000,000 collected by the insurance companies was impounded to await judicial verdict on the controversy.

In 1935, R. Emmett O'Malley, superintendent of the Missouri Insurance Department, agreed upon a compromise settlement with the major companies. The policyholders of Missouri were to receive 20 per cent of the impounded funds, the insurance companies 50 per cent, leaving 30 per cent to cover the cost of litigation. When Stark became governor, he clashed with Tom Pendergast over the bargain made by O'Malley. The Governor flatly refused to reappoint this friend of Pendergast as head of the Insurance Department. In November, 1938, Judge James M. Douglas of St. Louis, appointed by Governor Stark to complete an unexpired term in the Missouri Supreme Court, ran against a candidate put forward by Tom Pendergast and won by a plurality of 119,498.[8]

Enmity between Harry Truman and Maurice M. Milligan was in a large degree personal. Truman opposed Milligan's appointment as federal district attorney, during Franklin D. Roosevelt's first administration. When Senator Clark joined with Burton K. Wheeler of Montana in a fight against Roosevelt's Supreme Court policies, the President cut off all federal patronage from the Missouri senior senator, but did not transfer that patronage to Harry Truman.

Federal prosecution for vote frauds was under way when Roosevelt appointed Milligan for a second term in 1938, and Truman again had to decide whether to support the choice or to oppose it. The press was praising Milligan's vigorous efforts, which were helping to uncover corrupt practices of a Democratic organization. The Republican newspapers were especially flattering in their accounts of Milligan's part in the investigations. Truman still disliked Milligan, and he took the unpopular position of opposition to confirmation. The reasons were good and sufficient, in the opinion of Senator Truman.

In a Senate speech he accused Milligan of accepting illegal fees in bankruptcy cases and a great variety of other unethical practices. He also referred in bitter terms to judge Albert Reeves and Judge Merrill Otis, declaring that their attitude in the trials in Kansas City was "violently partisan." He compared them with the Federalist judges of Jefferson's time, calling attention to Reeves' appointment by "that great advocate of clean, nonpartisan government, Warren G. Harding," and to the appointment of Otis by "that other great progressive nonpartisan, Calvin Coolidge." He

[8] Reddig, *Tom's Town*, 185, 261–64, 312–17; *Messages and Proclamations of the Governors*, XIV, 9–11; Williams and Shoemaker, *Missouri*, II, 471; Maurice Milligan, *The Missouri Waltz*, 129–31; *Official Manual* (1937–38), 21, 173, 178, 196; Helm, *Harry Truman*, 42–47.

called upon the Senate to support his stand against Milligan's appointment; but a second term for the attorney of the Western District was approved by the *Kansas City Star*, the St. Louis *Post-Dispatch*, and many other powerful newspapers, some of which enjoyed a degree of liberal reputation.

The district attorney had taken a positive stand against the criminals of Kansas City and had been especially active in finding evidence of fraudulent voting. "The implication is that any good lawyer I would recommend . . . would not do his duty in regard to the vote fraud prosecutions," Senator Truman said. "Every good lawyer and decent citizen in Jackson County is just as strongly opposed to vote frauds as the *Kansas City Star* and Mr. Milligan." The time of this Senate speech, not deliberately chosen by Truman but selected for him by the circumstances of Milligan's reappointment, was unfortunate. The senators and the President as well were bound by the image of a great reformer, created by the intensive publicity of newspaper stories. The romantic picture of a fearless knight, fighting for justice without a thought for his own personal safety, had caught the public fancy.

If Senator Truman was correct in his estimate of Milligan, the *Star* had made a hero of a demagogue; but the senators could not back up the opinion of their colleague and the appointment was quickly confirmed. Four years later Roosevelt was to name Milligan again for attorney of the Western District; but by 1946, Truman would be President and his friend Sam Wear of Springfield would be a natural choice for the post.

Perhaps Truman, as senior senator from Missouri, underestimated Milligan and made his criticism unduly sharp. Certainly Milligan's book on the "Pendergast Machine," published in 1948, was grossly unfair and inexcusably partisan in its attack upon the President, who was making his campaign for a full term.

Truman's loyalty to his friend Tom Pendergast, who was definitely not in a position to give political favors during the last days of his life (while Truman was still Vice-President), is presented by Milligan as a blot upon Truman's character. Appearing during the year of an election with partisan intentions veiled but slightly, the book probably damaged the author's reputation more than it did Truman's, in Missouri and elsewhere. The attempt to discredit the Senator who had dared to speak out against his confirmation as district attorney, on the ground that he attended "Boss" Pendergast's funeral, was a cheap attack. Truman "affirmed his loyalty to the boss who had raised him to power," Milligan wrote. The statement provides a warped concept for men who must have partisan ammunition to fire against a leader whose influence grows with the years. Milligan's reference to President Truman's "close personal and political association with James Pendergast, the boss's nephew and political heir," has the odor of a literary bill of attainder.

There is no evidence to support the theory that Tom Pendergast dictated the policies of Senator Truman or that he even attempted to influence Truman's votes on Senate bills. The Senator needed the power of a highly organized party in western Missouri, and the Pendergast forces needed the prestige of having supported a man of his caliber. A vigorous and independent senator who had won promotions by intelligent and honest service was worth more to the Pendergasts than a senatorial lackey would have been.

The influence of the Kansas City organization from 1930 to 1940, outside of Kansas City, has been vastly exaggerated. The corruption of the "machine" has been dramatized, the toughness of the Kansas City toughs has been emphasized, the heroism of the people who opposed the "machine" has been publicized, often by the heroes themselves, all for the sake of making a good newspaper story or providing material for an interesting lecture, until a balanced view of Missouri politics in the era has become difficult if not impossible to achieve. Americans reared on the traditions of Jesse James and Wild Bill Hickok find it burdensome to have facts injected into the current of the historical record.[9]

Kansas City election frauds were established by the federal investigations which culminated in a district court trial in February, 1937. It was federal prosecution which provided the most serious check to Tom Pendergast's career as a political boss.

Insurance graft in the amount of $315,000 could be traced by the court to Pendergast, where it seemed to vanish. The "boss's"

[9] *Ibid.*, 48–58; Milligan, *Missouri Waltz*, xiii, 4–11, 109–66; Reddig, *Tom's Town*, 174–84.

expenses in benevolences and "oil for the machine" were high; but persons who took the trouble to learn details about his daily life have decided that the real basis of his exposure was the need of money to pay gambling losses. Rabbi Samuel Mayerberg, perhaps the most effective of the preachers who braved the boss's wrath, is convinced that Pendergast's losses on horse races, distributed widely across the country, amounted to vast sums and provided the chief motive for his greedy acceptance of bribes.[10]

Homer S. Cummings, the first attorney-general for Franklin D. Roosevelt, and Frank Murphy, who filled the same office in 1939 and 1940, gave solid support to the investigations in Kansas City. A federal grand jury indicted O'Malley for income tax evasion and found a true bill against Pendergast on the same charge. Edward L. Schneider, secretary-treasurer for seven companies in which members of the Pendergast family held stock, disappeared. Among the seven companies were several in which city contracts provided major items of income—such as Tom Pendergast's Ready Mixed Cement Company and the Sanitary Service Company, in which 40 per cent of the stock was held within the Pendergast family.

Schneider's body was pulled out of the Missouri River and suicide notes in his car revealed the probable manner of his death, although some of his associates believed he had been murdered. On a smaller scale, the violent episodes in the breaking up of Tom Pendergast's empire were repetitions of the events connected with Warren G. Harding's decline.

R. Emmett O'Malley on a guilty plea was sentenced to a term of one year in prison and fined $5,000. A. L. McCormack, an agent in the insurance frauds, gave testimony that was helpful to the government's case as a means of obtaining a light sentence, two years on probation. Matthew S. Murray, W.P.A. director for Missouri, was convicted of income tax evasion and sentenced to serve a term of two years; Otto Higgins, McElroy's police director, received a sentence of two years for tax evasion; and John J. Pryor, a contractor, two years on the same charge.

Judge Otis sentenced Tom Pendergast on two counts to serve

[10] *Ibid.*, 323–24; address by Rabbi Mayerberg (Nov. 6, 1961); Garwood, *Crossroads of America*, 300.

terms in the federal penitentiary. The amount of his unpaid income tax, including interest and penalties, was fixed at $830,494.73; but the Treasury Department agreed to accept $350,000 as payment in full. On one count his term in prison was set at fifteen months with a fine of $10,000; on the other count it was three years with probation for five years.

The city manager, H. F. McElroy, resigned, and while his income tax payments were still under federal investigation, died. The financial affairs of Kansas City under his administration had been managed with fantastic disregard for public interest. One item in his weird bookkeeping was an "emergency fund" established to provide ready cash. The audit, after his resignation, disclosed that the "emergency fund" had contained $5,843,643.56 during the seven years of his administration.

The adventures of his daughter, Mary, who always stoutly maintained that her father was innocent, received more space in the great newspapers of the day than was devoted to the controversial paintings of Thomas Hart Benton, grand-nephew of the illustrious Missouri senator. Included in Mary's escapades, after she was kidnaped when she was in her middle twenties in 1933, were her fight to get the sentence of the leader of her abductors, Walter McGee, reduced; a denial of romantic attachment for any of the four criminals, but a fluttery account of their consideration while she was a captive, an account which suggested no limits upon the writers of melodrama; and a disappearance in 1935, apparently connected with her worry over the sentences imposed upon the kidnapers.

Back in her Kansas City home, Mary was disturbed by the increasing tension of her father's position, by the evidences of wealth acquired by irregular means, and by the absence of discipline in her daily life. Every public contact that she made, including her appearances in court against the McGees and her conferences with newspaper reporters at various times and on a great variety of topics, provided evidence of her unstable character, egotism, insatiable desire for publicity, her immature, maudlin ideas of social justice, and her dangerous confusion in regard to basic principles. She made a point of attending the funeral of the slain gangster Johnny Lazia and disclosed mawkish sympathy for the "torpedoes" who killed four law enforcement officers and a captured fugitive in the "Union Station Massacre," a machinegun ambush typical of the desperate cowardice of gang killers.

Perhaps one of McElroy's gravest offenses against society was his neglect of his daughter. At twenty-five she had the mental outlook of a spoiled adolescent, and at thirty-two she shot herself. Mary made the headlines again, but only for a short time.[11]

SENATORIAL ELECTION, 1940

Harry Truman became a member of the Interstate Commerce Committee in his first session as a senator and was appointed vice-chairman of a subcommittee. He also served on the Appropriations Committee and later on the Military Affairs Committee. Well prepared on transportation, especially on railroad matters, he was to take a leading part in writing the Transportation Act of 1940. His first report to the Senate called sharp attention to abuses in railroad management, with emphasis upon the losses sustained by stockholders and the public in bankruptcy cases.

Senator Truman recognized the difficulty of legislation to improve farm-commodity prices and gave much thought to the problems of farmers in his own state. He followed New Deal farm policies, in general, because the real income of Missouri farmers was steadily improving. He supported the Guffey Bituminous Coal Act as a measure designed to better the conditions of miners and mining, and voted for the Neutrality Act of 1937 along with Bennett Champ Clark. Later, both Missouri senators were advocates of revision, to meet new conditions brought about by the outbreak of war in Europe.

Franklin Roosevelt's Civilian Conservation Corps appealed strongly to Senator Truman and had his full support. The President's tariff policy with flexible rates within limits set by Congress also had his hearty approval. Downward revision of tariff rates was gaining favor and the excessively high rates of the 1930 revenue act seemed to be completely abandoned.

11 Reddig, *Tom's Town*, 324–57; Garwood, *Crossroads of America*, 295–318; Milligan, *Missouri Waltz*, 109–66; Henry C. Haskell and Richard B. Fowler, *City of the Future*, 131–58.

The loan to railroads provided by Truman's and Lowenthal's Transportation Act of 1940 resulted in new vitality for many roads. With funds borrowed from the public at 2 per cent, the Reconstruction Finance Corporation made loans to the railroads at 4 per cent with a total profit of $500,000,000.

The campaign of 1940 for the Missouri seat in the United States Senate was no ordinary political fight. There have been various interpretations of the results, but the facts of the voting are clear. In a three-cornered primary, Truman defeated Governor Stark by a small margin—7,476. In the general election he beat the able and popular Republican candidate, Manvel H. Davis, by 44,399. In the contest for the governorship the Republicans elected Forrest Donnell by a narrow plurality over the Democratic candidate, Lawrence McDaniel.

The factors in the Senate election are interesting and revealing. Maurice M. Milligan, who ran as "the man who smashed the Pendergast machine," had little to recommend him except his vigor in the Kansas City exposures. His tendency to dramatize his success in the prosecution of criminals and his intemperate claims with respect to his part in the great project marked him as a relatively small man who was out of his depth in a political campaign against Lloyd Stark and Harry Truman. In addition to the impression of egotism with which he reduced his chances of success, Milligan proved to be a weak campaigner. The method of the prosecutor is not well adapted to successful wooing of the reluctant voter.

Senator Truman devoted some attention to the organization of his campaign for re-election. His secretary, Victor Messal, came to Missouri and began the difficult task of establishing order among the Truman supporters. The exposures of crime and graft in Kansas City, linked with a machine which had supported Truman for the Senate in 1934, definitely hurt his chances for renomination and re-election.

Although the Pendergast organization had aided in the election of Governor Stark in 1936 and had swung the Kansas City vote for Democrats in some other contests, it was Truman who was vulnerable to attack. He was a target for Republicans of all kinds, naturally—in particular for politicians who felt the need of an antidote for the Harding scandals or similar obstacles to public confidence. Democrats whom Harry Truman had offended, not geographically connected with the Kansas City electorate, could afford to regard injury to the Senator with secret elation and outward fairness on a high, nonpartisan level. The Truman campaign would have to be fought with vigor and skill.

Messal set up his base of operations in Sedalia and busied himself with determining who among Truman's followers could be depended upon for loyal support. Messal had been secretary to Frank Lee of Joplin when he served in Congress. Lee agreed to act as one of the eleven vice-chairmen of the Truman campaign committee. Sam Wear of Springfield became chairman of the advisory board.

For re-election, Truman needed the support of organized labor, and he needed the help of certain key men in Missouri: Robert Hannegan, who seemed reluctant to commit himself; and Bennett Champ Clark of St. Louis, who appeared from the beginning to prefer Truman over Stark. Many of Truman's former supporters, who believed in his personal honesty and admired his loyalty and courage, feared the political effects of the determined effort that was being made to link his name with the downfall of Tom Pendergast.

Mayor Dickmann of St. Louis was leader of a powerful Democratic machine that favored Stark, a resident of nearby Pike County. President Roosevelt did not openly support either candidate; but Truman had disagreed with administration policies in a few instances and the disclosures of fraud in Kansas City had been a blow to the Democratic party as a whole. Governor Stark was confident, perhaps with the knowledge of his influence in a dependable state organization containing an effective core of officeholders.

While Truman's record in the Senate was not spectacular, his six years in Washington had produced intangible political assets. He voted independently when he had a deep-rooted conviction against a party policy. He gave diligent, intelligent, effective support for New Deal legislation. A. F. Whitney and Alvaney Johnston, heads of the two great railroad brotherhoods, were enthusiastic admirers of his activities in the Senate. Intelligent

[385]

Negroes recognized the fundamental honesty of his views on civil rights. Truman had spoken with pride of the New Deal appointments of Negroes to high positions and had lost no opportunity to speak out for the equal rights of Negroes as citizens of the United States. Negro voters in Missouri regarded him fair-minded and friendly to their interests.

Missouri Democrats gave 19.4 per cent of their votes to Milligan, 36.69 per cent to Stark, and 40.91 per cent to Truman. In the city of St. Louis, Truman had a margin of 8,411 votes over Stark and 52,408 over Milligan. In Jackson County, including Kansas City, Truman won by 23,907 over Stark and by 20,528 over Milligan. This impressive vote of confidence in his home county after the recent elimination of ballot frauds would seem to dispose of the charge that Truman owed his high office to ghost votes. The district attorney's motives in attacking Truman were questioned by the Senator's neighbors, even before Milligan's book appeared; afterwards, his partisan interest was obvious. The absence of high officials of the giant insurance companies from the lists of men prosecuted gave emphasis to the one-sided nature of the movement.

In the grand jury investigation of insurance frauds, Milligan recorded that the "head officials of some of the most powerful insurance companies in America" were present. Clearly, he was awed by the fact of being in the same room with so much power. The laws which forbid giving bribes, as well as accepting them, did not impress him nearly so much. The evidence before the grand jury soon established that Tom Pendergast was guilty of handling bribes amounting to almost $500,000. Was that sum charged loosely to "additional legal expenses" on the records of the insurance companies?

These were men who had a keen sense of values, who would not pay out a small fraction of the sums named in the indictments without knowing the purpose and destination of the money. At least one and probably more of these "most powerful" insurance officials shared the guilt of Pendergast and his associates. Probably the "boss" passed money on to his confederates; probably he lost part of it at the race tracks, thus providing a concrete example of the evils of gambling.

[386]

Mr. Charles R. Street, whom Milligan accused of collecting $100,500 of the bribe money in the form of checks and additional sums in cash amounting to $330,000, very conveniently died on February 2, 1938. Thus Street could not tell his "sordid story of intrigue and scandal." The honorable prosecutor and the high-minded judges who had faced the hoodlums of Kansas City with such fearless words seemed to think that Street's death took care of the responsibility of the insurance companies. "Reach for all, even if you find them in high authority. Move on them," said Judge Reeves to the grand jury on December 14, 1936. The instructions were specifically directed to the vote-fraud investigation, and few people who read the judge's words doubted his sincerity. Perhaps there was food for thought, however, in Senator Truman's charge that no judges since the Federalists of Jefferson's day, Samuel Chase and his colleagues, have been so violently partisan as Reeves and Otis, one appointed by President Harding, the other by Calvin Coolidge.

A. L. McCormack, who acted as a messenger during the period of insurance bribes, received a suspended sentence of two years. Before all the evidence he could give was extracted from him, he was quite intimate with the prosecutor. "Mac, let's have the story," Milligan quotes his own words to the "stoolie." The two years on probation that "Mac" received would have been regarded a "very light rap" in Johnny Lazia's territory. Perhaps Charles Street's death, if he had been a Lazia lieutenant, would have gone down as something more than a thoughtful and timely gesture.[12]

The statement that Milligan's entry into the senatorial race elected Truman is open to serious doubt. We do not know how many Milligan supporters would have voted for Stark, how many for Truman, or how many would have neglected to vote. The general election did not show a strong distrust of Truman. On the contrary, Missouri voters returned him to office by a margin of more than 40,000 while they were electing a Republican governor, Forrest Donnell. Truman carried Jackson County by 28,485 and the city of St. Louis by 46,272. All the Democrats who voted in

[12] *Official Manual* (1937–38), 224–30; Milligan, *Missouri Waltz*, 167–214; Reddig, *Tom's Town*, 318–23; Helm, *Harry Truman*, 57–75.

the primary election, for Milligan, Stark, and Truman, were 274,274 fewer than the voters who supported Truman against the Republican candidate in November. It is not certain that Missouri Democrats would have mustered a majority for Governor Stark over Manvel H. Davis, the Republican candidate in the senatorial campaign.[13]

[13] *Official Manual* (1941–42), 236–42, 366–67.

17

THE TRUMAN ERA

NATIONAL CAMPAIGN, 1940

THE REPUBLICAN CONVENTION opened at Philadelphia on June 24, 1940. The names of Senators Robert Taft of Ohio, Charles L. Mc-Nary of Oregon, and Arthur H. Vandenberg of Michigan were often in the headlines. Thomas E. Dewey, district attorney of New York City, was highly regarded by men of his party who wanted a youthful candidate with attractive personal traits. Before the first convention session a corporation lawyer of New York City, Mr. Wendell Willkie, began to be heard from as a promising new Republican.

Willkie had broken with the Democratic party in 1938 after a contest with Tennessee Valley Authority. As attorney for various utilities companies and as head of Commonwealth and Southern Corporation, he had made a place for himself in the business world. His personal qualities were positive assets for hard political campaigning. At forty-eight Willkie was full of vitality, a good public speaker, though not so good that he was able to invite comparison with the President, and liberal enough to appeal to dissatisfied Democrats and borderline Republicans who looked back upon Theodore Roosevelt as their greatest party leader.

Willkie ran ahead of Taft and Dewey in the convention and began to pick up the votes of candidates who fell out. Dewey released his support on the fifth ballot, and Willkie's lead over Taft rose to 52. Vandenberg's delegates, numbering 76 on the first bal-

[389]

lot, came over to Willkie on the sixth. The stampede was joined by Pennsylvania, and the choice of Willkie by unanimous consent was soon accomplished. The delegates then named Senator Mc-Nary candidate for Vice-President.

At Chicago the Democratic national convention on July 15 began the customary forms of presenting and considering candidates; but a third nomination for Roosevelt had been agreed upon in advance by party leaders. Vice-President John Nance Garner, relying upon the traditional limit of two terms for a President and perhaps hopeful that Roosevelt would refuse to run, announced that he would be a candidate. Senator Tydings of Maryland, opposed to a large part of Roosevelt's program, and Burton K. Wheeler, hostile to many New Deal principles and erratic in his support of contrasting policies, were eager to try for nomination.

Roosevelt was placed before the convention by Senator Lister Hill of Alabama, and the reaction to his name left small doubt about his place in the Democratic party. James Farley, John N. Garner, Millard Tydings, and Cordell Hull were presented, but the third-term tradition was about to be discarded. On the first ballot Roosevelt had 946 votes to a combined total of 149. A resolution to make his choice unanimous carried without opposition.

Roosevelt's preference for Henry A. Wallace of Iowa as candidate for Vice-President was challenged briefly, but in the end he too was nominated. A large factor in the President's support was the big city bosses who were fighting for survival against liberal revolts and were in need of New Deal prestige. Mayor Kelly of Chicago, the Pendergast heirs in Kansas City, Mayor Hague of Jersey City, and other strong Democratic leaders hastened to join the force that seemed most likely to stop the Republican threat.

Roosevelt carried Missouri again, but by a smaller margin than the Democratic sweep of 1932 and less than one-fourth the plurality of 1936. Roosevelt received 958,476 votes in Missouri to 871,009 for Willkie. The city of St. Louis was two to one for Roosevelt, and Jackson County (including Kansas City) gave Roosevelt 137,285 votes to 101,568 for Willkie.

All the states of the Old South, all of the former slave states of the border, and most states of the North and West were carried by

Roosevelt. The states for Willkie were Maine and Vermont, Indiana, Michigan, and Iowa, Kansas, Nebraska, the Dakotas, and Colorado. With 54.7 per cent of the popular vote, Roosevelt received 449 electoral ballots to 82 for Willkie.

An important factor in the Democratic victory was the skill of the President himself as a campaign speaker. In the corn belt states Henry Wallace took the lead in the Democratic campaign. Roosevelt spoke to large audiences in the vicinity of each new national defense project, carefully avoiding partisan issues. Perhaps the idea was sound, but the enormous volume of Republican propaganda seemed to demand more skillful rebuttal than Wallace and the other Democratic speakers could provide.

Willkie and Roosevelt were agreed on a policy of giving all possible aid to Adolph Hitler's enemies, immediate attention to a rearmament program, and selective draft for military service. Both candidates denied the intention of sending troops to Europe except in defense of American liberty, and both knew with certainty that the war would involve the United States unless one group of belligerents promptly crushed the other. With greater newspaper support and a huge campaign chest, however, the Republican managers determined to place Roosevelt before the public as a warmonger.

Wendell Willkie announced his intention of holding campaign expenses to the limit set by the Hatch Act—$3,000,000. In Pennsylvania alone, however, Republican campaign expenditures reached a total of $2,500,000, administered by state and local authority and by volunteer organizations. Huge expenditures were obvious in every part of the country in a wide variety of advertising. The "Mothers of America," financed by the Republican National Committee, made its appeal for Willkie and Peace. "Democrats for Willkie" made an effort to capitalize the Republican candidate's former party connections. No great pains were taken, of course, to spread the information that he had once served on a Tammany committee.[1]

Former Democrats who disapproved a third term for Roosevelt

[1] Roseboom, *Presidential Elections*, 460–70; *Official Manual, State of Missouri*, (1941–42), 236–42.

included James A. Reed of Missouri—who had, in fact, repudiated the New Deal when it first dawned upon him that it was a new deal and had worked for the election of Landon in 1936. Alfred E. Smith of New York, George White of Ohio—Democratic national chairman during the bungling campaign of James M. Cox in 1920 —John J. O'Connor of New York, and the lame-duck Nebraska senator, Edward R. Burke, all took a stand for Willkie.

Bennett Champ Clark of Missouri accepted his party's choice reluctantly, yielding to the inevitable, and finally made a radio address in which he indorsed the entire Democratic ticket. Glass and Byrd of Virginia were of no help to the Democratic campaign, and the Northwestern isolationist, Burton K. Wheeler, was grumpily silent. Garner of Texas was silent. All in all, however, the total influence of the Democrats who revolted and those who engaged in the cold war against Roosevelt was small.

A greater political threat was the announcement of President John L. Lewis of the C.I.O. that Roosevelt had forfeited his right to be regarded the champion of labor. Lewis said that he would resign as head of the C.I.O. if Roosevelt were elected. The immediate approval of his announcement by Harry Bridges and other labor leaders suspected of attachment to World Communism had the effect of weakening Lewis's stand. The fact that Tom Girdler, head of the Republic Steel Corporation and known as the antilabor spokesman for big business, favored Willkie further weakened the attempt of John L. Lewis at party revolt. Most labor leaders remained staunchly for Roosevelt and the Democratic program.[2]

GOVERNOR FORREST C. DONNELL

The primary election of 1940 in Missouri provided an interesting study in state politics. Allen McReynolds of Carthage had strong support in the rural areas and substantial backing in Kansas City for the Democratic nomination as governor. Lawrence McDaniel of St. Louis enjoyed the support of the city organization there, approximately half of the Democratic strength in Kansas City, and

[2] Roseboom, *Presidential Elections*, 471–74.

the advantages of highly skilled publicity direction. McDaniel's plurality in the city of St. Louis was 71,430 and in the state of Missouri, 71,154. Probably the issue of the old-age pension was the most potent factor, aside from organization, in the election. The St. Louis candidate offered the more attractive prospect for the aged.

The Republicans nominated Forrest Donnell in a relatively light vote of 189,069. In the general election, however, Donnell made a deep incursion into Democratic ranks and defeated McDaniel by the margin of 911,530 to 907,917. The Democratic State Committee petitioned the General Assembly for an investigation of the election; and on January 10, 1941, both houses passed Joint Resolution No. 3, providing funds for a "general and sweeping investigation." Governor Stark vetoed the resolution, thus cutting off a partisan contest that probably could have served no useful purpose.

Stark's farewell address to the Assembly in 1941 contained a message closely related to his final veto. "In these perilous times," he said, "it is doubly necessary that every public official should . . . serve the people strictly according to the constitution and the laws of the land, without partisan bias and with only the welfare and the safety of our democratic form of government in mind."[3]

Forrest C. Donnell was born in Nodaway County, Missouri, in 1884. He was an honor student at each level of his education: valedictorian of his high school class in Maryville, elected to Phi Beta Kappa as an undergraduate in the University of Missouri, and member of the Order of the Coif in law school. The campaign for governor in 1940 was his first political race. In his last year as governor he was to be elected to the United States Senate for the term 1945–51.

The contest that arose over Donnell's election postponed his inauguration as governor until February 26, 1941. He had waited for a decision of the Missouri Supreme Court, carefully refraining from defiance of the Assembly. He sought a writ of mandamus in the high court which would require the Speaker of the House of Representatives to declare Donnell's election. The Supreme Court

[3] *Official Manual* (1941–42), 366–67; *Messages and Proclamations of the Governors of Missouri*, XIV, 3–14, 167–69.

decided by unanimous vote that Joint Resolution No. 3 was unconstitutional and directed the Speaker to make the declaration of election. Every member of the court at the time of this decision (*State* ex rel *Donnell* versus *Osburn*) had been elected as a Democrat—a fact which added weight to Governor Stark's refusal to be drawn into an unjust, partisan attack upon the successful Republican candidate for governor.

After Donnell was seated, Lawrence McDaniel filed a legal petition for recount of the ballots. By May 21, 1941, the Democratic candidate was convinced by results of the recount to that date that Donnell had been elected, and he notified the contest committee that he was ready to accept the original election returns.[4]

A constitutional amendment adopted by the people in the election of 1940 provided that judges of the appellate courts and circuit judges of Jackson County and the city of St. Louis should not be required to run for office on party tickets. Another change that was incorporated in the new constitution of 1945 transferred the function of canvassing election returns of executive officers from the speaker of the House to a board composed of the secretary of state and two judges of a court of record.

In December, 1941, the Japanese attack on Pearl Harbor altered the plans of the Donnell administration. The war against Japan and her European allies became the principal business of every American governor. However, a second movement of major importance was taking place in Missouri. The people authorized a constitutional convention in 1942, and Governor Donnell set April 6, 1943, for the election of delegates.

One Republican and one Democratic delegate from each of the thirty-four senatorial districts and fifteen delegates-at-large were elected. The convention assembled at Jefferson City on September 21, 1943, and ended its work on September 29, 1944. This wartime constituent assembly, like the convention of 1875, worked with great diligence. Among the delegates-at-large were Robert E. Blake of St. Louis, who was elected president of the convention,

[4] *Ibid.*, XV, 3–9; *State* ex rel. *Donnell* v. *Osburn*, 347 Mo. 469; *State* ex rel. *Donnell* v. *Searcy*, 347 Mo. 1052; *Mo. Hist. Rev.*, Vol. XXXV, 470.

Leo T. Daniels of Ellington, and Allen McReynolds of Carthage. Among the district delegates were former Mayor B. F. Dickmann of St. Louis, John C. McVay of Trenton, Howard Potter of Springfield, former Governor Guy Park of Platte City, Thomas C. Hennings of St. Louis, and Richard Nacy of Jefferson City.

In the special election of February 27, 1945, the voters cast 312,032 ballots for the constitution to 185,658 against it. Fifty-four counties voted for its adoption; sixty-one counties, for the most part counties of small population, voted against it. St. Louis County and the city of St. Louis were for it, three to one, Jackson County gave it four to one. Other units of dense population carried the Constitution by large majorities: Buchanan County, two to one; Greene County and Boone County, nearly two to one. Apportionment of members in the Assembly was the issue that was most debated and perhaps the decisive factor in determining the popular vote. In the state at large, 62.7 per cent of the voters were in favor of adopting the new constitution, 37.3 per cent against it.

The section that contained the apportionment provision of the new constitution directed the secretary of state to take the initial step in apportionment. The constitutional language was positive, leaving no loophole of discretion for the officer. "On the taking of each decennial census of the United States," the clause provided, the secretary of state "shall forthwith certify to the county courts" the number of representatives to be elected in each county. Counties entitled to more than one representative were to be divided by the county court into single-member districts.[5]

MISSOURI AND THE SECOND WORLD WAR

Missouri took a major part in the second global war of the twentieth century, both in the actual combat and in production of war goods. General Omar N. Bradley of Moberly, Missouri, commanded the Twelfth Army Group in the invasion of Europe. This army, with 1,300,000 combat troops, was the largest American

[5] *Messages and Proclamations of the Governors of Missouri*, XV, 4, 5; *Official Manual* (1945–46), 144–79.

force that has ever served under a single field commander. Bradley was to become chief of staff in 1948 and one of the two Generals of the Army in 1950.

More than fifty Missourians attained high rank in the army or the navy during the war—that is, the rank of general or admiral. Bradley, who became known as the "doughboys' general," was probably the ablest field commander produced by the United States since General John J. Pershing. In addition to the many officers of every grade, Missouri provided for the armed services, between 1941 and 1945, some 450,000 men and women. In December, 1944, the United States Army had a total number just over 8,000,000, of whom 220,881 were residents of Missouri.

Omar N. Bradley was born in Clark, Missouri, in 1893. He was admitted to the United States Military Academy at eighteen and attained the rank of major general at the age of forty-nine in 1942. After the surrender of General Krause with 25,000 men in the Tunisian campaign, Bradley received a Distinguished Service Medal and advancement to the rank of lieutenant general.

In the Sicilian campaign, Bradley took Troiana, Randozzo, and Messina in thirty-eight days, and was awarded the Legion of Merit. For the final great American and British drive into Western Europe, General Eisenhower was made supreme commander, General Bernard Law Montgomery was given command of all British and Canadian troops, and General Bradley all American troops in the field. Invasion of the Normandy coast began on June 6, 1944, and Germany surrendered on May 8, 1945.

Chester W. Nimitz, American naval commander in the Pacific, moved into Asiatic waters and reached Saipan in the Marianas as Bradley invaded Normandy. The fall of Saipan was followed by American reconquest of Guam, a colony which Japan had occupied as the war began. American bombers attacked military installations in Formosa and Japan, dropping bombs on Tokyo in November, 1944, from planes based in Saipan. Iwo Jima, six hundred miles closer to Tokyo, fell to the American forces early in 1945; and Okinawa, after an epic battle that began on April 1 and ended in the middle of June, also came under the control of United States naval and land forces.

In the meantime an army commanded by General Douglas Mac-Arthur, covered by Admiral William F. Halsey's fleet, landed on the island of Leyte in the Philippines and began the reconquest of the American province. Under the terms of an act passed by Congress in 1934, the Philippines had been well on their way toward independence when they were occupied by Japan in 1941 and 1942.

The battle of Leyte Gulf, beginning on October 25, 1944, resulted in the destruction of a major part of Japanese naval power. MacArthur's land forces, advancing upon Japanese positions in Samar, Mindoro, and Luzon, began the march to Manila in January, 1945, and entered the city on February 3. By June 30, Mindanao had been occupied and reconquest of the Philippines was practically complete.

As American forces closed in upon Okinawa and the other islands on the way to Tokyo, the Japanese began extensive use of *Kamikaze*, a device for the destruction of major American naval units. Japanese pilots bore down upon American ships with planes heavily laden with bombs, attempting to ram them from the air. These desperate, suicidal flights resulted in heavy losses; but the American war vessels, surface and submarine, tightened the circle about the Japanese homeland.

United States casualties in the battle for Iwo Jima, fifteen square miles of fortified power that could not be by-passed, numbered 4,900 killed and over 15,000 wounded. The Japanese had 20,000 killed in the action.

On August 6, 1945, four months after Harry S. Truman became President, an American plane dropped the first atomic bomb ever used in war upon the city of Hiroshima, Japan. Of 344,000 inhabitants, nearly 130,000 were casualties, including 78,150 killed. Three days later an atomic bomb was dropped upon Nagasaki (population 252,630), with similar results. On August 10 the Japanese news agency Domei put out a broadcast indicating that the island empire was willing to surrender, unconditionally. Emperor Hirohito agreed to take orders from the Allied commander during discussions of permanent terms by the belligerents. On September 1, a delegation representing the United Nations met with Japanese officials on board the U.S.S. *Missouri* and signed formal terms of surrender.[6]

The part played by Missouri in the manufacturing of war goods and the training of soldiers was definitely more adjusted to the state's potential of production than it was in 1917. The generally cordial relation between the Roosevelt administration and the Missouri members in both houses of Congress was a factor in the contrast. The insistence of Senator Harry S. Truman upon war production in the West as well as the East had its effect. The recognition of little producers, in their total output, also a prominent feature of Truman's plans, was an aid to Missouri.

The spirit of co-operation in all phases of war work was plain to be seen throughout the state. Mayor Gage of Kansas City, appearing in a giant rally at Swope Park, launched a war manpower drive. Mrs. Martha Franklin as head of the women's division added charm and vivacity to the Citizens' War Manpower Committee, which set a goal of 30,000 workers by September 1, 1941. Within five weeks Kansas City had enlisted 24,094 in war industry.

In the fifth war loan drive, St. Louis was the first city of its population class to reach its quota. Total sales were $181,665,605 —nearly one million above its quota. Omar Bradley's home town, Moberly, sold more than its quota in six hours of the first day of the war loan drive.

In his Senate speech on the investigation of war contracts, Senator Truman pointed out that the distribution of work in World War I had been sectional, that from 70 to 90 per cent of the contracts had been awarded in an area smaller than New England. The concentration of war production in the hands of large firms had been so pronounced as to discourage small companies, resulting in great loss in total productive capacity.

Two Republicans and five Democrats made up the Senate committee, with Truman as chairman. Selection of members was made after Truman had held conferences with Alben Barkley, Vice-President Wallace, and Charles McNary. In addition to the chairman the Democratic members were Connally of Texas, Hatch of

[6] *Official Manual* (1949-50), 3-7; Dorothy Dysart Flynn, "Missouri and the War," *Mo. Hist. Rev.*, Vol. XXXIX, 53-70.

New Mexico, Mead of New York, and Wallgren of Washington. The Republican members were Ball of Minnesota and Brewster of Maine.

Over a period of forty months the Truman Committee attacked abuses inherent in lobbying and contract brokers, "peddlers of influence," and investigated waste and corruption in the building of army camps, the relation of labor disputes to the cost of war goods, and similar vital problems. The original appropriation of $15,000 for committee expenses grew to a total of $400,000 during the forty months, in recognition of the savings effected by the investigations—savings that amounted to $250,000,000 by conservative estimate.

In a labor dispute involving John L. Lewis and the coal mine operators the Truman Committee appealed to both parties and to the operators' bankers with the question: Which comes first, national safety or the wage dispute? A labor racket was found in army camp construction. The unions were collecting fees from non-union applicants for jobs and were able to block work permits for men who would not pay the fee. Truman stopped the fee racket by addressing to the labor leaders a three-word suggestion: "Cut it out." The committee found three billion dollars in the contracts of four large companies, with priorities which cut off supplies for hundreds of little firms. Seventeen senators went to the War Department with a strong demand for more equitable distribution of war contracts and priorities.

"Dollar-a-year men" were responsible for some unethical allotments of contracts. The Truman Committee found that sixty-six companies, represented in Washington by these superpatriots, in eleven months ending April 30, 1941, made government contracts that totaled $2,880,450,000.[7]

In 1944, Missouri plant facilities for war goods were valued at $513,700,000. At the end of that year the plants of Kansas City alone employed 332,000 workers in war industry. North American Aviation Company manufactured its famous heavy armed Mitchell bombers in the Kansas City plant, and at Kaw Point on the Mis-

[7] Helm, *Harry Truman*, 153–89; Flynn, "Missouri and the War," *Mo. Hist. Rev.*, Vol. XXXIX, 485; *Official Manual* (1945–46), 13–23.

souri River, Harry Darby's shipyard produced a fleet of landing craft, 135-foot boats for landing tanks and smaller mechanized craft for landing men.

War supplies from Missouri at the end of June, 1945, reached a value of $4,192,774,000. Of this total, St. Louis had produced goods valued at $2,319,870,000, and Jackson County, $1,120,605,000. Small plants in the cities and throughout the state had made their contribution, which prevented enormous waste in the skills of localized laborers and utilized management and facilities of little businesses.

The Atlas Powder Company operated its plant near Webb City, producing essential war goods. The Weldon Springs Ordnance Works, thirty miles west of St. Louis, employed a maximum of 5,215 workers in producing TNT for war use. Mine La Motte Corporation sold its entire output to the St. Joseph Lead Company for the production of pig lead.

In November, 1942, the United States government set up a Smaller War Plants Corporation with Lon E. Holland of Kansas City as chairman. Little plants were enabled to make their contribution in the form of simple machine parts, such as cover plates, nuts, bolts, and screws. Women workers were numerous in the small centers of production, as in the larger plants. The Donnelly Garment Company of Kansas City produced 7,000,000 garments for the armed forces, with 99 per cent of its employees women. The Producer's Produce Company of Springfield, which increased its labor force from 250 to a maximum of 617, employed 75 per cent women. This firm produced frozen and powdered eggs, live poultry, and dressed poultry for the military camps. The efficiency of women employees was very high in many kinds of war work —radio, laundry, restaurant, woodwork, welding, and power-machine operating.

The Midland Bearing Company of St. Joseph produced cartridge dies. The Robinson Coal Company, operating a strip mine near Foster in Bates County, sold coal to army posts and war-production plants. The A. P. Green Fire Brick Company at Mexico, Missouri, produced fire brick for the boilers of war vessels and for other needs of the government. The boilers of the U.S.S. *Missouri* were lined

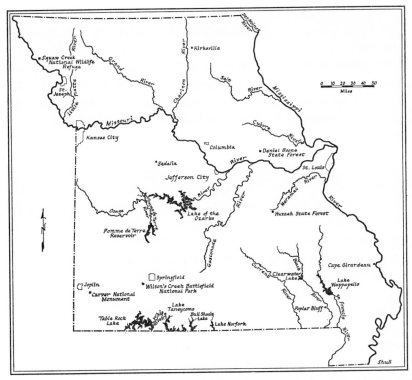

Based on a map from the State of Missouri
Commerce and Industrial Development Division

CHIEF WATER RESOURCES OF MISSOURI

with brick from the Mexico plant. Engineers trained by the Green Fire Brick Company helped in the construction of new plants in England.

Agricultural products were in strong demand in Missouri, as elsewhere in the nation. The Missouri Chemical Company at Joplin, with normal production of 30,000 tons of fertilizer a year, doubled its capacity by 1944 and two years later produced 120,000 tons.

Two army camps were built in Missouri: Camp Crowder in Newton County and Leonard Wood in Pulaski County. The former became the largest of all signal corps training centers, and the latter served a variety of military needs, providing training for some 300,000 soldiers during the war. Camp Crowder's barracks, constructed by 20,534 workers, had a normal capacity of 42,000 enlisted men and officers. A fieldhouse with a seating capacity of 4,000, an efficient fire department, post theatres, and well-lighted, paved streets were among the facilities of the "soldier city."

The military reservation at Camp Leonard Wood contained 86,000 acres, with barracks for 30,000 soldiers, a huge fieldhouse, a hospital with 1,700 beds, an airport, post offices, and 425 miles of paved streets. Brigadier General U. S. Grant III, commanding the Engineer Replacement unit, was the first to occupy the camp. Other units stationed at the camp during the war were the Sixth Infantry Division, Seventy-second Field Artillery Brigade, Eighth Infantry Division, Ninety-seventh Infantry Division, Seventieth Infantry Division, and the Seventy-fifth, "Missouri's own" division.[8]

THE ELECTIONS OF 1944: FORREST DONNELL AND PHIL DONNELLY

The mid-term elections at the beginning of America's second year in the war gave the Republicans ten additional seats in the United States Senate and an increase of forty-seven seats in the House. The Democrats still had majorities in both branches, but the margin was scant, particularly in the House of Representatives.

[8] *Ibid.*, "Army Posts in Missouri," 1085–87; Flynn, "Missouri and the War," *Mo. Hist. Rev.*, Vol. XXXIX, 56–72, 184, 216–43; *Congressional Record*, Vol. 87, Part II, *Appendix*, 77 Cong., 1 sess., A1475–77.

Southern conservatives under the leadership of Senator Harry F. Byrd of Virginia, by combining with Republicans on many domestic issues, reduced administration control of Congress to the vanishing point. Roosevelt's federal tax program, soldier voting by use of a federal ballot, antistrike legislation, a move to abolish poll tax restrictions on voting, and food-subsidy legislation, were all marked by defeat of the President, or by major compromise.

The Republican platform of 1944, presented to the Chicago convention by Robert A. Taft of Ohio, contained a pledge to stop government competition with private business, to halt regulation of farmers, businessmen, labor, and consumers, and to provide for federal aid but state control in a social security program. The Negro vote was sought in a proposal to abolish the poll tax restriction on voting by means of a Constitutional amendment and to take steps toward fair employment practices and toward control of mob violence. The platform also advocated a "fair protective tariff on competitive products."

Wendell Willkie had little chance to be nominated for a second time. He had forfeited all isolationist support by publication of his best-seller book, *One World*, following his trip around the world in 1942. The ultraconservatives had never trusted him, and his public statements were not becoming more colored by the views of Calvin Coolidge as he gained wider experience. The convention was most impressed by three outstanding governors: Harrold E. Stassen of Minnesota, Thomas E. Dewey of New York, and John W. Bricker of Ohio.

Governor Bricker withdrew from the race in favor of Dewey, Stassen quickly recognized the trend, and the convention nominated the New York governor by a vote that lacked only one of being unanimous. Bricker of Ohio, who was described by Theodore Roosevelt's daughter as "an honest Harding," became the Republican candidate for Vice-President.

The principal fight in the Democratic convention was on the selection of a candidate for Vice-President. Franklin D. Roosevelt was nominated for President on the first ballot, by 1,086 votes to 89 for Byrd of Virginia and 1 for James A. Farley.

The labor leaders, Philip Murray and Sidney Hillman, were

partisans of Wallace. Some of the liberals, such as Governor Arnall of Georgia, Senator Pepper of Florida, and Senator Guffey of Pennsylvania also were committed to Wallace. Southern conservatives who would not vote for Wallace found it possible to accept Truman, and labor chiefs, finding that the convention would not give a majority to Wallace, were willing to throw their support to Truman. After a noisy contest, the man from Missouri had 1,031 of the 1,176 votes, and became the candidate.

Funds expended by the two major parties are difficult to determine because national committee reports do not include contributions to state campaigns and independent organizations. The estimate of Eugene H. Roseboom indicates that Republican campaign expenditures were nearly double the Democratic outlay of money, through local, state, and national committees.

Roosevelt and Truman won with 432 electors to 99 for Dewey. The Democrats cast 53.4 per cent of the popular vote for President and elected majorities in both branches of Congress. Defeat of leading Republican isolationists—notably Hamilton Fish of New York and Gerald P. Nye of North Dakota—was a hopeful sign of progress toward international co-operation. President Roosevelt displayed his mastery of politics by including outstanding Republicans in the United States delegation to San Francisco, where the United Nations charter was to be drawn up. Senator Vandenberg, as a former moderate leader of the isolationists and perhaps the most intelligent man among them, was in an excellent position to help the United States avoid the blunders of the Harding and Coolidge era.

On April 12, 1945, President Roosevelt was stricken by a massive cerebral hemorrhage at his winter home in Warm Springs, Georgia, and died within a few hours. Harry S. Truman immediately took the oath of office as President.[9]

In the autumn of 1944 the Missouri Democrats had nominated Roy McKittrick for the United States Senate and Phil M. Donnelly for governor. The Republican candidate, Forrest Donnell,

[9] *Official Manual* (1945–46) (Democratic platform, 1944), 457–59; (Republican platform, 1944), 505–11; Roseboom, *Presidential Elections*, 477–91; Helm, *Harry Truman*, 224–32.

defeated McKittrick by a majority that was less than 2,000. The Democratic candidate won the race for governor, however, by a majority of 30,000. The vote was light, because of the absence of young men and women in the armed forces. The combined votes of the major parties in Missouri in the national as well as the state election were more than a quarter of a million short of the vote in 1940.

Phil Donnelly was an experienced politician at fifty-four, when he took the oath of office as governor. He was a native Missourian, educated in the public schools at Lebanon, and apprenticed in politics as city attorney and Laclede County attorney. He was a member of the lower house of the Assembly for one term and a member of the Senate for twenty years. In 1929 and 1939 he had served as chairman of a commission to revise the Missouri statutes.

Laclede County, with a traditional leaning toward the Republican party, supported Donnelly in his campaigns for office with enough persistence to suggest that independent voters had confidence in him. Among the high points of his administration were his efforts to retain state control of the Missouri Employment Service, and his reforms in penal institutions. Some major changes resulted, including the appointment of a new board for the Boys' Training School at Boonville.

Donnelly was to break a Missouri tradition in 1952 by winning a second term as governor. In many respects the second term was a continuation of the first, although the administration of Governor Forrest Smith intervened. Donnelly's conduct as chief executive during the prison riots of 1953 was courageous and intelligent, and the substantial reform measures that followed were a permanent gain for the state in penal control. A bond issue of $75,000,000 for new buildings and modernization of older structures met with Donnelly's approval.

In 1955 he vetoed twenty-six major bills, including a measure to expand credit through a new small-loan bill. His veto of Missouri Highway Commission reorganization was based upon what he called "disproportionate weight for rural areas" in the bill's provisions.[10]

[10] *Official Manual* (1953-54), 904, 910-12.

HARRY TRUMAN AS PRESIDENT, 1945–46

Harry Truman's investigation of exorbitant war expenditures had earned for him the respect of thoughtful men and had established a wider acquaintance for him among all classes of people. Men who had thought of Truman only as a name that appeared on the Senate roster were impressed by his refusal to "whitewash" unnecessary expenditures for the sake of party regularity. Hugh Fulton, the able young lawyer assigned to the Senate committee by Attorney-General Jackson, had accepted Truman's instructions as they came to him—to look for facts, "even if they should be hiding under the President's desk." The facts that came to light were of such value to the nation as to give new stature to the modest senator from Missouri. Only determined partisan foes, unwilling to give due weight to Truman's record of personal honesty, continued to sneer over his relations with the Pendergast organization.

Edward Stettinius, Frances Perkins, Henry Morgenthau, and Harold Ickes were replaced within one year by Truman appointees. James F. Byrnes became secretary of state, Fred Vinson of Kentucky took Morgenthau's place in the Treasury Department, L. B. Schwellenbach of Washington became secretary of labor, and Julius Krug replaced Ickes as secretary of the interior. Henry A. Wallace resigned in September, 1946, after a speech criticizing the State Department's failure to maintain friendly relations with Russia, and the President gave his post as secretary of commerce to W. Averell Harriman. Also in 1946, John W. Snyder of Missouri replaced Vinson in the Treasury Department.

The United Nations Charter was presented to the Senate of the United States by President Truman on July 2, 1945. The opposition from avowed isolationists was quickly overcome, Senator Vandenberg supporting effectively the President's appeal for ratification and the Democrats voting as a unit.

A comedy line of 1946 suggested, "The war in Asia ended and peace broke out." Labor contested for its wartime power; manufacturers scrambled for large profits and quick returns on their investments; an epidemic of strikes paralyzed American industry;

consumer goods were scarce, prices were high, and discharged veterans were unhappy. Republican party leaders adopted the slogan, "Had enough?" and scored heavily in the Congressional elections. Their program, loosely stated, was to "end controls, confusion, corruption, and Communism." The House of Representatives with a Republican majority of twenty-eight elected Joseph W. Martin of Massachusetts speaker. The Senate made Arthur H. Vandenberg president pro tempore and the isolationists found it impossible to put together any combination—Dixiecrats and America First zealots, or others—to reverse the progress indicated by American acceptance of the United Nations.

Missouri elected a Republican to the United States Senate, James P. Kem of Kansas City, to serve with Forrest Donnell of Webster Groves, the Republican senator elected two years previously. Laurance Mastick Hyde, who had been appointed to the Missouri Supreme Court in 1942 and elected without reference to party in 1944 to serve ten years, was making a nonpartisan record that would guarantee his re-election in 1954 for a twelve-year term. Born in Princeton, Missouri, in 1892 and educated in the public schools there and at the University of Missouri, Hyde had begun the practice of law in 1916. His experience included service on the Supreme Court Commission, to which he had been appointed in 1931, 1935, and 1939.

In September, 1947, Russia and the European nations most clearly under Communist control—Bulgaria, Hungary, Poland, Rumania, Yugoslavia, and, eventually, Czechoslovakia—held a conference in Warsaw and established a Communist Information Bureau for world-wide propaganda. Representatives from Communist groups in France and Italy met with this "Cominform," and Red Army units were stationed along the Russian-occupied territory in Austria and Germany as well as the frontiers of satellite countries. Complete control of France and Italy was clearly an objective of Soviet leaders. Across central Europe from the Baltic to the Adriatic a veil of secrecy was established for Russian-dominated countries—an "iron curtain" which shut out to a great extent the influence of American and British democratic ideas.

THE TRUMAN DOCTRINE AND THE MARSHALL PLAN

One of the areas selected by Soviet leaders for gaining ascendency was Greece. Control of the peninsula, islands, and adjacent shores of the Aegean would give Russia an advantage in any contest that might arise over the Mediterranean route to the Far East. President Harry Truman determined upon economic aid to Greece and Turkey as a means of blocking the rapid advance of Russia in Southeastern Europe, and gave his view to Congress on March 12, 1947.

Appearing at one o'clock in the afternoon for his message to a joint session of Congress, the President left the House chamber at 1:23 after explaining a policy that came to be known at once as the Truman Doctrine.

"I do not believe that the American people and the Congress wish to turn a deaf ear to the appeal of the Greek government," President Truman said.

"I believe that it must be the policy of the United States to support free peoples who are resisting subjugation by armed minorities or by outside pressures.

"I believe that we must assist free peoples to work out their own destinies in their own way.

"I believe that our help should be primarily through economic and financial aid which is essential to economic stability and orderly political processes.

"The world is not static and the status quo is not sacred. . . . The seeds of totalitarian regimes are nurtured by misery and want. . . . They reach their full growth when the hope of a people for a better life has died.

"We must keep that hope alive."

For Greek assistance the President recommended an appropriation of $300,000,000, and for aid to Turkey, $100,000,000. Congress passed the necessary legislation and the United States began shipments of supplies to Greece and Turkey. A Republican former governor, Dwight Griswold of Nebraska, was appointed by President Truman to administer the funds allotted to Greece. Both Turkey and Greece were prevented from falling under the control of the Soviet Union. Marshal Tito of Yugoslavia broke with Russia and closed its frontier to guerrilla troops that had formerly been encouraged by the Russians to conduct raids into Greece. Highly efficient military forces in Greece and Turkey, armed and equipped by means of American aid, greatly reduced the danger from internal disorder and outside pressure.

Leading Democrats supported President Truman strongly and Republican opposition was reduced to sniping operations. Even Alfred Landon, in a public address at Philadelphia, had words of praise for the economic-aid program. The President chose Warren R. Austin, former Republican senator from Vermont, as the United States member of the United Nations Security Council. Upon the resignation of James F. Byrnes as secretary of state, the President named former Chief-of-Staff George C. Marshall to fill the cabinet post.

Marshall had taken little part in politics as an army officer and was thoroughly nonpartisan in his attitude toward national policies. Together with Arthur H. Vandenberg, the later appointees— Griswold, Austin, and Marshall—gave a strong impulse toward nonpartisan decisions in American foreign relations. This freedom from narrow political motives was peculiarly valuable in diplomacy. In the President's thinking it was related to nonpartisan judicial campaigns in Missouri, aloofness from factional control such as Governor Stark's veto of Joint Resolution No. 3, and the Missouri Supreme Court's ruling in *State* ex rel. *Donnell* versus *Osburn*.[11]

The Marshall Plan (or European Recovery Plan) was the natural outgrowth of the Truman Doctrine. Secretary Marshall outlined his program in an address delivered at Harvard University on June 5, 1947. European nations, including Russia and her subject states, were invited to examine their condition, collectively and separately, to take all possible steps toward economic stability, and then to state in specific terms the aid they would need from

[11] Roseboom, *Presidential Elections*, 492–95; Helm, *Harry Truman*, 233–34; *Congressional Record*, 79 Cong., 1 sess., Vol. 91, Part V, 6981–85, 7118, 7941–50; 80 Cong., 1 sess., Vol. 93, Part II, 1980, 1981; Part XII, A2255, A3188, A3724, A3777; Part XIII, A4711; *Memoirs of Harry S. Truman*, I, 342, 558–59.

the United States. Western European nations received the Marshall announcement with enthusiasm, and each one began a study of its economic needs with reference to loans that would benefit Europe as a whole—to meet the specifications of the Marshall Plan. The Soviet Union and its satellites made no response to the offer.

American lend-lease to the Allies against Germany and Japan, between March, 1941, and August, 1945, had amounted to more than $40,000,000,000 above the lend-lease goods we received during the same period. By December, 1946, most Western European states had arranged satisfactory terms for settlement; but at the time the Marshall Plan was announced, the Soviet Union had not indicated any willingness to negotiate. The actual amount of the obligation, in every case, was much reduced by the principle that goods expended in the war were not to be paid for by the borrower. Goods used in postwar economic recovery were subject to repayment. After the war ended in 1945, Congress had voted an additional loan to Great Britain of $4,400,000,000 at 2 per cent interest. The principal was to be returned in fifty equal payments, from 1951 to the year 2000.

V. M. Molotov of Russia, in a meeting at Paris with Great Britain's Ernest Bevin and Georges Bidault of France, refused for the Soviet Union to take any part in the Marshall Plan. Sixteen nations of Western Europe established a Committee of European Co-operation and estimated their combined needs, over a four-year period, at $19,330,000,000. After consultation with President Truman's economic advisers, the committee reduced the figure to $17,000,000,000.

In November, 1947, Congress voted aid to France, Italy, and Austria in the total amount of $500,000,000 and to China $18,000,-000. In April, 1948, an appropriation of $5,300,000,000 was passed for continuing the economic aid. Instead of a pledge for the entire amount, as President Truman requested, Congress advanced the money in annual appropriations, maintaining legislative scrutiny of the plan in operation.

Italian elections brought the first test of the Marshall Plan's effectiveness in the explosive politics of Europe. The Communist "Popular Front" displayed about 30 per cent of Italy's voting strength, to 70 per cent aligned with anti-Communist groups. At the same time, General de Gaulle's rightist support in France gradually gained control, ended the period of strikes and disorder, and moved toward recovery. By January, 1949, when George Marshall resigned from Truman's cabinet because of ill health, the swift diplomatic conquest of Europe by the Soviet Union had been halted and an effective organization of Western European states had been achieved.[12]

THE ELECTION OF 1948

The fact that there were Republican majorities in both houses of Congress, indicating a strong trend toward the more conservative party since the elections of 1944, added to the responsibilities of Republican leadership. The principle of seniority gave some important committee posts to "Old Guard" members of the party who resisted all efforts of the liberals to meet public demands for reform. President Truman, who had been courageous and shrewd when he was a county judge, had learned political lessons of great value during ten years in the Senate and three years in the chief executive office. He regarded the Eightieth Congress as the worst in American history and relied upon his own judgment of the American people's position, between Toryism and reform.

In the Republican convention, Governor Dewey of New York obtained the lead over all the other candidates, and was chosen by unanimous vote on the third ballot. Warren of California was persuaded to make the race for Vice-President. Ultraconservative followers of Robert McCormick's *Chicago Tribune* were dissatisfied with both candidates. Warren, like Dewey, had moved forward with the broad current of the century on domestic issues. Neither candidate was a professional hunter of Communists-in-disguise, and neither was an avowed friend of tariff rates to match or surpass the protection of the Hoover era. The entire Middle West was dis-

[12] Department of State *Publication No. 3972, Our Foreign Policy,* 8, 9, 99, 100; *Congressional Record,* 80 Cong., 1 sess., Vol. 93, Part IV, 3693, 3694; Part IX, 11263, 11470, 11477; Arthur H. Vandenberg, Jr., *The Private Papers of Senator Vandenberg,* 337–98, 399–420; Pratt, *A History of United States Foreign Policy,* 694–709.

appointed by the failure of their section to name one of the Republican candidates.

The Republican platform approved in effect the United Nations, collective security, and bipartisan diplomacy. Some skill in evasion was required to avoid approval of President Truman's entire foreign policy. Senator Vandenberg, by his refusal to fall back upon isolationism, probably destroyed Senator Taft's opportunity for stampeding the convention; but he also gave new vitality to his party in the form of a moderately progressive campaign. The Republican resolutions took a stand against poll taxes as a voting qualification and a stand in favor of the Taft-Hartley Labor Act. Sweeping disapproval of the New Deal was recorded, generally without specific new solutions for old problems. Federal aid for low-rent housing projects to replace slums could be discovered in the Republican platform, carefully concealed behind restrictions.

A vociferous minority among Democratic leaders tried to displace Truman as the party's candidate for President by drafting General Eisenhower for the difficult spot. A variety of anti-Truman men appeared: Dixiecrats, labor leaders whom the President had offended, followers of Wallace who condemned the Marshall Plan, and many others. When Eisenhower refused to run, the most disgruntled of the Democrats turned to Justice William O. Douglas, but he also declined.

The convention gave Truman 947½ votes and the nomination on the first ballot. Senator Alben W. Barkley, who had delivered the keynote address and impressed the convention with his ability as a campaign leader, was seventy years old but full of fight. He was chosen as the candidate for Vice-President.

The civil rights provision as it came from the Democratic Committee on Resolutions was mild; but a Southern proposal to amend it led to debate, and the test of strength on the issue resulted in defeat of the sectional conservatives. A new civil rights provision, drawn up by Hubert H. Humphrey, Jr., of Minnesota, passed the convention by a substantial majority. When the result was announced, the Mississippi delegation and a part of the Alabama delegates walked out, waving a Confederate flag.

Later in July the anti-Truman Southerners held a convention

which nominated J. Strom Thurmond of South Carolina for President and Fielding L. Wright of Mississippi for Vice-President. This right-wing party was matched on the left by the followers of Henry A. Wallace, who nominated Senator Glen Taylor of Idaho for Vice-President to run with Wallace.

It was expected that both of the minor parties would reduce the Democratic vote. Many Democrats believed that Truman's campaign was hopeless, and this belief kept financial support unusually low and rendered the task of organizing the contest for votes doubly hard. National Chairman J. Howard McGrath and a small band of loyal regular Democrats planned an active drive for votes led by the President himself. Announcing that he would give the Eightieth Congress a chance to take immediate action on Republican campaign promises, Truman called a special session and placed before it the need of measures to halt inflation, provide housing, aid education, and promote health insurance, harmony in labor, and price supports for farm products. When the session adjourned without tangible results, Truman had new ammunition for his campaign.

He traveled 31,000 miles and spoke directly to 6,000,000 people. He called attention to the record of the Eightieth Congress, especially on housing, farm legislation, prices, and civil rights. Observers were astonished by the size of the Truman audiences and could not believe that the large, enthusiastic crowds meant voting strength. Wallace's campaign served to reduce the fear of conservative Democrats that Harry Truman was swinging too far to the left, particularly when a Communist party convention endorsed Wallace. Governor Thurmond took 39 electoral votes from Truman in the South, but the attention he brought to the Missourian's civil rights program probably gave him more than twice that many electors in the North. Truman carried Illinois by a relatively small margin, 1,994,715 to 1,961,103, and California by a similar close vote, 1,913,134 to 1,895,269. He won Ohio by a popular vote of 1,452,791 to 1,445,684 for Dewey, and lost New York by 60,959 in a total vote of nearly 6,000,000. Wallace, with a vote of 222,562 in New York, probably cost Truman that state.

When all the ballots were finally counted, Truman had carried twenty-eight states and held an electoral majority of 75 votes. Of the total popular vote, Truman received 49.6 per cent; Dewey, 45.1 per cent; and the minor party candidates, 5.4 per cent. Truman's margin over Dewey was 2,136,525 popular votes and 114 electoral votes.

Missouri cast 917,315 votes for Truman and Barkley to 655,039 for Dewey and Warren. Not only St. Louis and Kansas City, among the cities with large industrial population, but also many counties with smaller cities were carried by the Democratic candidates. Among these were Buchanan, Greene, and Jasper counties, containing such traditional Republican strongholds as Springfield and Joplin. The city of St. Louis gave Truman a margin of 100,000 votes over Dewey, and Jackson County (including Kansas City), a margin of more than 50,000. The Democratic candidate for governor, Forrest Smith, defeated Murray E. Thompson by a margin of 223,028. All Democratic candidates for state administrative offices were elected, along with twelve of the thirteen Democratic candidates for Congress. Only Dewey Short in the Seventh District won a seat for the Missouri Republicans in the Eighty-first Congress.

HARRY TRUMAN'S FOUR-YEAR TERM

Organized labor, unaffected by theories of the left wing and making a deliberate choice between Truman's moderate support and the active hostility of certain prominent Republicans, had played a major part in Democratic return to control of Congress. Truman's shrewd analysis of political forces in the nation was the principal factor in the election. He spoke directly to laboring men when he summarized in campaign speeches their gains since 1933, pointed out the injustices of the Taft-Hartley Law, and indicated other defeats that might be expected for labor in the event of Republican victory at the polls.

The agricultural states of the Middle West which had frequently voted for Republican candidates also entered strongly into the surprising returns of the 1948 election. Minnesota, Iowa, and Wisconsin were more than a counterweight for the loss of South Carolina,

Alabama, Mississippi, and Louisiana to Governor Thurmond; and Ohio, Illinois, Massachusetts, Missouri, and California, all with a large industrial labor vote, were needed for Truman's convincing election results. Paul Douglas of Illinois and Hubert Humphrey of Minnesota, both elected to the United States Senate by large majorities, and Adlai E. Stevenson, liberal Democrat who won the governor's office in Illinois, were typical by-products of the Truman campaign.[13]

Nearly everybody had underestimated Harry Truman's personal worth, even the people who voted for him; and the political experts underestimated the effectiveness of his campaign. With inadequate funds and a small corps of partisan workers, Truman planned wisely and worked with a diligence that has seldom been equaled. "With Truman's staff, Robert E. Lee couldn't carry Virginia," a journalist had commented during the campaign. Senator Vandenberg's statement on the day following the 1948 election was typical of Truman's fair-minded opponents: "You've got to give the little man credit. Everyone had counted him out but he came up fighting and won the battle. He did it all by himself. That's the kind of courage the American people admire."[14]

The Eighty-first Congress voted nearly $2,750,000,000 for slum clearance and new housing units. It voted to provide storage facilities for surplus crops and high supports for farm prices. It raised minimum wages from forty cents to seventy-five cents an hour. After a determined fight against a coalition of minority members and recalcitrant Democrats, Truman succeeded during the second session in extending social security benefits to about ten million additional workers. These were the President's principal victories in domestic affairs.

In diplomacy, President Truman's "Four-Point" program included full co-operation with the United Nations, adequate economic assistance for European recovery, participation in the North Atlantic Treaty, and a fourth proposal which he described as "a bold new program for making the benefits of our scientific

---

[13] Roseboom, *Presidential Elections*, 492–505; *Official Manual* (1949–50), 872, 874, 876; Vandenberg, *Private Papers*, 421–48, 450–52, 456–58.
[14] *Ibid.*, 460; *Yearbook of the United Nations, Annual Volumes 1946–47*.

advances and industrial progress available for the improvement and growth of underdeveloped areas."

The Eighty-first Congress supported the "Four-Point" program, in the main, although the opposition was persistent, long-winded almost to the extent of a filibuster. "We are at the crossroads" began Senator William E. Jenner of Indiana. His speech, with a few attempts at interruption by other senators, appears in twenty-two triple-column pages of the *Congressional Record*. It was inevitable that he should refer at some length to Washington's "Farewell Address" in this isolationist speech.

In spite of the determined efforts of men not entirely weaned from isolationism, Truman's policies had the votes. Full co-operation with the United Nations; aid for European recovery under the Marshall Plan, in the amount of $5,800,000,000; acceptance of the North Atlantic Treaty; and $1,300,000,000 for military support of our North Atlantic Allies—were among the diplomatic achievements of Truman's first two years. The policy of reciprocal trade agreements through the Department of State was continued. For national defense, Congress appropriated $15,000,000,000; and to support President Truman's Point Four, $10,000,000 for experimental steps in promoting the improvement of undeveloped areas.

The failures of Truman policies to gain acceptance by the Eighty-first Congress were numerous and costly. His civil rights program, aimed against suffrage discrimination and the lynching of Negroes, was blocked by a Southern Democratic filibuster aided by Northern Republican apathy. His social security program, which included expansion of benefits to more persons, compulsory health insurance, federal aid to education, and a new Department of Health, Education, and Welfare, was partially successful, as noted above. Federal aid to education was defeated and the new Department of Public Welfare had to wait for a later administration. Truman's attempt to balance the budget by means of a four-billion-dollar tax increase also met defeat.

The recognition of United States leadership in world affairs, shown by the selection of New York City as the permanent headquarters of the United Nations in 1946 and by the acceptance of the Marshall Plan in 1947, gave the Americans a new opportunity to prove the nation's fitness for leadership. During the period of the Eighty-first Congress (1949–51), developments in Europe and Asia made it clear that expressions of good will and peaceful intentions, even when backed by large appropriations, were not enough to guarantee harmony among the nations. The Soviet Union's readiness to challenge American leadership in southeastern Europe had brought about the announcement of the Truman Doctrine and the Marshall Plan in 1947. The Korean crisis in the summer of 1950, unquestionably caused by Russian influence in North Korea in opposition to American and United Nations influence in South Korea, provided another stern test for the United States government.

President Truman appointed General Douglas MacArthur supreme commander for the South Korean troops, supplemented by naval, air, and land forces from sixteen nations. After initial losses to the Russian-dominated North Koreans, the United Nations Army moved north beyond the thirty-eighth parallel and occupied the Communist capital, Pyongyang. Varying fortunes of the United Nations forces in the Korean Peninsula soon made clear the fact that General MacArthur's success or retreat depended upon the character of the aid received by North Korean forces, the air forces in particular, from Red China. A sharp difference of opinion developed between the President of the United States and the supreme commander in Korea in regard to Far Eastern policy.

General MacArthur, basing his opinions primarily upon military grounds, believed that an attack upon the Manchurian supply lines of North Korean troops and a blockade of the Chinese coast were necessities of his campaign. Opinion in the United Nations Assembly was strongly opposed to an attack upon Red China, however, because of the danger that such a course would bring on Russian intervention and a third world war. President Truman and his advisers, possessed of more information than General MacArthur and regarding the entire problem from a broader point of view, agreed that general adherence to the opinions of the European Allies of the United States was necessary in the interest of harmony.

Late in March, 1951, General MacArthur issued a statement to the effect that he was willing to confer with the North Korean commander on terms of peace. In the event that the Red commander would not make concessions, he added on his own authority, the United Nations might order an attack upon the coasts and bases of Red China.

For this flagrant violation of his instructions, General MacArthur was removed from command in Korea and in Japan and General Matthew B. Ridgway appointed in his place. Some difference of opinion existed in regard to the merits of the President's action. It is clear, however, that the popular and successful General was attempting to gain publicity for his stand on the Korean problem and trying to substitute his solution for that of the President; in short, he was extending his authority beyond its legal limits. The Constitutional power of the President to remove the officer from command was unquestionable and the need of asserting that legal civil authority over the military arm was never more urgent. The partisan character of the criticism heaped upon Truman and the continued efforts of General MacArthur to weaken the President's position on Korea have served only to lower the military man in the public estimation.

Senator George W. Malone of Nevada, in an extension of his remarks on General MacArthur in the Senate records had this to say: "The very same State Department officials who made the stupid blunders that invited the Korean war are cowardly [sic] attempting to smear General MacArthur by placing blame on him. . . . These left-wingers have been after General MacArthur's scalp for sometime."[15]

The elections of 1950 reduced the substantial Democratic margin in the Senate to a bare majority of two and added some thirty members to the Republican minority in the House. The opposition of labor to the Taft-Hartley Act was not strong enough to defeat Senator Taft of Ohio in his campaign for re-election. On another issue John Marshall Butler, running in Maryland for a Senate seat, defeated the incumbent, Millard Tydings, principally on the basis

[15] *Congressional Record*, 81 Cong., 1 sess., Vol. 95, Part I, 477–78; Part II, 1703, 1704; Part VII, 9552–74; 2 sess., Vol. 96, Part XVIII, A7228, A7230, A7231, A7232, A7233–49; *Yearbook of the United Nations, Annual Volumes, 1948–1951.*

of Senator Joseph McCarthy's propaganda. Senator Tydings was able and popular, but he had spoken in defense of Dean Acheson's appointees, and Butler found it possible to convey to the voters the ridiculous concept that both the Senator and the State Department were "soft" on Communists.

The issue of isolationism was not dead. Herbert Hoover found it possible late in 1950 and during the following year to arouse great interest by his public statements against sending troops to Europe as a part of the North Atlantic Treaty Organization's army. Senator Taft, always on the border of isolationism, gave Hoover the support of denying the President's authority to send troops abroad. The Truman Administration's proposal to send additional divisions of the army to serve in Europe with the NATO forces and the appointment of General Eisenhower as commander of the Allied army brought into Congress the "Great Debate" that had begun with Herbert Hoover's radio address in December, 1950.

Senator Taft had a strong following in both houses, and the regular Democrats had the support of the Secretary of State, who compared Hoover's attitude with that of one who "quivers in a storm cellar waiting for whatever fate others may wish to prepare . . . ." Senator Vandenberg was dying of cancer at his home in Grand Rapids, Michigan, but his influence among the Republicans was perhaps greater than that of Taft. Thomas E. Dewey, John Foster Dulles, General Eisenhower, and other leading Republicans made public statements which had the effect of cooperation with the President's efforts to put down the isolationist uprising.

Before the end of the Truman Administration the Allied army in Europe was sufficiently powerful to discourage aggression by the Soviet Union and its subject states. The European nations for their own defense against Russia planned an army of forty-three divisions—twelve each from Italy and West Germany, fourteen from France, and five from the countries of the Benelux Customs Union (Belgium, The Netherlands, and Luxemburg). The elections of 1952 may be regarded as the close of the Truman era in American political life. Although the President was not excluded by the terms of the Twenty-second Amendment from serving another term in the chief executive office, he had announced four months before the Democratic convention met that he would not be a candidate for re-election.

It was a blow to the Democratic party and a personal misfortune for President Truman that the old malady of popular governments, corruption, appeared in malignant form during the final years of the administration. The instances of bribery and undue influence that were clearly revealed by the investigations of Senator Kefauver, Senator Fulbright, and others were not attributed to officers of cabinet rank, as were some during the Harding administration. But the influential newspapers that had always been more or less hostile to Harry Truman seized the opportunity to link the scandals as closely as possible with the President. Some of the stories were, by their nature, first-class newspaper material, such as that of an expensive mink coat, lost during a function at the Mayflower Hotel by the low-salaried secretary of a Truman appointee.

Truman's appointment of William O'Dwyer of New York as ambassador to Mexico brought sharp partisan opposition in the Senate. After strong endorsements by Senators Herbert H. Lehman of New York and Dennis Chavez of New Mexico, O'Dwyer was approved, by a vote of forty-two to twenty-two. Both of the Republican senators from Missouri, Donnell and Kem, voted against the Truman appointee.[16]

Truman's great contests revolved around these issues: elimination of waste and corruption in public work; civil rights; social security; and national security against aggression. The Truman Committee during the preparation for World War II did work that was, by its nature, completed at the end of the war. It was a bold project attacked with vigor and pushed to completion by enormous effort. It was definitely not the work of a small man operating with narrowly partisan aims, but the work of a statesman.

The civil rights question is the most important civil issue of the present century. Essentially, the question is whether or not the

16 Vandenberg, *Private Papers*, 573–79; Pratt, *Foreign Policy*, 699, 699n.; Roseboom, *Presidential Elections*, 506–507; *Congressional Record*, 81 Cong., 2 sess., Vol. 96, Part XI, 14932, 14933, 14980, 14997–15011.

abolition of slavery and the acquisition of citizenship by Negroes as a result of the American Civil War in the nineteenth century are to be accepted as a part of the United States Constitution in the twentieth. It deals with a domestic situation that broadens into a world-wide problem in which the progress of the United States is not to be measured by the gains of our few million Negroes, although that alone is a matter of major importance. On all the continents of the earth racial intolerance is a problem of human society that still awaits solution. The United States is well on its way toward successful integration of schools, common carriers, and places of public entertainment, and toward equality in the vital matter of employment opportunity. The progress has been the result of work by many persons of diverse groups and different political backgrounds. Probably no person has done more than Harry Truman—as senator, President, and citizen—to move the nation toward an understanding of its most difficult racial problem.

In the decade following the Harding-Coolidge-Hoover era, social security was a reform movement in which the late Franklin D. Roosevelt played the leading role. He accomplished part of his aim when Congress passed the Social Security Act of August, 1935, which made about 25,000,000 workers eligible for retirement benefits and 27,500,000 eligible for unemployment insurance. The opposition to Truman's Social Security Act in 1950 was composed largely of the same groups—in some instances the same persons—who had fought against Roosevelt's reform. By the end of Truman's term as President, social security was firmly established, beyond the reach of partisan attack.

In diplomacy, it was President Truman's lot to make the great decisions that most clearly determined America's place among the nations. By turning his back upon isolationism, he indicated a choice for active participation in world affairs in preference to fighting wars brought upon us by conditions beyond our control. By accepting the responsibility of world leadership, he accepted the fact of enormous cost. But again it was a choice. The possibility of peace under American leadership was to Truman an attractive prospect, making the personal attacks by isolationists and spy-hunters of little significance. After all, wars are costly in many terrible ways. The Truman Doctrine, the Marshall Plan, and NATO have provided for the nations of the earth a fair chance to work out the riddles of international harmony.

-•≼ **18** ≽•-

POLITICS AND SOCIETY, 1952-1962

THE ELECTION OF 1952

SENATORS HENRY CABOT LODGE of Massachusetts, Frank Carlson of Kansas, and James H. Duff of Pennsylvania became the leaders of a Rump Caucus committed to the Republican nomination of General Eisenhower for President. As the former candidate most likely to divert votes, Governor Dewey was welcomed to the cause. Former President Hoover was not a natural adherent of the "Draft Eisenhower" movement. He was quite at home in the more conservative atmosphere of the campaign for "Mr. Republican," Senator Robert A. Taft.

In January, 1952, the New Hampshire primary disclosed an emphatic preference for Eisenhower over Taft and Stassen. The General, who still had command of the NATO Army in Europe, reluctantly agreed to resign and come home in June for personal attention to the campaign. His early news conferences disclosed an astonishing lack of information and absence of constructive views on political issues; but the people found his personality refreshing, and from the time of his first speech at Abilene, Kansas, popular support grew rapidly. The *Chicago Tribune*, still supporting Taft as the Republican candidate, referred to Eisenhower's discussions of issues as "five star generalities."

The Republican convention meeting in Chicago on July 7 quickly nominated General Eisenhower for President and Richard M. Nixon of California for Vice-President. At thirty-nine, Nixon had

[423]

become junior senator from his state after gaining some distinction in the House as a member of the Un-American Activities Committee. That the anti-Communist agitation had some value as a vote-producer had become apparent in the mid-term elections. Nixon's youth and vigor, in contrast to Eisenhower's advanced age, and the Californian's potential appeal through television added to his value as a candidate. An attractive wife with a flair for making a good public appearance was a further asset for Nixon.

For the Democratic nomination, Governor Adlai Stevenson of Illinois had a large following in the Middle West. His name was familiar to many elderly Democrats and to all readers of American history, and he possessed many of the personal qualities of an effective candidate. His grandfather, Vice-President Adlai Stevenson, had served with Cleveland from 1893 to 1897. The Governor was a fluent speaker with a keen sense of humor, enough understanding of complex issues to give his audiences an intellectual challenge, and enough experience as a politician to make him a dangerous opponent. He refused to run, declared that his only political ambition was to win a second term as governor of Illinois, and had to be drafted for the convention race.

On the first ballot of the Democratic convention, also at Chicago, Senator Estes Kefauver of Tennessee was in the lead, with Stevenson, Richard Russell of Georgia, Harriman, Kerr, and Barkley following, in that order. On the third ballot Stevenson had 617½ votes and a majority. The unanimous vote as an indication of party harmony was only a gesture, since extreme factions had not developed in the convention. Stevenson's acceptance speech was a masterpiece of convention eloquence, and President Truman's appeal for a fighting Democratic campaign was one of his best. For Vice-President the Democrats chose, on Stevenson's recommendation, Senator John J. Sparkman of Alabama.

The Republican resolutions denounced the "negative, futile, and immoral" policies of the Democrats, condemned corruption and Communism, opposed government in business, recognized the necessity of preserving states' rights, and gave carefully restricted approval of social security. The offshore oil resources were declared to be properly under control of the states. Compulsory health insurance and "Federal socialistic valley authorities" were strongly condemned. The section on diplomacy, written by John Foster Dulles, accepted Truman's policy of collective security, but at the same time condemned his "policy of containment of Communism."

The Democratic resolutions praised Truman's record of Communist containment by means of collective security, commended the Democratic exposures of disloyalty and dishonesty in public office, and lauded the security screening devised by Truman's advisers. Tax reduction was advocated when it could be done with adequate provision for national defense. On civil rights the platform proposed federal guarantees of employment equality, personal security, and political activity. The Senate filibuster as a means of defeating majority legislation was condemned.

Perhaps Eisenhower's great reputation as a military leader was the largest single factor in the Republican victory on election day. Americans had been impressed deeply by the effectiveness of their commander in the invasion of Europe, and his service as head of the NATO forces had given him added prestige. However, the General's personal qualities made his political campaign a triumph in a new field. His speeches, whether written in large part by advisers and phrase-makers or delivered as short, extemporaneous talks at the whistle-stops of his campaign, had a powerful appeal for common folk. Sincere and patriotic interest in the general welfare were combined with his natural conservatism in a convincing succession of popular talks. He did not find it necessary or important to launch a personal attack against Truman or against Adlai Stevenson.

Governor Stevenson began his campaign with vigor and skill. He spoke with deep understanding and sound common sense on current issues. His approach was not that of an "egg head" or a "highbrow." He was simple and direct when dealing with issues that could be defined in short sentences and plain words. Many of the intellectuals who were attracted to his camp were nonconformists in various fields and in some instances were liabilities to his campaign.

In Texas he spoke against state control of offshore oil and lost the support of a great industry that was attached to state control and of a multitude of persons who looked with suspicion upon any exercise of national authority, new or old. In Virginia he stated frankly his belief in equal civil rights for all citizens, regardless of their color. "I should justly earn your contempt if I talked one way in the South and another way elsewhere," he added.

Eisenhower demonstrated real ability in adjusting his campaign to the varied political views held by different wings of his party. Taft seemed ready to adopt an attitude of silent disapproval when it became clear that the amateur had defeated him for the nomination. In September, however, Eisenhower agreed with Taft on a public statement of unity on all major issues, except for some "differences of degree" on foreign policy. From that time on, the Taft men were working for Eisenhower's election.

Although Senators Jenner of Indiana and McCarthy of Wisconsin had been guilty of partisan attacks upon the loyalty of men whose loyalty could not be reasonably questioned, Eisenhower found that he was able, in the interest of party harmony, to make a common cause with the two powerful leaders of reactionary principles and unethical conduct. He appeared with each of the senators in his own state. Jenner had called Eisenhower's old personal friend from military life, Secretary of State George C. Marshall, "a front for traitors" and "a living lie." As the top spy-hunter among those Republicans who depended upon wild accusations of well-known Democrats as a means of keeping their own names in print, McCarthy had surpassed Jenner in vituperation by a wide margin. Acceptance of the Taft wing of the party must have been a severe test of General Eisenhower's forbearance.

Senator McCarthy made a radio assault upon the loyalty records of Adlai Stevenson and his campaign managers. Senator Nixon, well versed in McCarthy's technique, added sly suggestions concerning Stevenson's leftist tendencies. Nixon himself became the object of careful investigation by his own party leaders. The *New York Post* discovered that Senator Nixon had made use of an $18,000 fund over a period of eighteen months to pay the costs of travel, radio and television time, printing, and similar expenses incidental to the career of a rising young politician. A group of wealthy Californians had provided the fund and kept its existence secret, no doubt to avoid misunderstanding by citizens who might suppose that the California industrialists expected to get $18,000 worth of special service, or more, out of the youthful senator. Republican leaders were in a quandary for a time whether to keep Nixon on the ticket or drop him.

The Californian's future was in jeopardy, but his skill in television appearances enabled him to withstand the charges and the doubts that had been raised against him. When he had completed his televised explanation of the fund, which consisted mainly of avoiding that ugly subject and diverting his spellbound audience with a dramatic account of his personal rise from poor but honest boyhood to position and power, he was cleared. Some Americans, educated by lavish acquaintance with Horatio Alger and his successors, demanded that their hero provide a contest, preferably a spectacular fight against the plot to prevent his success. Some saw in the fund that started Nixon's trouble only a scheme to prevent the clean-cut young American from realizing his ambition. His rise to the Senate made him a hero; his continued ascent to a position of such affluence as to rate a bit of side money from rich constituents made him irresistible. His race for the vice-presidency, made in spite of adversity, high water, and the Communists, threw his critics into the role of villains.

Nixon's attractive, newsworthy wife and his children and their dog—a good, honest American dog with no taint of leftist philosophy—entered naturally into the story. Not only had the young Californian cleared himself; he had shot up as a potential candidate for President, at some future time when his more famous running-mate would become tired of the high office and its responsibilities.

General Eisenhower decided that the fund story had been a "very unfair and vicious attack" upon a courageous and honorable man.

The Republicans won all the states but nine in 1952. Stevenson carried only North Carolina, South Carolina, Georgia, Alabama, Mississippi, Arkansas, and Louisiana—former Confederate states and a part of the Democratic "Solid South"—together with West Virginia and Kentucky on the border of the Old South. It was similar to the Republican sweep of 1920, except that Harding, who carried West Virginia, did not carry Texas, Florida, and Virginia. Eisenhower had the electoral votes of the entire North and West, in addition to strong support from the Deep South and the Border.

The winner's electoral vote was 442 to 89 for Governor Stevenson, and the Republican margin in popular votes was 33,936,252 to 27,314,992. Eisenhower had 55.4 per cent of the popular vote, Stevenson nearly 44.6 per cent. In the absence of Dixiecrat separate voting, the minor party support was negligible.

Missouri's electors were won by Eisenhower with a very narrow margin of the large popular vote: 959,429 to 929,830. Jackson County and the city of St. Louis gave Stevenson a small majority while most other counties were carried by the Republican candidate. The Missouri Democrats elected W. Stuart Symington as senator over the Republican incumbent, James P. Kem, by a vote of 1,107,701 to 849,179—a total of 1,956,880 ballots, which was even higher than the vote for President. In the same election seven Democrats and four Republicans were elected to represent the state in the Eighty-third Congress. Phil M. Donnelly was elected for his second term as governor, with 976,092 ballots to 879,969 for his Republican opponent, Howard Elliott.[1]

THE ELECTION OF 1956

In August, 1956, the Republican national convention in San Francisco by unanimous decision nominated Eisenhower and Nixon to run for second terms. The Democrats, meeting in Chicago on August 13, had also chosen Adlai Stevenson for the second time as their candidate for President. It was Stevenson's wish that the convention (rather than himself) should select the candidate for Vice-President. After a sharp contest among five Democratic leaders, Estes Kefauver won the nomination by a small majority over John F. Kennedy of Massachusetts.

The anti-Communist activities of Senator McCarthy had received a stinging rebuke from the Senate after his investigation of an alleged spy ring in an army signal corps laboratory in 1954.

[1] *Official Manual, State of Missouri* (1955–56), 944–45; (1957–58), 194, 195; Roseboom, *Presidential Elections*, 508–23.

President Eisenhower's Secretary of the Army, Robert T. Stevens, charged that attempts had been made to obtain special favors for a draftee who was employed by McCarthy's legal adviser. The hearings on the charges and countercharges were televised. Perhaps most Americans were getting tired of McCarthy's single refrain and were becoming eager to find an official who would risk public condemnation in a clash with him. It was clear that McCarthy had become a liability to the administration.

Arthur V. Watkins, Republican senator from Utah, became chairman of a special committee to investigate McCarthy's methods and conduct. Upon hearing the Watkins committee's report, the Senate voted a resolution of censure against the Wisconsin member by a majority of sixty-seven to twenty-two. One Independent and twenty-two Republicans joined forty-four Democrats in the rebuke to McCarthy.

Vice-President Nixon, with the recent action of the Senate fresh in his mind and with Harold Stassen's attempt to have him dropped from the Republican ticket serving as a further warning, conducted his campaign with surprising dignity. He still had a strong hold upon the American public; and President Eisenhower, recovering from a heart attack and a subsequent bout with ileitis, was as popular with the voters as he had been in 1952.

The results of the balloting were similar in most respects to the Eisenhower landslide of the previous election. Again Eisenhower received a large popular majority and again the electoral majority was decisive, 457 to 73. Stevenson lost Kentucky, Virginia, and Louisiana which he had carried in 1952, and won Missouri from the Republicans. The urban Negro vote shifted toward Eisenhower, because intelligent Negro voters feared the influence of James O. Eastland, Democratic leader of segregation in Mississippi. As chairman of the Senate Judiciary Committee, Eastland could be depended upon to block the progress of civil rights for Negroes by factional combinations or by any possible device. Congressman Adam Clayton Powell, Jr., Negro Democratic leader from New York, had discussed the racial issues in politics with President Eisenhower before the election and decided to support the Republican campaign.

Both Missouri members of the Senate were Democrats: Stuart Symington, elected in 1952; and Thomas C. Hennings of St. Louis, first elected in 1950 and re-elected in 1956. All but one of the eleven Missouri representatives elected to Congress in 1956 were Democrats, Thomas B. Curtis of the Second District being the single Republican.[2]

Missouri voted for Democratic electors in 1956 by an extremely small margin, 918,273 for Stevenson, 914,289 for Eisenhower. The city of St. Louis gave the Democratic candidate a majority of 72,000. Jackson County was carried by Stevenson, 133,522 to 122,182. Buchanan, Greene, and Jasper counties gave Eisenhower small majorities, and St. Louis County, outside of the city, also voted Republican, 138,111 to 121,881.

In the race for the seat in the United States Senate the Democratic incumbent, Thomas C. Hennings, Jr., was returned by a plurality of 230,888. Strong support for Senator Hennings came from his home city, St. Louis, which he carried by a margin of nearly 120,000, and from Jackson, Buchanan, Jefferson, Boone, Clay, and some other counties of large population. St. Louis County also gave Hennings a plurality of more than 33,000.

James T. Blair, the Democratic candidate for governor, was elected over Lon Hocker by a margin of nearly 75,000 votes. The city of St. Louis was carried by Blair, 197,010 to 130,978 for Hocker. The county of St. Louis, however, voted for Hocker by a margin of 35,000. Jackson, Boone, Buchanan, Clay, and Jefferson counties gave majority votes to Blair; Greene, Jasper, and St. Francis, to Hocker. The party division of the Assembly in 1957 was as follows: Senate, 13 Republicans, 21 Democrats; House of Representatives, 64 Republicans, 93 Democrats.[3]

THE ELECTION OF 1960

The mid-term elections of 1958 in Missouri strengthened Democratic control in both houses of the Assembly, with an increase of fifteen seats in the House and four in the Senate. Stuart Symington,

[2] *Ibid.*, 524–42; *Official Manual* (1957–58), 84–92, 194, 195.
[3] *Ibid.*, 980–89, 1096, 1097; *Collier's Encyclopedia Year Book, 1957*, 385–86.

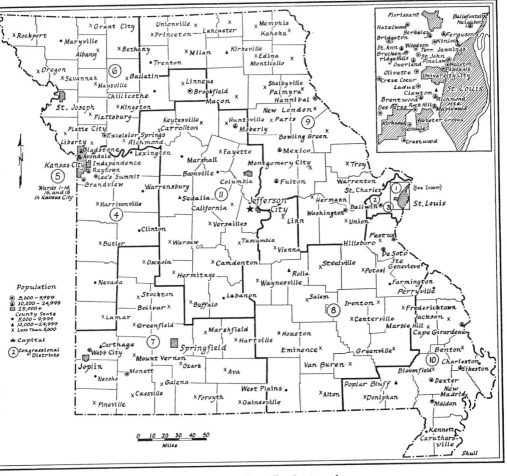

Based on a map from the Official Manual
of the State of Missouri, 1959–60

POLITICAL DIVISIONS, 1961

[431]

running for re-election to the United States Senate, won by an overwhelming majority—780,083 to 393,847 for Palmer, the Republican candidate.

Between 1953 and 1959 the Democratic members in the national House of Representatives increased in three consecutive elections, from 213 in the election of 1952 to 284 in 1958. The Eighty-sixth Congress, with 31 senators elected in 1958 along with the 437 members of the lower house, contained the following party divisions: Senate, 65 Democrats, 35 Republicans; House of Representatives, 284 Democrats, 153 Republicans. In 1958, Missouri elected ten Democrats and one Republican to Congress.

In July, 1960, the Democratic national convention assembled in Los Angeles. Senator John F. Kennedy of Massachusetts had entered seven state primary elections and won all of them. Two of his rivals for the nomination, Senators Lyndon Johnson of Texas and Stuart Symington of Missouri, had entered no primaries. Johnson obtained permission from the legislature of Texas to run for a national office and at the same time for re-election to his seat in the Senate. Former President Truman gave his support to Symington.

On the first ballot in the convention, Kennedy received 806 votes and the nomination. Johnson had 409 votes; Symington, 86; and Stevenson, 79½. The nominee chose Johnson to make the race for Vice-President, and the Texan accepted.

In the Republican convention at Chicago, Vice-President Nixon clearly enjoyed top rank, since he received 1,321 of the 1,331 votes on the first ballot. His choice for Vice-President was Henry Cabot Lodge of Massachusetts, son of the isolationist senator who took the lead in defeating President Woodrow Wilson's efforts toward international co-operation in 1920.

Vice-President Nixon at forty-seven and Senator Kennedy at forty-three each had a strong appeal for American voters simply because of physical vitality and attractive personal traits. The opponents met in televised debate, and in this phase of their contest Kennedy's vastly greater range of information and better reasoning ability gave him the advantage. The Massachusetts candidate's Roman Catholic background might have been a serious handicap in a less tolerant decade. In fact, many thousands of voters in the more backward sections of the rural South, reared in a tradition of "Protestant Supremacy," did consider religion an issue in the election; but Kennedy's anticlerical record, together with the growth of tolerance across America, reduced to a minimum the effectiveness of the "whispering campaign." Republican leaders, including Nixon, were too shrewd in their estimate of the American electorate or too much influenced by personal tolerance to make religion the major basis of attack.

When the final tabulation of votes was complete, Kennedy had been elected President by an extremely narrow margin. In a new record for total number of ballots cast, the Democrats had supported Kennedy with 34,082,289 votes to 33,881,866 received by his opponent. Votes for unpledged delegates in a few Southern states, together with other examples of unbridled individualism, amounted to 448,554 and raised the total to 68,412,709.[4]

Missouri gave its thirteen electoral votes to Kennedy and Johnson by a plurality of approximately 26,000. The religious issue probably had some weight in the voting. Kennedy's best pluralities were in St. Louis County, city of St. Louis, and Jackson County. Catholic population might have influenced the vote in some areas, just as traditional "Protestant supremacy" probably did in favor of Nixon in regions where Roman Catholics were few. It is worthy of note, however, that Stevenson in 1956 received a large block of votes in the same city districts. The election of 1960 was the third consecutive national campaign in which the winner's margin over his major opponent was under 30,000 in Missouri.

John M. Dalton, the Democratic candidate for governor, was elected over Edward G. Farmer, Jr., by a vote of 1,020,694 to 729,773. In the race for the seat in the United States Senate, formerly held by Thomas C. Hennings, the Democratic candidate was Edward V. Long. After the death of Senator Hennings in September, 1960, Governor Blair had appointed Lieutenant-Governor Long to occupy the place until the general election. Long defeated his Republican opponent, Lon Hocker, by a vote of 934,861 to 814,087. Dalton's majority in the race for governor,

4 *Collier's Encyclopedia Year Book*, 1958, 415; 1961, 404, 405, 661–67 (article on "Politics," by Paul Niven); *Official Manual* (1959–60), 961–67, 972, 1048–49.

nearly 300,000 over the Republican candidate, was more than twice the margin held by Long in the Senate race and nearly twelve times as large as Kennedy's margin over Nixon.

The Republicans re-elected Thomas B. Curtis in the Second Congressional District and won another race in the Seventh District. Dr. Durward G. Hall, basing his campaign upon issues similar to those of the former Republican representative from the same district, Dewey Short, won a decisive victory over the Democratic incumbent, Charles H. Brown. The other districts, nine in number, were won by the Democratic candidates.[5]

EDUCATION IN MISSOURI

Public education, organized under the authority of the state of Missouri, was provided by the original constitution. The office of state superintendent of schools was created by the Assembly in 1839, but after two years the duties of this office were incorporated with the functions of the secretary of state. By 1850 the population of Missouri had grown to 682,044 and was increasing at the rate of 50,000 a year. The General Assembly again established the office of state superintendent separately in 1854, abolished it upon the outbreak of the Civil War, and re-established it in 1865. The constitution of 1875 provided that the state superintendent of schools should be elected by the voters for a term of four years.

Another major change in organization was provided by the constitution of 1945. A state Department of Education was created to administer the schools under policies of the General Assembly. An appointed body of eight members, the state Board of Education, was placed over the department and given the responsibility of investment and apportionment of school money, certification of teachers, and general supervision over administration and teaching. The board appoints a salaried commissioner of education, who acts as its chief executive officer and administers the school system of the state. Ollin Drennan of Kirksville became president of the

[5] *Collier's Encyclopedia Year Book, 1958*, 415; *1961*, 404, 405; *Official Manual* (1957–58), 49, 75–81.

[434]

state Board of Education in 1955 for an eight-year term. The commissioner of education is Hubert Wheeler.

By 1959 the public school enrollment in Missouri had grown to 805,000, of whom about three-fourths were in elementary and one-fourth in secondary schools. The elementary school teachers numbered 20,391, the high school teachers 8,589.

The institutions of higher learning in Missouri, public and private, are listed together in the following table:

Senior Colleges

Name	Location	Type	Date of Establishment
Central College	Fayette	Coed.	1854
Culver-Stockton College	Canton	Coed.	1853
Drury College	Springfield	Coed.	1873
Evangel	Springfield	Coed.	1955
Kansas City College of Osteopathy	Kansas City	Coed.	1916
Kansas City, University of	Kansas City	Coed.	1929
Kirksville College of Osteopathy	Kirksville	Coed.	1892
Lincoln University	Jefferson City	Coed.	1866
Lindenwood College	St. Charles	Women	1827
Missouri, University of	Columbia	Coed.	1839
Missouri School of Mines and Metallurgy (division of the University)	Rolla	Coed.	1870
Missouri Valley College	Marshall	Coed.	1888
Park College	Parkville	Coed.	1879
Rockhurst College	Kansas City	Part Coed.	1910
St. Louis College of Pharmacy	St. Louis	Coed.	1864
St. Louis University (junior colleges, inc.)	St. Louis	Coed.	1818
St. Teresa College	Kansas City	Women	1916
Tarkio College	Tarkio	Coed.	1883
Washington University	St. Louis	Coed.	1853
Westminster College	Fulton	Men	1851
William Jewell College	Liberty	Coed.	1849

TEACHERS' COLLEGES

Name	Location	Type	Date of Establishment
Central Missouri State College	Warrensburg	Coed.	1871
Harris Teachers College	St. Louis	Coed.	1857
Northeast Missouri State Teachers College	Kirksville	Coed.	1867
Northwest Missouri State College	Maryville	Coed.	1906
Southeast Missouri State College	Cape Girardeau	Coed.	1873
Southwest Missouri State College	Springfield	Coed.	1906

JUNIOR COLLEGES

Name	Location	Type	Date of Establishment
Christian College	Columbia	Women	1851
Cottey College	Nevada	Women	1884
Flat River Junior College	Flat River	Coed.	1922
Hannibal-LaGrange College	Hannibal	Coed.	1858
Joplin Junior College	Joplin	Coed.	1938
Kansas City Junior College	Kansas City	Coed.	1915
Kemper Military School	Boonville	Men	1844
Moberly Junior College	Moberly	Coed.	1927
St. Joseph Junior College	St. Joseph	Coed.	1915
Southwest Baptist College	Bolivar	Coed.	1878
Stephens College	Columbia	Women	1833
Trenton Junior College	Trenton	Coed.	1925
Wentworth Military Academy	Lexington	Men	1880
William Woods College	Fulton	Women	1890

THEOLOGICAL AND BIBLE SCHOOLS

Name	Location	Type	Date of Establishment
Central Bible Institute	Springfield	Coed.	1922
Concordia Seminary	St. Louis	Men	1899
Eden Theological Seminary	St. Louis	Men	1848
Kansas City Bible College	Kansas City	Coed.	1932
Kenrick Seminary	St. Louis	Men	1869
St. Pauls College	Concordia	Coed.	1883

TECHNOLOGICAL, ART, AND MUSIC SCHOOLS

Name	Location	Type	Date of Establishment
Central Technical Institute	Kansas City	Coed.	1931
Kansas City Art Institute	Kansas City	Coed.	1894
Music and Arts College of St. Louis	St. Louis	Coed.	1947
St. Louis Institute of Music	St. Louis	Coed.	1924

The University of Missouri, established on the basis of the Geyer Act passed by the General Assembly in 1839, was the first state university in the region west of the Mississippi. The columns on the campus at Columbia mark the location of the first building constructed for use of the University, the cornerstone of which was laid on July 4, 1840.

The Missouri School of Mines and Metallurgy, at Rolla, is a division of the University of Missouri. Rolla is situated 110 miles southwest of St. Louis on the St. Louis and San Francisco Railroad and at the intersection of United States Highways 63 and 66. The location is easily accessible to important mining operations, including mines of the Tri-State lead and zinc area around Joplin, the iron, lead, and zinc mines of southeastern Missouri, and the brick and tile works of Missouri and adjoining states. Ceramic developments in St. Louis and Kansas City, in Vandalia and Mexico on United States Highway 54, and in towns beyond the borders of Missouri on United States Highway 66 have provided a great additional interest for students at Rolla.

The oil fields of Oklahoma, Kansas, and Arkansas are also readily accessible by railroad or highway to the campus at Rolla. Modern research laboratories are provided for students of petroleum engineering as well as of electrical, mechanical, and mining engineering. An experimental mine, situated at a distance of one and one-half miles from the campus, is of particular value to students of mineral surveying and mining methods.

Agriculture is another field in which the University has adjusted its program to one of the great economic interests of Missouri people. With 1,500 students regularly enrolled in the College of Agriculture at Columbia and many times that number receiving the benefits of research and instruction through short courses and extension activity, Missouri farmers are making better use of scientific methods than ever before. The resident staff devotes approximately 60 per cent of its time to research, 40 per cent to teaching.

Other divisions of the University have achieved national prominence. The School of Journalism, from its organization as a pioneer in the field in 1908, has been unique. The School of Medicine and the School of Law, both dating back to 1872, have enjoyed recent substantial growth. The College of Arts and Sciences and the Graduate School have done work of particular merit. Combined university enrollment in Columbia and Rolla reached 14,991 in 1959.

The colleges with largest endowments in Missouri are Washington University of St. Louis, with an endowment of $52,296,242, and St. Louis University, with $10,096,693. The enrollment at Washington University in 1959 was 11,727, and at St. Louis University, 8,688. Both of these institutions are of early origin among western colleges: St. Louis University, 1818; Washington University, 1853. Both have excellent libraries and the faculties of both have made distinguished records in research and instruction.

Enrollment in the teachers' colleges in 1959 was as follows: Central, 3,292; Harris, 1,210; Northeast, 2,521; Northwest, 1,736; Southeast, 2,135; Southwest, 2,256; aggregate, 13,150. Drury College in Springfield, founded in 1873, has a student body of more than 700 and a faculty of 69. Kansas City University, established in 1929, reached an enrollment of 3,000 in thirty years. Lincoln University, established for Negroes at Jefferson City in the age of segregation (1866), had an enrollment of 1,364 in 1959. Culver-Stockton at Canton, Central College at Fayette, and Park College at Parkville are among the older colleges of Missouri. Rockhurst College at Kansas City, barely fifty years old, has an enrollment of more than 1,400.

Among the privately endowed junior colleges and denominational schools offering two years of college instruction, Stephens College for women at Columbia, established in 1833, is the oldest and also the largest. In 1959 the student body numbered 1,525, the faculty 154. Cottey College for women at Nevada, established in 1884, has maintained a limited enrollment and high standards of instruction. Under the administration of President Blanche Dow, who has directed the college since 1949, Cottey has long-range plans for continuing development.

The municipal junior colleges, all of recent origin, have done notable work in meeting the increased demand for instruction above the high school level. With meager funds, these colleges have achieved remarkable results in the development of libraries, laboratories, and instructional facilities. For example, the college at Joplin, which opened in 1938, has an enrollment above 500 and a faculty of 33. Under the early leadership of Dean H. E. Blaine, whose undergraduate work was done at Drury College in Springfield, the institution had a mildly progressive start. Among other notable developments, selected at random, this college gave some of its students an opportunity to discover their talents in chromatic art, under the direction of Arthur Boles; won distinction for its orchestra, under T. Frank Coulter; and wide recognition for its students of drama, under the direction of Miss Jetta Carleton. Harry C. Gockel, instructor in geography, has been on this faculty for many years, and has made a record of solid achievement with students who have gone on to advanced study.[6]

MISSOURI CULTURE

The people of the Crossroads State have characteristics that set them apart. In the early days of statehood, as in the territorial period, people came from many sections of the country and from Europe to settle in Missouri. The patterns of travel, largely though not entirely confined to the great rivers, affected the flow of population to such an extent that the majority were immigrants from Southern states. Gradually changes appeared in the prevailing background of the settlers, as the Conestoga wagons brought more people across Ohio, Indiana, and Illinois. With the coming of rail-

[6] *Ibid.*, 381–532, 710; *Collier's Encyclopedia Year Book, 1957*, 386; *1961*, 405; Orpha Stockard, *Cottey College*, 1–118; Helen de Rusha Troesch, *The Life of Virginia Alice Cottey Stockard*, 44–101, 220–98. See also annual catalog of each college. The *Constitution of the State of Missouri* as amended to 1960, reprint of Report No. 5, Committee on Legislative Research, 1960, pp. 117–22.

roads, the northern part was filled largely by free white farmers from the North, giving an increasing degree of cosmopolitanism to the population.

The growth of St. Louis, particularly the additions of Europeans to the population, and the immigration of Europeans to other parts of the state brought increased urbanity. As a center of the great fur trade and an important outlet for overland freight from the Southwest, St. Louis molded the character of Missouri's culture in many ways. Other river towns on both of the great inland waterways made their cultural contributions. The distances people had to travel in sparsely settled areas and the limited means for earning a living in those regions determined occupations and set boundaries on the production of wealth; and the industries of special skills and business techniques—lead and zinc mining, meat packing, the cultivation of apples, strawberries, and tomatoes, wheat, corn, livestock and poultry growing—all contributed to the state's position in the culture of modern America.

A great variety of manufacturing enterprises with a total employment of nearly 400,000 in 1960 has gradually added a long list of occupations in Missouri. Transportation equipment ranks first among the manufactured products with workers numbering 57,400. Food products, apparel, printed material, leather goods, prefabricated metals, machinery, chemicals, and clay products, among other manufactured goods, became important in shaping the lives of Missouri citizens. A total well over three billion dollars is added annually by manufacturing to the value of products in the state. The relative importance of this figure may be seen by comparing it with the total value of mineral production, $157,000,-000 in 1959, or with the total farm income, $1,093,493,000. Of the 4,319,813 residents, approximately two-thirds were classified in 1960 as urban and one-third as rural.[7]

Thomas Hart Benton, the painter, once suggested that the Missouri mule was more important than the career of his great-uncle, Senator Thomas Hart Benton, in the history of the state. Perhaps the observation serves to explain why the painter's fame must rest

[7] *Official Manual* (1959–60), 277–87, 1308–15; *Collier's Encyclopedia Year Book, 1961,* 36–43, 393–402, 404–405.

upon his art rather than his grasp of historical values or his philosophy, but it does open a field for speculation.

The political life of Missouri is related to the democracy that swept the West, from Jefferson to Jackson, and came to the new state in the development of new figures in national life—Senator Benton and N. Beverly Tucker, Frederick Bates and his brother Edward, David Barton, John Scott, and William Henry Ashley. Greatest of the political figures before the Civil War, with no close competitor, was Thomas Hart Benton.

The ideas of democratic government that Benton represented are still potent in Missouri. As the more liberal of the two major parties, the Democrats have frequently elected their candidates to office; but independent voting is a persistent trait in Missouri politics, and liberal Republicans have frequently enjoyed state-wide support. Between 1901 and 1961, Republicans have won the office of governor in one-third of the campaigns. Of the five Republican governors elected, Hadley and Donnell have been distinguished by liberal views, and none has been excessively partisan or ultra-conservative.

The party support given by Missouri voters is made up, for both major parties, of many elements besides intelligent adjustment to current issues on the basis of democratic ideals. Many Republican votes are still based upon the Whig principles of Abraham Lincoln with a touch of sectional opposition to Rebellion; and many Democratic votes are strongly related to one or another of the vague concepts that arose in Missouri concerning the Southern Confederacy of the 1860's. Theories of states' rights that were repudiated by the Philadelphia convention in 1787 and severely rebuked by the military failures of Sterling Price, Joseph E. Johnston, and Robert E. Lee during the late months of the Civil War are still revived by lame ducks and minority leaders of both parties. Disgruntled Democrats are especially prone to go back to the interpretations of Thomas Jefferson when he was leader of the minority; but the anachronistic approach, which is in fact a retreat, is not confined to Democrats or to the state of Missouri.

In Missouri, as in other states, there are voters who swing abruptly from extreme radicalism on the left to the views of Alexander Hamilton—untouched by adjustment to the current situation—on the right. There are religious zealots who fear attacks upon their church or who hope to promote their peculiar views by party organization. And finally, there are professional politicians who would seize any opportunity to build or bolster a career by adopting as their own any prejudice of current popularity. Fortunately, the Civil War voters, the persons of radical disposition, the Protestant and Catholic advocates of clerical authority, and the opportunists are in minority.

The typical Missouri voter is a firm believer in the rights of the citizen. He is fair-minded and moderate but stubbornly independent. If his party fails to carry out its avowed purposes when it is in power, he is likely to follow the example of Carl Schurz and announce a change in his party support. Such a shift is not, as a general rule, adopted hastily. The Missourian is cautious by nature, and he is inclined toward progress in his intellectual outlook. No state but Missouri could have produced William Joel Stone, Herbert S. Hadley, Judge Laurance Mastick Hyde, Lloyd Stark, or former President Truman.

Aside from politics, the culture of Missouri has features of sharp distinction, the best examples of which have been produced by well-known persons. Mark Twain, dealing with the subject of the Mississippi and the territory adjacent to it, wrote with deep understanding. Needless to say, no other person could have expressed such basic familiarity with Hannibal and its people; but the relation of Mark Twain's humor and certain other characteristics of his work to the environment of his boyhood is not so obvious.

The elements that make his work great have universal appeal. He wrote for the people he knew, with a steadily widening circle of acquaintances. The whimsical exaggeration that would send a ripple of laughter through a party in Judge Thatcher's parlor, that was intended to bring forth a chuckle and perhaps a directed excursion of the imagination, proved effective with an extensive and varied group of readers. And always the humor was colored by his early environment. Villagers and river men, a few Indians and many Negroes, citizens and officials, the poor and the affluent, and settings that expand far beyond the limits of Missouri are all presented with the concept of interest and humor that was a part of the thinking of Little Sam Clemens.[8]

George Caleb Bingham was a great Missourian who was born in Virginia. When he was eight, his parents moved with their family to Franklin, Missouri, and upon the death of his father in 1823, George moved again with his mother to a farm in Saline County. At the age of twelve the boy had displayed an interest in art, and when he was twenty-four, the editor of the *Missouri Intelligencer*, visiting the Bingham studio in Columbia, found in his portraits "many evidences of deep, native originality."[9]

In the course of his career as a self-trained artist, Bingham found time to serve in the Missouri Assembly and during the later years of the Civil War as state treasurer. Contemporaries generally mentioned honesty in connection with his administration of the treasury, and competent critics found that same quality in his painting. As the result of a bout with the measles at the age of nineteen, Bingham had lost his hair, and his wig-covered head became a familiar sight in many parts of Missouri.

River scenes, election incidents, landscapes, and portraits made up the most of his long list of paintings. *The Squatters, Shooting for the Beef, Raftmen Playing Cards, Boatmen on the Missouri, Fur Traders Descending the Missouri,* and *The Jolly Flatboatmen* are a few of his well-known river pictures. *Canvassing for a Vote, County Election, Stump Speaking,* and *Verdict of the People,* all completed during the period 1852 to 1855, are among the most distinctive of the political incidents. In regard to his landscapes, his biographer says, "He painted at least forty such pictures, with or without cattle." The landscapes include a wide range of subjects, such as *The Storm, Mountain Scene with Deer, Mountain Gorge,* and *Moonlight Scene.*

For students of history, the portraits and historical events have particular value. Prominent Missourians were the subjects of most of his portraits. Dr. John Sappington, Mrs. John Sappington,

[8] Gladys Carmen Bellamy, *Mark Twain as a Literary Artist,* 3–54, 67–79, 149, 281, 320–23; Minnie M. Brashear and Robert M. Rodney, *The Art, Humor, and Humanity of Mark Twain* (Norman, 1959), 181–304.

[9] John Francis McDermott, *George Caleb Bingham, River Portraitist* (Norman, 1961), xxi–xxviii, 3–9, 402–11; *Dictionary of American Biography,* II, 274–75.

Meredith M. Marmaduke, John Thornton, Samuel Bullitt Churchill, and Mrs. Robert Aull were among the personages who sat for him between 1834 and 1837. *The Dull Story*, the portrait of a beauty napping in a chair, painted probably in 1840, is reproduced in John Francis McDermott's book on Bingham and credited to the collection of Charles van Ravenswaay. A portrait of John Quincy Adams, produced in 1850, is in the Detroit Institute of Arts. John Howard Payne, 1841–42, John Cummings Edwards, 1844, Mrs. John Darby, 1852, Dr. Benoist Troost, 1859, and Mrs. Thomas W. Nelson, 1862, are also among the portraits. The likeness of James S. Rollins, *The Palmleaf Shade*, and Mrs. James T. Birch belong to the latter part of Bingham's productive career.

Order No. Eleven, painted in 1868, is the Civil War picture in which Bingham presented his view of General Thomas Ewing's controversial removal order. As a Union state official (1862–65) and a personal enemy of General Ewing, the federal military officer, the painter's guiding motives must have been complicated; but his skill produced one of the great masterpieces of the war period. All that can be said in regard to Ewing's dilemma, his provocation for the use of harsh means, and the cruelty of war on both sides of the line, have had little weight to counteract the stern-visaged, heartless demeanor of the Union officers shown in the removal scene, the supplication of the Confederate ladies, the fearless mien of the brave old planter, and the faithful attitude of his Negro retainers. The picture is great, and its version of *Order No. Eleven* is generally accepted.[10]

Thomas Hart Benton, the artist, was the eldest son of Colonel M. E. Benton, a Missouri congressman who was the nephew of the great pre-Civil War senator. Colonel Benton settled at Neosho in southwestern Missouri, married after he was forty, and began the practice of law. The first of his four children was named for the child's great uncle, the Senator.

In his early life the lad displayed more interest in drawing and chromatic art than in the mental calisthenics that are generally

[10] McDermott, *Bingham*, 18–193; 197–275 (paintings); 279–390 (drawings). This book contains the most complete and accurate account of Bingham's life, together with reproductions of his works of art.

accounted useful preparation for law and politics. Perhaps his father's suggestion that young Benton should get acquainted with his great-uncle's sixteen-volume *Abridgment of the Debates of Congress* determined the boy's career—in favor of art. The Benton home at Neosho was one of the finest in town; and at the age of seven, according to a tradition often repeated, the son began his career as a mural artist by decorating the entire stairwell with a long freight train, drawn on the cream-colored wall paper with charcoal. Perhaps some of Benton's later murals prompted more widespread criticism, but it is questionable that any brought more intense disapproval.

Champ Clark and William Jennings Bryan were visitors at the Benton House in Neosho. Instead of acquiring from those great partisans a taste for politics, young Thomas seems to have been impressed with Clark's habit of chewing his cigars and Bryan's enormous consumption of food. By the time he was fifteen, the Benton heir had become a great disappointment to his father, who regarded his preference for painting over the practice of law a serious defect of character. Other evidences of imperfection came to light. Young Benton began to "go with girls"; and he developed a taste for "boilermakers," which led him, occasionally, into brawls.

At nearby Joplin he visited a saloon called the House of Lords when he was seventeen, and showed an interest in a painting of a nude woman. The men at the bar roared with laughter at the stripling's interest, and he loftily informed them that he was an artist and his study of the painting was strictly professional. The incident led to his meeting the editor of the Joplin *American* and his employment by the newspaper. His drawings for the *American*, likenesses of local celebrities for the most part, were clearly the work of a young man of talent but without training.

At eighteen Benton enrolled in the Chicago Art Institute and at nineteen managed to overcome paternal prejudice, through maternal intervention, to such effect that he received money from home to study art in Paris. After three years he returned to New York and settled down to the task of making a living by means of his skill with the brush. He was able to earn his way by a variety of artistic enterprises. He enlisted in the navy during World War I, and again gained experience—as a coal shoveler, which he did not enjoy; as a fighter, at which he was good but not good enough to be a professional; and as an architectural draftsman, where he discovered new interests and new techniques in drawing.

In New York after the war, Benton became the leader of a new school of painters, the "American Scene" movement. At the age of thirty-five he returned to Neosho to be with his father in his last illness. The old acquaintances of Colonel Benton, southern Missouri men and others, inspired in the artist a desire to know more of his native land. He began work on a history of the United States, to consist of sixty-four mural panels, a task that was not completed on his original plan.

For ten years, Benton crossed the continent annually, visiting and studying a great variety of American scenes: Pittsburgh steel mills, Illinois farms, plantations in the Deep South, "hill-billy" communities of Arkansas and Missouri, the Pacific states, and others. His greatest interest was in the back-country folk, although his absorption with the rural scene—mountain cabins, country inns, little towns, hash-houses, and cheap country dance halls—was by no means exclusive. He acquired a vast store of material in the form of sketches and notebooks.

In 1930 he received an assignment to do a series of murals at the New School for Social Research in New York. On the basis of this work, which he did without fee, he was commissioned to paint the *Arts of American Life*, a set of murals for the Whitney Museum of American Art in New York. Horseshoe pitching, bronco busting, country dancing, mule driving and Holy Roller worship, all of which had impressed him as essential parts of American life, were featured in these murals.

His mural history of Indiana for the Chicago Century of Progress, 12 feet high by 250 feet long, the work of a lifetime for a man of ordinary energy, gave permanence to his reputation. In 1935 the Missouri Assembly employed him for the sum of $16,000 to paint a series of murals for the Capitol at Jefferson City, and at the same time the Kansas City Art Institute employed him at $3,000 a year as a teacher. Special preparation for the Missouri murals included sketches of country dances, night clubs, burlesque shows; the rich and the poor; Tom Pendergast and J. C. Nichols; the Nelson Gallery of Art; Huckleberry Finn and Nigger Jim; steamboats, the Santa Fe Trail; and a political meeting in Pike County, with a poster of Speaker Champ Clark above the platform.

The completed murals, which Benton contended were true rather than complimentary, brought down upon him a tornado of criticism. In his efforts to defend his art, he did not in every case choose words that conveyed his meaning with accuracy, which is only to say that he was not an artist in the use of his mother tongue. He seemed to have no desire to be tactful, and he did not give to the public a clear view of the honesty that dominated his thought.

"Are you proud of your state?" a heckler asked him.

"I am not proud of it, merely interested," Benton replied.

"Give us your opinion of art museums," a New York reporter suggested, when Benton was on the verge of being fired by the Kansas City Art Institute.

"If it were left to me, I wouldn't have any museums," declared the painter. "Museums don't buy enough of my painting in an average year to pay for my boy's music lessons. Who looks at paintings in a museum? I'd rather sell mine to saloons, bawdy houses, Kiwanis and Rotary Clubs, Chambers of Commerce—even women's clubs. People go to saloons but never to museums, unless they happen to be tourists anxious to 'do' the place and get it over with." His Kansas City employers severed his connection with the Institute at the end of his sixth year, in 1941.

The painter was carried away by the daring of his assault on an important source of his own income, and he overestimated the weight of his attack. In his slightly distorted view, placing living art in a museum was "the delivery of the living to those trained professionally as caretakers of the dead." The psychology of the undertaker was essential to the conduct of such an institution, he said. "The typical museum is a graveyard run by a pretty boy with delicate curving wrists and a swing in his gait," Benton added.

When Billy Rose offered to exhibit Benton's *Persephone* in his New York night club, the "Diamond Horseshoe," the painter accepted. Rose estimated that forty-three thousand people saw the painting in the first three weeks of the special exhibition.[11]

George Washington Carver, born in 1864 near Diamond Grove, between Carthage and Neosho in Newton County, made unique contributions to the culture of the nation. His parents were Negro slaves, on the farm of Moses Carver in his mother's case. During the confusion and disorder of the war's last year, the Negro mother and her infant son were stolen from the Carver farm. The owner searched for them and with the aid of a bushwhacker recovered the child, for the return of whom he gave his agent his best horse. The mother, for whom Moses Carver was willing to pay forty acres of land and all the money he possessed, was not found. George the boy lived at the Carver place until he was nine, when he was put to work as a houseboy in Neosho. There he was permitted to attend school. In the following years he wandered over into Kansas, where he made brief acquaintance with the public schools of Fort Scott, Paola, and Olathe.

At Indianola, Iowa, young Carver attended Simpson College for three years, paying his expenses by means of laundry service. He was admitted to Iowa State College at Ames, where he received the B.S. degree in 1894 and the M.S. degree two years later. Agriculture and botany were the subjects that interested him most. The college found it possible to give him limited employment, and in 1905, Booker T. Washington made him director of the Department of Agriculture at Tuskegee Institute in Alabama.

Carver's work in diversification of crops, soil conservation, and salvage of waste products brought him wide attention and many honors—the Roosevelt Memorial Association Award, honorary degrees from Simpson University and the University of Rochester, and appointment as a collaborator in the Bureau of Plant Industry, United States Department of Agriculture. He became a Fellow of the Royal Society in London. His work in the discovery of new uses for a wide variety of plants was a fundamental approach to diversification. Cottonseed, sweet potatoes, soybeans, and peanuts

[11] Garwood, *Crossroads of America*, 275–94; Legislator's Lounge, State Capitol, Jefferson City, Murals; *Official Manual* (1955–56), 4, 5; Jesse Stuart, *Taps for Private Tussie* (illustrations by Thomas Hart Benton).

were among the objects of his careful and long-continued attention.

Like many other distinguished scientists, Carver was a keen observer of human traits, racial characteristics, and social phenomena. Perhaps no man has provided more data for the discard of fictitious estimates concerning the Negro. A common supposition in Alabama when Carver taught and engaged in research at Tuskegee was that the minds of bright Negroes at a certain period in their youth—twelve, thirteen, or fourteen years of age—ceased to develop. The "Wizard of Tuskegee" made the theory hard to defend.

As a distinguished guest in a hotel with a segregated dining room, Carver was served meals in his room by the proprietor. Eager to compromise between paying due respect to a great man and giving necessary weight to the social customs of his city, the proprietor took pains to give alert service and to point out choice dishes on the extensive menu. After he had recited tempting items on the list, with comments to prove his respectful attitude under the handicap of segregation, the guest suggested with equal courtesy: "Please just fetch me some turnip greens and a little bit of fat pork."

Southern men who could not call the great chemist "Mister" because of social distinctions hanging over from the days of slavery, did not hesitate to address him as "Doctor" Carver. An editor of a London magazine wrote of the Tuskegee scientist: "If I were asked what living man had the worst start and the best finish, I would say Dr. Carver. It is a great loss to us that we have no one like him in England."[12] Before the end of Carver's life it was generally agreed among Missourians and Americans from all sections that the Plant Doctor of Diamond Grove who became a great research scientist was a credit to the Negro race. It is also becoming widely recognized that his work entitles him to a more inclusive description: he is a credit to the human race.

Missouri must share the honor of her great citizens with other states. Senator Benton was born in North Carolina, introduced to politics in Tennessee, and adopted by Missouri. Carl Schurz and

12 Rackham Holt, *George Washington Carver* (Garden City, N.Y., 1954), 279–89.

Joseph Pulitzer were Europeans by birth. Stuart Symington is an "immigrant" of high rating from Massachusetts. Mark Twain was born in Missouri, steeped in the lore of his native land, and stamped with the indelible marks of the Mississippi River country; but he learned his art in a wider field and he wrote for a world public. Bingham was a Virginian before he was a Missourian. Benton the painter was born in Neosho, educated in Missouri and elsewhere, and rejected by the Kansas City Art Institute for belligerent honesty. In Missouri, George Washington Carver probably could not have obtained the scientific training necessary for his career as an agricultural chemist, but he did become the citizen of a federal republic, with the right to move from one state to another. For Carver's schooling, Kansas and Iowa must have the major share of the honor; for Carver's opportunities at Tuskegee, establishment of the institute in 1881 on the basis of an enlightened act of the Alabama legislature and the work of a great Negro educator, Booker T. Washington, were mainly responsible.

For want of knowledge and lack of space the great orchestras and choral groups, even of contemporary Missouri, cannot be touched upon here. Painters, philosophers, and writers of fiction, architects and creative artists in many fields, nuclear scientists, students of surgery and psychiatry, law, and the whole wide range of human knowledge are now engaged in work which may rival or surpass any achievements of the past. The examples given above of great contributions to the culture of Missouri cannot introduce the subject properly, as a history in each field might do. The work of the statesmen and the schools that have been described in brief are merely selections from a vast store of Missouri history that is available in the libraries and the archives.

EXAMPLES OF CURRENT CULTURAL DEVELOPMENT

The Missouri Farmers Association is an organization of enormous importance in the shaping of Missouri life. The early interest of Missouri farmers in the Patrons of Husbandry and Farmers Alliance and the continuing importance of agriculture in the state were evidences of the people's need for organization. William

Hirth, working after 1917 with materials already familiar to him, demonstrated the positive capacity of Missouri people for co-operation. He had published *The Statesman* at Columbia from 1906 to 1911 and the *Missouri Farmer* after he sold *The Statesman.*

A meeting of several hundred farmers at Columbia, Missouri, in January, 1917, began the organization of M.F.A. A convention at Sedalia in August, attended by 340 delegates from thirty-eight counties, made the association official and permanent. The purpose, as defined by the charter and by-laws, is the "benefit and advancement of members as producers of agricultural products." It is a nonprofit organization, and it has undertaken to furnish supplies to its members at cost and to market farm products of its members, charging only for necessary expenses.

The association is aloof from party control but active in farm legislation. By 1950 the M.F.A. was the largest business in Missouri and the largest co-operative in the United States. The list of its activities under the charter is extensive, including "marketing, selling, preserving, harvesting, drying, processing, manufacturing . . . or utilization of any agricultural product, including livestock, or the manufacturing or marketing of the by-products thereof." F. V. Heinkel, who had been vice president four years, succeeded to the presidency after William Hirth's death in 1940.

Representative Clarence Cannon, who wrote the introduction to Ray Derr's recent book on the M.F.A., is an example of the nonpartisan trend in Missouri politics. Although he runs for office as a Democrat and supports party policies with fair regularity, he is frequently engaged in service that is not partisan in character. The people of his district have elected him to sixteen consecutive terms in Congress, beginning during the administration of Herbert Hoover.

Born in Missouri in 1879, he was educated in the public schools and at La Grange College (now Hannibal–La Grange Junior College), William Jewell College at Liberty, and the University of Missouri. Between 1904 and 1908 he taught history at Stephens College. During the first world war he served in the United States Army. His first election to Congress was in 1930 and his sixteenth in 1960. In the House of Representatives he is chairman of the

Appropriations Committee. He edited the *Manual and Digest of the House of Representatives*, and is the author of two books on parliamentary rules—*Cannon's Procedure* and *Convention Parliamentary Manual*. He has a thorough acquaintance with the people of the Ninth Congressional District and a deep understanding of the democratic ideals of Missouri.[13]

The Linda Hall Library in Kansas City is a notable addition to the facilities for scholarship in Missouri. Founded by Herbert F. Hall in 1946 and housed in the Hall residence for ten years, the collection of books and serial publications on science and technology outgrew the available space, and in January, 1956, occupied the new building. Measuring 225 by 100 feet, the new Linda Hall Library was designed to house 500,000 volumes.

Joseph Collins Shipman, the librarian, is an example of Missouri's continued dependence upon the migration of persons of specialized knowledge from other states and from foreign countries. Born in Winnepeg, Manitoba, in 1908, he came to the Linda Hall Library in 1946, five years after he had become a naturalized citizen. His training in library science was acquired at Western Reserve University and his experience as a librarian at Cleveland Public Library, Union College, Toledo Public Library, and Enoch Pratt Library at Baltimore.

Some other distinguished librarians in Missouri came from other states. Ralph H. Parker, director of the library at the University of Missouri and ex officio president of the state Library Commission, came to Missouri in 1947 after seven years as director of the library at the University of Georgia. His academic training was at the University of Texas and the University of Chicago. Andrew J. Eaton, who became librarian at Washington University in 1953, was born in New York, received graduate degrees at the University of Michigan and the University of Chicago, and held a variety of positions in New York, Louisiana, and Florida. He came to Washington University at the age of thirty-nine. Paxton P. Price, state librarian, is a native of Arkansas. He studied library science at George Peabody College and Columbia University, served as

[13] Ray Derr, *Missouri Farmers in Action*, Introduction, ix–xi, 1–5, 16–32, 120–55, 188–93.

librarian in New Mexico and at Northwest Missouri State College before he was chosen for his present position in 1949.

Every special field of education in Missouri has drawn heavily upon the talent of other states and of foreign countries for recruits. Among the notable families in the field of higher education is that of Ernest Wentworth Dow, who came to Missouri from Maine. He became head of the little college at Louisiana, and of the Pierce City Baptist College. He also served as president of the Southwest Baptist College at Bolivar.

His daughter, Blanche Hinman Dow, was born at Louisiana, Missouri. The family returned to New England, and Blanche had the advantages of Massachusetts schooling, with undergraduate work at Smith College and the Boston School of Expression. She attended Columbia University, where she earned the M.A. and Ph.D. degrees. She taught college classes—French at Milwaukee-Downer, French and drama at Grand River College, and modern languages at Northwest Missouri State College. She received honorary degrees at Culver-Stockton and Missouri Valley College, and served the state in a variety of functions. From 1948 to 1952 she was a member of the executive committee of the Missouri Co-ordinating Council of UNESCO. In 1949, she became president of Cottey College at Nevada, Missouri.

Elmer Ellis came to the University of Missouri History Department in 1930 at the age of twenty-nine. He was born in North Dakota, educated in the elementary schools of the state, with undergraduate work and a master's degree from the University of North Dakota. He received the Ph.D. degree at the University of Iowa. For sixteen years his main occupation at the University of Missouri was classroom instruction, with the added duties of junior college visitor and acting dean of the Graduate College. He became dean of the College of Arts and Science in 1946, acting president of the University in 1954, and president in 1955. He has an extensive reputation among American universities as an occasional speaker and has served as visiting lecturer at Amsterdam and at Salzburg. He is president of the board of directors of the Harry S. Truman Library at Independence.

The Truman Library is one of the newest of the great book and manuscript collections in the state. The city of Independence provided thirteen and one-half acres of ground for the enterprise and the public subscribed $1,750,000 for the building, which was presented to the National Archives on July 6, 1957. Together with other executive papers belonging to the former President, the library contains three and one-half million documents relating to the Truman administration.

Both St. Louis and Kansas City have creditable public library collections, and each of the great schools—Washington University at St. Louis, the University of Missouri, and St. Louis University—has important collections of books, periodicals, and manuscripts. The Missouri State Library at Jefferson City serves the 20 per cent of the state's citizens, over 800,000, who have no other public library facilities. The state Library Commission (Mrs. Raymond Young, president; Mrs. Frank Steury, Mrs. Albert H. Thoma, Mrs. Philip H. Strop, members, 1960; and ex officio members Ralph Parker and Commissioner of Education Hubert Wheeler), since 1946 has elevated Missouri to a high place among the states in this phase of public library development. The Commission selected Paxton P. Price as librarian in 1949, and he has been directly responsible for administration of the progressive policies of the state. Demonstration Bookmobile service and the delivery of books, magazines, pictures, and films to schools, clubs, and individuals—by various means of transportation—are the most obviously useful of the library's activities.

The new Knights of Columbus Vatican Film Library at St. Louis University marks the high point in manuscript materials covering a vast field of European history. Upward of eleven million pages of longhand documents from the Vatican Library are made available to American scholars. Jesuit documents from the Americas, Medieval and Renaissance texts used in the universities, and commentaries on the works of ancient scholars such as Socrates, Galen, and Hippocrates are among the microfilms. The Vatican collection contains smaller libraries of European families—lawyers, medical men, and others—kept as separate collections. These are the sources for a great variety of specialized manuscript study. The four-million-dollar building of the Pius XII Library, with all of its excellence of lighting and refinements of conveniences, is by no means the only notable feature of the University's progress in scholarship.[14]

Missouri has the advantages of two great historical societies, the Missouri Historical Society at St. Louis and the State Historical Society of Missouri at Columbia. The society with headquarters in St. Louis was organized in 1866 by a group of newspapermen, educators, and industrial leaders. In 1913 it moved to the Jefferson Memorial Building in Forest Park and enjoyed a revival of interest and activity. The society's museum contains a valuable collection of portraits, Creole furniture, costumes, the apparatus of a century-old volunteer fire department, the Charles A. Lindbergh Collection of trophies, the pilot wheel from a river steamer, and a collection of early American firearms.

Its library contains manuscripts extending back to the Louisiana Province, numbering over one and one-half million, in addition to books and newspaper files. Support for the Missouri Historical Society is from individual and corporate membership dues, which numbered 4,073 in 1959. The materials of the society are concerned with St. Louis, the state of Missouri, and Louisiana Territory, with emphasis upon regional rather than local affairs. Charles van Ravenswaay of Boonville held the position of director from 1946 until 1962, when he resigned. George R. Brooks became director on June 1, 1962.

The State Historical Society of Missouri, with headquarters in the library of Missouri University at Columbia, has been in existence since 1898. A group of promoters met in Eureka Springs, Arkansas, approved the work of a committee that had been selected to write a constitution, and chose officers. E. W. Stephens of the Columbia *Herald* was made president, Isidor Loeb of the University of Missouri, secretary. During the following session of the Missouri General Assembly, an act signed by Governor Lon V. Stephens made the State Historical Society trustee for Missouri's official historical records.

14 *Official Manual* (1957–58), 521–25; (1959–60), 545–49; Lowrie J. Dally, "Manuscripts in Microfilm," *Library Journal*, Vol. 86, No. 15 (Sept. 1, 1961), 2756–57; *2000 Years of Man*, bulletin of the Pius XII Library, St. Louis University; *Milestones in the History of Science to 1800*, bulletin of the Linda Hall Library, 1956; *Kansas City Star*, March 4, 1956.

In 1955, State Senate Resolution No. 98 honored the fortieth anniversary of Floyd C. Shoemaker as secretary of the society. Recent statistics provide evidence of the organization's healthy growth. In 1934–35, a steady increase in membership had made it the largest of all the state historical societies, and it has not surrendered first place since that time. By 1957 the membership had passed 10,000 and by May 1, 1960, had reached 11,912. An oil portrait of the secretary, painted by Daniel L. MacMorris, was presented to the society on the occasion of Shoemaker's retirement. Richard S. Brownlee of Missouri University was chosen to fill the position of secretary and librarian.

The art collections of the State Historical Society have become famous. Among the portraits of historical persons, in addition to the MacMorris painting mentioned above, are the following: the President Harry S. Truman Family, by Greta Kempton; Isidor Loeb, by J. Scott MacNutt; John Woods Harris, Baron Alexander von Humboldt, Thomas Jefferson, Vinnie Ream, and James Shannon, by George Caleb Bingham; Senator Thomas Hart Benton, Francis P. Blair, Daniel Boone, Samuel L. Clemens, James B. Eads, and Lewis F. Linn, by Henry C. Thompson. William Knox's *Fort Osage*, Thomas Hart Benton's *Negro Soldier* and *Year of Peril*, and landscapes by Bingham receive the attention of thousands of visitors annually. For want of space it is impossible to mention other notable examples of Missouri art in this collection.

The library of the State Historical Society contains 25,000 books, 3,412 bound volumes of newspapers, 8,031,870 microfilm pages of newspapers, and a collection of rare maps. Among the longhand manuscripts, which contain 223,574 pages of diaries, letters, journals, and state archives salvaged from the capitol fire in 1911, are such sources for historical research as the letters of General Guitar, the Leonard Papers, and the Autobiography of Charles D. Drake.[15]

The phases of cultural development in Missouri reviewed here

[15] *Official Manual* (1957–58), 515–21; (1959–60), 535–44, 1338–41; *Mo. Hist. Rev.*, Vol. LIV, No. 4 (July, 1960), 375–83 (cover picture, *Fort Osage*, by William Knox).

are no more than suggestive of the state's resources in art and learning. Every library and art gallery, every editorial desk, musical studio, and chemical laboratory, every schoolboy engaged in composing an essay on the excavations of an ancient Indian mound or on the Constitution is an adventure in culture.

For presenting this short history of the Crossroads State, I have selected some persons and incidents that you would not have chosen. If my characters and events were the same as yours, then reading my story of Missouri would be pointless for you. The persons who have made notable contributions to the state's history who are omitted from this volume must of necessity be more numerous than the persons included. A book devoted exclusively to rural landscapes of colorful beauty and endless charm would be incomplete without a description of the pleasant hill above Clear Creek near Pierce City, that I knew in some detail more than half a century ago; yet it would be impossible to include in the book of descriptions every such fascinating scene.

The purpose of this volume has been to present a view of the state's past, selected from material that I have found in the records or in the narratives of other writers or met in a lifetime of acquaintance with Missouri, that will add to the reader's understanding of the state. Perhaps it should be pointed out that one man's acquaintance is not long enough or thorough enough for the task. That must be admitted at once, for the assignment is large.

No book that has yet appeared on St. Louis or Kansas City or St. Joseph has completely covered the historical significance of those cities. No account of Missouri banks or railroads or parks or highways has exhausted the subject. Many separate districts of St. Louis are worthy of deep and detailed historical study; and many sections of hurrying, sprawling, brawling, beautiful, and thoughtful Kansas City have yet to be thoroughly examined.

And across the state are hundreds of unique communities. No city in the nation is quite like Joplin; none is a duplicate of Hannibal, Independence, Springfield, or Louisiana. Doniphan, with its irregular streets, oddly shaped buildings, and friendly, ingenious people, has in it an unlimited appeal to the imagination and a powerful urge toward the study of human society. Osceola and Cassville, Clinton and St. Charles, Cape Girardeau, Moberly, and Nevada—each has its special character and unique place; and each is but an example of the endless variety of the state.

AFTER 140 years of statehood, the sources for a survey of Missouri's history are of necessity secondary, to a great extent. To the author of this volume, however, it seemed desirable to rely upon primary materials for certain areas in which he has ventured to disagree with earlier writers and for other phases which needed fresh examination. The Library of Congress, the Missouri State Historical Society in Columbia, the Missouri Historical Society in St. Louis, the Mercantile Library in St. Louis, and the National Archives in Washington, D. C., contain vast sources for research in the history of Missouri. Furthermore, interesting and important new materials are appearing daily in the great libraries recently established and in unexpected treasures of family archives, newspaper files, and local records.

Three collections were especially useful for this book: the Manuscript Division of the Library of Congress, the manuscripts in the Missouri State Historical Society, and the National Archives. Papers dealing with the activities of the Bates, Blair, and Ewing families, deposited in the Library of Congress, provided material directly related to Missouri problems for which the author has attempted to offer fresh treatment. The records of the War Department and the Legislative Reference Division of the National Archives were used for items connected with the Civil War. The manuscripts consulted in the Missouri State Historical Society included the "Autobiography" of Charles Daniel Drake, the Abiel Leonard Collection, and the Odon Guitar Manuscripts.

Most useful of the printed documents were the following: *American State Papers*, 38 volumes (Washington, 1832–61); *Official Records, War of the Rebellion*, 130 volumes (Washington, 1880–1901); *Messages and Papers of the Presidents*, 20 volumes (Washington, 1897–1922); *United*

States Census Reports (7th, 8th, 11th, and 17th, especially); *Messages and Proclamations of the Governors of Missouri,* 18 vols. (Floyd C. Shoemaker, ed.), with Buel Leopard, I–III; Grace Gilmore Avery, IV–VI; and Sarah Guitar, VII–XVIII; *Official Manual of the State of Missouri,* biennial publication beginning 1907–1908.

The books and articles listed below are intended as suggestions to supplement the footnotes.

BOOKS

Ayres, Leonard P. *The War With Germany.* Washington, D. C., 1919.

Barclay, Thomas S. *The Liberal Republican Movement in Missouri, 1865–1871.* Columbia, Mo., 1926.

Bates, Edward. *The Diary of Edward Bates.* Howard K. Beale, ed. American Historical Association *Annual Report, 1930.*

Bellamy, Gladys Carmen. *Mark Twain as a Literary Artist.* Norman, 1930.

Benton, Thomas Hart. *Historical and Legal Examination . . . Dred Scott Case.* New York, 1858.

Brackenridge, Henry M. *Views of Louisiana; together with a Journal of a Voyage up the Missouri River in 1811.* Pittsburgh, 1814.

Brownlee, Richard S. *Gray Ghosts of the Confederacy.* Baton Rouge, 1958.

Byars, W. V. *An American Commoner: The Life and Times of Richard P. Bland.* Columbia, Mo., 1900.

Cable, J. R. *The Bank of the State of Missouri.* New York, 1923.

Chambers, William Nisbet. *Old Bullion: Senator from the New West.* Boston, 1956.

Chittenden, Hiram Martin. *The American Fur Trade of the Far West.* 3 vols. New York, 1902.

———. *History of Early Steamboat Navigation on the Missouri River.* 2 vols. New York, 1903.

Cole, Arthur C. *The Whig Party in the South.* Washington, 1913.

Connelley, William E. *Doniphan's Expedition and the Conquest of New Mexico and California.* Topeka, 1907.

———. *Quantrill and the Border Wars.* New York, 1956.

Coues, Elliott. *Forty Years a Fur Trader on the Upper Missouri.* 2 vols. New York, 1898.

Culmer, Frederick Arthur. *A New History of Missouri.* Mexico, 1938.

Darby, John F. *Personal Recollections of Many Prominent People I Have Known.* St. Louis, 1880.

Derr, Ray. *Missouri Farmers in Action.* Columbia, Mo., 1955.

De Voto, Bernard, ed. *The Journals of the Lewis and Clark Expedition.* Cambridge, 1953.

Doherty, William T., Jr. *Louis Houck, Missouri Historian and Entrepreneur.* Columbia, Mo., 1960.

Ellis, James F. *The Influence of Environment on the Settlement of Missouri.* St. Louis, 1929.

Ellis, Roy. *A Civic History of Kansas City.* Springfield, 1930.

Ewers, John C. *The Blackfeet.* Norman, 1959.

Frémont, Jessie Benton. *Souvenirs of My Time.* Boston, 1887.

Frémont, John Charles. *Memoirs of My Life.* 2 vols. Chicago, 1887.

French, Benjamin. *Historical Collections of Louisiana.* 5 vols. (I, New York, 1846; II, Philadelphia, 1850).

Garwood, Darrell. *Crossroads of America: The Story of Kansas City.* New York, 1948.

Gayarré, Charles Étienne Arthur. *History of Louisiana.* 4 vols. New York, 1854–66.

Gregg, Josiah. *Commerce of the Prairies.* Max L. Moorhead, ed. Norman, 1954.

Hagan, William T. *The Sac and Fox Indians.* Norman, 1958.

Hammond, Bray. *Banks and Politics in America, from the Revolution to the Civil War.* Princeton, 1957.

Harding, Samuel Bannister. *Missouri Party Struggles in the Civil War Period.* American Historical Association *Annual Report*, 1900.

——. *Life of George R. Smith, Founder of Sedalia, Missouri.* Sedalia, 1904.

Haskell, Henry C., and Richard B. Fowler. *City of the Future.* Kansas City, 1950.

Helm, William F. *Harry Truman: A Political Biography.* New York, 1947.

Hopkins, Vincent C. *Dred Scott's Case.* New York, 1951.

Houck, Louis. *A History of Missouri from the earliest Exploration and Settlement until the Admission of the State into the Union.* 3 vols. Chicago, 1908.

——. *The Spanish Régime in Missouri.* 2 vols. Chicago, 1909.

Jackson, Andrew. *The Correspondence of Andrew Jackson.* John Spencer Bassett, ed. 6 vols. Washington, 1926–33.

Loeb, Isidor. "Constitutions and Constitutional Conventions in Missouri," *Journal of the Missouri Constitutional Convention, 1875,* Vol. I.

———, and Floyd C. Shoemaker. *Debates of the Missouri Constitutional Convention of 1875.* Columbia, 1930.

McClure, C. H. *History of Missouri.* Chicago, 1920.

———. *Opposition in Missouri to Thomas Hart Benton.* Warrensburg, 1926.

———, and Marguerite Potter. *Missouri: Geography, History, and Government.* Chicago, 1951.

Margry, Pierre. *Découvertes et établissements des Français dans l'ouest et dans le sud de l'Amérique Septentrionale (1614–1754).* 6 vols. Paris, 1878–88.

Meriwether, Lee. *Jim Reed: "Senatorial Immortal."* Webster Grove, Mo., 1948.

Milligan, Maurice M. *The Missouri Waltz: Inside Story of the Pendergast Machine.* New York, 1948.

Million, John Wilson. *State Aid to Railways in Missouri.* Chicago, 1896.

Monaghan, Jay. *Civil War on the Western Border, 1854–65.* Boston, 1955.

Moore, Glover. *The Missouri Controversy, 1819–21.* Lexington, Ky., 1955.

Moorhead, Max L. *New Mexico's Royal Road: Trade and Travel on the Chihuahua Trail.* Norman, 1958.

Nevins, Allan. *Frémont, the West's Greatest Adventurer.* 2 vols. New York, 1928.

Parkman, Francis. *La Salle and the Discovery of the Great West.* 6 vols. New York and Boston, 1893–1903.

———. *The Oregon Trail.* New York, 1931.

Peckham, James. *General Nathaniel Lyon and Missouri in 1861.* New York, 1866.

Pike, Zebulon Montgomery. *The Expeditions of . . . .* Elliott Coues, ed. 3 vols. New York, 1895.

Reddig, William M. *Tom's Town.* Philadelphia and New York, 1947.

Roseboom, Eugene. *A History of Presidential Elections.* New York, 1957.

St. Louis Metropolitan Survey. *Path of Progress for Metropolitan St. Louis.* 1957.

Scharf, John Thomas. *History of St. Louis City and County, from the Earliest Periods to the Present Day.* 2 vols. Philadelphia, 1883.

Schurz, Carl. *Life of Henry Clay*. 2 vols. Boston, 1888.

Shaner, Dolph. *The Story of Joplin*. New York, 1948.

Shoemaker, Floyd C. *Missouri and Missourians*. 5 vols. Chicago, 1943.

Simms, Henry A. *A Decade of Sectional Controversy*. Chapel Hill, 1942.

Smith, Elbert B. *Magnificent Missourian*. Philadelphia and New York, 1958.

Smith, William Ernest. *The Francis Preston Blair Family in Politics*. 2 vols. New York, 1933.

Stanwood, Edward. *A History of the Presidency*. 2 vols. Boston, 1916.

Stockard, Opha. *The First Seventy-Five Years*. Nevada, 1961.

Thwaites, Reuben Gold. *France in America*. New York and London, 1905.

——— (ed.). *Original Journals of the Lewis and Clark Expedition*. 8 vols. New York, 1904.

——— (ed.). *Early Western Travels*. 32 vols. Cleveland, 1904–1907.

Trexler, Harrison A. *Slavery in Missouri, 1804–1805*. Baltimore, 1914.

Truman, Harry S. *The Truman Program*. New York, 1949.

———. *Memoirs*. 2 vols. Garden City, N. Y., 1955, 1956.

Vandenberg, Arthur H. *The Private Papers of Senator Vandenberg*. Arthur H. Vandenberg, Jr., ed. Boston, 1952.

Violette, Eugene Morrow. *A History of Missouri*. Boston, 1918; Reprinted by Ramfre Press, Cape Girardeau, 1953.

Whitney, Carrie Westlake. *A History of Kansas City, Missouri*. 3 vols. Chicago, 1908.

Williams, Walter, and Floyd C. Shoemaker. *Missouri, Mother of the West*. 5 vols. Chicago and New York, 1930.

Woodward, Ashbel. *Life of General Nathaniel Lyon*. Boston, 1862.

Zornow, William Frank. *Kansas: A History of the Jayhawk State*. Norman, 1957.

ARTICLES

Aiton, Arthur S. "The Diplomacy of the Louisiana Cession," *American Historical Review*, Vol. XXXVI (1931), 701–20.

Anderson, Hattie M. "The Jackson Men in Missouri in 1828," *Missouri Historical Review*, Vol. XXXIV (1940), 301–35.

Bieber, Ralph P. "Some Aspects of the Santa Fe Trail, 1848–80," *Missouri Historical Review*, Vol. XVIII (1924), 158–66.

Castel, Albert. "Kansas Jayhawking Raids into Missouri in 1861," *Missouri Historical Review*, Vol. XLIV (1959), 1–11.

Connelley, William E. "The Lane-Jenkins Claim Contest," *Collections of the Kansas Historical Society*, Vol. XVI (1923–25), 21–176.

Clark, Victor S. "The Influence of Manufactures Upon Political Sentiment in the United States from 1820 to 1860," *American Historical Review*, Vol. XXII (1916), 58–64.

Cotterill, R. S. "The National Railroad Convention in St. Louis, 1849," *Missouri Historical Review*, Vol. XII (1918), 203–15.

Denison, W. W. "Battle of Prairie Grove," *Collections of the Kansas Historical Society*, Vol. XVI (1923–25), 586–90.

Dietzler, John P. "Major General Samuel Ryan Curtis—City Engineer," *Missouri Historical Review*, Vol. XLII (1957), 354–61.

Dorfman, Joseph, "The Jackson Wage-Earner Thesis," *American Historical Review*, Vol. LIV (1949), 296–306.

Dugan, Frank H. "An Illinois Martyrdom," Illinois State Historical Society, *Papers in Illinois History and Transactions* (1938), 111–57.

Flanagan, John T. "Reedy of the Mirror," *Missouri Historical Review*, Vol. XLIII, 128–44.

Forbes, Cleon. "The St. Louis School of Thought," *Missouri Historical Review*, Vol. XXV (1931), 85–101, 289–305, 461–73, 609–22; Vol. XXVI (1932), 68–77.

Frémont, Jessie Benton, "Senator Thomas Hart Benton," *Independent*, Vol. LV (1903), 240–44.

Gratiot, Adele de P. "Adele de P. Gratiot's Narrative," *Collections of the State Historical Society of Wisconsin*, Vol. X (1888), 261–75.

Garraghan, the Rev. Gilbert J., S. J. "The Beginnings of St. Louis University," *St. Louis Catholic Historical Review*, Vol. I (1919), 85–102.

Griffith, G. W. E. "The Battle of Black Jack," *Collections of the Kansas State Historical Society*, Vol. XVI (1923–25), 524–28.

Grissom, Daniel M. "Personal Recollections of Distinguished Missourians," *Missouri Historical Review*, Vol. XVIII (1924), 129–45.

Hamilton, Bray. "Jackson, Biddle, and the Bank of the United States," *Journal of Economic History*, Vol. VII (1947), 1–23.

———. "Banking in the Early West: Monopoly, Prohibition, and Laissez faire," *Journal of Economic History*, Vol. VIII (1948), 1–25.

Missouri Historical Society. *Glimpses of the Past*, Vol. VIII (1941), 7–9, "Earliest History of St. Louis."

McCandless, Perry. "The Significance of County Making in the Elections of Thomas Hart Benton," *Missouri Historical Review*, Vol. XLIII (1958), 34–38.

Magers, Roy V. "An Early Missouri Political Feud," *Missouri Historical Review*, Vol. XXIII (1929), 261–69.

Merkel, Benjamin. "The Slavery Issue and the Political Decline of Thomas Hart Benton," *Missouri Historical Review*, Vol. XXXVIII (1944), 388–407.

Nelson, James Warren. "Congressional Opinion in Missouri on the Spanish American War," *Missouri Historical Review*, Vol. XLII (1957), 245–56.

Nolen, Russell M. "The Labor Movement in St. Louis Prior to the Civil War," *Missouri Historical Review*, Vol. XXXIV (1939), 18–37.

Oliphant, John R. "Recollections of Thomas Hart Benton," *Missouri Historical Review*, Vol. XIV (1920), 433–35.

Pierson, W. W. "The Committee on the Conduct of the War," *American Historical Review*, Vol. XXIII (1917), 550–76.

Power, Richard Lyle. "A Crusade to Extend Yankee Culture, 1820–65," *New England Quarterly*, Vol. XIII (1940), 638–53.

Ray, P. O. "The Retirement of Thomas Hart Benton from the Senate and Its Significance," *Missouri Historical Review*, Vol. II (1907–1908), 1–14, 97–111.

Raybeck, Joseph G. "The American Workingman and the Antislavery Crusade," *Journal of Economic History*, Vol. III (1943), 152–63.

Remeck, Samuel. "The Depression of 1819–1822," *American Historical Review*, Vol. XXXIX (1933), 28–47.

———. "The Social History of an American Depression," *American Historical Review*, Vol. XL (1935), 662–87.

Ryle, Walter H. "Slavery and Party Realignment in Missouri in the State Election of 1856," *Missouri Historical Review*, Vol. XXXIX (1945), 320–32.

Shepherd, William R. "The Cession of Louisiana to Spain," *Political Science Quarterly*, Vol. XIX (1904), 439–58.

Shoemaker, Floyd C. "Traditions Concerning the Missouri Question," *Missouri Historical Review*, Vol. XVI (1922), 253–62.

———. "Some Colorful Lawyers in the History of Missouri," *Missouri Historical Review*, Vol. XLIII (1959), 125–31.

Soulard, Amadée. "The Bloody Island Cross Mark," *St. Louis Globe Democrat*, June 25, 1899.

Squires, Monas N. "A New View of the Election of Barton and Benton to the United States Senate in 1820," *Missouri Historical Review*, Vol. XXVII (1932), 28–45.

Stephens, F. F. "Banking and Finance in Missouri in the Thirties," *Proceedings of the Mississippi Historical Association*, Vol. X (1920), 122–34.

Sternberg, Richard R. "Some Political Aspects of the Dred Scott Case," *Mississippi Valley Historical Review*, Vol. XIX (1933), 571–77.

Sullivan, William A. "Did Labor Support Andrew Jackson?" *Political Science Quarterly*, Vol. LXII (1947), 569–80.

Thomas, A. B. "The First Santa Fe Expedition, 1792–93," *Chronicles of Oklahoma*, Vol. IX (1931), 195–208.

Van Ravenswaay, Charles. "The Tragedy of David Barton," *Bulletin of the Missouri Historical Society*, Vol. VII (1950), 35–36.

Viles, Jonas, "Population and Extent of Settlement in Missouri Before 1804," *Missouri Historical Review*, Vol. VI (1911), 189–213.

Violette, Eugene Morrow. "Spanish Land Claims in Missouri," *Washington University Studies, Humanistic Series*, Vol. VIII (1921).

Waddell, James R. "Thomas Hart Benton," *International Review*, Vol. XII (1882), 480–96.

Wilson, Charles R. "The Lincoln-Blair-Frémont Bargain of 1864," *American Historical Review*, Vol. XLII (1957), 71–78.

MISCELLANEOUS

Angus, James Thomas. "The Attitude of Missouri Toward Slavery from 1850 to 1860." Unpublished M.A. thesis, University of Missouri, 1932.

Dictionary of American Biography. Allen Johnson, Dumas Malone, Harris E. Starr, Robert Livingston Schuyler, eds. 22 vols. New York, 1928, 1936, 1944, 1958.

Dictionary of American History. James Truslow Adams, ed. 6 vols. New York, 1940.

Encyclopedia of the History of Missouri. 6 vols. St. Louis, 1901.

Geiger, Louis George. "The Public Career of Joseph W. Folk." Unpublished Ph.D. dissertation, University of Missouri, 1947.

March, David de Armand. "The Life and Times of Charles Daniel Drake." Unpublished Ph.D. dissertation, University of Missouri, 1949.

Nelson, Earl John. "The Passing of Slavery in Missouri." Unpublished M.A. thesis, University of Missouri, 1932.

O'Neil, Emily Ann. "Joseph Murphy's Contribution to the Development of the Great West." Unpublished M.A. thesis, St. Louis University, 1947.

Smith, Bert A. "The Senatorial Career of James A. Reed." Unpublished M.A. thesis, University of Missouri, 1950.

MISSOURI
A History of the Crossroads State

was set on the Linotype in eleven-point Caledonia with two points
of leading between the lines. This typeface was designed by the
distinguished American typographer and lettering artist, the late
William Addison Dwiggins. His deviation from the basic Scotch
Roman form has complemented the inventive Dwiggins touch.

THE UNIVERSITY OF OKLAHOMA PRESS
Norman

45551

F
466
M2

McREYNOLDS, EDWIN
    MISSOURI.

DATE DUE

Fernald Library
Colby-Sawyer College
New London, New Hampshire

GAYLORD   PRINTED IN U.S.A.   PRINTED IN U.S.A.